THE POLITICAL ORIGINS OF RELIGIOUS LIBERTY

The issue of religious liberty has gained ever-increasing attention among policy makers and the public at large. Whereas politicians have long championed the idea of religious freedom and tolerance, the actual achievement of these goals has been an arduous battle for religious minorities. What motivates political leaders to create laws providing for greater religious liberty? In contrast to scholars who argue that religious liberty results from the spread of secularization and modern ideas, Anthony Gill argues that religious liberty results from interest-based calculations of secular rulers. Using insights from political economists dating back to Adam Smith, Gill develops a theory of the origins of religious liberty based on the political and economic interests of governing officials. Political leaders are most likely to permit religious freedom when it enhances their own political survival, tax revenue, and the economic welfare of their country. He explores his theory using cases from British America, Latin America, Russia, and the Baltic states.

Anthony Gill is Associate Professor of Political Science at the University of Washington, where he specializes in the study of religion, economics, and politics. He is the author of *Rendering Unto Caesar: The Catholic Church and the State in Latin America* and numerous articles on religion and politics. Professor Gill was awarded the University of Washington's Distinguished Teaching Award in 1999 and is a nonresident scholar at Baylor University's Institute for Studies of Religion.

Cambridge Studies in Social Theory, Religion, and Politics

Editors

David C. Leege, *University of Notre Dame*
Kenneth D. Wald, *University of Florida, Gainesville*

The most enduring and illuminating bodies of late-nineteenth-century social theory – by Marx, Weber, Durkheim, and others – emphasized the integration of religion, polity, and economy through time and place. Once a staple of classic social theory, religion gradually lost the interest of many social scientists during the twentieth century. The recent emergence of phenomena such as Solidarity Poland; the dissolution of the Soviet empire; various South American, Southern African, and South Asian liberation movements; the Christian Right in the United States; and Al Qaeda have reawakened scholarly interest in religious-based political conflict. At the same time, fundamental questions are once again being asked about the role of religion in stable political regimes, public policies, and constitutional orders. The series *Cambridge Studies in Social Theory, Religion, and Politics* will produce volumes that study religion and politics by drawing on classic social theory and more recent social scientific research traditions. Books in the series offer theoretically grounded, comparative, empirical studies that raise "big" questions about a timely subject that has long engaged the best minds in social science.

Titles in the Series:

Joel S. Fetzer and J. Christopher Soper, *Muslims and the State in Britain, France, and Germany*

Pippa Norris and Ronald Inglehart, *Sacred and Secular: Religion and Politics Worldwide*

For Victor H. Gill and his shining city on the hill.
Never forget the value of freedom.

The Political Origins of Religious Liberty

Anthony Gill
University of Washington

CAMBRIDGE
UNIVERSITY PRESS

CAMBRIDGE UNIVERSITY PRESS
Cambridge, New York, Melbourne, Madrid, Cape Town, Singapore, São Paulo, Delhi

Cambridge University Press
32 Avenue of the Americas, New York, NY 10013-2473, USA

www.cambridge.org
Information on this title: www.cambridge.org/9780521848145

First published 2008

Printed in the United States of America

A catalog record for this publication is available from the British Library.

Library of Congress Cataloging in Publication Data
Gill, Anthony James.
The Political origins of religious liberty / Anthony Gill.
p.   cm. – (Cambridge studies in social theory, religion, and politics)
Includes bibliographical references and index.
ISBN 978-0-521-84814-5 (hardback) – ISBN 978-0-521-61273-9 (pbk.)
1. Freedom of religion. I. Title. II. Series.
BL640.G55   2008
323.44′209–dc22   2007012288

ISBN   978-0-521-84814-5 hardback
ISBN   978-0-521-61273-9 paperback

Contents

Preface   *page* ix
Acknowledgments   xiii

1   Introduction: Of Liberty, Laws, Religion, and Regulation   1

2   The Political Origins of Religious Liberty   26

3   Colonial British America   60

4   Mexico and Latin America   114

5   Russia and the Baltics (with Cheryl Žilinskas)   168

6   We Gather Together: The Consequences of Religious
    Liberty   224

    Appendix: List of Definitions, Axioms, and Propositions   231

Bibliography   235
Index   255

Preface

I am not sure how many people read prefaces, but if you have made it this far I urge you to continue. In the course of the next few short paragraphs, I hope to provide you with a little insight into why this book was written and how to read it.

This work is an extension of my earlier research that began while I was in graduate school and which resulted in a dissertation and a previously published book, *Rendering Unto Caesar: The Catholic Church and the State in Latin America*. The primary conclusion of that book was that religious competition, primarily from evangelical Protestants, prompted the Latin American Catholic Church to pay attention to the needs of its parishioners more closely. In countries where the number of Protestants was expanding rapidly, the Catholic Church tended to take a more preferential option for the poor and denounce governmental institutions deleterious to the nation's citizenry. In the final analysis, I concluded that this is a good thing. However, the one question that I never got around to answering was why Protestants happened to be more numerous in some countries than in others. In a subsequent article published in *Rationality and Society*, I discovered that religious liberty accounted for the varying growth rates of Protestants throughout Latin American countries. This finding would seem rather mundane; of course minority religions would expand where there were fewer laws preventing them from expanding. Despite this obvious conclusion, some early reviewers of that manuscript commented that such logic was counter-intuitive. Nonetheless, I persevered in my belief that religious freedom and religious vitality were linked.

The next question that naturally arose from my course of study was why some countries would have more liberal regulations governing religious groups and others would maintain stricter laws. The fact that there were significant degrees of difference throughout countries with similar cultural backgrounds and religious traditions ruled out the possibility that culture was at work. Moreover, other research I conducted with my graduate student Arang Keshavarzian revealed that similar patterns of church-state relations could be seen in countries with radically different cultural traditions, most notably Mexico and Iran. All of that set me to thinking about the role that political interests play in regulating religions. Because religious liberty is really just the accumulation of numerous laws telling churches and believers what they can and cannot do, it would make sense that the interests of lawmakers would be of crucial importance in determining the shape of those laws.

The process of exploring this idea led me first to examine Mexico and a few other countries in Latin America. I then turned my attention to the United States, realizing that the writing of the First Amendment of the U.S. Constitution was a major milestone in the history of religious liberty, at least in the modern era. I found great joy in going back and reading U.S. colonial history, and I found additional pleasure in the fact that it took me back into European history. Finally, I decided to pursue an exploration of Russia, which in 1997 implemented a highly restrictive set of regulations on religious minorities. Though not an expert in Russian politics or history, I gathered up the courage to move ahead, realizing that this case offered up a remarkable test of my hypothesis. Fearing my lack of knowledge would inhibit me in this area, I recruited a graduate student who was taking one of my classes at the time – Cheryl Žilinskas. Cheryl suggested that the Soviet-dominated Baltic States would also make a great case study, and because she was planning a dissertation on the topic, I agreed to let her help me. The result of my thinking on this topic is what you now hold in your hands. I hope you enjoy it.

And speaking of enjoyment, I hope that this work finds a broader audience than most scholarly books. I think it will. The topic is of great concern to the waves of religious believers who have refused to go away despite the coaxing of Karl Marx, Friedrich Nietzsche, Steve Bruce, and others. The book should also provide good reading to those interested in the general topic of liberty. Because freedom of conscience is often considered the "first freedom," understanding how it flourishes (or is repressed) should help us understand how other liberties are won or lost. To reach out to this wider audience, I tried to minimize the use of jargon wherever possible, or at least to explain that jargon when it appears in the text. I firmly believe that lay readers are capable of reading whatever academic scholars can dream up, so long as the language they write in does not come from some esoteric secret society. Too much scholarly writing today is thick with pedantic meanderings. If you are a lay reader of this work, I invite you to contact me and let me know if you found this work inspirational. Of course, if you are reading this work some sixty years from now, I probably won't be around, but you could always try a séance.

To further help the cause of reaching a broad audience, I have also tried to include some wit in the text and footnotes.[1] Deciding whether I have succeeded in this task will be up to the reader, but I sincerely hope that you get at least one chuckle. As with my concern over arcane writing, I also think that too many scholars take their work far too seriously, particularly in the social sciences and humanities. I understand there are serious topics that demand a serious mind, but part of the reason I enjoy my profession so much is that it gives me the joy of discovering new things, including all varieties of human quirks and foibles. Being a person who is not immune from possessing such quirks and foibles, I figure it is best to celebrate them. And the bottom line is this – on average, human beings get about seventy-five years to enjoy life. If I cannot find the opportunity to smile in the course of that time, including the portion of it when I am at work, then I sincerely wonder if I spent my time wisely.

---

[1] Speaking of footnotes, I encourage readers to read them. For graduate students and other interested parties, I have put a number of unanswered questions in the footnotes. Many of these would make great dissertation topics or research projects.

Acknowledgments

Standard operating procedures in academic circles require me to thank all of those who helped shape my ideas. Personally, I would like to take all the credit for everything that is correct in this work and pass blame for all errors on to some unsuspecting soul. Alas, my internal moral compass tells me that this is not a good thing to do. Moreover, I am truly a grateful person deep down inside and all the acknowledgments here are sincere and heartfelt. I may forget a few people who helped me along the way, so let me start by apologizing for this shortcoming.

First, I would like to recognize Roger Finke, whose 1990 article in *The Journal of Church and State* was a significant inspiration for this work. Roger also provided exceptionally thoughtful comments on the prospectus for this work and the completed manuscript. Larry Iannaccone and Rod Stark also deserve major praise for being sources of continual inspiration in my work and models whom I seek to emulate. Each of these three scholars – Roger, Larry, and Rod – have been influential in my intellectual development, and they have been good mentors and friends to boot. Even though they don't know this, they have been responsible for keeping me in the academic profession when times looked tough. But let's keep that as our little secret.

Several good friends and colleagues – Steve Hanson, David Leege, Matt Manweller, Steve Pfaff, Ken Wald, and Carolyn Warner – read significant chunks of this manuscript and presented helpful comments on both content and style. I didn't always take their suggestions (this is my book after all), but I greatly appreciate the time and effort it took to slog through my various drafts. All of these folks have been strong confidantes over the years, finding ways to tolerate this academic misfit (and several of them know what I mean by that). Steve Pfaff deserves special mention; he's a great storyteller and an even better friend.

Many other people have read portions of this work and/or have been forced to sit through tedious and monochromatic Microsoft PowerPoint presentations outlining the various arguments posited here. These include John Anderson, Robert Barro, David S. Brown, Paul Froese, Kirk Hawkins, Michael Hechter, Wade Jacoby, Stathis Kalyvas, Edgar Kiser, Ahmet Kuru, Margaret Levi, Chris Marsh, Rachel McCleary, Michael Mousseau, Dan Nielson, Mark A. Smith, Murat Somer, Bill Talbott, Clyde Wilcox, and John Witte Jr. I also thank all of those who participated in the various university seminars at which I presented this work, including Arizona State, Baylor, Brigham Young, Emory, Harvard, Koç University (Istanbul), and Rice. I particularly enjoyed the enormous hospitality shown to me at Brigham Young University, which has a remarkably energetic and prolific political science department. The good folks at the University of Washington's Political Economy Drinks and Discussion group also provided needed commentary at the early stages in this process. The University of Washington's Royalty Research Fund provided funding for my research in Latin America.

Several students were instrumental in a variety of ways in bringing this book to fruition. My greatest appreciation here goes to Cheryl Žilinskas, who not only read my manuscript and provided commentary but also crucially assisted in writing the chapter on Russia and the Baltics. This was Cheryl's first foray into the world of academic publishing, and I know that she put enormous pressure on herself to do a good job. The result was a truly amazing job, and I could not have finished this book without her help. I also took inspiration from her missionary work, which showed a great deal of courage and faith. Cheryl's husband, Rimas, also provided a couple of noteworthy comments and proved to be tolerant of Cheryl's heroic late-night efforts to finish her portions of the chapter. They both earned themselves a movie night. Other graduate students helped me research portions of this book including Stefan Hamberg, Erik Lundsgaarde, Diana Pallais, and Anthony Pezzola. Some hard-working undergraduates also lent a hand in the research for this book (and on related topics). Recognition goes to Ivan Barron, Etan Basseri, Franklin Donahoe, Monya Kian, Kim Mabee, Erica Monges, Lech Radzinski, Don Rasmussen, Lindsay Scola, and Claudia Zeibe. Many more undergraduate and graduate students were exposed to my ideas in various courses that I taught at the University of Washington.

Lew Bateman, David Leege, and Ken Wald gave me an incredibly long leash as editors at Cambridge University Press. I really appreciate that. Any author should feel blessed if they get a chance to work with these fine folks. Lew even took me out for breakfast when I was in New York City. Who could ask for anything more in an editor? Monica Finley and Shelby Peak did a great job shepherding this manuscript through the production process and putting up with my jocular e-mails. And Christine Dunn did a fantastic job copyediting the manuscript and had a great sense of humor. I recommend DunnWrite Editorial for all copyediting jobs. A few other people deserve mention for listening to my ideas, offering encouragement, being an inspiration, or just being plain old good folks that kept me going: Chris and Janet Campton, Katie Carlton, Charles Daniels, Greg and Jill Esau, Christopher Gibson, Joel and Mary Green, Lois Gustafson, Barbara Kautz, Dave and Mary Kautz, Ted Lester, Brian and Theresa Pedersen, Tim and Kathy Sinclair, Kirby and Trina Wilbur, and Shelly and Steve Young. Bullet, "C," and Quinn also provided support in their own particular ways. None of these folks know they've helped so let's keep that a secret too.

And who can forget the family? My wife, Becky, put up with this thing causing me all sorts of angst over the past six years. She allowed me to complain and take more than a few extra weekends to devote work to this effort. She was always there for support. My parents – Jim and Arlene – were also there to keep asking if I had finished yet. Apparently writing a book is a lot like mowing the grass when you're a teenager. And then there's my son, Victor. He has given me lots of hugs and kisses when I needed them most and has never been at a loss for inspirational and funny words at just the right time. His excitement over me writing a book that was dedicated to him has certainly made an impression on him. He even sat down to write his own book at age six just to be like his daddy. And he keeps telling me how he wants to go to college wherever I happen to be working so that he can become a scientist and have lunch with me. Now how cool is that? I hope he still shares that goal in some form or another as he grows up. But as for the immediate future I think he and I earned some good fishing time together next summer.

Finally, special gratitude goes to the greatest cowboy of them all. We've talked a lot over the past few years and these conversations have definitely made me a better, stronger, and more patient person. But I'm still trying.

CHAPTER 1

Introduction: Of Liberty, Laws, Religion, and Regulation

In a free government, the security for civil rights must be the same as that for religious rights. It consists in the one case of the multiplicity of interests, and in the other in the multiplicity of sects. The degree of security in both cases will depend on the number of interests and sects.

– James Madison, *Federalist 51*

ON APRIL 13, 1598, King Henry IV of France signed a remarkable document. In a nation where the Roman Catholic Church reigned supreme, the Edict of Nantes gave French Protestants – the Huguenots – a guarantee that they would no longer be persecuted for their dissenting religious beliefs. Although it did not provide the Huguenots with a legal status equal to that of Roman Catholics, this document represented an important step toward greater freedom of conscience in Europe. Unfortunately, it would not last. Less than a century later (in 1685), King Louis XIV would rescind the Edict of Nantes, an act that resulted in a rush of violence directed at the Huguenots and the subsequent emigration of nearly four hundred thousand French Protestants to various parts of Europe and the British American colonies. Yet, while France was backtracking on its movement toward religious liberty, a neighboring country was moving forward.

Across the English Channel in Britain, King William of Orange proclaimed the Act of Toleration (1689), which marked a significant step

1

toward the gradual implementation of religious liberty in Great Britain. The rapid expansion of dissenting Protestant denominations (e.g., Presbyterians, Quakers, and Anabaptists) in England during the 1600s made a policy of continued persecution costly and impractical. Efforts to curtail the liberties of Catholics and Protestant dissenters early in the century resulted in an extended period of internecine warfare that hindered economic progress and made unification of the British Isles a difficult task. Not only was the Act of Toleration a response to the religious strife that tore violently at the fabric of English society during the seventeenth century, but also it was a reaction to the growing religious toleration shown by one of Britain's main economic rivals – the Netherlands. Dutch Protestants, having suffered persecution under Spanish rule, ensured that minority religions were protected after the Netherlands gained independence in 1579. Not only did this facilitate trade with other nations, enriching the Dutch economy, but also the Netherlands served as a safe haven for religious sects fleeing persecution in England. These religious refugees, which included the famed Pilgrims, were often the most creative and industrious citizens in their home nations; England's loss was the Netherlands' gain. The English Toleration Act helped address this situation.

Ironically, although dissenting sects long fought for religious toleration in England, some were rather hesitant to extend it to others in the American colonies. The Pilgrims may have found a haven from persecution by fleeing to America, but Quakers and Baptists did not fare well in the Puritan strongholds of New England. Anglicans, too, were quick to declare their religious dominion. Virginians were required to pay taxes to support the officially established Church of England, a fact that the followers of other denominations found to be quite distasteful. And Catholics were never much liked anywhere in the colonies outside of their enclave in Maryland. But by the dawning of U.S. independence, the environment had shifted noticeably. The rise of religious pluralism and tolerance in Pennsylvania pressured the New England assemblies to back away from the most egregious forms of religious persecution. Beginning in 1776, the Virginia Assembly suspended the payment of tax-supported salaries to Anglican priests and placed the official status of the Church of England in limbo. A decade later, a series of contentious debates in the Virginia Assembly finally resulted in the passage of Thomas Jefferson's Bill for Establishing Religious Freedom, which eventually served as the template for the First Amendment of the U.S. Constitution. Even Catholics witnessed improvement in their legal and social status by the late 1700s. During the Revolutionary War, colonial Catholics once derided as "papists" and "antichrists" quickly became allies in the war against King George III. Nonetheless, Catholics still remained on the "least tolerated" list of denominations and faced ongoing discrimination throughout the nineteenth century.

Catholics fared better to the south in the Spanish colonies, albeit at the expense of Protestant freedoms. Roman Catholicism was granted an exclusive and privileged position in colonial Latin America. The Spanish Crown guaranteed that only one faith would be permitted in its section of the New World. Tithes were collected by the colonial government, Church officials tended vast landholdings granted to them by the Crown, and clergy were tried for misdeeds in separate ecclesiastical courts (*fueros eclesiásticos*), where they often received more favorable treatment. The *quid pro quo* for all of these benefits was that the Spanish monarch had the ability to appoint Church officials and approve of papal decrees that would apply to the colonies – a loss of religious freedom that the Vatican was willing to pay for its advantaged position. Circumstances changed dramatically for the Catholic Church in the decades following Latin American independence. During the mid-nineteenth century, Church landholdings were seized (often without compensation), and the rights of the clergy to conduct and collect fees for marriage and funeral services were revoked. Ecclesiastical *fueros* were abolished and priests came under the jurisdiction of civil courts. By the turn of the twentieth century, a handful of Latin American governments were allowing Protestant missionaries greater access to their countries, though enforcement of religious liberty was highly selective. Growing liberty and toleration throughout the mid- to late twentieth century led to a Protestant "explosion" in several parts of the region.

The Mexican Revolution ushered in perhaps the most dramatic change in church-state relations in Latin American history. The revolutionary constitution of 1917 prohibited the Church (and other religious denominations) from owning any property and clergy lost the right to run for office or vote, effectively making them second-class citizens, a situation immortalized in Graham Greene's classic novel *The Power and the Glory*. Passions ran high over this new church-state regime. Enforcement of these constitutional provisions ignited a short-lived civil war in the country during the late 1920s. However, conflict between the Church and state eased by the 1930s and by 1992 the Mexican episcopacy, with help from the Vatican, compelled the government to rescind the most restrictive anticlerical provisions in the constitution. These changes not only benefited the Catholic Church but also helped non-Catholics seeking access to the country.

Anticlericalism wasn't restricted to Mexico during the twentieth century. The fates of religious groups under the yoke of Communist rule are well known. Although it did not completely eliminate religious practice in Russia and Eastern Europe, the Soviet regime implemented such highly restrictive conditions on churches that religious participation became a rarity in most of these nations. Then in 1989 the Berlin Wall crumbled. The Kremlin no longer controlled Eastern Europe. The Soviet Union collapsed two years later. Along with the process of constructing new democratic constitutions, politicians throughout the region set about drafting laws governing religious groups. Although the United Nations' (UN's) Universal Declaration of Human Rights served as a general template for codifying religious freedom in each country, the specific regulations emanating from the policy-making processes varied quite substantially throughout the region. In Russia, an initial regime of religious freedom gave way to restrictive legislation that primarily favored the Russian Orthodox Church (ROC) just a half decade later. The most interesting irony of this legislation is that it was supported by former members of the Soviet Communist Party who had previously suppressed the rights of Orthodox clergy. Although the Russian Orthodox hierarchy celebrated the new laws that came into being in 1997, religious minorities heard the door to a promising new mission field slam shut.

The Baltic States of Lithuania, Latvia, and Estonia offer an instructive comparison.[1] Admittedly, these three nations differ in terms of their religious and ethnic makeup and their historical experiences predating the Communist era. Nonetheless, all three suffered under a similar repressive Soviet rule devoted to reducing religious influence in society from the end of World War II to 1990. The leadership arising from the ashes of Communist rule in each nation faced a "blank slate" for writing laws regulating religious groups. Yet the regulatory regimes taking shape by the mid-1990s differed dramatically. Lithuania had one of the most aggressive activist groups promoting religious liberty for Catholics *and* religious minorities (such as Pentecostals) in the 1970s and 1980s, advocating their positions through the largest underground publication in the Soviet Union – the *Chronicle of the Lithuanian Catholic Church*. Yet when the newly independent Lithuanian government finally instituted its laws governing religious bodies in 1995, Pentecostals (and several other prominent religious minorities) did not make the list of nine officially recognized "traditional" religions receiving special legal status. A concordat with the Vatican firmed up the preferential status of the Roman Catholic Church five years later. Neighboring

---

[1] I am deeply indebted to Cheryl Žilinskas for her knowledge, insight, and work on Eastern European religiosity.

Latvia imposed similar restrictions on religious minorities, only providing legal recognition for six traditional religions and not allowing more than one organization within the same confession – that is, an officially established church – to register, making it all but impossible for highly splintered evangelical and Pentecostal faiths to gain equal status. Like their southern neighbor, the Latvian government claimed that the influx of dangerous sects was a primary motivation for its lack of flexibility with particular religious groups. By contrast, as of 2006, Estonia – with a mix of Orthodox and Lutherans and a smattering of other denominations – possessed no officially recognized religion and maintains comparatively minimal requirements for the registration of new religious communities, making it the most religiously free country in the former Soviet bloc according to a recent Freedom House ranking (Marshall 2000, 26). Despite this, the Estonian parliament has considered tightening regulations on religious groups in recent years.

The aforementioned cases represent significant historical changes in religious liberty. In most instances, the path has been toward expanded freedom for religious organizations. But the march of religious liberty certainly has had its setbacks over time, as witnessed by the revocation of the Edict of Nantes and the 1917 Mexican Constitution.[2] And a casual glance at nations today reveals significant variation in the nature and extent to which churches are regulated, as can be seen in the Baltic States. All of this raises a series of important questions central to this book. What accounts for the origins and development of religious liberty over time? How can we explain the differences in the nature of laws regulating religions throughout countries? Related to these questions, we must ask why governments would ever want to place restrictions on the free worship of its citizens in the first place. Why would politicians favor one confession over other denominations, effectively guaranteeing a religious monopoly over a population? And once a religious monopoly is established, what factors would motivate politicians to deregulate the religious economy (i.e., introduce religious liberty)?

The issue of religious liberty garnered growing attention in the latter decades of the twentieth century. The UN saw fit to reaffirm its commitment to religious liberty in 1981 with Resolution 36/55, the Declaration on the Elimination of All Forms of Intolerance and Discrimination Based on Religion and Belief. Seventeen years later, one hundred fifty representatives from various countries and religious groups gathered in Oslo to declare the

---

[2] Even in the United States, perhaps the cradle of religious liberty, the cause of religious liberty has arguably had its setbacks, a subject that will be examined in Chapter 6.

importance of religious freedom yet again. A plethora of nongovernmental organizations (NGOs) has arisen during this time to monitor religious freedom throughout the world, including the International Coalition for Religious Freedom, the International Religious Liberty Association, International Religious Freedom Watch, the Religious Liberty Commission and the Rutherford Institute (cf. Moreno 1996). Even the prestigious Freedom House, which has monitored economic freedom and civil liberties since 1941, created a separate division specifically for monitoring religious freedom in 1986 – the Center for Religious Freedom (cf. Marshall 2000).

Policy makers have turned their attention to the issue of religious liberty, largely responding to pressure from constituents interested in the issue. In 1998, the 105th Congress of the United States passed the International Religious Freedom Act (P.L. 105–292) requiring the U.S. Department of State to provide an annual overview of religious liberty and persecution around the world for consideration in foreign-policy making. It has factored into debates surrounding the economic trade status of several countries, most notably the People's Republic of China (PRC) where groups such as the Roman Catholic Church, various Protestant missionaries, and Falun Gong have suffered serious persecution. Domestically, a series of U.S. Supreme Court decisions throughout the 1990s prompted federal policy makers to pass legislation aimed at specifically defining and protecting the rights of religious individuals and institutions.[3] Other countries such as Sweden have substantially modified the way in which religious groups are regulated and a number of other countries in Europe are trying to find ways to legally incorporate the Islamic faith of immigrants into their highly secular societies. Finally, the salience and increased visibility of religious-based conflict at the beginning of the twenty-first century has served only to reinforce our desire to understand all facets of religion, including the interactions between church and state – the institutional nexus of religious freedom.

To date, however, few scholars have sought to explain the rise of – or, more precisely, the change and fluctuations in – religious liberty in any theoretically systematic way. Most studies have either emphasized the consequences of varying forms and levels of religious liberty or regulation (cf. Monsma and Soper 1997; Stark and Iannaccone 1994; Chaves and Cann 1992), discussed the normative implications of varying interpretations

---

[3] The two major pieces of legislation passed by the U.S. Congress were the Religious Freedom Restoration Act (1993), which was declared partially unconstitutional by the Supreme Court four years after its implementation, and the Religious Land Use and Institutional Persons Act (RLUIPA) (2000).

of religious freedom (cf. Segers and Jelen 1998; Instituto de Investigaciones Jurídicas 1996),[4] or provided detailed historiographies (cf. Curry 1986; McLoughlin 1971) with little attempt to develop a generalizable theory for the emergence of religious liberty throughout time and space.[5] Only a few scholars – such as Roger Finke (1990),[6] Charles Hanson (1998),[7] and John Anderson (2003) – have attempted to provide theoretically developed explanations for the rise of religious freedom, though each focused on specific case studies and did not seek greater generalizability for their ideas. Part of this general scholarly neglect can be attributed to the fact that the answer to this puzzle (if it is considered a puzzle at all) is thought to be obvious. The secularization paradigm, which has dominated social scientific studies of religion until recently, appeared to provide the solution. From this perspective, religious liberty was concomitant with religious pluralism and a general decline in spirituality and was considered a natural outcome of the process of social, political, and economic modernization. The question about the origins of religious liberty was not seen as much of a question at all. This book attempts to remedy the neglect of this important topic by providing a general theoretical framework for studying the origins and development of religious liberty.

Although the path toward religious liberty has often been considered a natural outgrowth of more "modern" thinking (i.e., the triumph of Enlightenment philosophy) over traditional thought, the overarching thesis presented here argues that *interests* play an equally important if not more critical role in securing legislation aimed at unburdening religious groups from onerous state regulations. Specifically, I will focus on the political and

---

[4] The normative literature on religious freedom, centering mostly on interpretations of the U.S. Constitution's First Amendment, is too voluminous to cite here. For the broad parameters of the debate, see Clarke Cochran's detailed preface to Segers and Jelen (1998). Or, should the reader be more adventurous, I suggest a stroll down the BR and BX aisles of any major research library.

[5] There are several edited volumes such as Sigmund (1999), Helmstadter (1997), and van der Vyver and Witte (1996) that deal with religious freedom in different eras and countries, but the nature of these volumes – with different authors emphasizing different aspects of religious liberty – make the promulgation of a reasonably unified theory difficult. This should not be seen as a critique of these volumes as they provide a wealth of detailed information in their own right. Moreover, had any of these works attempted to provide an overarching theory of the origins of religious liberty, I would not be writing this book.

[6] Finke's article on the *origins* and *consequences* of religious liberty tended to focus more on the latter than the former, though his initial thoughts on the topic of origins was a major inspiration for this work.

[7] Hanson's explanation for why American colonists yielded greater tolerance to Catholics during the Revolutionary War might be considered more of an emphasis on a particular factor – the need to win French support – than a deductive theory.

economic interests of politicians (rulers)[8] and the institutional interests of religious leaders in the policy-making arena. As such, this book discusses the *political*, as opposed to the *intellectual*, origins of religious liberty. This is not to say that ideas are irrelevant when formulating policy; ideas do matter as will be discussed in Chapter 2. However, when competing ideas exist in society, it is often *political interests* that tip the balance of the debate in one direction or another.

The interests at play in determining the nature of religious liberty come from both the side of religious actors (church leaders, clergy, and parishioners) and secular rulers (legislators, presidents, monarchs, and dictators). Leaders of a dominant religion in society, I contend, are inclined to prefer a regulatory regime that discriminates against religious minorities, making it difficult for them to worship and/or gain converts.[9] In contrast, religious minorities will favor regulations that make it easier for their clergy and members to openly practice their faith and proselytize.[10] The degree of denominational pluralism in a society thus affects the likelihood that greater religious liberty will prevail. A religious market with a plurality of denominations (i.e., where no majority denomination exists) will be most favorable to the expansion of religious freedom, something that James Madison recognized in *Federalist 51*. An environment wherein religious minorities are gaining significant ground will also be amenable to the growth of religious freedom but not without conflict or attempts to restrict that freedom by leaders of the dominant religion. Societies where one denomination is hegemonic and religious minorities are of no consequence will tend toward a highly regulated environment favoring the dominant church. The one important exception to this latter situation is where political leaders see the dominant church as a potential threat to their political survival and seek to limit its societal influence. Such situations will also tend toward a highly regulated (less free) religious environment that does not favor the dominant church nor most other denominations.

---

[8] The term *politician* will be used throughout the text in a generic manner to refer to any type of political actor – be it a democrat or a dictator.

[9] As will be noted in the following text, this discrimination can be subtle yet very powerful. Although proclaiming favoritism toward religious freedom as a general principle, it is still possible to favor microregulations that inhibit an upstart church from gaining foothold in a certain area. Battles over land-use law and zoning regulations are common in religious freedom cases.

[10] The scope of this book is largely limited to religious liberty in Christian societies wherein most of the religions examined are proselytizing. I realize that some faiths (e.g., Judaism) and denominations do not aggressively seek members. Nonetheless, the arguments made in this book still apply.

But religious leaders and activists are not the only ones who determine the degree of religious freedom in society. The role of government officials is essential too. After all, these secular rulers – be they democrats or dictators – are the ones who put pen to paper and define the legal parameters under which churches and their members operate. Understanding the motives and incentives of these rulers thus becomes crucial in understanding the origins of religious liberty. Moreover, policy makers do not make laws and regulations on a specific topic in a vacuum; in other words, policy makers often consider factors seemingly unrelated to the specific topic under debate when passing legislation. This is important to realize considering that many of the discussions related to religious liberty tend to center on the moral arguments surrounding different legal configurations of religious freedom (e.g., Harmin 2005; Pufendorf [1687] 2002; Segers and Jelen 1998; Tierney 1996; Locke [1689] 1955).[11] This leaves the impression that the nature of religious liberty is the result of an intellectual (and often esoteric) debate. To the contrary, I contend that political actors consider a set of other *interests* when deciding how to regulate religion. Specifically, I argue that politicians take into account their own political survival (i.e., ability to get reelected or stave off a coup), the need to raise government revenue, and the ability to grow the economy when writing laws pertaining to religious freedom. Whenever a rather restrictive set of laws governing religious activity affects any of these three interests, secular rulers will be more apt to liberalize regulations on religion – that is, promote religious liberty.

Defining the Scope of Religious Liberty

What constitutes religious liberty? As an outside observer, how can one tell whether or not a country has religious freedom? This latter question is perhaps misleading in that it assumes religious liberty is a simple dichotomy – that is, it is something that a nation either possesses or does not possess. Constitutional declarations pronouncing a "right to conscience" enhance this perception that religious freedom is an "either/or" concept. In reality, religious liberty is a large umbrella concept that covers a wide array of policies that affect worshipers, clergy, and spiritual institutions. Methodist Bishop G. Bromley Oxnam, in a 1947 article for the magazine *Churchman*,

---

[11] Again, this is most common in scholarly discussions about the First Amendment of the U.S. Constitution and the various cases that have come before the U.S. Supreme Court related to the subject of religion.

laid out what might be the best definition of *religious liberty* and helped to elucidate the scope of policies that affect such freedom:

> When we speak of religious liberty, specifically, we mean freedom of worship according to conscience and to bring up children in the faith of their parents; freedom for the individual to change his religion; freedom to preach, educate, publish, and carry on missionary activities; and freedom to organize with others, and to acquire and hold property for these purposes. (Cited in Stokes 1950, 20–1)[12]

What Oxnam reveals here is that religious liberty involves more than the right of personal conscience; it includes a host of policies concerning property rights, education, media ownership, and public speech. The ability of congregants to come together, build a church, and reach out to nonbelieving members of the community is an essential part of religious freedom. Although religious freedom can certainly be framed in moral imperatives, it is important to understand that religious liberty is a matter of government regulatory policy and can touch on issues as diverse as citizenship requirements and land-use restrictions.

From this point forward, I will view religious liberty as a matter of government regulation. Thinking of religious liberty in regulatory terms has several analytical advantages. First, following up on the work of scholars studying regulatory policy, the analysis can be cast in terms of cost-benefit analysis. Government policies impose various costs and benefits on different individuals and groups. In a world where people have unlimited goals and face scarce resources, any increase in cost can be thought of as a restriction on one's liberty; making some activity more expensive reduces the ability of a person with fixed resources to pursue that activity.[13] For instance, a

---

[12] The original citation is attributed to G. Bromley Oxnam, "Liberty: Roman or Protestant," *Churchman* (November 15, 1947). No page numbers provided.

[13] I am aware of the argument that without a minimal restriction of liberty imposed by some form of government, humans would be living in a Hobbesian state of nature wherein life is solitary, nasty, brutish, and short. Such a world – free from all government restrictions – would not be conducive to liberty at all given that we would live in a perpetual state of fear of others. As such, some basic restrictions upon behavior – e.g., laws preventing murder, theft, and jaywalking – are necessary for humans to realize a more comfortable and expansive freedom. Institutions such as an independent judiciary are also necessary to guarantee that freely made economic contracts are respected. In order to recoup the costs for a government to provide the public good of security, it is necessary to coerce citizens into paying taxes. Paying taxes is a restriction on liberty in an absolute sense, but the sense of security that tax revenue buys does enhance our ability to enjoy freedom. The optimal level of taxation needed to provide for basic public goods that allow us to enjoy a comfortable freedom is up for eternal debate. Suffice it to say that I do not intend to resolve that debate here.

regulation requiring auto manufacturers to produce cars that meet certain mileage standards or pollution requirements limits the freedom of those firms to build the cars that they want. It also limits consumer choice. Drivers who prefer heavy and fast cars will have fewer options in the marketplace when car makers produce only light, slow cars to meet the new regulations. Moreover, the additional costs of making more fuel-efficient cars may mean that some individuals will no longer have the financial means to purchase a car and will be restricted to public transportation. A zoning law requiring church buildings to be no more than a specific size (e.g., 20,000 square feet) or located in a certain area are also likely to impact the abilities of clergy to attract the number of adherents they would like to. Regulations impose costs on Chrysler and Christians alike. Non-Christians are also subject to onerous government regulations (cf. Fetzer and Soper 2005).

Second, conceptualizing liberty as a matter of government regulation allows us to see the issue in multidimensional terms. Proclaimed freedom in one arena may be cut short by restrictions in another policy area. A government may allow its citizens to own land and build private houses. However, land-use requirements or zoning restrictions may limit the ability of people to choose where they want to live, how much of their land they can develop (as opposed to leaving it in a natural state), and what type of house they would like to build. Mandates on certain types of building materials (e.g., slate roofing) or construction features (e.g., energy-efficient windows) may also raise the cost of homes, thereby excluding some poorer individuals from the housing market. Conceiving of liberty as a multidimensional concept subject to numerous regulatory restrictions reveals that liberty is not simply a dichotomous variable – that is, something you either have or don't have. A constitutional guarantee of freedom of speech does not mean an absolute lack of restrictions on public speech. Laws punishing slander, prohibitions on copying intellectual property, and restrictions on campaign advertising all put limits on free-speech rights.

Understanding that religious liberty is multidimensional allows us to conceive of it as existing on a continuum. Fox (2005), Grim (2004), Grim and Finke (2006), Norris and Inglehart (2004), Barrett et al. (2001), Gill (1999a), and Chaves and Cann (1992) have recognized this fact as they have attempted to construct indices measuring religious freedom. Laying aside whether these indices are adequately comprehensive, covering all possible dimensions of religious liberty,[14] they should be a reminder that

---

[14] I should note that I have the utmost admiration for the efforts of all these scholars in measuring religious freedom and my comment here by no means implies a critical attitude toward their achievements. It is just that the mere fact of trying to capture every possible

subtle changes in any one dimension of religious freedom can move a country toward greater *or lesser* freedom. It is not necessarily the case that countries ultimately move toward greater freedom in a unilinear fashion, as evidenced by the revocation of the Edict of Nantes. A brief discussion of the various areas of regulation affecting religious organizations and their adherents will help illustrate the point that religious liberty is a multifaceted concept and how such regulations impact the cost-benefit calculations of religious individuals and institutions.

The broadest regulation relating to religious liberty would be a constitutional declaration stating freedom of conscience. Most, but not all, nations of the world maintain some statement of religious freedom in their constitutions. Even countries like the PRC and Cuba provide a constitutional guarantee for freedom of conscience, but it would be difficult to consider these nations as bastions of religious liberty. To use a worn cliché, when it comes to religious liberty, the devil is in the details. Let us further examine those details.

Regulations that affect the liberty of religious individuals and groups can be grouped into two broad categories – negative restrictions and positive endorsements of select denominations. The former category is relatively self-explanatory and includes specific regulations telling certain (or all) religious groups that they cannot undertake certain activities, making it difficult for them to gather for worship or proselytize. Positive endorsements of select denominations have a more subtle effect when it comes to restricting religious liberty. Here, favoritism shown to one faith tradition may make it implicitly more difficult for members of other groups to gain new adherents, as will be shown in the following text.

Negative Restrictions on Religious Liberty

Throughout history, governments have found a number of ways to limit the presence and/or expansion of "undesirable sects." Simply banning religious clergy from living in or entering a country is probably the most obvious manner of achieving this goal. Immigration restrictions on Protestant missionaries were common in Latin America during the first half of the twentieth century (Pierson 1974, 177; Lodwick 1969, 103; Goff 1968, 3/27–36) and the current Russian and Chinese governments are careful about handing out visas to individuals seeking to spread their faith. One

dimension of religious liberty is an extremely difficult task, and one that I avoid. Grim (2004) constructs the most sophisticated of the indices. See also Grim and Finke (2006).

can clearly see how this would be a restriction of religious freedom; without leaders, churches are unlikely to get off the ground. Such restrictions also affect consumer choice and the ability of individuals to fulfill their own freedom of conscience. If clergy from certain denominations are prohibited from proselytizing, individuals who might prefer a certain type of religion (e.g., Pentecostalism and Mormonism) will not be able to easily find a group of like-minded believers. Such restrictions on consumer choice are difficult to see in practice given that it is hard to determine whether a person has a preference for a certain type of religion when that religion is not present. How can one know that they enjoy evangelical Protestantism when no evangelical Protestant options exist for them to try? Leaders of historically dominant religions in a nation often resort to claims that a nation's populace subscribes only to one true faith and that prohibitions on foreign sects are required to protect the citizenry from cultural contamination (cf. Kuznetsov 1996; Consejo Episcopal Latinoamericano 1984). This raises an interesting dilemma. If one religion truly defines a national culture, and people are deeply steeped in that culture, restrictions on foreign missionaries would be unnecessary; the populace would reject the new sect out of hand. In reality, such restrictions are often necessary because there is a variety of preferences for different types of religion in a society and because the dominant church has not done a sufficient job in capturing the loyalty of the citizenry, leaving the "unchurched" ripe for the picking.[15] In addition to banning foreign religious personnel, governments have also been known to ban some of the primary equipment of those missionaries. In Latin America, many countries prohibited the importation of the Bible as it was commonly used by Protestant missionaries to teach people to read (Montgomery 1979, 89).

Once inside a country, politicians still control several policy levers that allow them to raise significant barriers to the religious freedom of both minority and historically dominant religious groups. Registration requirements for churches are a common avenue for government leaders to discriminate among denominations. Most governments require that various groups – both religious and nonreligious – register with the government to receive certain perquisites, which may include tax-exempt status, the ability to be represented as a corporation in legal proceedings, the ability to

---

[15] Kutznetsov does acknowledge that although the "Russian nation has traditionally been Orthodox and considers itself belonging to the Russian Orthodox Church" (indicating that there is a unified national religious culture) the religious soul of Russians had been "spiritually weakened by the seventy-year onslaught of atheism" (1996, 10).

purchase property as a corporate body, and access to certain public institutions such as prisons, state-run hospitals, and the military.[16] After strug-
gling nearly a decade for a legal status that would put them on par with the
Catholic Church and give them access to prisons and the military, Protestants in Chile finally obtained such recognition in 1999 (Isaacson 2003).[17]
In part, legal registration requirements are a matter of public safety. No
government to my knowledge is willing to allow the legal registration of
a religion that practices human sacrifice or may in any other way violate
basic civil laws. This reveals that religious liberty is not absolute.[18] But
beyond simply restricting groups that could do public harm, the nature of
registration requirements can subtly, yet significantly, affect the operating
costs of churches and hence their freedom to practice their faith. Some
governments mandate that a church must have a certain number of followers before it gains legal recognition. Setting this number high can exclude
small startup sects or denominations that operate on a highly decentralized
and congregational basis (e.g., Pentecostals), as compared to groups that
have a more episcopal nature and can claim broad membership throughout
distinct subunits such as parishes (e.g., Catholics). For example, the Czech
Republic's parliament, overriding a presidential veto, recently increased the
standards a church must meet for legal recognition.

> [A] church seeking registration must submit a petition containing the personal
> data and signatures of at least 300 Czech Republic residents. In order to obtain
> additional specific rights, however, the church must have existed for at least
> 10 years and must have a membership equal to at least 0.1 percent of the
> population of the Czech Republic. Priests' confessional secrecy is protected
> only after a church has existed for 50 years. (Pajas 2003)

Membership of 0.1 percent of the Czech population in 2003 would be
roughly equivalent to ten thousand adherents, a figure that even the largest
independent "megachurches" would have a difficult time achieving. Not
surprisingly this requirement favored the Catholic Church, the largest

---

[16] Religious personnel frequently seek access to such public institutions. Oftentimes prisons,
hospitals, and military barracks are places where people need consoling due to stressful
situations. They also offer a potential recruiting ground for new converts.

[17] I confirmed this in a number of interviews conducted in Santiago, Chile in 1999.

[18] One of the problems with the short-lived U.S. Religious Freedom Restoration Act (1993–
7) was that it allowed for the proliferation of nonmainstream sects and cults that maintained
practices allowing incarcerated felons to opportunistically avoid prison regulations or make
onerous requests upon penitentiary administrators. For examples, consult the following
U.S. District Court cases: *Hamilton v. Schriro*, 863 F. Supp. 1019; *Rust v. Clark*, 851 F.
Supp. 377; and *Campos v. Coughlin*, 854 F. Supp. 194.

religion in the Czech Republic.[19] The inability to achieve legal status for small or congregationally based groups may imperil their survival as they would have to pay taxes (which are not an insignificant cost for organizations that often rely on voluntary contributions) and might not receive permission to obtain a church building. Governments can also set historical restrictions on churches, requiring them to have had an institutional presence for some designated period before granting them legal status. The 1992 legal reforms in Mexico imposed such a historical requirement, putting many Protestant congregations in a Catch-22 situation – in order to gain legal status church groups needed to show they had a historical presence of five years, but such a presence could not be easily verified because those organizations were not legal before the reforms took effect (Gill 1999; Scott 1992a).[20]

Although allowing the legal presence of religious groups, governments can also have a negative effect on religious liberty by banning specific religious practices. In the infamous *Smith v. Oregon* case, the Supreme Court ruled that the state of Oregon could legally prevent Native Americans from using a sacramental drug (peyote).[21] France currently prohibits Muslim women from wearing the traditional head scarf in public schools, and Turkey bans the wearing of Islamic head scarves in public institutions altogether (Kuru 2006). Some have argued that prohibitions on prayer in public school – whether it be a public prayer or time allocated for private reflection – also violates the basic tenets of religious freedom by discriminating against religion in general in favor of secularism (Monsma and Soper 1997, 33).[22]

---

[19] Jews did not meet the 0.1 percent requirement because they are not numerous in the Czech Republic and do not have an overarching organization. Nonetheless, the state granted Jewish synagogues legal status because they were recognized by the state prior to 1989. Muslims have not received similar recognition to date. See U.S. State Department (2004).

[20] See also Chapter 4.

[21] The full title of the case is *Smith v. Employment Division, Department of Human Resources of Oregon*, 484 U.S. 872. The actual issue being contested involved two employees who worked for a drug rehabilitation center and were fired for using peyote during their off hours. The employees were denied unemployment benefits because the firing was considered just according to Oregon law.

[22] This author, although admittedly a proponent of religious freedom generally, takes no normative position on the issues of sacramental use of controlled substances or of prayer in public schools. But even without taking a position, it is still possible – in a positivist sense – to see how such prohibitions restrict religious liberty. One's normative opinion regarding the legality of a certain practice need not stand in the way of determining whether criminalizing those practices would be a restriction of freedom. In this way, I can both oppose human sacrifice on normative grounds and contend that making that practice illegal is a restriction of someone's religious freedom.

Property-rights regulations offer another means wherein the freedom of churches can be restricted. Manipulation of property rights represents one of the most common areas wherein government officials affect religious liberty. As the quote from Bishop Oxnam reveals, the ability to hold and use property as one sees fit is crucial to a church's goal of serving its parishioners and expanding its membership. This is crucial not only to religious leaders who would like to construct church buildings but also for individual believers who wish to have a place where they can meet on a regular basis. Outright property-ownership restrictions on religious organizations present an obvious example of a restriction on the freedom of churches, particularly if other similar organizations (perhaps private nonprofit groups or government services) are granted ownership. Turkey forbids private ownership of mosques; all (officially recognized) mosques are closely regulated by the state (cf. Kuru 2006). The same was true for Christian churches in Mexico prior to the 1992 reforms. The inability of Catholics to build new churches put costly limitations on the clergy's outreach efforts. It was even more difficult for Protestant missionaries who could only meet in rented gymnasiums or someone's private home. Such space limitations obviously restricted church growth. In former Communist countries, the restitution of church property seized by dictatorial governments has become a major issue of contention and one that many clergy see as a fundamental issue of religious freedom (Földesi 1996, 250).

Although outright restrictions on property ownership for churches represent fairly obvious violations of religious liberty, other more subtle property regulations can be just as deleterious. Zoning laws may represent one of the most frequently used forms of legislation used to curb the freedom of churches. Simply dictating where a church can build, and how big the building must be, can have a dramatic impact on church growth. In the United States, zoning regulations have been used to prevent Jehovah's Witnesses – who require adherents to evangelize door-to-door – from constructing church buildings near residential communities and from canvassing neighborhoods.[23] A 2001 moratorium on church construction in unincorporated King County (Washington), followed by a size restriction of twenty thousand square feet, drew such furor among religious leaders that the county executive had to back down from his plan (Lewis 2001; Modie 2001). In Europe, obtaining the proper building permits for nontraditional religious groups can take nearly a decade (cf. Fetzer and Soper 2005; Stark

---

[23] See the U.S. Supreme Court cases *Martin v. Struthers*, 319 U.S. 141 (1943), *Murdock v. Commonwealth of Pennsylvania*, 319 U.S. 105, and *Watchtower Bible v. Village of Stratton*, No. 00-1737 (2002).

and Iannaccone 1994). And in Latin America, local governments have been known to block the construction of Mormon temples,[24] prohibit loud-speakers from being placed outside of Pentecostal churches, and prevent evangelicals from parading around a neighborhood singing (Scott 1992b), two techniques often used to attract new adherents (cf. Gill 1999b).

Ownership issues not only relate to buildings but also to media access. Because many religions seek to "spread the Word," possessing an efficient means of spreading – through print or electronic media – is often crucial. As Finke and Iannaconne (1993) note, changes in U.S. telecommunications laws in the 1960s had a dramatic effect in advancing the evangelical movement in the United States and giving rise to televangelism. In Latin America, evangelicals have had difficulty obtaining broadcasting permits for religious radio programs.[25] The Mexican government maintained an outright ban on religious broadcasting and other forms of media for most of the twentieth century (Gill 1999c), and the regime of Juan Perón did so selectively against Protestants for several years in the 1940s and 1950s (Canclini 1972, 84–5). And the British parliament stirred controversy in 1996 when it promulgated a new law regulating digital media that excluded religious groups from entering that burgeoning market (Blackman 2003). Yet despite significant changes various evangelical groups still find it difficult to purchase broadcasting licenses (Wilson 2003).

On top of all of this, governments can impose office-holding restrictions on individuals, requiring them to be a member of a particular faith (or not a member as it may be) to hold a public office (Hutson 1998, 62–3; Curry 1986, 79–80). This was quite common in colonial America where only members of the Church of England in good standing were permitted to sit on legislative councils. The same was true in parts of New England where Puritans were the favored denomination. Likewise, Lutherans (or members of the Reformed Church) were the only individuals who could hold civil-service positions in the Nordic countries for most of the nineteenth century.[26] Until recently, the Argentine constitution barred any non-Catholic (sometimes interpreted broadly as non-Christian) from becoming president (Bonino 1999, 199), a situation that was mildly troubling for Carlos Menem who was rumored to have an Islamic heritage (Marshall 2000, 56). The situation was reversed in the former Soviet Union wherein known membership in a religious organization was grounds for denying one access

---

[24] "Temple Construction Blocked," *National Catholic Reporter* (April 26, 1996), 7.
[25] Interview with Paul Finkenbeiner, Director of Hermano Pablo Ministries, Costa Mesa, CA (March 16, 1993).
[26] I am grateful to Steve Pfaff for this observation.

to Communist Party membership. Given that membership in the Communist Party was a necessity if one wanted to have improved housing and job prospects, this requirement created a huge disincentive for affiliating with any denomination.

All told, there are numerous regulations and requirements that increase the costs of practicing religion on individuals and organizations. Any increase in such costs due to government policy should be viewed as a restriction on religious liberty, for better or worse.[27] It should be remembered that because most religions tend to be community oriented, any restriction that raises the costs to a religious organization or institution will have a negative impact on the individual members (or potential members) of that group.

Positive Endorsement of Specific Denominations

Government policy in the religious arena not only centers on negative prohibitions on groups but also can involve positive actions toward religious groups. Such positive actions usually imply an official endorsement (beyond the basic registration requirements noted in the preceding text), financial subsidization, and/or some other form of public assistance in promoting the faith. When all religious groups in a country are given equal endorsement and/or equivalent subsidization (in proportion to their share of the population) then no significant infringement on religious liberty exists, although the matter of whether secular and atheist groups are included in this mix becomes a sticky definitional issue. Monsma and Soper (1997), in their examination of such policies throughout five nations, do make the case that secularism should be considered akin to a religion. They further note that in places like the United Sates secularism tends to get preferential endorsement in the public square, whereas countries like the Netherlands and Australia do a reasonable job in balancing religious and secular interests in public policy.[28]

---

[27] To reiterate, I do not take a normative stand here on whether a restriction of religious liberty is good or bad. I simply seek to show that an increase in regulatory costs on religion represents an infringement on religious liberty. Although I personally find the practice of human sacrifice to be objectionable, government policies that forbid such practice are considered a limitation on religious freedom. The same could be true of sacramental drug use or other activities that governments deem unacceptable.

[28] I would like to note that the work by Monsma and Soper (1997) provided a major impetus for this current study. Their detailing of religious policies in five democratic nations, and what that implied for religious freedom, was an eye-opening experience for me, and the text remains one of my favorite works in the study of religion and politics.

It is possible, however, that positive endorsements of a specific denomination (or denominations) to the exclusion of others can impose a significant
cost on the nonfavored faiths. For instance, some governments provide substantial financial assistance to official state churches or to churches that have
had a long historical presence in the nation. These funds may be paid for
clerical salaries, church building maintenance, or other programs. This was
common in many parts of Latin America during the nineteenth and twentieth centuries (Mecham 1966, passim). The administration of Juan Perón
even went so far as to purchase limousines for Catholic bishops (Sweeney
1970, 11), and the Argentine government to this day provides funds for
refurbishing Catholic churches.[29] Although this may not seem to be a substantial burden on any other religion's religious liberty, it does contain an
implicit cost. If a portion of an individual's tax dollars are being used for
the maintenance of a specific denomination, those individuals will be less
likely to join another denomination that will require them to pay (through
voluntary contributions) for the upkeep of that church. This goes under
the common economic principle that government subsidization of some
activity will have a "crowding out" effect of an equivalent service in the
private sector (Gill and North 2005; Hungerman 2005, 2004). An official
government endorsement of one religious group as a "state church" (e.g.,
the Church of England) could have a similar effect. The psychological or
social costs of associating with a dissenting sect could be significantly high
as to prevent some people from joining a denomination that they may more
likely prefer; if one decides to join a religion other than the official state
religion, they may feel less attached to that particular nation and may be
ostracized from their community.[30]

The issue of state-assisted tax collection poses a related issue in the realm
of religious liberty. Religious groups rely heavily on voluntary contributions
to pay their clergy and maintain their facilities (see Chapter 2) and therefore
often have difficulty in raising revenue (cf. Della Cava 1993; Harris 1993).
Having the help of the state with its coercive tax-collecting power can prove
to be an enormous asset to a church. If the state provides this service for
some historical religions but not other, particularly newer, denominations,
those "upstart sects" may have a hard time "up and starting." Not only
would the new religious groups have to convince potential adherents that

---

[29] Author's observation of a sign outside of the Argentine National Cathedral (Catholic) in
Buenos Aires declaring that public funds were being used to renovate the building.

[30] No study of this possible effect exists to my knowledge, but the relationship is possible. An
enterprising graduate student might consider this as a thesis topic worthy of exploration.

their "religious brand" is better but also they would have to convince those same people either to pay additional financial contributions to the new church or find a way to opt out of the current tax structure. Germany is a case in point. The German government collects a mandatory tax from individuals for the Evangelical (Lutheran) Church, the Catholic Church, and Jewish synagogues (Monsma and Soper 1997, 173–4). Although it is relatively easy to opt out of this system, it poses a similar (if not more direct) set of incentives as public subsidization of religious groups – if I'm already paying for one religion, why bother to join another? One of the disadvantaging aspects of this type of policy is that it is difficult to implement for congregationally organized or decentralized religions, such as Pentecostals or Muslims. Monsma and Soper detail the problem and show how it can create a situation wherein a government tries to impose a situation on a religion that religious leaders don't want.

> The failure of the Muslim community to attain public corporation status [and be eligible for tax collection], given the fact it is the third largest religious community in Germany, is especially noteworthy. This failure is due, not primarily to overt discrimination against Islam, but to the fact that the Muslim organizational structure does not fit the prevailing German pattern. Both the Catholic and Evangelical churches are hierarchical in nature and thus they have centralized councils and leaders who can deal with centralized governmental bureaucratic bodies and leaders. But Islam is not hierarchical in nature.... This has led to an impasse, with German authorities for the most part saying the Muslims need to organize themselves in such a way that they can qualify for public corporation status and many Muslims saying the Germans need to make allowance for their organizational structures. (1997, 172–3)

A similar situation troubles leaders in the Netherlands.

Finally, the issue of public education is another key arena where public favoritism toward one faith, even in an environment relatively free of negative restrictions on religious minorities, can lower the general level of religious liberty in society. One of the enduring principles in the sociology of religion is that individuals who are steeped in a religious tradition early tend to stay in that tradition as they mature (Iannaccone 1990). If a government allows children to be taught one specific "brand" of religion in public schools or if generic religion classes are only taught by the clergy of a specific faith (a practice common in Latin America until recently), it will become difficult for minority sects to recruit them later on. Although imposing no normative claim on this practice, it is possible to see how preferential access to public education given to one religion is viewed as a significant disadvantage by other religions. Beyond schooling, governments can also give special recognition to some religious marriages, but not others, creating disincentives for lovebirds who might otherwise want to join a different denomination from converting. Such was the case in much of Latin America until the late twentieth century (Mecham 1966, passim).

The Separation of Church and State

It should be noted that up to this point I have avoided using the phrase "separation of church and state," which is frequently bandied about in conversations of religious liberty. In the United States, Thomas Jefferson's famous "wall of separation" is frequently seen as commensurate with religious freedom; the higher and more impenetrable the wall, the more religious liberty supposedly exists. However, as Monsma and Soper (1997) and Mary Segers (Segers and Jelen 1998) argue, a strong wall that excludes religion from the public square can have the effect of privileging secularism over religion in general, a potential violation of religious liberty. In more extreme cases, such as the Soviet Union, an aggressive separation of church and state can be consistent with severe restrictions on religious liberty. In short, "separation of church and state" does not tell us much about the differential costs and benefits imposed on religious groups and individuals, which forms the primary basis for a definition of religious liberty here. For these reasons, I will endeavor to avoid the phrase "separation of church and state."[31]

Nor do I intend to address theoretically the issue of religious persecution and harassment in this work. Although I provide instances of such persecution in the discussion to come, I am not concerned primarily with the psychological or social motivations that make one individual or group hate another. My main concern is to understand why politicians would legally commit themselves on paper to changing the way they manage religious groups. The issue of persecution, if not a matter of legal policy,[32] raises concerns regarding the enforcement of rules. This is a fascinating topic

---

[31] There are instances in the discussion of Latin America where I will use the term *separation of church and state* to indicate when a government ended official (often constitutional) recognition of the Roman Catholic Church. Likewise, the term *disestablishment* as used in the case of the United States will refer to a "church-state separation." The separation of church and state does not necessarily imply religious freedom.

[32] Few countries to my knowledge actually have laws that state they will persecute religious individuals. Even places such as Saudi Arabia and the PRC, which place severe restrictions on certain types of religious practice, do not have laws that state they will physically harm or harass dissenting sects.

unto itself – why do governments choose to ignore enforcement of laws they have written down? However, my more immediate concern is with official policy making, and I do not intend to devote much attention to the important topic of persecution in so far as it relates to nonenforcement of existing law. I do understand, however, that many religious groups consider written legal restrictions on their behavior to be a form of persecution, so in that regard I do address this concern.

Scope and Methodology

With the main topic and thesis of this work and a definition of religious liberty out of the way, it is now time to elaborate on the goals of this book. The primary intent of this book is to propose a general deductive theory regarding the political origins of religious liberty that incorporates the role of human agency through the use of rational choice theory. This theory places interests, as opposed to ideas (or culture), at the center of the analysis. Without denying a role for ideational factors (e.g., values, ideologies), rational choice theory provides a useful starting point – the self-interested, utility-maximizing individual – from which to build more complete theories. Assuming that humans have some degree of control over their own history (as opposed to having their actions predetermined by some structural arrangement), it makes sense to begin with a theory that places human agency at its core.

The success of building a general theory not only will rest on its empirical accuracy but also will be determined by its ability to be applied widely throughout space and time. This approach yields an immediate tension. Placing emphasis on empirical validity and human agency pushes one in the direction of "thick description," wherein the specific actions of individuals in unique historical situations become all-encompassing in the explanation. Generality is hard to achieve because individuals (with varying interests and calculating capacities) change over time, and historical situations rarely repeat themselves exactly. Nonetheless, it is reasonable to assert that humans behave in patterned ways, and any pattern is subject to generality. Striking a balance is critical to gaining maximum explanatory "leverage" (cf. King, Keohane, and Verba 1994; Lave and March 1975). The theory laid out here attempts to strike such a balance by arguing that, in general, political actors respond to changing opportunity costs that affect their ability to remain in office and maximize revenue. It will be argued that these are relatively ubiquitous goals that are shared by almost all political actors irrespective of time or place. Laws pertaining to religious freedom will be affected by how politicians respond to these changing opportunity costs and some specific historical conditions. As for the latter, I will outline a general set of conditions that appear to have a general impact on the degree to which religions are regulated. I hope this theory will be useful as a general framework for scholars examining specific cases and in building a broader research agenda designed to examine the issue of religious liberty (and "liberty" more generally) from a more theoretical perspective.

In terms of methodology, I will be employing a technique recently termed *analytic narrative* (Bates et al. 1998). The point is to wed historical description with a deductive theoretical framework that guides the historical tales told. Given that I am interested in exploring the dynamic emergence of religious freedom over time, this is an ideal method. Although I am a partisan of quantitative methods in teasing out statistical relationships (cf. Gill and North 2005; Gill and Lundsgaarde 2004; Gill 1999a), the subject matter here is more amenable to qualitative methods. This is not to say that religious liberty cannot be measured and examined in a quantified manner. Several noble and informative attempts have been made in this direction (Grim and Finke 2006; Fox 2005; Barro and McCleary 2004; Grimm 2004; Gwin and North 2004; Norris and Inglehart 2004; Barrett et al. 2001; Marshall 2000; Chaves and Cann 1992). However, given the focus and spatial and temporal dimensions of this project, quantifying religious freedom would not necessarily be fruitful. First, although the aforementioned attempts to measure religious freedom are instructive, it remains difficult to weigh the different components of the indices that different researchers create. Who is to say that the relaxation of immigration restrictions on missionaries is more important than altering the property rights imposed on religious organizations? Second, and perhaps more importantly, the focus here is on the political decisions to deregulate (or in some instances reregulate) the religious market in whatever form that regulatory change may take – whether it be altering registration requirements for religious groups or rolling back financial subsidies to state churches. This study is rather ambivalent as to which type of regulatory reform took place, although the general realm of policy making (e.g., immigration law, property-rights regulations) may be of historical interest.

The cases chosen here represent identifiable and significant changes in religious regulation and provide a wide range of spatial, temporal, and cultural variation to test a generalized theory regarding the origins of religious liberty. The United States is an obvious place to start given that the U.S. Constitution's First Amendment represents a major landmark in the legalized establishment of religious freedom (cf. Jaffa 1990). Nonetheless, events in the American colonies and Europe prior to 1789 played a significant role in shaping the interests involved in the emergence of religious liberty in America. Latin America was chosen as a second area of examination because the cultural, political, and economic conditions there differed substantially from the United States. As compared to a country that arose amid an environment of religious pluralism (the United States), Latin America came to independence with a dominant religious monopoly – the Catholic Church. The course of religious liberty in Mexico is given specific attention because of the dramatic changes in religious regulations – from a period where the Catholic Church was favored, to an era where extreme anticlerical laws were enacted constitutionally, and, finally, to a general environment of religious freedom for both Catholics and non-Catholics. Finally, I (with the help of Cheryl Žilinskas) examine the former Soviet bloc, with a detailed comparison of the Baltic States of Estonia, Latvia, and Lithuania. The rise of Communism in this region ushered in an era where religious organizations were crushed under the weight of state control and attempts at annihilation. Following the collapse of the Soviet empire, the independent nations that emerged were faced with what were essentially a "blank slate" and the task of writing new laws that regulated religious groups. No uniform system emerged, and examining the variation throughout states comes as close to a natural experiment that any social scientist studying history is going to get.

My empirical examples are chosen primarily for historical interest. This opens up the study for a critique based on biased case selection. The fact that I restrict my examination to countries that are predominantly Christian may also be a matter of concern for someone claiming the mantle of generalizability. Likewise, even among Christian nations, I could have chosen to examine a number of countries and historical situations to which I devote little or no attention. The intriguing case of the Netherlands is given only brief treatment in Chapter 3. Admittedly, it could have easily served as a case deserving of a chapter unto itself. The reader can undoubtedly think of numerous other examples that are not addressed here. Nonetheless, in the spirit of Harry Eckstein's (1975) oft-cited chapter on case studies, what I hope to do here with my case selection is to show that the theory advanced in the following chapter presents a plausible explanation for a wide span of historical situations. Should this theory seem adequate to the reader, it is hoped that it will inspire further case studies and other forms of methodological inquiry. I welcome such inquiries and would be most enthused by scholarly efforts to extend this research agenda into the non-Christian world.

The evidence presented in the case studies primarily relies on secondary sources although some primary documentation and interviews are used.[33] My extensive reading on the subject of religious liberty has shown me that evidence for the theoretical hypotheses I wish to test are scattered throughout historical literature. What I claim to do is not to discover these empirical nuggets for the first time but rather to put them into a well-developed theoretical framework and give the understanding of those facts some logical consistency. This has been the methodology of some of my favorite works in the social sciences, including Barrington Moore's *Social Origins of Dictatorship and Democracy* (1966) and Rodney Stark's *The Rise of Christianity* (1996), *One True God* (2001), and *For the Glory of God* (2003). I can only hope to aspire to the influence that their scholarship has inspired in me.

With all this stated, it is now time to explain the political origins of religious liberty.

---

[33] I decided to exclude the possibility of conducting interviews for my chapter on colonial America with the reasonable expectation that many of the most interesting people that should be interviewed are not talking anymore.

CHAPTER 2

The Political Origins of Religious Liberty

The laws concerning corn may every where be compared to the laws concerning religion. The people feel themselves so much interested in what relates either to their subsistence in this life, or to their happiness in a life to come, that government must yield to their prejudices, and, in order to preserve the publick tranquillity [*sic*], establish that system which they approve of. It is upon this account, perhaps, that we so seldom find a reasonable system established with regard to either of those two capital objects.

– Adam Smith, *The Wealth of Nations*

IN HIS TIME and day, the great political economist Adam Smith considered laws regulating the conduct of religious individuals and institutions as akin to agricultural subsidies and the free trade of grain. Since his time, economists and political scientists have devised numerous theories to explain the origins of free trade. But substantially less attention has been paid to developing theories regarding the regulation and deregulation of religion. This is perhaps understandable given that the preceding passage from Smith's classic work has all but disappeared from library shelves. Abridged versions of *The Wealth of Nations* are quick to cut his musings on religion.[1] It was in these sections that Smith discussed the sovereign's proper

---

[1] These musings were developed in *The Wealth of Nations*, ch. V, pt. III, art. II and III.

role in maintaining public education and other institutions. Given the large role that the Church of England had in the educational infrastructure of Britain at the time and the fact that spiritual instruction was considered an important part of the education for all Britons (schoolchildren and adults alike), it was natural that Smith's discourse on religion would be found in that section of his book.

The theory regarding the origins of religious liberty proposed here is inspired in large part by the writings of Adam Smith. As evidenced by my conceptualization of religious liberty in Chapter 1 and the following text, I declare kinship with Smith in seeing similarities in the laws regulating religion and other forms of economic activity. Laws restricting religious liberty should be conceived of as raising the costs associated with practicing a religion just as tariffs are associated with raising the costs of economic trade. The presentation developed in the following text, then, is rooted in a classical (or perhaps neoclassical) economic view of the world wherein interests predominate over ideas. This is not to say that ideas (including values and moral imperatives) are irrelevant (a topic that I will briefly discuss later in this chapter). Smith was a proponent of the important role of ideas in his other major work, *The Theory of Moral Sentiments*. However, I owe my intellectual (but not blind) allegiance to a school of thought that economists since Smith's time have developed to study interest-based behavior and to which Nobel Laureate Gary Becker has extended more broadly into the social sciences – rational choice. Scholars such as Rodney Stark, Laurence Iannaccone, Roger Finke, Steve Pfaff, Paul Froese, Carolyn Warner, and I have extended the rational choice perspective to encompass the study of religion.[2]

It may seem odd to study religion from a rational choice perspective. Mancur Olson, one of the great economists of the twentieth century who helped extend rational choice theory to other social sciences, declared that economics had little to say about religious groups and behavior (1965, 159–61). Religion, after all, is about faith. It concerns itself with philosophical (theological) ideas about the meaning of life and death and the moral imperatives – the "shalls" and "shall nots" – that humans need to obey. These ideas and moral directives guide the behavior of people adhering to them and generally are not subject to empirical evaluation. And without the ability to empirically evaluate those ideas, the behavior that results cannot possibly be subject to the cost-benefit analysis of which economists are so fond. Moreover, it may be the case that a firmly held religious belief may

---

[2] See the bibliography for references to their work.

prompt a person to act against what otherwise might be in his best self-interest. A person may be discouraged from stealing money (a net financial gain) by a religious belief even in a situation where the probability of being caught and punished is zero. In other words, when people behave under the influence of religion and religious institutions it is commonly believed that they are not calculating the self-interested costs and benefits of their actions.

Rational choice theory, at its essence, is simple.[3] The theory assumes that people have varying needs and desires – that is, preferences. Rational choice has little to say about the content of those preferences. Some people prefer to drive blue Jeeps to work, while others prefer pedaling red bikes. Some people prefer to sing the praises of God for hours on a Sunday morning, while others would rather stay at home and watch football. What rational choice theory says, though, is that *given those preferences*, people will try to achieve their goals (i.e., their preferential needs and desires) in the least costly manner possible given the various environmental and strategic constraints that they face.[4] Everybody faces constraints; it is a fact of life. No matter how rich a society or an individual is, there is never enough time or resources to achieve everything we want in life. Rational choice theory is concerned with analyzing how individuals make choices to achieve their goals through a cost-benefit calculation determined by the constraints that they face. As constraints change, so do the cost-benefit incentives faced by different individuals, and hence the strategic choices they make.

Rational choice theory can easily be applied to religious individuals and the institutions that they staff. Remember, rational choice theory says little about the content of an individual's preferences; it is incumbent on the research to assume a reasonable set of preferences for the various actors under investigation. In the case of religious behavior, we can start with an assumption that priests and parishioners alike seek to learn about, live according to, and possibly spread[5] the Word of God. Not all individuals in

---

[3] I have discussed rational choice theory more extensively elsewhere (Gill 1998, 193–202), and there are a number of excellent summaries of the approach as pertains to religion (Stark and Finke 2000; L. Young 1997; Iannaccone 1995).

[4] Examples of environmental constraints include such things as one's financial resources, inherent skills, and limits on time. Strategic constraints involve the fact that other individuals are trying to achieve goals that may or may not be similar to your own; the goal-oriented actions of others may affect your own cost-benefit calculations for achieving your objectives. For instance, an incumbent politician facing a charismatic challenger may force that incumbent to vote for certain policies to appease critical constituents; whereas the incumbent may not have supported such policies in the past.

[5] As will be discussed later, not all religions are proselytizing.

society will have these same goals, and many people who consider themselves religious may share different intensities for achieving these goals.[6] Nonetheless, this information can be worked into a rational choice account of religious behavior. Once we make our assumptions about the preference content of various individuals, our analysis focuses on the abilities, resources, and constraints that face those individuals in their pursuit of their goals.

Religious believers live in the real world. And life in the real world is constrained in a number of different ways including limited time, money, and other resources. A devout churchgoer will have to make decisions about how much time to commit to volunteer activity at church and how much money to tithe given other commitments and budgetary constraints (cf. Azzi and Ehrenberg 1975). Iannaccone (1990) demonstrates how church participation is more likely to be time intensive (i.e., volunteering) when individuals have low income earning potential (i.e., for youth or retired folks); people in the prime of their professional careers show a higher propensity to participate through financial donations. As the different demands on our time change as we move through the life cycle, we often change the way we are involved in religious organizations. Iannaccone also shows that in mixed religious marriages, one spouse is more likely to convert to the other's faith as it simplifies the mundane costs of traveling to two different churches on Sunday.

Likewise, a pastor seeking to increase attendance at Sunday services may have different options available to him – for example, direct mail advertising, hiring popular musicians, providing an extensive youth ministry, or building more comfortable pews. Each option has different costs and is likely to yield different outcomes (benefits). And each of them must be weighed against one another in accordance to budgetary constraints. Trade-offs must be made. Capital improvements on the actual church building might have to be delayed while the pastor hires a youth ministry staff. Church leaders must also consider the various costs and benefits of sending missionaries to

---

[6] This relates to the concept of "price elasticity," which asserts that individuals will react differently to changes in price depending on how much they value or need the good. A person who will do anything to live the Word of God can be considered someone who has an inelastic demand for religion. If the price of one's faith requires meeting with lions in a Roman coliseum, they will be there. Such folks – often referred to as zealots or martyrs – are often crucial to the early success of a religious movement (cf. Stark 1996, 163–90). Somebody who has an elastic demand for religion will balk at the prospect of going to church if there is a half inch of snow on the ground and the Steelers are playing an early Sunday game.

different nations around the world, a fact that is illustrated by the presence of Christian-owned firms that specialize in "missionary insurance."[7] If you are seeking souls for God, you have to weigh the different payoffs between sending missionaries to China or Saudi Arabia, where Christian proselytizers are likely to be jailed or killed (and hence largely ineffective), or placing them in countries like Uruguay or a more liberalized Hungary. In short, just because religious individuals are people of deep faith and may be motivated by desires that are hard to empirically verify (e.g., obtain salvation) does not mean they are immune from worldly considerations of trying to manage budgets and achieve goals.[8]

The benefit of rational choice analysis is that it begins by examining the simple cost-benefit calculations and trade-offs posed under different conditions (or constraints). When conditions change, we can readily calculate the general changes in costs and benefits and predict how individuals may alter their behavior. For instance, if long-term gas prices rise, we could predict that consumers will switch to more fuel-efficient cars or ride public transportation in order to save money. We could further predict that people with more discretionary funds to spend (i.e., rich people) will be less affected by increases in gas prices and hence will be slower to trade in their gas guzzlers or jump on the bus. If real gas prices fall over time, our interest-based prediction would suggest that people would switch back to less fuel-efficient cars.[9] If our prediction is not supported by the evidence then we might be

[7] One firm is even called the Missionary Insurance Group, Inc. (http://www.migi.net, accessed May 15, 2007) and offers such services as policies that cover the price of cancelled mission trips.

[8] I often illustrate this to my classes with an example involving Mother Teresa, a person most folks would recognize as being deeply spiritual and guided by altruistic motives. I ask students to imagine that they are Mother Teresa and that they received a substantial monetary reward from the Nobel Peace Prize committee – e.g., $1 million. I ask them how they (Mother Teresa) would use that money. The students invariably come up with a number of creative ideas, which we then evaluate for their effectiveness. Some students say they would simply "give the money to the poor." I ask them if they should give one dollar to one million people or ten dollars to one hundred thousand people. They begin to see the trade-offs involved. Other students suggest using the money to build a school or improve a hospice. Each solution has a different set of short-term and long-term payoffs. We then discuss which strategies would yield the greatest benefits, which is the essence of cost-benefit calculation. Mother Teresa's altruism did not exempt her from making difficult decisions about how best to serve the poor.

[9] This appears to have been the case between the 1970s and 1980s. As real gas prices rose in the 1970s, smaller, more fuel-efficient cars became popular. But as real gas prices fell in the late 1980s and 1990s, consumers tended to purchase larger sports utility vehicles (SUVs). Had there been a general shift in societal attitudes toward more fuel-efficient cars, SUVs would not have become as popular as they did in the 1990s. The underlying explanation

encouraged to consider other, nonrational choice explanations. The same holds with religious and political leaders. As I will assert in the following text, clergy and politicians possess a number of easily identified personal and institutional goals that they seek to achieve. Given that theologies and ideologies tend to be relatively resistant to change, particularly in the short term, we would first look for some policy change to be the result of some environmental change that has affected an individual's interests. If behavior changes in the predicted way according to the new environmental incentives, we probably can attribute the change to interest-based behavior. If behavior is not in accordance with the predicted interest-based calculations, the role of ideas can likely be accorded with greater explanatory power. The critical task will be to properly specify the interests of both religious and political actors.

In this chapter I briefly review some of the previous perspectives on the origins of religious liberty to keep the rational choice explanation advanced here in perspective. I then propose a theory of why religious liberty would emerge in a society based on a rational choice perspective.

Secularization, Modernity, and the Rise of Religious Liberty

The primary alternatives to an economic approach to human behavior are ideational and structural. An ideational approach emphasizes the (largely independent) role of ideas in shaping conduct. Creative and thoughtful people develop new ideas about how the world operates (through scientific reasoning) or should operate (through normative argumentation). These

---

of this would appear to be that consumers like powerful engines that burn more gas but are more willing to trade them for fuel-efficient autos when gas prices rise. An alternative, ideational (i.e., nonrational choice) explanation for the switch to fuel-efficient cars in the 1970s would focus on shifting preferences. Rather than the high cost of gas and limited household budgets being the cause for the shift, an ideational argument would assert that individuals have shifted their priorities (or values) toward more environmentally friendly vehicles. This, however, would create a difficulty in explaining the movement of consumers back to SUVs in the 1990s, when gas prices fell. Of course, there is always the possibility that a synergy exists between changes in external constraints and shifting preferences (cf. Elster 1983) – e.g., high gas prices pushed individuals into fuel-efficient cars whereupon those same people discovered that they preferred such vehicles. Sorting out that synergy can be a difficult methodological task for researchers, so the usual approach is to hold one of these elements constant (preferences) while allowing the other to vary (environmental constraints) and make predictions based upon those changes. Should those predictions not hold up to empirical scrutiny it would be incumbent on the researcher to investigate the factor that was held constant.

ideas then are disseminated throughout society in some manner (e.g., news media, parliamentary debate). If the new ideas are convincing to others, traditional behavior patterns will change. For instance, if colonial American Quakers developed a belief that slavery is immoral and argued forcefully for its abolition, and if they were successful in spreading these beliefs, the institution of slavery would have withered away.[10] Structural explanations emphasize large social processes and relationships that tend to have automatic behavioral outcomes. Karl Marx was probably the preeminent structuralist in that he argued the way a society produces and distributes goods leads to certain social and political outcomes. To Marx, the logic of capitalism and the profit motive drove employers to suppress the wages of workers to the point where a proletarian revolution was inevitable. Other structuralist theories have emphasized a variety of "large structural" variables that influence behavior, including industrialization, urbanization, and population growth.

One of the most dominant social scientific theories of religious behavior in the past century – secularization theory – shares, in its various forms, elements of both ideational and structural explanation (cf. Norris and Inglehart 2004). Not surprisingly, secularization theory has often formed the basis for how we understand religious liberty and may be a reason why a general theory of religious liberty has not been promulgated. To a large extent, a general theory for the rise of religious liberty has not been advanced in the social sciences largely because the reason for the spread of religious freedom seemed to be rather obvious – it was the natural outgrowth of the secularization process. Secularization theory, which dominated the sociological literature on religion for more than a century, conditioned the scholarly belief that religious freedom was the natural outgrowth of the demise of spirituality in the public square. Commenting on the general state of the field, Richard Helmstadter notes that

> secularization, in the sense of putting the secular aspects of life at the center and marginalizing religion, has been fitted into the master narrative as a kind of extension of Protestantism, progress, and modernization. To see the decline of religion and the secularization of society as inevitable, was ... the logical postscript to the narrative in which *liberalism and religious freedom are seen as predestined goals in the progress of mankind.* (1997, 7; emphasis added)

[10] Consider Rodney Stark (2003, 291–366). Although Stark is categorized as a rational choice scholar, he undoubtedly recognizes the powerful role that ideas play in society and develops a detailed theory of how such ideas can matter.

The "inevitable" and constant global process of modernization is seen as the principal cause of religious freedom. From a structural perspective, modernization produces greater functional differentiation of social roles and results in a multiplication of state agencies and bureaucracies staffed by experts and charged with specific tasks – for example, child welfare services, mental health services, monitoring business practices, and environmental protection. Traditionally, many monarchs and rulers relied on religious institutions to provide many of these goods, and states would often support these religious institutions. With the rise of the bureaucratic expertise and the modern welfare state came the elimination of the public need for church-provided welfare services. Separation of church and state became the first step toward religious liberty (as it is difficult to have true religious liberty where there is one officially sanctioned church).[11]

At the ideational level, modernization purportedly coincides with a certain set of values privileging the role of individual (as opposed to communal/corporatist) choice. Such choice is not possible without freedom of conscience. José Casanova summarizes this uniquely Western notion:

> [R]eligious freedom, in the sense of freedom of conscience, is chronologically "the first freedom" as well as the precondition of all modern freedoms. Insofar as freedom of conscience is intrinsically related to "the right to privacy" – to the modern institutionalization of a private sphere free from governmental intrusion as well as free from ecclesiastical control – and inasmuch as "the right to privacy" serves as the very foundation of modern liberalism and of modern individualism, then indeed the privatization of religion is essential to modernity. (1994, 40)

Other scholars have emphasized the development of particular theological notions that justified the movement toward religious freedom. Historian Fred Hood, for example, in explaining why Virginia was the heart and soul of religious liberty in the American colonies, argued somewhat paradoxically

> that conservative Protestants, as represented by a majority of the Presbyterians in Virginia, conceived of religious liberty as a religious dogma compatible with an established religion and that the legal separation of church and state did not alter that belief or its influence. The dogma of religious liberty emphasized the Protestant belief that every man had the right to interpret the Bible for himself and affirmed the authority of Scripture for the common life of the

[11] See Monsma and Soper (1997) for the nuanced exceptions in Europe. Ironically, many of the states that are considered to be highly secular still manage social welfare programs through traditional confessions (e.g., Germany, Belgium).

> nation. The government's surrender of coercive powers in matters of religion, while viewed as a less than satisfactory solution was nevertheless understood as the acceptance of this religious dogma as the law of the land. (1971, 171)

If Hood is correct in his description of Presbyterian views during the late eighteenth century, the logical pretzel twists needed to explain how a religious establishment was compatible with religious freedom seem more of a post hoc accommodation to a reality – religious pluralism – with which Presbyterians were uncomfortable.

Consider also W. Cole Durham's argument. He puts forth the idea that the spread of Enlightenment philosophy (most notably that of John Locke) was the principal determinant for religious freedom:

> Contrary to what might initially be thought (and what had been thought for centuries), Locke contended that respect for freedom of choice in matters of religion (and more generally with respect to comprehensive world views) is a source of both legitimacy and stability for political regimes. This insight constituted a kind of Copernican Revolution in political theory.... Locke revolutionized politics by suggesting how religious (and by extension, political) freedom could sow political order from religious seeds that had always been assumed to be the ultimate source of anarchy. The Lockean insight thus opened up the possibility of seeing the political cosmos from a new perspective. By placing respect for freedom at the center of the constellation of values, and by recognizing that respect for freedom and dignity of individuals is itself a moral and religious truth of the highest order, this revolution transformed the grounds for legitimizing and stabilizing political communities.... This idea was initially theoretical, but it became a central aspect of the "lively experiment" with religious freedom in the United States. (1996, 8–9)

Durham continues by noting that a general process of "globalization" (a structural process caused by expanding technology) is facilitating the acceptance of this ideal:

> Growing consensus on religious freedom reflects a more general need to address the reality of pluralism in the global setting.... [G]lobalization itself is enhancing our sense of pluralism.... These patterns of global demographic pluralism are likely to be conducive to religious freedom and application of the Lockean insight into the stabilizing force of respected pluralism in much the same way that American pluralism paved the way for meaningful institutions of religious freedom two centuries ago. (1996, 11)

Other such explanations (cf. Chadwick 1975, passim; Sandler 1960; Pauck 1946) have a similar ideational and structural bent.

The ideational perspective of Hood and Durham is clearly echoed by two legal scholars of the U.S. First Amendment – albeit with a focus on different sources from where the notion of liberty came.

> The American Founders were *influenced greatly by theologians and philosophers* who reflected on the religious conflicts that occurred in the wake of the Reformation. From Martin Luther and John Calvin they *inherited the view* that God had instituted "two kingdoms" – a heavenly one where the church exercised spiritual authority and an earthly one where the civil magistrates exercised temporal authority. A liberal Roman Catholic tradition represented by Erasmus and Thomas More *also exerted influence* in the colonies, inspiring the Lords Baltimore and the Carrolls of Maryland *to rethink* the proper relationship between church and state.... From [Roger] Williams, John Clarke, and William Penn, the Founders *learned* that state control of religion corrupted faith and that coercion of conscience destroyed true piety. From the theorists Algernon Sidney and John Locke, they *appropriated concepts* such as inalienable rights, government by popular consent, and toleration for the religious beliefs of others. (Adams and Emmerich 1990, 3; emphasis added)

The term "rethink" is critical in the preceding passage as it reveals the primacy that the authors place on the role of intellectual debate. McConnell (1990) presents a similar view of why religious freedom developed most extensively in the United States by arguing that Locke's ideas combined with evangelical thought during the First Great Awakening (ca. 1730–50)[12] to provide a more radical notion of "religious free exercise." McConnell asserts that the most fervent evangelicals (i.e., Baptists and Quakers) developed "essentially religious arguments based on the primacy of duties to God over duties to the state in support of disestablishment and free exercise" (1990, 1442). Combined with Locke's more secular notions in favor of toleration, this new evangelical line of thinking created a potent ideological milieu – a perfect ideological storm, so to speak – in the American colonies that helped shape the eventual drafting of the First Amendment. Marc Arkin (1995) follows suit by emphasizing the influence David Hume had on James Madison in the late 1700s.

It is also noteworthy that Adams and Emmerich recognize that theologians and philosophers developed their ideas by looking at European religious wars. This reveals that ideas do not necessarily pop up in a vacuum isolated from harsh reality; ideas come from reflecting upon reality and, as

---

[12] Scholars debate the exact beginning and end of the Great Awakening, though the most fervent period of revival occurred with the wanderings of George Whitefield in the 1730s and 1740s (see Finke and Stark 2005).

I will argue, reality is filled with self-interested behavior. Historian Charles Mullett recognized how ideas were often the function of interests, specifically in reference to the writings of the Enlightenment philosophers. "The struggles for religious toleration in England show that this idea [religious freedom], like others, cannot be treated *in vacuo*. No writer on liberty of conscience, to be sure, failed to emphasize his belief in abstract toleration, yet often the ideal was conceived in self-interest, born in faction, and grew up amid indifference" (Mullett 1938, 24). In other words, political and social context matters.

In contrast, Owen Chadwick, in his classic work *The Secularization of the European Mind in the 19th Century*, places even more emphasis on the role of ideas than Adams and Emmerich, downplaying the influence of historical events on the thought of great philosophers.

> The ultimate freedom was liberty to worship God as the conscience called. Modern ideas of freedom, as they stemmed from John Locke in the later seventeenth century, were founded in religious toleration. Locke's intention, after the age of intolerance and party conflict which he experienced as a young man, was to justify religious toleration. *He based his argument, not upon policy – such as, we cannot hold England together as a state unless we allow Protestant dissenters to worship God as they please – but upon the principle of a natural right.* . . . Of course Locke depended on a long tradition of political thought in Europe. But his statement of it founded liberal convictions in the form in which they conquered the Europe of the nineteenth century. The expression of them was widened, adjusted, expanded to new circumstances. But this way of thinking about freedom and the power of government ran henceforth in a continuous tradition. (1975, 25; emphasis added)

Although Chadwick implies that the English Civil War (1642–9)[13] impacted Locke to some degree, he emphasizes Locke's thinking on the "principle of natural right" and deemphasizes the role of "policy." Secular philosophers then influenced the dominant religious thought, which had previously favored rather illiberal forms of regulation over confessions.

> Part of the development of Christian doctrine was forced upon the churches by *advances in knowledge* which in other directions made men's minds more 'secular.' And part of the development of Christian doctrine, during the nineteenth century, contributed to the growing 'secularity' of men's minds. (Chadwick 1975, 17; emphasis added)

[13] Scholars differ upon the exact start and end dates for this conflict. The boundaries mark the beginning of military fighting and the execution of Charles I.

Chadwick thus sees a dialectical pattern of new ideas giving way to secularization, not only within the society but also within the churches, which all in turn pushes the separation of church and state, and religious liberty, further.[14]

In all the aforementioned explanations, the process giving rise to religious freedom is relatively straightforward. Modernity – a result of various structural variables including urbanization, industrialization, and technological progress – gives rise to certain ways of thinking (namely, Enlightenment liberalism), which, when adopted by a sufficient number of people, alters the political environment in favor of religious liberty. The thesis linking modernity, secularization, and religious liberty is a close cousin to modernization theory popularized in the social sciences during the 1950s and 1960s. However, whereas modernization theory has come under critical scrutiny at both the theoretical and empirical levels, secularization theory has come under attack only in the last two decades of the twentieth century (cf. Swatos and Olson 2000; Berger 1999; Warner 1993).[15] However, ideational explanations for the rise of religious liberty, heavily influenced by secularization theory, have yet to face such strict examination.

Although this type of explanation is seemingly convincing at a general level, particularly when one considers the role of intellectuals and philosophers in justifying religious toleration, it has a number of theoretical and methodological problems. First, methodologically speaking, a constant cannot explain variation. Both the degree and nature of religious liberty have exhibited extensive variation across nations and throughout time. Modern countries have dramatically different forms of church-state relations and policies on religious freedom (cf. Monsma and Soper 1997). The obvious countercritique is that "modernization" also varies throughout spatial and temporal dimensions. Yemen is much less modern today than the United States on a number of different measures (e.g., per capita income, literacy rates, accessibility of telecommunications); therefore we should not expect the two to have similar degrees of religious freedom. Unfortunately, without using independent measures of "modernization," this explanation risks becoming tautological: The presence of modernity is associated with religious liberty, whereas one of the conditions for being "modern" is having religious liberty. Moreover, a casual glance at variations

---

[14] Admittedly, Chadwick does not deal with the issue of religious liberty directly, but his account of the secularization of the European mind certainly conflates the issues of religious freedom, separation of church and state, and the secularization of society.

[15] Also consult the extensive work of Rodney Stark dating back to the 1960s. Stark was perhaps the first and most fervent opponent of the secularization thesis.

in religious liberty using relatively commonsense measures of "modernization" (e.g., level of industrialization, gross domestic product [GDP] per
capita) suggests that little if any correlation exists between these two variables. Stephen Monsma and Christopher Soper (1997) detail how five Western nations,[16] all of which could be considered equally "modern," maintain
distinctly different forms of church-state relations. Some of these relationships, they argue, lead to distinct disadvantages for some denominations in terms of religious liberty.[17] Mark Chaves and David Cann (1992)
and Rodney Stark and Laurence Iannaccone (1994) note similar variation
across highly modernized West European countries. In prior work (Gill
1999a), I have quantified the substantial variation in religious liberty across
countries in Latin America and noted that more "modern" nations such as
Argentina, Colombia, and Mexico possess substantially lower levels of religious liberty than "less-developed" countries such as Ecuador, Guatemala,
and Nicaragua. Although none of these studies measure "modernization"
comprehensively,[18] a casual examination of the different data used to measure this amorphous concept suggests a poor correlation between the level
of "modernity" and religious freedom.

   Cross-national comparisons are not the only piece of evidence to cast
doubt on ideational explanations of religious freedom. These explanations
also run into problems when viewed over time. If modernization is considered to have a unilinear direction, we should not anticipate any setbacks
with religious liberty once it is institutionalized. Yet we know that the Edict
of Nantes, giving French Protestants greater legal protections, was revoked
nearly a century after it was decreed, despite the promulgation of liberal

---

[16] The countries are the United States, the Netherlands, the United Kingdom, Germany,
and Australia.

[17] Monsma and Soper argue that in the cases of Germany and the Netherlands, state spon-
sorship of multiple denominations is potentially discriminatory toward Islamic groups,
which, because of their decentralized nature, cannot be worked into the traditional means
of financing these groups. Likewise, they argue that in the United States, a strict separationist interpretation of the First Amendment privileged secularism over religion, thereby
acting in a potentially discriminatory manner. Without commenting on the normative
implications of their study, the central point I want to make for this study is the substantial variation in how religious organizations are regulated (including subsidization) by the
state.

[18] Gill (1999a) includes various measures of "industrialization" and "urbanization" in a regression analysis in which religious pluralism was the dependent variable, though the intent was
not to measure "modernization" per se but to measure "social anomie." The theoretical
argument under scrutiny was that rapid industrialization leads to social anomie, which in
turns prompts people to convert to new religious movements. Although the link between
industrialization and religious liberty was not tested explicitly, no significant collinearity
existed between these variables when included in the same regression.

ideas from Locke and Montesquieu, and the increasing bureaucratization (read: modernization) of the French monarchy under Cardinal Richelieu. Religious toleration for minority denominations also took a negative hit in Argentina during the latter half of the twentieth century, both under Juan Perón and subsequent military governments.[19] And early efforts in the Baltics and Eastern Europe to provide new religious groups with legal status equal to that of historical confessions fell apart as registration requirements were made more onerous.[20]

Another pitfall of ideational explanations of religious liberty is that they often do not consider the presence of opposing viewpoints floating about in society, and, if they do, they fail to provide an explanatory mechanism detailing why one argument won out over the other in the intellectual debate. James Madison and Thomas Jefferson are widely credited with promoting the disestablishment of the Anglican Church in Virginia and promoting religious liberty in the new U.S. republic. However, they were not the only voice in the debate; none other than the great orator Patrick Henry took a position against general disestablishment.[21] The vote count favoring Madison's side was by no means secure when the issue was brought before the Virginia legislature in 1776, which left the status of the Anglican Church in limbo for several years (Buckley 1977, 38–70). Likewise, liberal reformers in Latin America during the nineteenth century favored significant restrictions on the privileges of the Catholic Church, but they were opposed both by Catholic prelates and Conservative politicians who saw the maintenance of exclusive Catholic status as a central feature of Latin culture. Why did one side or the other prevail in these debates? Saying that the winning ideological position was more convincing to the winning majority simply becomes a circular and irrefutable argument.

A final weakness befalling secularization-based theories of religious liberty relates to the preceding point and an affliction that affects all broadbased systemic and structural-functionalist arguments: the problem of missing agency.[22] In many of the theories presented in the preceding text, the process of secularization, church-state separation, and the resulting religious freedom is presented as a "natural occurrence," independent of human choice. Although it is doubtful that any scholar would admit to such a crude

---

[19] See Chapter 4 for a more extended discussion of this case.
[20] See Chapter 5.
[21] Madison was not known for his fiery oratory skills and hence one would give the debating advantage to Henry in this case, especially considering his huge popularity in Virginia in the 1770s and 1780s (Buckley 1977, 71).
[22] See Cohen (1994) for an excellent discussion of the weaknesses of structural functionalism.

rendering of history, the lack of a rigorous causal explanation of the origins of religious freedom leaves us with the sense that little human agency is involved. We are left with an intriguing and important question: How do the victors in the great debates over religious freedom eventually prevail to get their policy vision written into law? Relying on rational choice and the economic concept of opportunity costs, I now present my theory of the political origins of religious liberty.

A Theory of the Political Origins of Religious Liberty

Religion has long been considered beyond the purview of economic analysis. Scholars typically assume that the behavior of religious actors derives from a set of ideational (theological) principles that transcend the self-interested motivations of *homo economicus*. Yet, although religious actors may be motivated by "high ideals," it is still obvious that they exist in a world of scarcity wherein difficult choices about how to allocate resources must be made on a daily basis.[23] For example, a Catholic bishop might face a difficult choice of whether to spend his limited budget on putting more priests through the seminary or expanding day-care facilities in his diocese. The latter may have the effect of immediately increasing the attendance of young families at services, while the former option has a longer-term (and more risky) payoff of improving the quality and perhaps the quantity of religious services offered. An evangelical Protestant organization might face a difficult choice of whether to send its one hundred eager missionaries to Brazil or Russia. Where are more converts likely to be made? Even Mother Teresa, perhaps the noblest of souls, had to make tough decisions about how to divvy up her scarce time and energy to help the most people (Kwilecki and Wilson 1998).[24]

---

[23] Whether actors are motivated by "high ideals" or "economic rationality" may be a moot point. "High ideals" typically inform a person's fundamental preferences (i.e., ends), while "rationality" speaks more to means. A person who maintains the most altruistic of goals is still limited by scarce resources and must make difficult (economic) choices as to how to best realize those altruistic goals. For the analyst, the trick is first to determine what a person's basic preferences are, then to specify the constraints the person faces. Ideational perspectives are typically useful in discerning the former; rational choice theory is superior in the latter.

[24] Although a provocative application of rational choice theory, Kwilecki and Wilson's analysis of Mother Teresa commits a fatal methodological error by seeking to explain a single case. Rational choice theory relies on probabilistic and marginal analysis. In other words, the goal of rational choice theory is to explain the average behavior of the typical consumer/producer when faced by a marginal alteration in their environmental constraints. Specific exceptions to rational choice predictions will always exist, but unless those

Moreover, religious actors also must deal with individuals who might not share their high ideals. Scoundrels, scalawags, and rogues roam throughout government and society. Successful interaction with such nefarious individuals often requires sacrificing strict obedience to high principle for strategic expediency. This is *not* to say that religious actors are hypocrites when it comes to living in the secular world; it merely notes that high principles do not always guide behavior. A Jesuit president of a Catholic university may decry the crass materialism of modern society and the neglect of the poor yet aggressively pursue financial contributions to sustain his university, often diverting those funds from other philanthropic causes (e.g., building homeless shelters). A preacher calling for greater ecumenical relations between faiths might also lobby to have restrictions placed on "cults" that are stealing members from his flock. All told, rational choice theory provides us with some leverage in explaining tough decisions of resource allocation. The theory does not tell us much in the way of what a specific individual's high ideals or other preferences might be, but many general preferences can be assumed safely as the basis for theory testing. Thus to the extent that religious actors and institutions exist in a world of scarcity, economic theory can have some bearing on explaining behavior in this realm.

The Religious Marketplace

To begin the process of building a theory of the origins of religious liberty, it is first worthwhile to begin with a number of definitions. These definitions will help to delineate the scope of the study and help to place the issue of religious liberty in a framework analogous to that of economics.

> *Definition 1: Religious goods* are fundamental answers to the deep philosophic questions surrounding life that have as their basis some appeal to a supernatural force.[25]

---

exceptions constitute a significant proportion of the cases examined, they do not necessarily destroy the predictive power of the theory. For instance, the existence of martyrs who are willing to give their life for a cause does not detract from the rational choice prediction (and empirical finding) that most people stop well short of zealous actions in their personal religious practice. Nonetheless, idiosyncratic anomalies and outliers may often serve as a basis for examining the assumptions and logic of a theory and provoke modifications to that theory (cf. Froese and Pfaff 2005, 2001). Therefore, it would be negligent for a scholar to simply neglect an anomaly.

[25] Stark and Bainbridge provide a more specific definition of religious goods based on a theory of compensators (1987, 25–42).

Definition 2: A *religious firm* (i.e., a church or denomination) is an organization that produces and distributes religious goods.[26]

Definition 3: A *religious marketplace* is the social arena wherein religious firms compete for members and resources.[27]

Axiom 1: Religious preferences in society are pluralistic.

People normally do not think of churches as equivalent to manufacturing plants or retail stores. Yet these organizations do supply things that people want, as evidenced by the fact that people attend religious services voluntarily. These consumers (parishioners) purchase these goods with their financial contributions and time commitments.[28] As with most marketplaces, religious markets can be monopolized or highly competitive. Given the natural low barriers to entry into the religious marketplace,[29] and assuming a variety of religious preferences in society, the "natural" state of the religious market is one of competitive pluralism (Gill 2003a; Stark 2003: 15–120; Stark 1992). This assumption differentiates this analysis from cultural explanations. Culturalists tend to assume a high degree of homogeneity in religious beliefs within national boundaries. For purposes of this analysis,

---

[26] *Produces* could also mean "interprets from divine revelation." The question of where religious beliefs come from or their ultimate validity is not the focus of this study. Also, the author acknowledges that the term *church* carries Christian connotations, but it will be used interchangeably with *religious firm* for the sake of rhetorical simplicity.

[27] Gill (1998) makes the argument that proselytizing religions are primarily market-share maximizers. I.e., churches seek to win over as many parishioners to their spiritual message as possible.

[28] The very nature of religious goods make them difficult to price. Because they are largely ideas and it is difficult to prevent their diffusion, free riding is a common problem with religions: People can learn about the answers to life without paying for the provision of those ideas. However, exact pricing is not a requirement for the existence of a market. As the computer age has demonstrated, pricing intellectual property and policing intellectual property rights are difficult tasks. Theology, in many respects, represents the ultimate intellectual good. For a discussion of how the medieval Catholic Church priced its theological goods (including indulgences), see Ekelund et al. (1996).

[29] It is relatively cheap to create an ideology and start disseminating it. There are very few capital costs associated with startup religions. However, low barriers to entry do not guarantee market success, as many Internet firms are now discovering. And although low barriers to entry exist in the religious marketplace, there still may be a significant economy of scale in the production of religious goods. Because religious goods are credence goods and require credible testimony about the quality of the good, there may be "strength in numbers." The adage that "five hundred million Muslims can't be wrong" applies here. As for an economic analogy, anybody can start an e-commerce Web site, but it helps to be Amazon.com.

we will take the "varied preferences" assumption as an untested axiom.[30] The main implication of the varied preferences assumption is that such apparent homogeneity (e.g., Catholicism in Latin America) is due to the presence of a religious monopoly. Such a monopoly can be maintained only by governmental regulation, as Stark and Bainbridge assert:

> No religion can achieve a monopoly out if its own resources alone. No faith can inspire universal, voluntary acceptance, except, perhaps, in time, primitive societies. . . . [U]nmet religious needs will prompt competing religious groups in a society as long as a free market exists. Religious monopoly can be achieved only by reliance on the coercive powers of the state. Neither Roman Catholic nor Protestant clergy could prevent religious dissent (heresy). Only the king's soldiers, or the threat of the king's soldiers, could suppress religious dissent (and then only to a degree, for even at the height of Catholic dominance of Europe, dissent flourished in all the cracks and crannies of society and constantly burst forth). (1985, 508)

Observation of the relationship between religious pluralism and government coercion sets up the definition of religious liberty.

Definition 4: Religious liberty (or freedom) represents the degree to which a government regulates the religious marketplace.[31]

Such a definition might seem trivial, but it shifts the analysis toward the examination of specific regulatory laws aimed at religious organizations. Broad-based ideational theories of religious liberty shy away from

---

[30] It is possible to test this assumption. One possible methodology would be survey research. However, in a monopolized market, respondents might not be aware of religious alternatives and would claim either a preference for the monopoly faith or no preference at all. If many respondents reply the latter yet indicate a strong belief in God or "importance of religion," this could be taken as indirect evidence that a plurality of religious differences exist that the monopoly religion cannot satisfy (cf. Gill 2003b). Alternatively, a historical study could be conducted. When laws regulating nonmonopoly religions are relaxed, religious activity and pluralism would tend to increase if the varied preferences assumption holds (cf. Froese 2003; Stark and Iannaccone 1994; Finke and Iannaccone 1993).

[31] Although not central to the thesis, *religious toleration* can be defined as the level to which norms in society allow for the operation of dissenting sects. It is possible to have a deregulated religious economy with high levels of religious intolerance. As religious intolerance can impose significant costs on religious minorities – from social ostracism to outright violent attacks – these social norms and values can play a substantial role in limiting their religious activity. The foregoing analysis is restricted, however, to the origin of actual legislation. To the extent that governments do not choose to monitor and enforce their own laws pertaining to religious freedom, this study could intersect with the study of religious intolerance.

examining specific laws and see the level of religious liberty in society as a function of the general ideological milieu. Such laws can be as encompassing as constitutional declarations of the right to free conscience or as specific as zoning regulations on church property, as discussed in Chapter 1. Today, almost every country provides some constitutional guarantee of religious freedom. On closer examination, however, the specific manner in which religious groups are regulated can vary extensively (Gill 1999a; Monsma and Soper 1997; Chaves and Cann 1992).

Just as commercial businesses have different preferences for the degree of regulation in society (e.g., preferences about tariff rates), so do religious firms. By adding one additional axiom, we are able to derive a proposition related to these preferences:

> *Axiom 2:* Proselytizing religious firms are market-share maximizers; they seek to spread their brand of spiritual message to as many followers as possible.

Although most economic analyses take firms to be profit-maximizing entities, here I take the declared goal of proselytizing religions at face value – that is, religious leaders want to spread the Word of God to as many people as possible (given the limitations of their own resources). This keeps the spirituality within religion and avoids critiques of materialistic reductionism (cf. Stark 2000). (Remember, an economic analysis does not necessarily imply that an actor is out for material gain; it merely says that the actor is trying to maximize some given goal.) By way of Axiom 2, it becomes possible to derive policy preferences. Spiritual monopolies that have a captured market prefer to keep the barriers to entry in the religious marketplace high. Although rhetorically in favor of freedom of conscience, they will seek laws that require minority religions to gain the government's official permission to proselytize, restrict visas on foreign missionaries, impose zoning and impose media restrictions on alternative faiths, and so on. This tendency did not escape the attention of Adam Smith as early as the late 1700s, when he wrote of the dominant religion in any given country:

> The sect which had the good fortune to be leagued with the conquering party, necessarily shared in the victory of its ally, by whose favour [*sic*] and protection it was soon enabled in some degree to silence and subdue all its adversaries. . . . The clergy of this particular sect having thus become complete masters of the field, and have their influence and authority with the great body of the people being in its highest vigour [*sic*], they were powerful enough to over-awe the chiefs and leaders of their own party, and to oblige the civil magistrate to respect their opinions and inclinations. [The clergy's] first demand was generally, that he [the civil magistrate or ruler] should silence

and subdue all their adversaries; and their second, that he should bestow an independent provision on themselves [i.e., subsidize the dominant faith]. ([1776] 1976, 792)

By contrast, minority religious groups that could potentially win converts in an undersupplied religious economy will seek legislation that lowers restrictions on "religious trade." Hence:

> *Proposition 1:* Hegemonic religions will prefer high levels of government regulation (i.e., restrictions on religious liberty) over religious minorities.[32] Religious minorities will prefer laws favoring greater religious liberty.[33]

An interesting test case for this proposition is the Roman Catholic Church. Here we have an institutionalized faith that exists in nearly every part of the world yet varies in whether it is a majority or minority religion. An ideational model of preferences for religious liberty would predict a consistency in the Church's policy across nations, perhaps harking back to the Second Vatican Council's declaration in favor of religious liberty (*Dignitatis Humanae*). Alternatively, the interest-based proposition in the preceding text would lead us to expect variations in Catholic policy positions as determined by the Church's market position. In Latin America, where Catholicism has been dominant for five centuries, the Church has actively sought restrictions on Pentecostals and other upstart evangelical groups (Gill 1999b, 1998). However, in post-Soviet Russia, where Catholics are an expanding denomination, the Vatican has been pressing for greater access against the cries of the historically dominant Orthodox Church (Anderson 2003, 128; Kutznetzov 1996). Likewise, in Asia, Catholics are seeking fewer restrictions on religious activity.[34] These empirical observations favor the interest-based hypothesis as presented in Proposition 1. Here we have an

---

[32] This proposition is an example of how rational choice theorists can derive logically the preferences of actors rather than merely stating them as given. As is noted elsewhere (Gill 1998: 195–6), a major critique of rational choice theory is that it takes preferences as given. However, this does not mean that preferences simply are asserted in an ad hoc or tautological fashion. Careful attention must be paid to justifying the assumed preferences, as I have attempted to do here. Being explicit about these assumptions allows other scholars to modify the assumptions and play out the theoretical logic to see whether alternative, testable implications can be advanced.

[33] In the case in which a traditionally dominant religion exists under a state with an explicit "atheistic" (or anticlerical) ideology (e.g., the Soviet Union, Mexico 1917–94), the dominant religion can be thought of as a minority player in that it does not wield the coercive power to counter the dominant producer of social values and norms.

[34] "Pope urges China to allow religious freedom" (December 3, 1996), Cable News Network, http://www.cnn.com/WORLD/9612/03/briefs.pm/pope.china/ (accessed September 8, 2005).

instance of an institution whose leaders' preferences are determined by their self-interested position in the religious marketplace rather than by some constant theological precept. If theology were dictating policy preferences in this case, we would expect the Catholic Church to maintain a consistent position across countries.

We can further derive the preferences of religious groups under pluralistic conditions from Proposition 1, in which no one firm commands a majority market share; that is, every denomination is a minority denomination. In such situations, all religious firms will prefer a minimum level of religious liberty that allows all *existing* faiths to practice freely (within reason).[35] Imposing restrictions on one faith could potentially lead to religious conflict wherein one's own denomination finds itself under repressive legislation.

> *Proposition 1a:* In an environment where no single religion commands a majority market share, the preferences of each denomination will tend toward religious liberty.

Nonetheless, religious leaders in such an environment are likely to oppose a completely laissez-faire religious market that allows new religions to arise.[36] Ecumenical relations among existing denominations are most likely to develop under such pluralistic conditions – an implication that follows directly from Stark's work (2001, 119–20) and was observed by Adam Smith:

> [H]ad the conquering party never adopted the tenets of one sect more than those of another, when it had gained the victory, it would probably have dealt equally and impartially with all the different sects, and have allowed every man to chuse [*sic*] his own priest and his own religion as he thought proper. There would in this case, no doubt, have been a great multitude of religious sects. . . . The teachers of each sect, seeing themselves surrounded on all sides with more adversaries than friends, would be obliged to learn that candour [*sic*] and moderation which is so seldom to be found among the teachers of those great sects, show tenets being supported by the civil magistrate, are held in veneration by almost all the inhabitants of extensive kingdoms and empires, and who therefore see nothing round them but followers, disciples, and humble admirers. ([1776] 1976, 792–3)

---

[35] "Within reason" is important here, as it is unlikely that Lutherans or Catholics in the United States would argue favorably for the unrestricted rights of a religion that practices human sacrifice.

[36] Mainstream Christian reaction to the creation of Mormonism is an example. Likewise, most established faiths are skeptical of laws that allow prisoners to declare religious belief systems that allow them exemptions from various prison regulations, one of the unique consequences of the short-lived Religious Freedom Restoration Act.

Smith's analysis further points out that religious tolerance, supported by laws that do not favor a dominant faith, will lead to increased religious pluralism ("a great multitude of religious sects") and increased religious civility,[37] as confirmed by contemporary research linking denominational pluralism to religious freedom (Stark 2005; Gill 1999a; Stark and Iannaccone 1994; Finke and Iannaccone 1993; Finke 1990). The initial presence of religious pluralism – particularly at the time of a nation's founding – would make the state hesitant to impose any form of legislation that would favor one minority sect over any other minority sect. This, in turn, would encourage the immigration of religious dissenters from other parts of the world and/or schismatic denominational growth in the domestic arena. In other words, religious pluralism begets religious freedom, which in turn enhances the prospects for greater pluralism. Noting this prompts us to consider the interests and incentives facing those who make the laws regulating the religious marketplace.

Political Incentives in the Religious Marketplace

As defined in the preceding text, religious liberty is a matter of governmental regulation. Therefore we should expect the interests and incentive structures of politicians to play a significant role in determining the level (and form) of religious freedom in society. Why would politicians want to regulate (or deregulate) religious organizations? This moves us to the central question regarding the origins of religious liberty (i.e., the deregulation of the religious marketplace). We begin with two basic assumptions about the general preferences of policy makers common in the political science literature (Geddes 1994; Ames 1987; Mayhew 1974):

Axiom 3: Politicians are primarily interested in their personal political survival.

Axiom 4: Politicians will also seek to maximize government revenue, promote economic growth, and minimize civil unrest.

Axiom 5: Politicians seek to minimize the cost of ruling.

Policy makers may be driven by a plethora of ideological influences, but their goals are largely unachievable if they are not in power. Also they may seek power for power's sake or the fame and possible fortune it bestows.

---

[37] As noted in Axiom 1, Smith implicitly assumes that religious tastes in society are latently pluralistic. If he had assumed such preferences were monolithic, no "great multitude" would arise.

In whichever case, retaining power is the primary (instrumental) goal to achieving these other ends. Beyond political survival, rulers will also attempt to maximize government (i.e., tax) revenue. The more revenue that they have at their disposal, the more policy goals they can achieve – be it building a strong military, extending health care to more individuals, or filling the coffers of their Swiss bank accounts. Enhancing government revenue is also a function of economic growth; the more the nation's economy grows, the larger the tax base and the more revenue politicians have to spend.[38] As a side benefit, a growing economy often means greater employment and rising standards of living, all of which make the citizenry happy and more willing to keep the present rulers in power. Thus, politicians will favor policy decisions that promote *general* economic growth all the while balancing the need to stay in power by satisfying *specific* constituencies (Olson 1993).[39] And, obviously, civil unrest is potentially threatening to a political leader as it may mean the possibility of being overthrown in a revolution or coup. Consistent levels of civil unrest usually mean slower economic growth, if not economic devastation, in that entrepreneurs are less likely to invest in politically unstable environments, and workers are having their time and energy diverted into other activities (e.g., protesting government policies, fighting a civil war).

Politicians are constantly aware of the trade-offs between guaranteeing political survival, enhancing tax revenue, and achieving policy goals (Levi 1988). Staying in office requires resources. The more resources that are expended to retain power, the less are available for achieving other goals, *ceteris paribus*. Politicians have three general mechanisms for ensuring the compliance of a population: coercion, patronage, and ideological legitimacy. Coercion simply means threatening and carrying out punishment to those who fail to obey the leader's will. Patronage represents some form of mutual exchange – for example, providing a public works project in exchange for electoral support. And ideological legitimacy involves citizens obeying the

---

[38] Raising government tax revenue is not simply a function of raising the tax rate as there may be decreasing absolute returns on very high marginal tax rates. Cutting taxes need not necessarily mean a loss of government revenue if the incentives provided by lower taxes produce an economic expansion, a phenomenon illustrated by the Laffer curve (Wanniski 1978).

[39] This is the age-old political economy problem of free trade versus tariffs. Although free trade generally improves the general welfare of a trading nation in the long term, reducing trade barriers can harm specific sectors of the economy in the short term. Economic protectionism tends to win out because political survival is often determined in the short term (e.g., frequent elections).

demands of their leaders based on a belief that those demands are just and proper. Of these three means, the last is the least costly,[40] leading us to the following proposition:

> *Proposition 2:* Politicians will seek ideological compliance of the population when possible.

Patronage is undeniably costly as it entails paying critical groups of citizens for their support. One would imagine that the price demanded for support by the citizenry will be in direct proportion to the value that the ruler places on that support. Moreover, over time, bargaining power in patronage relationships tends to flow to the recipients as they can threaten to withdraw support unless payments increase. Think of it as political extortion. One might believe that coercion is less costly than patronage, but that is not necessarily so. Reliance on repressive means entails paying a large security force (that can also demand increasing resources for continued support), giving rise to a terrified work force that may not have an incentive to be productive (cf. Sharansky 2004), or exacerbating existing divisions within the ruling coalition between those who favor coercion and those who prefer more liberalized forms of rule (cf. Drake and McCubbins 1998). Overuse of the military or police may also cause resentment among those running those institutions (as few soldiers actually prefer to be constantly in harm's way) and lead to a possible coup (Stepan 1988). Winning the "hearts and minds" of the citizenry – that is, gaining ideological legitimacy – is most likely the cheapest route to ensuring political survival in office (cf. Hechter 2000; North 1981). As Nobel laureate Douglass North has argued, "A common belief system which embodies social norms consistent with the policies of the ruler will reduce the use of coercion" (2005, 104) and presumably lower the need for patronage.

The preference of political leaders to enhance political survival through ideological legitimacy naturally provides an incentive for church-state cooperation in that religions tend to be the primary producer of societal norms and values (Gill 1998: 52–3). To the extent that citizens agree that obedience to the government is morally correct or in their best interest, politicians need not devote resources to coercion or paying off

---

[40] For an extended discussion of this assumption, see Gill (1998, 50–2) and Taylor (1982, 11–20). Again, I refer to the maestro of political economy and religion Adam Smith, who noted that "management and persuasion are always the easiest and the safest instruments of government, as force and violence are the worst and most dangerous" ([1776] 1976, 799).

constituents. The conveyance of ideological legitimacy frequently comes from the endorsement of religious leaders.[41] Clergy tend to be among the most trusted officials in society. In large part this is due to the inherent nature of producing religious goods. Because religion is a credence good, at its essence, consumers may tend to be skeptical about purchasing such goods unless they have some signal about the good's future quality. Suppliers of these goods maintain a strong incentive to develop credit-worthy reputations. Clergy frequently live austere lives, make other sacrifices (e.g., celibacy), and engage in rather costly rituals to cultivate an aura of trust among parishioners. In situations of uncertainty, people will look to trusted leaders for guidance. It can be expected that a priest will give carefully considered advice that is in the best interest of his parishioners. If the priest constantly makes poor political decisions, thereby leading his flock to harm, it is unlikely that he will be successful in "selling" his spiritual message. In other words, clergy often act as guiding voices in the secular realm, providing information that would otherwise be costly or unavailable to citizens.[42] Having trusted priests endorse a government, or governmental policies, is one means of reducing the costs of ruling. This endorsement comes at a price. Clergy are likely to ask for favors in return, which may entail significant regulations on other religions or government subsidies. As I shall

[41] As usual, Adam Smith was one of the first to point this out. "Articles of faith, as well as all other spiritual matters, it is evident enough, are not within the proper department of a temporal sovereign, who, though he may be very well qualified for protecting, is seldom supposed to be so for instructing the people. With regard to such matters, therefore, his authority can seldom be sufficient to counterbalance the united authority of the clergy of the established church. The publick [sic] tranquility, however, and [the ruler's] own security may frequently depend upon the doctrines which they may think proper to propagate concerning such matters. As he can seldom directly oppose their decision, therefore, with proper weight and authority, it is necessary that he should be able to influence it; and he can influence it only by the fears and expectations which he may excite in the greater part of the individuals of the order" (Smith [1776] 1976: 798).

[42] This leads to a number of testable propositions that are tangential for this study, such as the proposition that people with little access to information about politicians (e.g., because of illiteracy, lack of access to televised news) will tend to place more credence in the recommendations of clergy when considering political action. Also, it should be noted that this hypothesis builds on the political economy of interest groups, which suggests that such groups act as information conduits for rationally ignorant voters. Because religious clergy tend to reflect a wide range of class and sectoral interests, their recommendations should be more pertinent to broad, general issues that do not affect an individual's specific welfare. Occupational groups (e.g., the trial lawyers association) usually provide more finely tuned information on these issues. This general hypothesis also suggests that professions that deal more in credence goods will have a stronger reputation for trustworthiness than those that deal with more tangible goods.

argue, a religion's ability to obtain these demands is a function of the religious market structure.

Understand that churches are not only a source of ideological legitimation but also can represent a source of rival authority. In line with the political survival axiom mentioned earlier, politicians seek to neutralize rivals. Churches offer one potential focal point from which a rival ruler or party can rally opposition. The main reason is that religious organizations possess several features that are helpful in mobilizing collective action, the basic problem inherent in any (mass-based) opposition movement (Lichbach 1995). First, members of a religious community typically hold shared values and mutual expectations about behavior. This enhances trust among individuals, which in turn lowers the uncertainty associated with mutually cooperative behavior (Chong 1991). Trustworthy leadership is also essential for collective action. Leaders who advocate risky action (e.g., protesting a government) will be successful only to the extent to which their followers trust their choices of action. People rarely follow strangers blindly into dangerous situations. As previously noted, religious organizations require trustworthy leadership to accomplish their goals of enticing individuals to contribute to a credence good. Numerous other factors also enhance the ability of religious groups to quickly mobilize collective action, including regularized meetings, financial resources, common religious idioms, and established networks of communication (cf. Chwe 2001; Chong 1991). For rulers who are concerned with their political survival, maintaining a tight regulatory control over this potential rival source of authority provides a strong incentive to tamper with laws regulating religion in order to enhance their own political position. This might entail restricting the freedoms or reducing the exclusive legal privileges of particular denominations, especially those that are institutionally aligned with, and unable to back away from a commitment to, a strong rival. Alternatively, it might entail co-opting the support of a religious group with preferential legislation that directly benefits the church in question or restricts the activities of competitive denominations.

Predicting which situation is more likely will depend on a more detailed specification of the political and religious environment in question. The bargaining power of the relevant actors, both secular and religious, will condition the outcome for regulatory legislation. Nonetheless, the discussion in the preceding text points us in the direction of several testable propositions about the relative bargaining power of church and state that can then form the basis for a more historically based analytic narrative.

The first proposition establishes a general prediction about the deregulation of the religious marketplace and is based on the opportunity costs facing secular leaders:

> *Proposition 3:* To the extent that political survival, revenue collection, economic growth and social stability are hindered by restrictions on religious freedom or subsidies to a dominant church, religious regulation will be liberalized or not enforced (de facto liberalization). In other words, when restrictions on religious liberty have a high opportunity cost as measured in terms of political survival, government revenue, and/or economic growth, deregulation of the religious market results. Concomitantly, restrictions on religious freedom will increase if it served the aforementioned political and economic interests of policy makers.

This hypothesis challenges the notion that religious liberty is the result of a shift in political philosophy (or the victory of one group that holds a more liberal political philosophy). One of the central failings of ideational explanations is that they typically view the debate over religious liberty in isolation from other concerns in the polity; religious liberty is simply a question of two sides debating "right" versus "wrong," with one side eventually prevailing. In reality, though, legislation is rarely considered in isolation. Positions on one issue condition another. The reason for specific policy choices in one arena may be connected to seemingly unrelated issues. This proposition directs scholars to look for evidence of potential policy trade-offs, something that ideational perspectives do not do effectively.

In economic terms, politicians are said to be calculating their opportunity costs. An opportunity cost is the price paid for a foregone opportunity. Implementing one policy necessarily means not implementing its opposite, and that opposite policy comes with a set of potential costs. For instance, assume politicians have a choice between jailing religious minorities (limiting religious freedom) and allowing them to move about a territory freely (enhancing religious liberty). The opportunity cost of the imprisonment decision might be a loss of economic trade by merchants from other territories that want to hawk their wares. Moreover, it could also mean a drop in immigration or prompt an exodus, which is a significant cost for a government seeking to attract and/or retain skilled laborers. Alternatively, allowing dissenting sects access to one's territory may irritate the established religious authorities and cause a loss of public support (or even a religious insurrection). A politician will have to weigh the various costs and benefits of the different policies to determine how each would affect his personal goals of political survival, collecting revenue, economic growth, and minimizing civil unrest.

Proposition 3 is admittedly broad. The general vagueness of Proposition 3, however, is both its principal strength and its principal weakness. By not identifying more specific trade-offs, the proposition can be used to examine a wide array of political settings, both longitudinal and latitudinal. It is argued that political goals annunciated in Axioms 3–5 generally hold true for all rulers – both democrats and dictators – throughout time and space. The guiding theoretical principle is that some policy trade-off that affects a politician's self-interest will be in play during periods of religious deregulation or increased regulation. The specific nature of the policies and policy trade-offs will largely be determined by the historical context. Unfortunately, by not being more specific, Proposition 3 risks tautology. Observation of a change in religious policy can be taken as evidence that political survival is at risk. Although the careful use of an analytic narrative can help to alleviate this problem in historical and comparative case studies, I will attempt to lay out additional propositions that delineate more-specific environments in which religious deregulation (or increased regulation) might occur.

Situations of Political Competition

I begin this exercise by noting that political survival varies according to the presence of viable opposition candidates for power, that is, the level of political competition (which in turn affects the prospects for political survival). Politicians facing intense rivalries tend to have shorter time horizons (higher discount rates) and less bargaining power relative to organized social actors. These factors are likely to affect policy-making decisions.

Proposition 4: The presence of viable secular rivals to power increases the bargaining power of religious organizations, *ceteris paribus*.

Proposition 4a: If one religious organization commands hegemonic loyalty among the population[43] and is not tied to any secular political actor, the bargaining power of that church increases, *ceteris paribus*. Regulatory policy

---

[43] The issue of hegemonic loyalty will become an important issue. In contemporary Latin America, the Catholic Church is considered to be hegemonic, and a majority of people nominally affiliate with Catholicism. However, in several countries, the active, churchgoing Protestant population equals, and perhaps even exceeds, the active Catholic population – Brazil, Chile, and Guatemala are the central examples. Calling the Catholic Church *hegemonic* in these instances might be a misnomer.

toward religion is likely to favor the dominant church and discriminate against minority denominations.

Proposition 4b: If a church is institutionally linked (or credibly committed) to one political faction, regulatory policy will favor that denomination if the affiliated faction holds power. Conversely, religious deregulation, which punishes the dominant church and rewards spiritual competitors, is likely when the church's favored faction loses.

Proposition 4c: If several competing denominations exist (none with hegemonic dominance), regulatory policy will tend not to discriminate among them (i.e., increased religious liberty). In other words, the presence of competing religious denominations reduces the bargaining leverage of any one particular group, leading politicians to curry favor with all.

When a politician faces political uncertainty, he is more likely to cut deals with individuals or groups that can enhance his position of power over rivals. A religious group that commands the loyalty of the vast majority of a population would be in a good position to make certain demands (e.g., access to public schools, prohibitions on minority sects) of this politician in exchange for public support.

However, the ability of church leaders to deliver the promised support will shape the credibility of their bargaining position. Religious leaders who have always been visibly supportive of one political faction will have a difficult time convincing politicians of the rival faction and of the citizenry that they have switched sides. Such switching often means rejecting moral arguments that were made in favor of the old ally. Strong institutional linkages between the church and the old ally (e.g., favored political appointments for clergy, large financial subsidies) only exacerbate the credibility problem facing church leaders. Remember, churches are in the business of producing and distributing credence goods. Quickly switching political parties would likely appear opportunistic and would reflect poorly on the credibility that the church has when it proclaims that it is looking after the eternal well-being of its parishioners. In situations where the church is closely linked with a political faction that has fallen out of power, the new rulers have little incentive to reward the church because they know any church support would appear opportunistic and not be worth much to members. Moreover, depending on the bitterness of the political rivalry that brought the new faction to power, the new rulers may seek to punish the standing religious leaders by revoking their favored official status, which may mean providing greater access to the religious market to dissenting denominations. Or, in the case of the Soviet Union and Mexico (ca. 1920s), it may mean a crackdown on all religious activity.

If secular leaders facing stiff political competition exist within an environment where there are multiple denominations, it may behoove these politicians to treat all religions equally. Even a small religious group that may only represent 5 percent of the population could potentially make the difference in a tight election. Of course, those politicians may take a chance and support the larger denomination in the hopes of securing more votes, but this may be a risky strategy if the religious minorities are actually growing. Opposition rulers may be able to make headway on the incumbents by rallying these religious minorities with the promise of equal treatment. The optimal position then for the incumbent would be to promise equal treatment (to neutralize their opponent's policy advantage) or to try avoiding the problem altogether. Any particular church in a pluralistic environment would do well to avoid any specific attachment with a single political party as they may risk disadvantageous legislation when their faction is out of power.[44]

Situations of Minimal Political Competition

Where political rivalry is minimal, the goal of political survival becomes less pressing, and time horizons lengthen. The opportunity costs of various policies are likely to shift. Policies that bought a politician immediate support under intense competition but that harmed long-term economic growth and revenue collection are likely to be more costly relative to longer-term policies in a new, less competitive environment. For instance, candidates who are running for election are more likely to propose tax cuts than are political leaders with secure tenure. These shifts in political opportunity costs can potentially affect church-state relations.

> *Proposition 5:* As political tenure becomes more secure, the bargaining power of a religious group wanes.

> *Proposition 5a:* Given that restrictions on religious liberty entail monitoring and enforcement costs, politicians will be less likely to enforce them as their political tenure becomes secure.[45]

> *Proposition 5b:* As enforcement of restrictions on religious freedom decreases, religious pluralism increases in society (by way of Axioms 1 and 2).

[44] A similar argument is being made with labor unions in the United States. Given the strong affiliation between unions and the Democratic Party in recent decades, labor leaders cannot expect much favorable legislation when Republicans dominate the different branches and geographic levels of government.

[45] Likewise, subsidization of religious groups becomes more expensive in that as political survival becomes secure supporting an established church yields increasingly fewer benefits to the politician.

In reality, supporting an established church and keeping legal restrictions on minority religions are relatively inexpensive tasks.[46] For most politically secure governments, the matter of church regulatory policy will simply become a moot issue.[47] So long as religious minorities do not become politically or socially disruptive, entrenched incumbent politicians are more than likely to be indifferent to their growing presence (cf. Mullett 1938). Should secular leaders become uninterested in enforcing laws restricting new sects, the innate religious heterogeneity within most societies will result in a gradual increase in denominational pluralism, particularly if the dominant church lacks the institutional muscle to punish "heresy." And, as Rodney Stark (1992) has argued, most religious monopolies do not have the resources to effectively stamp out religious pluralism without the support of a coercive state.[48]

If religious pluralism increases to some visible threshold[49] and political competition reappears, we are likely to see movement toward religious freedom (as per Proposition 4c). In other words, Propositions 5, 5a, and 5b provide for a means wherein the incentive structures of both secular politicians and religious actors can change over time, allowing for gradual progress toward religious pluralism and freedom. As the aforementioned propositions imply, increasing political competition among growing religious pluralism is the best environment in which to foster religious liberty.

---

[46] A casual glance at the budget of any state that has an established church will reveal a pittance spent on supporting that church. Enforcement costs of religious regulations are more difficult to measure, but the lack of major incidents in which people are arrested for nonviolent forms of religious worship seems to provide initial evidence that such costs are low.

[47] As much as I would like to think that my research on church-state relations is a central topic in political science, I readily admit that other matters, such as managing the economy and fighting wars, are probably more important to political leaders. That is the gist of the argument presented here. Although the regulation of religion is something that will pique a ruler's attention, especially if clergy are whispering in his ear, his decision to regulate or deregulate the religious economy will be contingent on more important matters – staying in power, growing the economy, and raising tax revenue.

[48] The medieval Catholic Church may appear to be an exception given the relative weakness of the state system in Europe at the time. Nonetheless, feudal lords were willing to act on the behalf of the Vatican to preserve the Church's hold over the population. See Ekelund et al. (1996) for an interesting discussion on how the Catholic Church maintained its relative hegemony over a politically fragmented medieval Europe.

[49] This threshold may not be as large as one would intuitively expect. My previous work (Gill 1998) indicates that if religious minorities can reach about 4–5 percent of the population, they will rouse the passions of the dominant religion and become a political issue. The rapid, albeit initially small, influx of evangelical missionaries and other "nontraditional" denominations in Eastern Europe and Russia created immediate cries for some regulatory action to slow or restrict these groups outright. See Chapter 5 for more details.

To the extent that "modernization" correlates with increasing political competition, this might help to explain the general trend toward religious liberty over the past several centuries. However, the opportunity costs approach to explaining religious liberty leaves a role for human agency and allows for potential reversals in the progress toward religious freedom.

The Role of Ideas: A Brief Discussion

One of my former colleagues once remarked, "Scratch an ideology and watch an interest bleed."[50] This statement may appear to summarize how most economists (and materialists more generally)[51] view the role of ideas and values in society – an individual's self-interest determines his or her ideological worldview. From this perspective, ideas are at best secondary causes of social phenomenon, if not simply ex post facto justifications of self-interested actions. There is some truth to the preceding statement. Brutal dictators often are known to justify their oppressive regimes with statements that they are looking after the best interests of their nation. Even democratic politicians have been known to cloak their pork-barreling policies in high-minded rhetoric. And the Catholic Church's support for religious liberty and ecumenical relations is often at odds with its actual behavior in certain parts of the world (as noted earlier).

In all fairness, not all rational choice theorists view ideas in such a simplistic or off-handed manner. Ideas do matter (cf. North 2005; Kuran 2004). We only need to scan the students sitting in our lecture halls to prove this; those pupils who place a high value on education tend to work harder and get better grades than those who view college as a diversionary pastime. And there are countless examples of political crusaders and zealots who go to great lengths to champion a cause – from antiwar activists who travel the country in VW minibuses to antiabortion advocates giving up their time to blockade clinics. Religious belief often inspires many of these social movements. Consider the Quakers' role in the abolitionist movement or the Baptists' role in promoting temperance. To claim that ideas have no influence over behavior would be misleading.

So what role do ideas play in a rational choice analysis? Technically speaking, rational choice theory is agnostic on the role of ideas in the sense

---

[50] The colleague was Pierre Van Den Berghe of the University of Washington's Department of Sociology. He has since retired. To the best of my knowledge, this was his original quote.
[51] For clarity's sake, I should note that not all economists and materialists are rational choice scholars and vice versa.

that our ideologies and values affect the preferences we hold. If a person is raised in a household that promotes the value of recycling, that person will likely place a high value on recycling in the future and behave in ways to maximize that goal. Likewise, a person raised Catholic who attended Mass and Sunday school every week would be more likely to place a high utility on religious practice later in their life, a phenomenon that economist Larry Iannaccone (1990) termed "religious human capital" (cf. Becker 1994). Hence, ideas (including values and norms) matter in that they form the basis for our preferences. Rational choice theorists, however, assume that preference formation is exogenous to their explanations. Although it is entirely plausible that preferences change over time and affect our behavioral choices (something that the advertising business counts on), a rational choice scholar will generally hold preferences constant and see if changes in external constraints lead to alterations in behavior.

Ideas, values, and norms can also act as constraints on human behavior. Certain types of behavior – for example, yelling at professors in class or throwing an aluminum can on the side of the road – are considered unacceptable practices by the culture at large. Even though I may realize that it is easier to throw a can out my car window than drive to the nearest trash can, social disapproval of such activity might prevent me from doing it. Likewise, religious prohibitions on out-of-wedlock fornication may lead to fewer sexual dalliances among the young. A constraint-based view of ideas is perfectly compatible with rational choice theory. A person seeking social acceptance among his peers will be less likely to engage in practices that violate set notions of appropriate behavior. Attending church in a pink fuzzy bathrobe and bunny slippers may maximize a person's physical comfort, but it certainly would isolate him or her from friends and family.

As pertains to this study, it is possible that ideas regarding the appropriate level of religious freedom within society change over time. It could happen through open and lively debate or through the actions of a few intellectual entrepreneurs. Changes in belief among significant players may constrain the actions of other individuals. For instance, a powerful governor may proclaim that it is no longer acceptable to persecute a religious minority and seek to implement laws that guarantee freedom from persecution. Individuals seeking to curry favors from that well-placed politician may fall in line on this policy, not out of any innate change in their worldview, but rather because they see such action as means to another end (e.g., a desirable political appointment or other favor). In this case, what may appear to be a general social shift in preferences simply is the result of self-interested behavior on two seemingly unrelated dimensions – religious liberty and one's political self-promotion. Of course, such a self-interested shift toward another ideological position may eventually expose one to another belief system and modify that person's intrinsic ideas or values. An uncommitted Methodist who begins attending a Mormon singles group out of a desire to find a date (or mate) may eventually end up internalizing that faith's theology, something implied by Iannaccone's (1990) analysis.

Disentangling whether or not a change in behavior is related to a genuine shift in preferences among some (or all) members of society or is simply a matter of interest-based behavior is difficult to do, particularly in historical analysis where the relevant people have passed from the scene. Interviews with the dead are notoriously difficult to obtain, usually have significant response biases, and grant-giving agencies are often reluctant to allocate money for séances.[52] Diaries and letters may help us sort out some of this entanglement, but it is not uncommon for individuals to justify self-interested behavior with the use of lofty rhetoric and an appeal to high ideals. Even living folk tend to do this. Finding predictive instances wherein the pursuit of apparent self-interest in one arena is closely related to a change in position in another arena would provide evidence that self-interest lay behind the change in the latter circumstance, as opposed to a shift in preferences or worldviews. The preceding deductive theory attempts to do this for the issue of religious liberty and seeks to relate it to a series of other policies on trade, economic growth, social conflict, and political survival. With that in mind, we now turn our attention to examine a series of historical instances of changes in religious liberty to see if such issues played a role.

---

[52] For the record, I am skeptical of séance methodology.

CHAPTER 3

Colonial British America

Tax all things, water, air, and light,
If need there is, yea tax the night
But let our brave heroic minds
Move freely, like celestial winds.
Make vice and folly, feel your rod,
But leave our consciences to GOD.
    – Anonymous[1] *Virginia Gazette* (October 11, 1776)

ON THE EASTERN SIDE of Boston's gold-domed State House sits a statue of a religious freedom fighter. The inscription on the pedestal reads:

Mary Dyer

Witness for Religious Freedom

How did this brave woman of the seventeenth century witness religious freedom? The next line on the statue's base provides the answer:

Hanged on Boston Commons 1660.

Hanging at the wrong end of gallows probably is not the most enjoyable way to witness religious liberty. A perplexed Boston tourist might ask how

---

[1] Quotation cited in Buckley (1977, 22). Buckley also cites Lohrenz (1970) as attributing this verse to David Thomas, a Baptist preacher.

Mrs. Dyer met such a distasteful fate. You see, Mary Dyer was a Quaker and the Massachusetts Bay Colony was Puritan country. In 1660, that was a bad combination.

The story of Mary Dyer's tragic fate exposes one of the darker sides of American mythology.[2] Grade-school history textbooks are filled with the noble story of the Pilgrims who fled religious persecution in England, traveled to the Netherlands for a spell, and finally received a charter to settle in the New World. Felicia Hemans penned a famous poem – "The Landing of the Pilgrim Fathers" – celebrating this historical journey:

> What sought they thus afar?
>   Bright jewels of the mine?
> The wealth of the seas, the spoils of war?
>   They sought a faith's pure shrine!
> Ay, call it holy ground,
>   The soil where first they trod;
> They have left unstained what there they found
>   Freedom to worship God.[3]

This portrait of early religious liberty in Britain's American colonies was a romantic notion at best. The harsh truth, as discovered by Mary Dyer, was "religious freedom for me, but not for thee" (cf. P. Miller 1935, 59). Restrictions on various denominations and outright persecution existed for nearly two centuries prior to the drafting of the U.S. Constitution's First Amendment. This observation sets up an intriguing question. If religious freedom was hard to come by and a lack of religious tolerance common, what factors eventually led the United States to be the first modern nation to firmly enshrine liberty of conscience in its principal document of governance? Before investigating this question more fully (with the help of the theory presented in the Chapter 2), it is worth taking a glimpse at the religious regulatory landscape in colonial America to place the historical accomplishment of the U.S. Constitution's First Amendment in historical context.

---

[2] This statement should not be taken as an indication of "revisionist history" or an attempt to denigrate the accomplishments of the American colonists. I remain skeptical of histographies that see any blemish in American history as an indication of the nation's inherent corruptibility. This book was partly inspired by the noble struggle for religious freedom in the United States, a story that contains heroes, villains, and a mélange of ambiguous characters.

[3] Cited in McCallum (1929, 26). Hemans's poem, now only familiar to schoolchildren of an earlier time, was initially published in *New Monthly Magazine* (November 1825).

Religious Intolerance and Regulation in
the American Colonies

The story of religious intolerance in colonial America – and the unfortunate
fate of Mary Dyer – begins in early-seventeenth-century England and aptly
illustrates the assertion of Proposition 1 – that minority denominations
prefer religious liberty while dominant churches tend to desire government-
imposed restrictions on upstart sects.[4] The ascension of James I to the
throne of England in 1603 ushered in a period of increased persecution of
both Catholics and puritanical Calvinists – known as Puritans – a policy that
carried over into the reign of King Charles I (1625–49) (Ahlstrom 2004,
93; Grell, Israel, and Tyacke 1991, 5). Although most Puritans in England
considered themselves still to be members of the Church of England, and
several of them actually sat in parliament at the time, a small subset of
Puritans saw the attempt at internal reform of the state-run English church
to be futile and sought separation. These "Separatists" – as they would
become known[5] – were specifically singled out for harsh punishment under
both King James's reign and that of his successor Charles. Seeking asylum
from this treatment, a group of Puritan separatists fled to the Netherlands
where the Dutch government showed a high level of tolerance for dissenting
religious groups (see following text). Despite greater religious liberty, these
English separatists were unable to obtain full economic and political rights
because they were not Dutch citizens. Moreover, the immoral seductions of
a port city and the looming prospect of war with Spain drove these spiritual
sojourners to search for a new home (Dillon 1975, 87–117; Bradford [1650]
1909, 19–23).

Be it either by historical accident or divine intervention, a golden opportunity presented itself to these wayward pilgrims. The Pilgrims, as they
would eventually be called,[6] were able to secure a contract with the Virginia

---

[4] McLoughlin (1968, 1406-7) notes this hypocrisy for Separatist Baptists in Virginia;
although chafing under mandatory taxation to support the Church of England in the
colony at large, once they became a majority within a township they were quick to impose
compulsory tithing on others, arguing that voluntary contributions could not provide adequate funds for a church. Curry (1986, 109) notes this for Anglicans in the Massachusetts
Bay Colony wherein clergy for the Church of England had to argue for exemptions to
tithes supporting Congregationalists while their denominational brethren in the colonies
to the south (and back in England) were promoting compulsory taxation to support their
church.

[5] Never let it be said that the British were not good at coming up with aptly descriptive
names.

[6] The name *Pilgrims* would not be widely used to describe this group until 1669, roughly a
half century after they made their pilgrimage to the New World.

Company to establish a settlement in the British Americas. King James I approved of this deal but only after the Pilgrims swore loyalty to the English Crown (Ahlstrom 2004, 105). James's willingness to give these religious nonconformists colonial land after having persecuted them at home was more than likely a concession to the realization that he needed to populate the American colonies lest they fall into the hands of other foreign powers, an indication of how economic and geopolitical considerations affect one's policy toward religious institutions (cf. Proposition 3).[7] Originally destined for the Virginia territories,[8] the ships carrying William Bradford and his disciples landed a bit farther north in the area now known as Plymouth, Massachusetts.

For the most part, the early colonists of Plymouth displayed a remarkable degree of liberal attitudes in both governance and religious toleration (Gura 1984, 34; Stokes 1950, 153). The latter was due in large part to the small number of non-Puritans in the colony; it is easy to be tolerant when there is no one around to be intolerant toward. The ironic problems of religious intolerance arose in the wider Massachusetts Bay Colony (which eventually absorbed the Plymouth colony in 1691). After allowing the separatist Pilgrims to leave England in 1607 and then settle Plymouth in 1620, King James turned his wrath toward the Puritans that remained behind in England, most of whom did not seek to separate from the Church of England.[9] As James Hutson describes it:

> The great majority of Puritans rejected headlong separation from the Church of England and sought instead to reform it from within. Their hopes were dashed in the late 1620s when the leadership of the church, backed by the civil

[7] Proposition 3 does not include considerations of geopolitical strategy per se, but such factors do fit within the spirit of that proposition.

[8] The actual target destination was Manhattan Island, which was part of the Virginia territories at the time, something that few New Yorkers would admit happily today.

[9] The fact that most Puritans still sought internal reform of the Church of England is evident by their actions within days of James I taking the throne. A group purportedly representing more than one thousand clergymen petitioned James with a list of demands regarding changes in the Church, including moderate adjustments to the episcopal structure of the institution (Tyacke 1991, 21-6). Seeing a significant outcry for reform within such a stolidly traditional institution coming on the heels of his coronation represented a major provocation to his authority. Hence it is understandable that James would unleash his wrath as a means of demonstrating his governing resolve. This could be taken as support for the general thesis of this book (Proposition 3) that political leaders decide their religious policy based on calculations affecting their political survival (among other things). The need to assert one's authority against a rebellion of dissenting clergy (who are themselves seeking limitations on a state church under control of the sovereign) in the first days and months of one's reign will push one to crack down on the dissenters.

authorities, insisted that they adopt religious ceremonies and practices that they abhorred. Puritan ministers who refused to conform were fired from their pulpits and threatened with "extirpation from the earth" unless they and their followers toed the line. Exemplary punishments were inflicted on Puritan stalwarts; one zealot, for example, who called Anglican bishops "knobs, wens and bunchy popish flesh," was sentenced, in 1630, to life imprisonment, had his property confiscated, his nose slit, and ear cut off, and his forehead branded S.S. (sower of sedition). (1998, 4)[10]

Not surprisingly, many Puritans decided to pack up and leave England for the land pioneered by their separatist brethren. The door to leaving was opened by King Charles I, who ascended to the throne in 1625 and continued his father's harassment of Puritans, but who nonetheless agreed to let Puritans emigrate as part of an agreement with the Massachusetts Company to establish a new colony and populate the territory north of the Virginia colony beginning in 1629.[11] More than two thousand Puritans under the leadership of John Winthrop took the opportunity to leave within the first year, and the colony, centered in Boston, grew unabated for the next decade and a half.

Having experienced a decade of increased persecution in Britain, one might expect that the Puritan settlers would be more empathetic toward nonconformist sects. This was not the case. Anson Philips Stokes, one of the most preeminent historians of church-state relations in the United States, observed in the Massachusetts Bay Colony that

religion, of an intolerant Calvinistic type, and government were to be closely associated in accordance with English tradition; a Puritan State-Church specially closely related to town government, gradually developing from nonconformist to take the place of the old Anglican State-Church to which they had been accustomed in England. The Church was a 'carefully selected group of communicants' who emphasized their prerogatives, and who would not brook serious dissent from their duly adopted tenets. They expected the State to support public worship and suppress heresy. They did not wish it to interfere in strictly religious questions, but recognized that in matters of Church government and ecclesiastical affairs State and Church should work together. (1950, 155; cf. Park 1954)

---

[10] The "extirpation" quote is attributed to Perry Miller (1956), and the "bunchy popish" quote was taken from *The Dictionary of National Biography* XI, 880.

[11] Plymouth Colony never had an official colonial status and was allowed to exist primarily through benign neglect. That fact that Plymouth remained a relatively small outpost of only a few hundred settlers made this an easy de facto policy.

The irony here is that a group of religious dissenters who were opposed to enforced religious conformity when they were a minority in England (cf. Tyacke 1991, 23–7; McLoughlin 1971, 13) were quick to establish it into law when they became a majority in their new homeland (Noonan 1998, 41–58), a phenomenon predicted by Proposition 1: religious minorities will prefer greater liberty while dominant religions favor restrictions on different sects. The fact that Puritans went from asking for greater tolerance in England to making life difficult for all non-Puritans in the colonies within the span of just a few years indicates that this change was more strategic (i.e., based on calculations of self-interest) than ideological.

It could be argued that the Puritans of the Massachusetts Bay Colony really did not go through a fundamental shift in their policy of religious freedom and tolerance but were merely implementing the policies of the Church of England in the colonies. After all, aside from the Pilgrim Separatists who sailed on the Mayflower, the majority of Puritans in England during the early 1600s still considered themselves to be members of the Church of England.[12] Their position was that they were working from within Anglicanism to reform it. Nonetheless, once removed from their close proximity to the Archbishop of Canterbury, the Puritan Congregationalists in colonial America became de facto separatists and developed laws that impinged on the freedom of others, including the Anglicans with whom they purportedly claimed brotherhood. Isaac Backus, a Baptist minister and champion of religious freedom in America, noted how in 1767 "the episcopal clergy appeared very earnest for having Bishops established in America . . . [and] that all they wanted, was only to have their church compleatly [sic] organized, without the least design of injuring others" (1787, 4). However, the response of one official – Dr. Chauncy – representing the colonial government in Boston was that "[w]e are, in principle, against all civil establishments in religion" (Backus 1787, 4). To this Backus declared "that corrupt reasonings have carried Dr. Chauncy's denomination on in a way beside Scripture rule for these hundred and forty years; for just so long have their rulers interposed their authority, to support their religious ministers by assessment and distress, to the unspeakable damage of other denominations, and contrary to the practice of the first planters [the Pilgrims] of the country, for eighteen years" (1787, 5–6).

---

[12] The non-Separatist Puritans were known variously as Presbyterians or Congregationalists depending on how much hierarchical organization they preferred. Both varieties were to be found among the early settlers of the Massachusetts Bay Colony, along with a smattering of Separatists (Dillon 1975, 209).

This became evident in the latter portion of the seventeenth century when Anglicans began chafing under rules that required them to pay mandatory tithes (taxes) to support Congregationalist churches in Connecticut and Massachusetts (Curry 1986, 109). As noted in Chapter 1, mandatory tithing to a specific established denomination makes an individual less willing to shell out extra money to support another denomination of his or her choosing; hence such taxes serve to inhibit the religious freedom of non-established sects to recruit members.[13] The claim by the Puritan Congregationalists that they were still one with the Church of England and abiding by England's laws governing it while ignoring the cries of more traditional Anglicans to be exempt from paying tithes to their reformist brethren, led to logical contortions on the part of colonial authorities. Secular leaders from George Winthrop to Cotton Mather and Benjamin Colman had to argue that all governing localities had rules in place to allow citizens to choose the single denomination they wished to support financially, in accordance with British law.[14] But as Curry explained,

> The [colonial authorities' arguments] that other ministers could be established remained a smokescreen to protect New England Congregationalism from possible English interference. The laws regarding the selection of ministers by the towns presumed a Congregational minister, and the composition of the population of Massachusetts at the time ensured that none other would in fact... be an established minister. Chastened by encounters with Anglican power by way of England, however, Massachusetts Congregationalists became increasingly discreet in their explanations of the system they determinedly practiced. (1986, 108)

Folks like Mather did have their theological justifications for establishing their brand of religion and not others, but it largely boiled down to the

---

[13] This may be aptly illustrated by the timing of exemptions given to Baptists and Quakers in the 1730s, and the emergence of Separatist churches during the Great Awakening beginning in 1735 is probably more than coincidental. Although various institutional features of the new churches and the creative marketing efforts of George Whitefield and other circuit riders should be given the lion's share of credit (Finke and Stark 1992, 75–108), being exempt from Congregational taxes would certainly provide an incentive to establish an independent church. Individuals who would normally not join an independent (non-Congregational) church because this would mean making voluntary contributions to one's new church in addition to the compulsory tax they paid to the Congregational establishment would now be more likely to join the new church because they would be exempt from the mandatory tithe. This linkage deserves greater investigation.

[14] Although I use the term *secular leaders* to describe Winthrop, Mather, and Colman this does not imply they were nonreligious (or antireligious) as it often does in today's vernacular. Quite the contrary, these men were professed believers. The term refers to their role in governing as a secular vocation.

case that theirs was the true religion of God while others' confessions were not (Gura 1984, 189–90). As shall be elaborated on in the following text, increasing religious diversity was already pressing colonial leaders to move toward greater religious toleration against their institutional interests, even if it was only in rhetoric. Administratively, though, the legal requirement that every town in the Massachusetts colony financially support an "able, learned and orthodox minister" meant that Puritan Congregationalists – who were the majority denomination in nearly every township – could get non-Congregationalists including Baptists and Quakers to foot their religious bills (McLoughlin 1971, 114). Although these denominations were able to petition for and win exemptions by the 1730s, a new wave of controversy over church taxes followed the First Great Awakening that began in 1735.[15] With a series of new and independent "separatist" congregations appearing at a rapid pace,[16] the New England Congregationalists and the secular officials who supported them tried preventing them from claiming the financial exemptions reluctantly yielded to the Quakers and Baptists.[17] The controversy over payment of taxes supporting Congregational churches lasted well into the eighteenth century (cf. Backus 1771) and wasn't truly settled until Massachusetts became the last of the original colonies to dismantle their denominational establishment in 1833.

Interestingly, mandatory church tithing was not the initial policy of the New England colonies. Voluntary contributions were the norm in Plymouth Colony, Massachusetts Bay, Connecticut, and New Haven for at least the first decade of their existence. Massachusetts installed compulsory tithing in 1638, Connecticut and New Haven did the same in 1640, and Plymouth followed suit in 1657 (Greene 1970, 59), albeit Plymouth was less forceful in its enforcement until it was absorbed by the Massachusetts Bay Colony in 1691 (McLoughlin 1971, 113). Of critical importance for this study is the sequential timing. The first colony to end voluntary contributions – Massachusetts Bay – was also the colony with the largest immigration at the time, with nearly twenty thousand Puritans settling in that

---

[15] See n. 13.

[16] These new Separatists, who started separating during the First Great Awakening, were variously called Separatists, Separatist Congregationalists, or New Lights.

[17] McLoughlin argues that in addition to the "stubborn determination" of the Baptists and Quakers, tithing exemptions were enacted because of the "new latitudinarianism of the Age of Reason" and "increasing affluence, materialism, and secularism of the colonies or, conversely, the waning of the Age of Faith and of the Puritan Revolution" (1971, 115). This ideational explanation is hardly satisfying considering that Baptist congregations were growing (despite a supposed waning of faith), and the Great Awakening was just about to lead to a burst in religious activity in such a "secular" environment.

area within the first decade (Hutson 1998, 5–7).[18] Obtaining voluntary compliance among such a large and increasingly diverse population was difficult and the strong arm of government was quickly put to use. Moreover, it wasn't just Puritans that flocked to Massachusetts. Members of other denominations began sprouting up, along with many nonbelievers, or at least nonpractitioners (cf. Finke and Stark 1992, 31–9). Plymouth, the last of these four colonies to impose and effectively enforce a compulsory religious tax, registered the slowest population growth, remaining in the hundreds for its first several decades of existence. That Plymouth remained a relatively isolated colonial outpost with a homogenous religious population in the early 1600s made "voluntary" contributions possible (Greene 1970, 59–60) .

Taxation wasn't the only limitation on religious liberty in the New England colonies. Although the American colonies were a crucible for participatory democracy, voting eligibility was generally restricted to church members in good standing (i.e., those who paid their tithes dutifully) (Greene 1970, 61; Mead 1956, 318). At its most restrictive, "good standing" meant an individual was a "visible saint," which entailed proof of conversion (or receipt of "saving grace") in adulthood (Ahlstrom 2004, 158). And it was also impossible to hold any political office if you did not belong to the proper (Congregational) faith. Considering the enticement of voting and being part of the lawmaking body in an era of expanding political participation, non-Congregationalists were at a significant legal disadvantage when it came to recruiting and retaining members. Just as mandatory tithing raises the costs of joining an independent church (wherein you also would be responsible for paying voluntary tithes to the new church), denominational requirements for citizen participation in governing also increase the barriers to entry for upstart sects; joining a non-Congregational denomination would put one outside the community to begin with, and exclusion from town council participation would only aggravate that exclusionary feeling.

If mandatory church assessments and limitations on civic participation were not enough to demonstrate colonial restrictions on religious freedom, a law implemented in 1646 "required all inhabitants [of Massachusetts], saints and sinners alike, to attend church . . . although . . . visible saints alone could participate fully" (Pope 1969, 4; cf. Dillon 1975, 209). The need for such a law only after a decade and a half following the onrush of Puritan

---

[18] Hutson notes that some of the Puritans settling in the Americas chose the West Indies as a destination, but the majority settled in New England.

migration indicates that many new immigrants were not of the churchgoing persuasion and that the zeal of the colony's original migrants was waning. A colony largely settled with the goal of creating a puritanical religious outpost for English dissenters was quickly becoming a mélange of individuals with varying religious tastes and levels of spiritual intensity. Strict laws to enforce religious unity were necessary to prevent the dilution of the colony's initial religious spirit. But even mandatory church attendance and tithing could not adequately solve the dilemma of growing religious pluralism and indifference. The strict requirement that only "visible saints" could participate fully in religious services and, hence, in local governance became problematic as generations passed. But this was difficult to come by for some, which resulted in two outcomes. First, the children and grand-children of many prominent families of the initial Puritan immigrants were being excluded from full church membership and hence privileged political positions, something that rarely sits well with the elite. Second, because women were more religious and apt to show signs of "visible sainthood," full church membership became increasingly dominated by women. Because men and "visible saints" were only allowed to participate in government affairs, the pool of fully activated citizens began to shrink as the population of the colonies continued to grow – a tension that did not coincide well with the democratic spirit of the initial colonial charters. Attempts to water down this high standard and accept infant baptism as acceptable for full church membership – a movement known as the "Half-Way Covenant" – was greeted with disdain by some of the more fervent Puritans during the middle of the seventeenth century and led to increasing levels of dissent (religious pluralism) within the Congregational community (Pope 1969).

The combination of compulsory taxation to support Congregational ministers, religious restrictions on the franchise, broad denominational limitations for public officials, and mandatory church attendance constituted religious establishment in New England and served as a barrier for any nonconformist sects. But despite the Puritans' best efforts and for reasons I shall reveal in the following text, New England grew in religious diversity as the population increased. This inspired another set of legal methods to deal with nonconformists – banishment, imprisonment, torture (including tongue boring and ear cropping), and death (Pestana 1991, passim). Dissenters from Congregationalist orthodoxy – particularly Quakers or Baptists – were routinely jailed and/or beaten, and ship captains caught bringing Quakers into the Massachusetts colony were financially penalized (Noonan 1998, 50–1).

Despite efforts to establish Congregationalism as the sole religious entity in the New England colonies, religious homogeneity eventually gave way to diversity. Along with diversity came the coercive means to combat new denominations. Maltreatment of minority sects was not uncommon (Pestana 1991). John Clark,[19] a Baptist doctor and preacher who settled in Rhode Island alongside the more famous Roger Williams in the mid-1600s, documented a typical problem that believers of his ilk faced in his treatise *Ill Newes from New England* (1652). It is interesting to note that one of the subtitles of the book was "That while old *England* is becoming new, *New England* is become [sic] Old," laying claim to the idea that while religious freedom was gaining in Britain under Oliver Cromwell's Commonwealth,[20] the migrant Puritans slipped into the heavy-handed ways of the Church of England.

Clark's *Ill Newes*, written in large part to stir Cromwell into pressuring the Congregational establishment in Massachusetts to allow greater liberty for Baptists, details the events surrounding a trip that he and two other Rhode Island Baptists took to perform a religious service on behalf of William Witter and to perform adult baptisms for some of Witter's neighbors (cf. Backus 1771; Clark 1652).[21] There they were removed by town constables and forced to attend a Congregational service wherein Clark refused to take off his hat and then chastised the congregants for not being proper Christians (McLoughlin 1971, 19). Clark and his two companions were then arrested the next day and accused of

> [meeting] at one William Witter's house at Lin, upon the Lord's day, and there did take upon you to Preach to some other of the Inhabitants of the same Town, and being there taken by the Constable, and coming afterward into the Assembly at Lin, did in disrespect of the Ordinances of God and his worship, keep on your Hat (the Pastor being then in Prayer) insomuch you would not give reverence in valing [sic] your Hat till it was forced off your head. (Clark 1652, 5)

[19] There seems to be some disagreement as to the correct spelling of John's surname, sometimes appearing as Clarke (cf. McLoughlin 1971). I will use the shorter version – Clark – as that is the name that appeared on the front cover of his *Ill Newes from New England*.

[20] The Commonwealth was established in 1649 following the execution of King Charles I. Cromwell, being a fairly radical Puritan himself, promoted the highest level of religious toleration England had seen to that point, although he was not particularly respectful of Irish Catholics.

[21] McLoughlin (1971, 19, n. 22) points out that the historical record is somewhat vague on who was baptized during Clark's visit to Witter's home, and Clark seems to downplay what actually went on during his time in Witter's home. For present purposes, it is enough to know that Clark was engaging in religious practices in a private residence.

Worse yet, when asked if he was an Anabaptist and had rebaptized adults, he refused to declare himself such even though Clark admitted to baptizing adults.[22] Similar charges were brought against John Crandall and Obadiah Holmes, his traveling mates. The resulting punishment for all three was jail and a substantial fine. Although supporters of Clark raised the money to pay the fine for the three men, Obadiah Holmes refused on principle to accept this charity whereupon he received a public whipping (Clark 1652, 20–2).

Mary Dyer met a much worse fate (see Pestana 1991, 33–5; McCallum 1929, 25–30). Dyer was a follower of Anne Hutchinson, a charismatic and radical Puritan who led discussions of the Scriptures in her Boston home in the early days of the Massachusetts Bay Colony. Hutchinson's radical antinomian views and growing popularity earned her banishment to Rhode Island, which was being settled by Roger Williams as a safe haven for religious dissenters and outcasts. During the trial that resulted in the banishment of Hutchinson in 1637, Mary Dyer was the one person who courageously stood with Hutchinson as she was led from the courtroom. For that act, Dyer too was banished and told never to return to Massachusetts. She heeded this advice for some two decades, whereupon she traveled to England and became a Quaker convert. In 1659, the arrest and subsequent death sentence of two male Quakers in Boston provoked Dyer to return to the city she was forced to leave twenty-two years earlier. Given her fame in the New England colonies, it didn't take long before she was arrested and escorted back to Rhode Island. Not one to back down so easily, particularly fervent in her faith, Dyer returned to Boston, was quickly arrested, and hanged alongside the two gentlemen for whom she had just pleaded clemency.

Although death sentences became rare, fines, imprisonment, and banishment were common for religious dissenters throughout the seventeenth and eighteenth centuries, often under the auspices that they read prohibited books or failed to attend religious services (McLoughlin 1971, 23). Isaac Backus detailed a number of unjust actions taken against Baptists in Massachusetts as late as 1770. In each case he details, the individual supposedly had been granted a certificate officially exempting them from paying church taxes (written here as the "Minister's rate").

---

[22] Puritan Congregationalists at this time were engaging in infant baptisms. When other groups not associated with the Congregationalists – namely the Baptists – performed adult baptisms, this was considered an illegitimate "rebaptizing." Clark, who rejected the theology of the Puritans, obviously did not recognize the Puritan baptism, and hence denied he was "*re*baptizing." Clark, Witters, and others were often referred to as *antipedobaptists*.

At South Hadley a Baptist Church was gathered some years ago, who took Advice of one of the best Lawyers in the County, and carried in their Certificate, yet they were rated to the Paedobaptist Minister [Puritan Congregationalist], and their goods strained away: The Case was carried to Court, and they were cast, and had the Charges of two Courts to pay, and then they gave the Town about twenty Dollars to let them be free for the future; and so with a *great Sum* obtained they their Freedom, who were truly *free born*. In the District of Montague is another Baptist Church, who carried in their Certificate by direction of a Lawyer, yet the Assessors put them into the Minister's rate: The Constable made Distress upon one of the Committee who signed the Certificate. When they came to Court, they were cast, because (said the Judge) he witnessed for himself, when yet there were two more to witness with him. They appealed to the Superior Court, and have attended two, and the Case is hung up to the third, and all this time they are left in the Hands of the Adversaries, who treat them in a most barborous [*sic*] Manner, driving away their Cattle and selling them at an Out-cry, for their Minister's rate. At Shutesbury, one Daniel Fisk, not withstanding his Certificate, was seized by two Constables at once, held under Keepers some Time and through the Assessors met and released him, yet not Recompence was made for his loss of Time and Charge. (Backus 1771, 14–15; emphasis in original)

Backus continues with several more cases and the harassment that Baptists received was generally widespread to others, most notably Quakers (Pestrana 1991; Gura 1984, passim).[23]

A similar pattern of religious regulation and harassment occurred in the southern colonies, most notably in the highly populated Virginia. There, the Church of England held sway. But unlike New England, where religious motives factored heavily in the initial *raison d'être* of settlement, the primary drive for settlement to the south was economic and strategic. Religious intolerance and persecution was less intense than the New England territory under the control of Puritans, but significant burdens were placed on the nonestablished churches. In Virginia, the Church of England was formally

---

[23] It may seem odd to the contemporary mind that Quakers would be the object of persecution. Our impression of them as jovial and peaceful often comes from the cover of oatmeal containers and is reinforced by their pacifist ways. But in addition to theological differences that may have spawned animosity toward this particular religious group, their behavior was often provocative in the early days of the movement as noted by William Lee Miller. "Some [Quakers] insisted on wearing long hair, and a few took simplicity to the point of wearing no clothes in public. They could be rude.... Their 'radicalism' in behavior and conduct made them somewhat more like the New Left or the youth culture of the late 1960s than like the peaceable middle-class Quakers we know today" (W. Miller 2003, 163). Miller even notes that the icon of religious tolerance – Roger Williams – even became irritated with the Quakers late in his life (2003, 163).

established, and colonists were obliged to pay for its maintenance (Curry 1986, 30), although colonial officials were not overly generous in their funding of the church providing an indirect indication that the government was not puritanically intent on perpetuating Anglican orthodoxy (Curry 1986, 51; Isaac 1973, passim). The continued funding of the Anglican clergy became one of the most hotly contested religious policies during the late 1700s, and the issue that directly gave birth to James Madison and Thomas Jefferson's promotion of the separation of church and state.

Beyond the issue of a mandatory church assessment, Virginia and the other southern colonies imposed restrictions on office holding and voting that privileged Anglicans over nonconformist sects. The permitting process for new church buildings and licensing process for qualified preachers was also used to restrict minority sects (Smith 1972, 31–4). These building restrictions were used to harass the circuit riders of the First Great Awakening who preached fire and brimstone not from a permanent structure but from tents that they erected from town to town or meetinghouses they tried to rent (often unsuccessfully). Other laws that regulated "disturbances of the peace," which required dissenters to keep their doors open[24] and prohibited night meetings, were used to disadvantage non-Anglicans (Smith 1972, 33–4). Smith also notes that "recognition of marriages performed by dissenting clergy and freedom from the necessity of patronizing the established clergy for burials" served as restrictions on religious freedom, as did the episcopal control over public welfare funds for the poor (1972, 35). Fines, imprisonment, and whippings frequently accompanied failure to comply with these rules (Buckley 1977, 14). A similar pattern of establishment and regulation favoring the Church of England existed in the Carolinas and Georgia, though it was "weak because of the lack of ministers, churches, organizations and resources" (Curry 1986, 153 and passim).

Some pockets of true freedom of conscience did exist, most notably in Rhode Island, Pennsylvania, and Maryland (for reasons that shall be discussed). The case of Maryland, however, presents us with one of the greatest ironies of religious freedom. An initial royal charter granted Cecil Calvert (a.k.a. Lord Baltimore) permission to set up a colony for Catholics but required religious liberty and toleration for Protestants, most notably

---

[24] Although Smith does not detail the reason for this regulation, it would seem that an "open-door" policy would allow townsfolk to see who was attending the services held by dissenters and hence may serve to increase the likelihood of social ostracism. Alternatively, requiring open doors would increase the likelihood that a religious service could be cited for disturbing the peace as music would be more likely to spill out into the streets.

Anglicans. This freedom allowed enough Anglicans to settle the territory that by the late 1600s they were able to legally enact restrictions on
Catholics, effectively disenfranchising them from their "own" colony! Jay
Dolan estimates that although Maryland was settled by a coterie of well-
heeled Catholics, and despite an effort by Jesuits to evangelize the Indians
in the colony, Catholics only numbered about 2,500 among a population
of 34,200 in the year 1700 (1992, 79). This certainly had ramifications in
terms of religious policy, even before the Church of England was formally
established as Maryland's official confession in 1702:

> Catholics had already been excluded from office, and in 1692 an act forbade
> them to act as attorneys. To limit Catholic numbers, a law of 1699 [sic] laid
> a poll tax of twenty shillings on each Irish immigrant.... In 1704 the Act
> To [sic] Prevent the Growth of Popery prohibited Catholic worship and for-
> bade priests to make converts or to baptize children of any but Catholic par-
> ents.... In 1718 Catholics were disenfranchised. (cf. Dolan 1992, 75; Curry
> 1986, 51)

Thus initial freedom of religion in Maryland gave Protestants the tools
needed to eventually rescind such liberty – one of the great ironies of American history.

To summarize, colonial British America was not the hotbed of religious
liberty that simplified stories or poems relating to the Pilgrim's quest would
lead one to believe. Mandatory taxation proved to be the biggest thorn in
the side of minority religions, along with prohibitions on citizen participation, restrictions on church buildings, and other regulatory nuisances.
Informal intolerance and formal restrictions on religious liberty generally
increased as the colonies became more populated and diverse in the mid-
to late 1600s, as indicated by the movement from voluntary to compulsory
tithing in Massachusetts. The dawn of the First Great Awakening in the
1730s presented the major entrenched denominations – Congregationalists
in New England and Anglicans to the south – with even greater difficulties
as independent circuit riders and the growth of Methodists and Baptists
chipped away at the loyalties the citizenry had to the established churches.
And by 1791, when the majority of colonies ratified the Bill of Rights, the
United States had ended up at a point where it had the most comprehensive and pithy statement on behalf of religious freedom – "Congress shall
make no law respecting an establishment of religion, or prohibiting the free
exercise thereof." Although it took a few more decades for some states to
disassemble their religious establishments (most notably Massachusetts in
1833), and realizing that the battle for religious liberty is truly an ongoing

struggle, it could be said that a major demarcation in the history of religious liberty had been reached. What were the principal reasons for this momentous sea change?

It took a little more than two centuries between the time the Puritans established a religious bulwark in Massachusetts in the 1620s and 1630s until the Congregational church was finally disestablished in Massachusetts in 1833. By the time the First Amendment of the U.S. Constitution was ratified in 1791, the intellectual climate in the country had shifted in such a way as to give an advantage to the forces who wanted a disentanglement of church and state and the general deregulation of the religious market that this entailed. Although one could argue that the primary cause for the rise of religious freedom in America was a result of a grand intellectual debate (which certainly did occur), I will argue that three principal non-ideational factors made politicians realize that religious establishment and other restrictions on religious minorities were not in their interest. These factors include (1) the need to attract immigrants and the ease and ability of people to migrate to other areas once in the colonies; (2) a growing religious pluralism resulting from immigration that made it difficult to favor one sect over another without endangering religious or political conflict; and (3) the desire to facilitate trade among the colonies and with other nations. My explanation for the rise of religious freedom in the British American colonies owes a great debt to Roger Finke's 1990 article in the *Journal of Church and State* that inspired this chapter. I will also mention a fourth cause specifically related to Catholics during the Revolutionary War era that was written about extensively by Charles Hanson (1998) – the need to cultivate French assistance in the war against England necessitated better treatment of Catholics, something Hanson called a "pragmatic" cause of religious liberty and a "necessary virtue." In each of these situations, the opportunity costs of continuing with strict regulations eventually became high enough that liberalization of those regulations became a political necessity. Our journey begins, though, not in America but on the opposite shores of the Atlantic.

The European Foundation of Religious Liberty in America

Although the First Amendment of the U.S. Constitution is noted as a landmark in the history of religious freedom – legally creating a degree of separation between religious and state officials that had not existed until that time – the lessons of Europe in regulating religion were important for the foundation of religious liberty in the United States. It could be argued that the issue of freedom of religious conscience has been ever present in Western civilization – from the Jews' Exodus from Egypt, to the struggles of early Christians to avoid persecution, to the attempts of various theological sects to break from the Catholic Church in medieval times. Our story, however, begins with the Protestant Reformation; an event that created for kings the problem of how to regulate a visible degree of religious pluralism.[25] France, the Netherlands, and England provide varying examples of how this pluralism was managed in ways that illustrate the various propositions advanced in the Chapter 2. These nations also had important effects in conditioning events within colonial America.

Pluralism and the Protestant Reformation

Although isolated by a large ocean, events in Europe dating back to the Protestant Reformation played an important role in setting the stage for religious freedom in America. It all started with a mallet, a nail, and ninety-five theses tacked on a church door in Wittenberg, Germany by a man named Martin Luther. The Protestant Reformation ushered in by this act set forth a proliferation of denominational pluralism that necessitated religious tolerance and, eventually, liberty. This is not to say that the European Roman Catholic Church didn't face the threat of pluralism prior to 1517. Quite the contrary, Popes since the time of the Edict of Milan (313 AD) played a constant game of religious whack-a-mole with heretical movements, an almost inevitable consequence of monotheistic religion (Stark 2003, 15–119).[26] With the rise of separate Protestant denominations,

---

[25] As noted in Axiom 1 (see Appendix), I assume that spiritual pluralism is a natural state for humanity. However, when one institution monopolizes and mandates the public expression of one version of spirituality, it is difficult to observe this pluralism. Pluralism only becomes visible when multiple institutions (churches) exist to give latent beliefs a public voice.

[26] For those without children or who have never visited a county fair, "whack-a-mole" is a game wherein mechanical moles randomly pop up out of holes, and a contestant must whack as many as possible before time runs out. Throughout the Middle Ages, gnostic sects and all variety of heresies popped up throughout Europe. Consider the Cathars, Waldensians, Lollards, and Hussites (Stark 2003, 52–68). These unorthodox groups often necessitated force by the Vatican to put them down through the creation of a permanent tribunal to deal with heresy and the use of force (Johnson 1976, 250–64). Martin Luther, thus, did not represent a "one-time" historical accident. Similar reformist rumblings could be heard in other parts of the continent, including Switzerland where Ulrich Zwingli was reaching many of the same conclusions about centralized religious power at the same time Luther was. Luther, however, was the first of several large moles – which included Calvin – that didn't get whacked hard enough. The whack-a-mole analogy should be attributed to me.

political rulers were now set with a task of choosing which groups would be allowed to practice within their sphere of influence – that is, the nature of the religious regulatory regime. Although the theological arguments may have swayed some of the kings and barons in feudal Europe, many of the religious regulations were made with an eye toward other political and economic calculations, as Proposition 3 would imply (see Appendix). As Stark notes,

> when [Martin] Luther nailed up his theses, the northwestern German princes and electors had no legal power to stanch the flow of funds to Rome or to limit the expansion of Church lands, a process that continued to eat away their tax bases. By turning Protestant and confiscating Church property and income, as Luther advocated, they reversed their unfavorable situation vis-á-vis the Church, which is precisely what most of them elected to do. This did not, of course, apply to the prince-bishops, since they already owned the Church property and netted most of the Church income, and not one of them opted for Protestantism. (2003, 114–15)

Financial calculations were also at the heart of King Henry VIII's break from Rome in 1534 (Stark 2003, 91). Thus, the first major regulatory decision that emanated from religious pluralism – whether to allow Protestants or Catholics to be the official majority religion to the exclusion of the other – was largely based on a desire by the ruler to maximize revenue. We could only expect, then, that future decisions regarding how to regulate religion would be based – in substantial part – on a similar political and economic calculus.

Just as Noah begat Shem so too did religious pluralism beget conflict. Initially, and only briefly, decisions to become Protestant or remain Catholic were territorially bounded. Feudal kings and lords simply chose the denomination for their fiefdom and the residents therein followed suit. However, population growth and mobility, the expansion of cities, and the fragmentation of Protestantism into numerous sects inevitably meant that people with different faiths would bump into each other, often times with swords (Johnson 1976, 292). France offers a case in point. It wasn't soon after Luther split from the Catholic Church that Protestant thought seeped into the French nobility and general population. Aristocratic rivalries and machinations for the throne quickly took on a religious tinge and sporadic denominational violence occurred throughout the middle part of the sixteenth century, finally erupting into a series of civil wars between 1562 and 1598, with residual conflicts lasting for another three decades (Holt 1995). England witnessed similar turmoil with persecution and violence emerging not only between Anglicans and Catholics but also among Protestants in the form of the Puritan challenge to the Church of England. The English Civil War (1642–9) partially resulted from King Charles's attempt to establish religious uniformity in Scotland and by a crackdown on vocal Puritan non-conformists. Other countries throughout Europe, including the Netherlands in the mid-1500s, experienced similar "religious growing pains" when denominational diversity increased.

From Conflict to an Uneasy Truce and Back Again: The Edict of Nantes

In the new age of religious pluralism, political rulers had to determine how to manage religious conflict. One way was to simply fight through it and hope that one side would prevail. As the Dutch, French, and British found out, that proved costly. Civil war, with its uncertainties and decreased incentives for economic activity, and the ability to conduct a war depended on taxing a healthy economy; prolonged wars tended to be self-defeating even for the victors. It was not uncommon for the persecuted religious minority to flee the country, taking with them some of the most productive and entrepreneurial individuals within society (as they are the ones who had the greatest mobility).

The other major option beyond persecution was peaceful coexistence. As the ravaging costs of religious war became apparent to all the parties involved, there was a realization that religious toleration was a better solution. In France, the connection between economic growth and religious toleration became apparent to the monarchy as the religious wars dragged on.

> Emphasizing the king's duty to foster the spiritual development of his subjects as well as their *economic prosperity*, a spokesman for the Reformed [Calvinist] religion insisted that persuasion rather than violence was the solution to ending religious division. The size of the Calvinist community was now such . . . that outright violence would only devastate the king's forces and the French economy. . . . *Political pragmatism rather than ideological insistence* upon individual religious autonomy underpins this Calvinist request for royal protection, and for understandable reasons: Catholics were perhaps willing to endure . . . the presence of Protestants in their midst for the sake of peace, but they were far from ready to recognize the legitimacy of the other faith. (Armstrong 2004, 11–12; emphasis added)

Even some of the most ardent opponents of the Huguenots eventually gave up the battle due to "[e]xhaustion and self-interest," realizing that peace was more profitable than war (Armstrong 2004, 165). The outcome of several decades of destructive religious battles was the Edict of Nantes in 1598, the first major document granting (limited) religious liberties to a religious minority in early modern Europe. Although not providing the Huguenots with the same state recognition as the Catholic Church, the Edict of Nantes did grant them freedom of conscience and the ability to publicly worship in a limited number of townships and on feudal estates (Baird 1895, 3–5).[27]

The promulgation of the Edict of Nantes fits with Proposition 3 wherein regulatory policies about religion are often made on the basis of political interests – the decision to grant religious liberties to the Huguenots originated from a desire to protect King Henry IV's hold on power and to prevent further damage to the French economy. The edict was born of political self-interest, not an ideological preference, although one might be quick to note that Henry IV was a Huguenot and, hence, more likely to support his own kind. As historian Roland Bainton summarized, "Henry IV . . . had come to the recognition that the welfare of the state is to be preferred to the victory of one religion" (1936, 431). During a time when the monarchy was seeking to extend and consolidate its territorial hold over France, religious conflict was an issue that needed some form of resolution (Scoville 1952, 296). An irresolvable war would only weaken the king's grip on power and require ever-increasing levels of taxation, something that the nobility was sure to resist. Although a uniform religious culture would have been the ideal situation for securing the king's domain, at least from the vantage point of Henry's Catholic advisors, the presence of religious pluralism necessitated a religious truce.

Pressure to immediately back away from the spirit, if not the letter, of the Edict of Nantes arose within a matter of a few years of its passage, particularly under the reign of Louis XIII. Nonetheless, Cardinal Richelieu – one of Louis XIII's closest advisors and an ardent Catholic who undertook a campaign to convert Protestants early in his career (Bergin 1991, 100–7) – expressed his concern over efforts to repeal the Edict of Nantes in a letter he wrote to the Count of Sault. His reasoning reveals that the cardinal was less concerned with the inherent justice of religious liberty than with bolstering political power and stability.

> I am of the opinion that, as we must not stretch in favor of the Protestants whatever may be contained in the edicts, so also we ought not to detract from

---

[27] The Edict of Nantes even allowed the Huguenots the right to bear arms, a considerable concession that apparently was meant to ensure the enforcement of the treaty (Baird 1895, 6–7).

the gracious concessions that are made to them. Especially at the present time, when, thanks to God, peace is so well established throughout the realm, too much care cannot be taken to prevent all these causes of popular discontent. I assure you that *the king's veritable intention is to enable all his subjects to live peaceably under the maintenance of his edicts, and that those who are in authority in the provinces will render him service by conforming thereto.* (cited in Baird 1895, 351; emphasis added)

Having their subjects render faithfully unto Caesar motivated the Bourbon monarchs more than any enlightened view of religious peace. In the immediate years following religiously inspired civil war, the most effective policy of consolidating royal power was a live-and-let-live policy toward the Huguenots, a pattern remarkably similar in other parts of the world during periods of political consolidation (cf. Gill and Keshavarzian 1999).

The truce that was the Edict of Nantes, however, lasted less than a century. During that time, the Huguenots rarely enjoyed full security from persecution. Although Calvinists represented a vital minority both economically and politically (Baird 1895, passim), the Catholic Church maintained greater control on the reigns of power. Even after the introduction of the *intendant* system, Catholic dioceses served as a key institution in royal tax collection (Bergin 2004, 42). Moreover, Catholics never gave up on the goal of religious uniformity (in accordance with Proposition 1 where hegemonic denominations prefer heavy regulation of religious minorities). As the "absolutist" position of the monarchy strengthened under Louis XIII and Louis XIV, the calculus of religious liberty slowly shifted away from tolerance. Despite Cardinal Richelieu's advice to "look objectively at the dangers and the real value of further anti-Huguenot campaigns [in the early 1600s]," Louis XIII listened to other advisors who sought to eliminate rival sources of authority to the crown and undertook a program of legal harassment against French Protestants (Bergin 1991, 227–8). Richelieu, ever the complex character and scheming politician, was complicit in some of this harassment despite his own advice (Bergin 1991, 100).

By the time of Richelieu's death in December 1642 (and King Louis XIII's expiration five months later), the House of Bourbon was in a remarkably strong position. Initially, Richelieu's replacement – Cardinal Mazarin – and the young Louis XIV maintained an uneasy truce with the Huguenots. However, the expanding military, bureaucratic, and financial power of the monarchy combined with the ongoing influence of Catholic officials within the regime led to increasing persecution of religious minorities. Although the Edict of Nantes remained untouched, a series of minor laws limiting the activities of Protestants was enacted that undermined the spirit of the edict, including limitations on property rights and office holding, expropriation of Huguenot schools and churches, and stricter requirements on the public activities of Protestant ministers (Baird 1895, 401–15).[28] Legal changes begat intensified violence, resulting in a series of emigrations from France by Huguenots (Baird 1895, 419–90). Many fled to other parts of Europe (e.g., Prussia) and the colonial Americas, with the Netherlands being a primary destination. By 1685, few Protestants remained in the country or within their old denomination, having converted (often half-heartedly) to Catholicism. In a move to please his Catholic advisors and supporters, and to create a uniformity of faith throughout the land, Louis XIV revoked the Edict of Nantes, revealing that the pathway toward greater religious liberty is not always one of steady progress. The political calculations of the powerful often determine the limits on the faithful.

France's loss was Holland's gain. In an effort to unify warring religious factions of Catholics and Calvinists against an undesired Spanish rule, Dutch leaders declared "every citizen should remain free in his religion, and no man be molested or questioned on the subject of divine worship" in 1579 (Dillon 1975, 88; cf. Zweirlein 1910, 9–35). Religious toleration came of political necessity, but it opened the door for an economic boom. French Huguenots began fleeing north beginning in the early seventeenth century and continued to arrive as King Louis XIV tightened the vice on them. These religious refugees "carried with them skilled manpower, technical know-how, and some liquid capital," and were "among the wealthiest and most industrious of France's middle class" (Scoville 1952, 295–6; cf. Temple 1690, 215–17). Although the fleeing Huguenots were not accorded with full rights of citizenship and religious liberty, they were allowed to exist in their own neighborhoods and go about their entrepreneurial business free from regular persecution. The result was a diffusion of new economic production processes and a source of revenue for the Dutch government (Scoville 1952). The Netherlands also offered refuge for a handful of radical Puritans fleeing a crackdown on their way of life in England. How the English crown managed its religious landscape, with an eye toward growing as a major European power is the logical next step in our story.

---

[28] The wide range of laws enacted to limit the freedom of the Huguenots presents a remarkable study of how small regulatory changes can have large impacts in terms of the ability to worship as one pleases. Baird (1895) provides a remarkably detailed discussion of all these laws, from prohibitions on Protestants from being midwives to the suspension of debts for any person converting to Catholicism while simultaneously imposing fines and taxes on Catholics converting to Protestantism.

The Rise of Toleration in England

The story of the growth of religious toleration in England during the seventeenth century can be set in contradistinction to the French case. Although the Edict of Nantes was allowing for a respite in religious conflict in France, English King James I began a crackdown on religious nonconformists that set the story of the Pilgrims in motion. However, as the century drew to a close the situations reversed themselves; the French monarchy rescinded the freedoms granted in the Edict of Nantes (1685) while the British crown proclaimed an official end to religious persecution in the Toleration Act (1689).[29] How Britain moved from persecution to toleration during the seventeenth century informs us a great deal about the emergence of religious liberty in America and demonstrates the role that seemingly tangential political and economic matters played in the rise of freedom.

Henry VIII's decision to sever ties with the Vatican established a precedent that religious dissenters soon began to follow. With the threat of papal excommunication off the table and new theological ideas filtering in from the continent religious heterogeneity flourished. Stagnancy within the established Church of England, which retained many "popish" trappings, led many devout believers – of the Ariminian, Calvinist, and Presbyterian varieties – to seek ways to purify the church. These nonconformists became known collectively as the Puritans and, along with the persistent Catholics, became a nuisance to the crown by the mid-1500s. In determining how to deal with a growing religious pluralism, the indomitable Queen Elizabeth I based her policies on political calculations – both the survival of her reign and the ascendancy of England in Europe – rather than on any ideational attachment to a particular philosophy (Lyon 1937, 21–4). As Jordan notes of the Elizabethan Settlement, diversity of religious thought was tolerated so long as it did not endanger a unified Britain:

> Every religious action was viewed and tested in the light of its relations to the security and well-being of the State. . . .There was no indication throughout the long reign that the Queen was motivated in any degree by those spiritual ideals which so largely dominated the public conduct of her sister [the

[29] The Toleration Act (1689) was designed mainly to relax tensions between Protestant denominations; Catholics both in Britain proper and Ireland (under the influence of the British crown) still did not fare well (Poynter 1930). Bossy (1991) argues that although the Act and King William, owing favors to his Catholic supporters, did help Catholics to some degree, a variety of parliamentary decisions made life difficult for Catholics. These decisions included double taxation, confiscation of weapons, and attempts to confiscate property (Bossy 1991, 370–1).

Catholic Mary Queen of Scots].... [T]he Government's mission lay in preventing and in curbing the appearance of faction. She was an exact observer of two State maxims, "never to force men's consciences" and "never to suffer factious practises [*sic*] to go unpunished."[30] Her primary aim was to secure peace abroad and quiet at home and to attain these ends she was willing to juggle with creeds and dogmas.... [N]o distinction had been drawn between inner belief and outward conformity. Every Englishman had been called upon to adjust his conscience as well as his conduct to the policy of the State. The Government, especially in its handling of Catholic dissent, refused to accept the moral responsibility involved in religious persecution for its own sake. To [Elizabeth's advisors] persecution was a necessary evil, which found its sole justification in political grounds. (Jordan 1932, 87–9)

The result of this policy was to allow dissent and pluralism to continue to grow underneath a patina of Anglican conformity, a policy that suited many of the Puritans who didn't necessarily seek a break from the Church of England but rather strove to change it from within. This set up an inevitable political tension. Although nonconformity was allowed to persist underneath the political surface, nonconformists grew to believe that they would eventually win the day and the Church of England would be reformed. It was merely a matter of time and the right monarch. Alternatively, the appearance of Anglican conformity meant that any outburst by dissenters would likely be seen as a threat to the Crown and would be dealt with harshly, particularly if the nonconformists misjudged the intentions of the new king.

This situation came to a head following Elizabeth's death in 1603. Puritan hopes ran high with the ascension of James I, who was raised in (and ruled over) Scotland as a Presbyterian. This was ostensibly good news for dissenters because Scottish Presbyterianism was less hierarchical than the Church of England, and it was Anglican hierarchy that was a primary irritant for Puritans. Surely, a Presbyterian would empathize with the plight of the dissenters and grant their vocal demands for greater freedom (McGrath 2001, 139). This was not to be the case, though. King James met the vocal challenge of the Puritans with an iron fist. Interestingly, but not surprisingly, James dealt with the Puritans more harshly than Catholics (Jordan 1936, 87–114) as the former represented a more direct challenge to the episcopal power brokers of the Church of England and hence the authority of the king to maintain control over the officially established church. The new king felt that royal authority went hand in hand with a formal

---

[30] Quotations in Jordan taken from Laurence Echard, *The History of England* (London: Jacob Tonson, 1720), 415.

episcopal structure. "'No bishops, no king' summarized admirably his view of the interrelationship between church and state" (McGrath 2001, 139). The creation of the now famous King James's Bible was largely an attempt to circumvent the popularity of the Calvinist Geneva Bible that was gaining popularity among nonconformists and others (McGrath 2001, 141–71). The unacceptable reaction of James to Puritan demands for church reform and greater freedom catalyzed radicalism among some sectors of the nonconformists, pushing some toward greater congregational organization (denying the need for any church hierarchy) and others (such as the Pilgrims) toward a separatist stance (Jordan 1936, 157–65, 223–8).

As fate would have it, the global political context allowed the English monarchs another option for dealing with religious dissenters that proved beneficial to both parties. The simple solution was to let the dissenters leave. This had the benefit of siphoning off the most vocal troublemakers in the country and, more importantly, enhancing the goal of colonization in the Western Hemisphere. Establishing a foothold in the Americas was geopolitically important. The Spaniards and Portuguese already dominated the territory south of latitude 30° north and the French were sneaking into portions of North America. It was thus vitally important for England, which was rapidly becoming a global power following the defeat of the feared Spanish Armada in 1588, to gather colonial holdings in the Western Hemisphere. King James's initial attempt to populate the Americas in 1607 – in the form of the eponymous Jamestown settlement – was a near disaster with roughly two-thirds of the original colonists dying within the first year (Schweikart and Allen 2004, 16–17). The lesson learned was simple – if Britain was to be at all a significant competitor with France and Spain in the Americas, it needed a large number of warm bodies to settle the land. Who better than a bunch of people that wanted to leave anyway? And if 60 percent of them happened to die in the process, well so be it; it was a risk the king was willing to take.

The strategy to ship religious rebels across the sea was beneficial not only for the king and Puritans but also for the trading companies. As long as the colonists agreed to swear allegiance to the English Crown, King James was willing to give commercial trading companies permission to ship religious nonconformists to the Americas. The trading companies, stocked with members of the new bourgeoisie class seeking entrepreneurial adventures, welcomed the dissenters with open arms. Dillon notes that the Plymouth "[C]ompany was only too glad to have the Pilgrims as settlers, because it was in a poor financial state and until it could get a plantation made, or a fishing and trading station manned, it was not in business. If it had settlers who had signed up for America it could attract capital from speculators" (1975, 109). The strategy was a bit less risky for the non-Separatist Puritans than it was for the Pilgrims, as the former religious reformers still saw themselves at least within the Church of England rather than a breakaway sect. As Dillon argues, Massachusetts Bay Colony's first governor John "Winthrop saw Separatism as wrong thinking in itself and as a grave political danger... because if Separatism became dominant, the bishops might get the king to revoke the Massachusetts Bay Charter" (1975, 209). But even the Pilgrims, who were never granted full citizenship rights in the Netherlands, and who feared being caught up in a war between the Dutch and Spanish, were willing to pledge loyalty in exchange for some space away from their real enemies – not King James per se but the bishops in the Church of England (Dillon 1975, 111).

In essence, King James pursued a somewhat contradictory policy toward religious groups that, in a perverse way, could be seen as granting religious liberty. The policy was "love it or leave it (or be jailed)." Although persecutions continued at home for those who didn't love the Church of England in all its official trappings, the policy of emigration did provide some freedom for those willing to brave the hardships of colonial life. Geopolitical calculations, therefore (and as predicted in Chapter 2), played a significant role in providing some degree of de facto freedom for religious minorities. More importantly, allowing all sorts of dissenters to migrate to America eventually sowed the seeds of religious pluralism and made the destination of religious liberty in the United States all the more likely.

The religious policy of allowing discontents to exit proved to be too successful for its own good. In the 1630s, an estimated fourteen thousand to twenty thousand Puritans fled old England for New England (Dillon 1975, 209). This represented a significant number in a time when transportation costs were high, and mass mobility was low. Schleps they weren't; a sizable portion of the émigrés represented the most entrepreneurial segment of the population, which impacted the economic health of the monarchy, and hence motivated a new set of regulations to deal with religious nonconformists.

Alarmed by the Puritan emigration, which was depopulating certain sections of England and which was seriously disturbing property values, the Government on April 30, 1637, issued a proclamation calculated to curb it strictly. Persons who were subsidy men, "or of their value," were required to secure a license from the Royal Commissioners for Plantations before emigrating, and those of lesser wealth were obliged to secure a certificate from two justices of their locality stating that they had taken the Oaths of Allegiance and Supremacy, and a testimony from their parish priest that they had conformed to the practices and doctrines of the Church of England. Thus the Government had closed the remaining safety-valve. (Jordan 1936, 163)

It was quite obvious that the economic interests of King Charles I (successor to James) motivated his religious policy. Parliament was already chafing under what was considered onerous and arbitrary taxation, and so it was imperative to prevent further erosion of the tax base.[31] Add to this the assertive Archbishop of Canterbury, William Laud, who – like Richelieu and Mazarin on the other side of the English Channel – sought to crush minority dissent within the Church,[32] and you have a volatile environment primed to explode in civil strife. And explode it did.

The causes of the English Civil War (1642–51) are undoubtedly numerous and complex, enough to keep more than a few historians gainfully employed for their entire academic careers. Economic, political, and military factors all played a significant role in the conflict. But suffice it to say that religion played an integral part (cf. Manning 1973). This was guaranteed by Charles I's insistence, guided by Archbishop Laud, on religious uniformity throughout Britain, with a particular concern with stamping out theological competitors within the Church of England. A decision in 1636 to force Presbyterian Scotland to use the Anglican *Book of Common Prayer* exclusively got the fireball of religious fervor rolling, resulting in two short "Bishops' Wars" between England and Scotland (1639–40). A series of religious libel cases against well-known Puritan clergy and persecutions against Baptists and others followed (Lindley 1998, 87–96; Jordan 1936, 157–65).

---

[31] One could reasonably argue that Puritan emigration was not a total loss to the king's tax revenue; the colonists did have to pay taxes, and the mercantilist structure of the relationship guaranteed that the crown could still collect revenue. However, the inherent difficulties in monitoring and enforcing tax policies for a colony that was a two-month ship voyage away and the low level of revenue generation at the outset of any new settlement invariably meant that there would be less revenue coming from the colonial Puritans than if they had stayed put.

[32] See Proposition 1 (Appendix) wherein a dominant religion normally will attempt to restrict the freedoms of religious minorities. Further evidence of the economic motivations behind the suppression of Puritan freedoms comes from McGrath who noted that the nonconformists' preferred Bible – the Calvinist Geneva edition – happened to be of higher quality and lower cost than early editions of the King James version. In order to protect the English printing industry, William Laud and Charles I sought a full ban on Geneva Bibles (McGrath 2001, 282–4).

The consequences of the English Civil War and the resulting period of Commonwealth rule for religious liberty were twofold. First, under the rule of Oliver Cromwell's Commonwealth (the governing outcome of the civil war), Puritans finally received the freedom and influence they had long sought and could celebrate, albeit without liquor or beer because Cromwell banned such libations.[33] Lord Protector Cromwell, himself a Puritan, fought a recalcitrant Parliament for a broadly defined policy of religious liberty (Jordan 1938, 160–75).[34] Despite his best intentions, intolerance was shown toward Anglicans and a variety of other sects whose behavior challenged the attainment of civil peace, most notably the Quakers (Jordan 1938, 174–253).[35] Nearing the end of Cromwell's reign, the ability to maintain a widespread tolerance began to break down, yet, for a brief moment in the 1650s, a great experiment in religious tolerance was tried.

Second, it was observed by many that this great experiment in religious tolerance was actually successful in preserving a modicum of civil harmony. Far from leading to a disintegration of faith in England as some had predicted, it actually fostered a relative degree of denominational peace. "The Government of the Lord Protector [Cromwell] grew in solidity and prestige as England came to realize that the policy of religious toleration had alone prevented the outbreak of an internecine struggle of bigoted and zealous sects for religious supremacy" (Jordan 1938, 171). Moreover, under this greater degree of religious toleration, religion flourished in many forms. This is not to say that all things were roses. Cromwell's military escapades in Presbyterian Scotland and Catholic Ireland did provoke resentment and hostility that had a religious overlay to it. But relative to what France had gone through and Louis XIV's policy of chasing out the Huguenots, England actually was making significant progress in its religious policy.

Following Cromwell's death and the short-lived reign of his third son, Richard, Britain once again came under the rule of the Stuart monarchy,

---

[33] No matter because good Puritans should not have been drinking to begin with!

[34] Proposition 1 would predict that minority sects that obtain political power would see an advantage in implementing many of the same restrictions on the previously dominant sect (and other minority groups) that they had suffered under. The first parliament to meet under the new Commonwealth was dominated by Presbyterians who sought to do just that (Jordan 1938, 160–9).

[35] Remember, despite the contemporary peaceful image the Society of Friends projects, early Quakers were known to disrobe and scream – behaviors that were not necessarily conducive to receiving public toleration. Given that the Quakers largely appeared on the scene in the late 1640s, this must have been a most curious sight to behold, and it is somewhat understandable that Cromwell and Parliament wanted to bring this sect under tighter control.

albeit one that was substantially weakened. The first Restoration king – Charles II – started to backslide from the policies of toleration adopted during the Commonwealth. Through the Corporation Act and Test Act, Charles II restricted Catholics and nonconformists from holding influential positions in local government, the military, and Parliament (Welsh 2002, 180; Grose 1937, 226; Hawkins 1928, 17–33). Other restrictions were placed on nonconformists, including the Act of Uniformity, requiring the exclusive use of the Anglican *Book of Common Prayer* in religious services, the Conventicle Act, which prohibited religious gatherings of more than five non-Anglicans, and the Five-Mile Act, which prevented nonconformists from living within a five-mile radius of a large town (Coffey 2000, passim; Grose 1937, 226–7).[36] This policy of favoritism toward the Church of England was interesting considering that Charles II was financially supported by his Catholic cousin who also happened to be the king of France (Louis XIV) at the time. But like his French cousin, this policy did represent a strong preference for a unitary state church under the control of the secular leader, irrespective of denominational affiliation.[37] Moreover, Charles's brother – James – was openly Catholic, and popular suspicions were aroused about his general course of religious action if and when he would take the throne (which he did in 1685).

Charles's logic in banning Catholics from office was probably designed to alleviate fears that he would return the nation to Rome's religion (Grose 1937, 229–30), while his clampdown on Protestant dissenters helped to shore up the hierarchical Church of England in a bid to reestablish religious order in an environment of burgeoning pluralism.[38] Charles II did not go so far as to ban religious dissent altogether, realizing that would have led to yet another civil war that he could ill afford to fight. Nonetheless, his policies whipped up anti-Catholic fervor among the population that was only held at bay by hopes that James II – Charles's successor – did not have any children of his own. Unfortunately for James, he did have a son in 1688, and his positioning of Catholics in influential posts during his brief reign

---

[36] These pieces of legislation are yet further examples of how creative religious monopolies can be in setting up barriers to entry in the religious marketplace.

[37] This astute observation was brought to my attention by Steve Pfaff and fits the general theoretical framework presented in Chapter 2 wherein rulers will prefer to control a hegemonic church when it is possible to do so without affecting one's political survival.

[38] Collins (1999) provides a different view of King Charles's relationship with the Anglican hierarchy, arguing that an underlying tension always existed between the two. This is entirely plausible given Charles's Catholic leanings, yet Grose's (1937) analysis leads one to view the king's favorable policies toward the Church of England as being politically expedient.

only sharpened the opposition to him (Welsh 2002, 180–2).[39] The result was the Glorious Revolution deposing King James II, installing the Dutch Protestant William of Orange on the throne and forcing the king to agree to the Toleration Act of 1688, which specifically guaranteed religious toleration for nonconforming Protestants in Great Britain. Having experience with religious pluralism in the Netherlands probably made his acceptance of this legislation all the more easy.

Britain's Toleration Act was a milestone in this history of religious liberty. First, it legally bound the monarchy to respect dissenting religious beliefs so long as they did not disturb the security of the nation. This document encoded the laws protecting Protestant nonconformists during the Commonwealth era and repealed the excessive restrictions on dissenters implemented during the Restoration. Given that the Glorious Revolution, in general, shifted power from the Crown to the Parliament, and religious nonconformists were common among parliamentarians, it would be difficult for future kings to backtrack on this agreement. Second, the Toleration Act set a new standard for religious dissent in the American colonies. Minority denominations in the colonies, such as the Baptists, Methodists, and Quakers, could use this document to support their claims for exemptions from general church assessments (i.e., taxes) that went to support only one denomination or to demand free passage and residency in certain territories (namely the Massachusetts Bay Colony, which was renown for making life difficult for anybody other than Congregationalists).[40]

The reasoning behind the enactment of the Toleration Act was not only to provide Protestant nonconformists with greater protection from Anglican harassment but also to ensure that the religious conflict that tore Britain apart during the Civil War would not be repeated again. As Thomas Buckley notes,

> Most important of all, the rapid multiplication of churches and sects made religious uniformity an impossibility. In granting Protestant dissenters the freedom to worship in peace, the Toleration Act of 1688, albeit grudgingly, recognized reality. Men agreed that a limited measure of religious liberty was imperative, not simply for the preservation of religion, but for the well-being of society. (1977, 3; cf. Jordan 1940, 472, 483)

[39] The obvious question that arises is how James II could become king with the Test Act in place. The answer was due to shrewd politicking and a series of fortuitous events. In politics, rulers often get to make and break the rules.

[40] Presbyterians also lived among the Massachusetts Bay colonists and were tolerated as a sister sect to the Congregationalists although the latter tended to be the more predominant of the two.

The political motivations behind the Act were clear. "James's authoritarian policies also forced Anglicans into a Protestant alliance with Dissenters, making Anglican leaders far more open toward the 'separated brethren'" (Coffey 2000, 209). Additionally, at a time when Britain was an ascendant world power, ongoing civil strife would only serve to weaken its international influence.

Although there was growing general ideological support for greater toleration in society, as witnessed by Locke's *Letter on Toleration* (1689), religious toleration was far from being the dominant thought of the day. "[T]he 1689 Act was not passed because a rising tide of tolerationist conviction made it inevitable. Radical tolerationists who condemned all forms of persecution were still a small minority. The [members of Parliament] who passed the Act were willing to grant relief to Dissenters who had stood against popery, but very few were radical tolerationists" (Coffey 2000, 208–9). The limits of an ideational explanation for the Toleration Act can be gleaned from its actual title – "An Act for Exempting their Majesties *Protestant* Subjects, Dissenting from the Church of England, from the Penalties of certain laws" (emphasis added). One must remember that toleration is not liberty; England was far from being a bastion of religious freedom even after the Act of Toleration (Finke and Stark 2005, 53–4; Smith [1776] 1976, passim). For instance, toleration did not legally extend to Catholics, who remained under the watchful eye of the Protestant majority in England (Leege 2004, 3). Given the machinations of the previous two Stuart kings, this was not surprising. To forestall any repeat of the problems associated with James II, Parliament passed the Act of Settlement in 1701 prohibiting future monarchs from being Catholic. A general intellectual climate of toleration indeed!

One other final consideration for the rise of greater religious liberty in Britain (at least for Protestants) reveals how political and economic interests shaped religious policy: the desire for trade and prosperity. This explanation takes us back to the Netherlands and will help us explain the growth of religious freedom in America. During the early seventeenth century, the Dutch managed one of the most dynamic and prosperous nations in the world. Their openness to trade and willingness to allow creative entrepreneurs (such as the Huguenots) were two of the primary factors for their wealth. Britain, with its efficient agricultural sector and increasing technological advantage over other nations, also sought to widen its trading networks. A clear connection was drawn between trade, prosperity, and religious toleration from the Dutch case. "The ill effects of persecution and civil war upon trade, the fact that dissent was especially prevalent among the commercial groups, and the supposed connection between Dutch prosperity and the religious freedom which obtained there exerted considerable influence in the direction of religious toleration" (Jordan 1932, 22; cf. Coffey 2000, 217). The lesson was becoming clear – religious tolerance was good for a nation economically and politically, a lesson that was beginning to take hold in the American colonies.

Economic and Political Factors Leading to Religious Liberty in the United States

Although the ideas of John Locke and other European liberals helped to shape the ideological contours of the Founding Fathers and the Constitutional Convention – leading to the eventual ratification of the First Amendment – a number of economic and political factors played a dominant role in nudging the colonies toward greater religious tolerance and liberty almost from the time of initial settlement in the early 1600s. As noted in the preceding text, the initial Puritan settlers were not keen on promoting liberty for those outside their denominational circles. Nor was the Church of England, which sent clergy to establish a church in the southern colonies, open to liberties for non-Anglicans. Resistance to the general idea of religious liberty continued well into the late 1700s, if not well beyond.[41] Accepting religious liberty because John Locke and James Madison thought it was a good idea was not sufficient to change laws. Instead, a liberalization of the religious market required that such a policy be in alignment with the other economic and political goals of government officials. In colonial America the primary factors driving the movement to deregulate religion were immigration, trade, internal migration, and the continued growth of pluralism (due to the difficulties in enforcing conformity), which meant a rise in new constituencies demanding tax relief from the general religious assessment common in many places. The mere fact that the forces favoring independence needed to unite a country and find allies for an uphill war against the British also pushed the country toward a more liberal spirit in religious affairs.

---

[41] Massachusetts did not disestablish the Congregational church until 1833, and Catholics faced constant harassment throughout the 1800s. Mormons also felt the wrath of legal restrictions on their faith, and many denominations still battle various legal barriers to religious freedom today.

Immigration

Setting up a colony in the Americas was not an easy task. Settlers and more settlers were needed to populate the new territory and make it profitable, both for the monarchy and the trading companies the king contracted. The Jamestown experience, expensive in both lives and money, proved this (Ahlstrom 2004, 105). Whatever could be done to attract settlers had to be encouraged. In many cases, this meant allowing individuals with different religious ideas to immigrate to the new territory, the first step on the road to denominational pluralism and eventual religious liberty.

As noted in the preceding text, one of James I's strategies for populating the Americas quickly was to allow religious nonconformists to stake a claim in the New World provided that they agreed to sign a loyalty agreement with the Crown. In the political trade-off between rapid settlement of the American colonies and enforcing religious conformity, the former trumped the latter. Such a trade-off was fairly easy to make because allowing religious dissenters to leave proved useful. Above all, it tended to mitigate the religious problem at home, at least in the short term; the most irritated and vocal malcontents are usually the ones to leave first (Hirschman 1970). Moreover, the nonseparatist Puritan reformers that left during the 1620s were still interested in staying within the Church of England, although they demanded specific changes to make the church more "pure." As such, the Puritans received what they wanted by having a colony away from the homeland to experiment as they saw fit. From the vantage point of the Anglican hierarchy, the results of the experimentation would be far enough away so as not to affect the core operations of the Church of England. The immediate position of Anglican bishops was safe as long as the more radical forms of Puritanism remained on the other side of the Atlantic.[42]

The monarchy's desire for settlement even allowed for Catholics to set up shop in the colonies. This came when King Charles I provided an entrepreneurial merchant named Cecil Calvert with a charter to settle the area around Chesapeake Bay in 1632 (just two years following the Puritans charter to populate Massachusetts). Although providing a golden opportunity for English Catholics to find a safe haven in which to worship, Calvert also understood that the economic success of the colonies required attracting immigrants. This lesson was reinforced by the experience of his

---

[42] This strategy did not work perfectly, as we know from the English Civil War and the emergence of other radical Protestant sects during the Commonwealth (cf. Manning 1973). Once the gates to the schism were opened, they were hard to close.

father – George Calvert – who failed to establish a long-term colony in Newfoundland a decade earlier (Curry 1986, 32–3). A colony's initial success is incumbent on attracting inhabitants, be they Catholics or Protestants. Thus, when Calvert's ships set sail for the Americas in 1633, Catholics represented a *minority* of the passengers; it was far easier to attract Protestant settlers in England at the time. Recognizing the tenuous position he was in, Lord Baltimore provided explicit instructions to maintain de facto religious toleration aboard ship and in the colonies. As quoted in Gaustad, Calvert said,

> Be very careful to preserve unity and peace among all the passengers on shipboard and suffer no scandal nor offence to be given to any of the Protestants.... [C]ause all acts of Roman Catholic religion to be done as privately as may be.... [T]reat Protestants with as much mildness and favor as justice will permit. And this to be observed at land as well as at sea. (1966, 72)

Historian Jay Dolan also noted this when he detailed the rather tumultuous beginnings of the Maryland colony. Following a brief period in 1645–6 when Puritan raiders wrested control of the territory from him, Lord Baltimore explicitly sought to establish social peace and the population growth and economic prosperity this would bring with it.

> The religious wars of the 1640s had underscored the need to keep religion out of olitics. . . . Thus, specific legislation had to be enacted that would prevent religion from becoming a socially disruptive force. For Lord Baltimore and the Maryland Assembly, the best way to achieve this was to guarantee the toleration of religion. This would safeguard the rights of the Catholic community, *make the colony more attractive to Protestants living in Virginia and elsewhere,* and undermine the charges made by Calvert's opponents that Maryland was a seedbed of Papists. (Dolan 1992, 76; emphasis added)

Similar to Virginia and New Amsterdam (see following text), "Maryland was established first and foremost as a commercial enterprise, with profit, not religion, the primary impulse" (Dolan 1992, 72; cf. Leege 2004). Once again (and as predicted in Chapter 2), the movement toward religious toleration and liberty resulted from an auxiliary political and economic calculation and not necessarily to any change in ideological temperament. As noted in the preceding text, though, the great irony of Maryland's early experiment with religious freedom sowed the seeds unto which an Anglican majority would grow and eventually deny Catholics their rights by the 1690s (Dolan 1992, 75).

The desire to allow religious dissenters to populate the new territory was augmented by the fact that colonization was carried out through the granting of commercial charters to private companies. The managers and stockholders of these companies were primarily concerned with making their investment profitable and less concerned with establishing a spiritual utopia. Even those with metaphysical motives realized that making a profit necessitated a more liberal policy toward religious pluralism. W. W. Sweet noted that

> [t]he Catholic proprietor of Maryland and the Quakers [sic] proprietors of New Jersey, Pennsylvania, and Delaware were undoubtedly liberal-minded gentlemen, and were sincere in their desire to establish in their several colonies a refuge for persecuted religious groups, especially the ones with which they were personally associated, but they likewise had vast tracts of land for sale. They were all engaged in a great business enterprise and if their vast wilderness estates were to prove profitable, people in large numbers must be attracted to take up land, establish homes and pay quit rent to the proprietors. (1935, 46–7)

Freedom was important, but money was money.

Economic motives also trumped religious establishment in the creation of the Dutch colony of New Amsterdam (later to become New York when the British took it over). New Amsterdam's initial charter was granted to the West India Company (WIC) with the goal of setting up a trading outpost, but that trading outpost required settlers.

> Turning a profit was the basic aim [of settlement]; the idea of establishing an outpost of Dutch society in North America was never first in the minds of the directors of the W.I.C. . . . [T]he W.I.C., beginning in 1629 with the "patroonship" idea, launched a series of experiments to attract immigrants to New Netherland [sic], not, however, with any marked success. Indeed, the inability of the company to populate the region was one of the chief reasons for its fall to the English in 1664. . . . New Netherland's [sic] commercial character gave birth, very early, to a situation of religious pluralism and the accompanying de facto toleration of a wide variety of religious viewpoints. Already in 1643 a Jesuit priest visiting at New Amsterdam observed, "No religion is publicly exercised but the Calvinist, and orders are to admit none but Calvinists, but this is not observed; for besides the Calvinists there are in the colony Catholics, English Puritans, Lutherans, Anabaptists . . . etc." The growing desire of the Dutch W.I.C. to populate the province added Jews and Quakers to this religious mélange. (G. Smith 1973, 12–13)

Further evidence that attracting immigrants was an important political factor pushing religious toleration in New Amsterdam comes directly from a communiqué between the WIC directors and Governor Peter Stuyvesant.

> Your last letter informed us that you [Stuyvesant] had banished from the Province and sent hither by ship a certain Quaker, John Bowne by name; although we heartily desire that these and other sectarians remained away from there, yet as they do not, we doubt very much, whether we can proceed against them rigorously without diminishing the population and stopping immigration, which must be favored at so tender stage of the country's existence. (cited in G. Smith 1973, 230; cf. Zwierlei 1910, 136–42)[43]

Similar pressure to attract settlers in the Restoration colonies of Pennsylvania, New Jersey, and the Carolinas also led to a greater degree of toleration for religious dissenters (Curry 1986, 54–7; Stokes and Pfeffer 1964, 7; Greene 1941, 53). William Penn actually advertised for settlers to his colony among non-Quakers in Germany promising them religious freedom if they came, and the colonists of the Carolinas followed a similar path (Sweet 1935, 50). By the time that the Carolinas got around to formalizing their political institutions, the diversity of the region made a formal establishment impractical.

> The proprietors of the Carolinas...intended some day to establish the Church of England in their domains, but from the beginning had to reckon with a hopeless variety of creeds, Puritans from England and from New England, Huguenots, Dutch Calvinists, Scotch Calvinists, Quakers and several sorts of Baptists. The uniformity for which the noble proprietors hoped was impossible, unless they were prepared to expel nine-tenths of their settlers. So religious principle gave way to economic interest; practical toleration became the rule. (Miller 1935, 60)

As Sweet also noted, the primary drive bringing most settlers to America was wealth, not worship, so it would be expected that colonial leaders would be more reactive to this desire. "Though the religious motive was strongly present in the establishment of a majority of the English colonies yet, as a matter of fact, the economic motive was undoubtedly far more powerful in bringing individual colonists to America" (Sweet 1935, 52). Religious liberty emerged gradually not from intellectual argumentation but from the necessities of the political economy.

---

[43] Despite the efforts of the WIC to secure a broad degree of religious freedom in order to attract settlers in what was not a territory with fertile land, the charter eventually granted by the Dutch crown and parliament required that the Dutch Reformed Church be officially established and the WIC pay for its maintenance. Nonetheless, the strict terms of the charter were ignored for a more laissez-faire policy that resulted in an explosion of religious diversity (Zwierlein 1910, 140–1).

The Church of England was able to plant its own established church in Virginian soil, but owing in large part to the commercial impulse behind the settlement of the colony, the Anglican establishment was relatively weak, and dissenters were able to move into that territory (Ahlstrom 2004, 184). This is not to say that immigration came conflict free; Anglican clergy were victorious in convincing colonial authorities to expel a group of Puritans in 1649 and ban Baptists a decade later (Ahlstrom 2004, 192). Nonetheless, the impulse for attracting immigrants drove the movement for religious liberty as late as 1776 with none other than James Madison, principal architect of the U.S. Constitution's First Amendment, making the connection between religious liberty and the need to attract laborers. Madison argued that "[i]f Virginia defied this growing pattern of religious liberty [seen in Rhode Island and Pennsylvania] by instituting a policy of establishment, it would be closing the door to immigration and encouraging dissenters to forsake the state for other, freer climes" (Buckley 1977, 99).[44] Considering that Madison's thoughts on governmental structure were well known to those at the Constitutional Convention, it can safely be said that the framers of the U.S. Constitution were well aware that restricting denominational freedom would impinge on social prosperity and opted for a general declaration of religious liberty, just as predicted by Proposition 3 in Chapter 2; decisions to deregulate the religious market were prompted by considerations of auxiliary issues such as a polity's economic well-being.

Trade and Commerce

There was another major economic motive at play in promoting religious freedom closely linked to immigration – promoting commerce and industry. As noted in Axioms 3 and 4 (see Appendix), political leaders prefer first to bolster their political survival and then promote economic growth (as a means of expanding tax revenue without raising tax rates and as a means of making the citizenry happy). If some policies tend to inhibit trade without affecting political survival, politicians will want to remove those barriers, *ceteris paribus*.[45] Restrictions on religious liberty did represent a significant

---

[44] Actually, Madison's argument could certainly apply to the late nineteenth century when industrialization in the United States necessitated attracting workers from Catholic nations such as Ireland, Italy, portions of Germany, and the Austrian-Hungarian Empire.

[45] Of course one might ask, then, why politicians ever favor tariffs. The easy example is that important constituents who support a given politician want those tariffs in place for their own self-interest. This is true for democratic politicians facing elections and for dictators who still need societal support.

barrier to trade within the colonies and, following the Revolutionary War, with other foreign nations. After all, if one routinely jails Methodist merchants passing through town, such merchants will choose to avoid the town in the future. That trade flourishes when members of minority denominations are allowed free passage was the lesson of the Netherlands (Curry 1986, 17). And as Stokes and Pfeffer observed, "[t]rade tended to distract colonies from their absorbing preoccupation with an exclusiveness in the matter of religion and encouraged their thinking relatively less of the Church and more of the State and of commerce. The colonists began, in turn, to see the enormous advantage commerce would derive from liberty" (1964, 29).

The role of commerce in gently pushing the intolerant to allow for greater toleration came early in U.S. history. The conflicting desires to cultivate commercial exchanges among the colonies while simultaneously promoting religious orthodoxy in defined territories nearly resulted in a trade war between New England and Rhode Island.

> In 1659 the [Puritan-dominated] United Colonies [of New Haven, Massachusetts, Connecticut, and Plymouth] wrote to Rhode Island to point out that Quakers were entertained there and asking that they be removed, lest the contagion spread. Otherwise, the letter hinted, the colonies might have to take further steps for their own protection. Rhode Island interpreted this as the threat of a trade embargo and was clearly frightened by it. Its president, Benedict Arnold,[46] replied in a conciliatory fashion, declaring that his colony wished to retain good relations with its neighbors.... Shortly thereafter, in a letter to John Clark, its agent in England, the Rhode Island Assembly revealed its real feelings. The letter acknowledged that the Quakers were indeed making themselves a nuisance to the other colonies, but that Rhode Island had no reason to charge them with breach of the civil peace.... As it turned out, the answer was almost anything short of economic sanctions, an answer that the perceptive Rhode Islanders might have gleaned from a look at New Haven laws, which permitted Quakers to trade in the colony as long as they did not preach. (Curry 1986, 22–3)

Obviously, the Puritans in New Haven realized that attracting trade was more important than quashing Quakers. No trade war resulted and several petitions submitted to King Charles II resulted in a decision favorable to the

---

[46] He was the great-grandfather of the better known traitor of the same name. Although one Arnold may have betrayed the cause of freedom, the elder's firm stance against intolerance helped – in a small but significance way – to make the United States one of the most religiously free nations on earth.

Quakers. An earlier petition by "divers [*sic*] merchants and others" resulted in ending the harshest restrictions against Anabaptists in Massachusetts (Curry 1986, 17). This, of course, did not result in immediate and complete freedom for minority sects; Puritan leaders devised numerous other ways to inconvenience non-Congregationalists (including the continuation of a religious tax and prohibitions on voting for permanent residents of the colony who felt a desire to worship differently).

Trade among the colonies expanded with time and population, and the pressure to allow uninhibited movement to merchants of different denominations increased in stride. The connection between religious toleration, commerce, and social wealth – a goal of all colonial leaders – became increasingly apparent. William Penn, one of the great champions of liberty in colonial America, clearly understood the relationship between trade and religious freedom. In his treatise on how to ensure social peace and prosperity in England presented to King Charles II, he laid out the foundation for what would become the political philosophy of his own colony:

> Consider Peace, Plenty, and Safety, the three great Inducements to any Country to Honour the Prince, and Love the Government, as well as the best Allurements to Foreigners to trade with it and transport themselves to it, are utterly lost by such Partialities [restrictions on religious freedom]. . . . Plenty will be hereby exchanged for Poverty, by the Destruction of many thousand Families within this Realm, who are greatly instrumental for the carrying on of the most substantial Commerce therein: Men of Virtue, good Contrivance, Great Industry; whose Labours, not only keep the Parishes from the Trouble and Charge of maintaining them and theirs, but help to maintain the Poor, and are great Contributors to the King's Revenue by their Traffick. This very Severity [restrictions on religious freedom] will make more Bankrupts in the Kingdom of England in seven Years, than have been in it upon all other Accounts in Seven Ages [*sic*]. (Penn 2002, 58)[47]

This argument by Penn was strategically brilliant; if the crown was reluctant to allow religious freedom solely on ethical grounds (which Penn argued too), then it was wise to make an appeal directly to the financial interests of the kingdom.

In a more specific treatise on religious liberty published four years later (and just two years prior to his colonial grant), Penn once again made the connection between religious liberty, commerce, and prosperity.

[47] This quote comes from William Penn's "England's Present Interest Considered, with Honour to the Prince and Safety to the People" (1675).

> That Way of Worship we are Commanded Conformity to, doth not make Better Livers, that is a Demonstration, Nor Better Artists, for it cannot be though that going to Church, hearing Common-Prayer,[48] or believing in the present Episcopacy, learn Men to Build Ships or Houses; to make Clothes, Shoes, Dials or Watches; Buy, Sell, Trade, or Commerce better, than any that are of another Perswasion. And since these Things are Useful, if not Requisite in Civil Society, is not prohibiting, nay ruining, such Men, because they will not come to hear Common-Prayer, &c. destructive of Civil Society? (Penn 2002, 238)[49]

And again arguing several years later for greater toleration throughout the English kingdom (in the homeland and abroad), Penn states,

> But as it [persecution] has many Arguments for it, that are drawn from the Advantages that have and would come to the Publick by it, so there are divers Mischiefs that must unavoidably follow the Persecution of Dissenters, that may reasonably disswade from such Severity. For they must either be ruined, fly, or conform; and perhaps the last is not the Safest. If they are Fuin'd in their Estates and their Persons Imprisoned, modestly compute, a Fourth of the Trade and Manufactury of the Kingdom sinks; and those that have helped to maintain the Poor, must come upon the Poor's Book for Maintenance. This seems to be an Impoverishing of the Publick. Bit if to avoid this, they transport themselves, with their Estates, into other Governments; nay, though it were to any of the King's Plantations [colonies], the Number were far too great to be spared from Home. So much principal Stock wanting to turn the yearly Traffick, and so many People too, to consume our yearly Growth, must issue fatally to the Trade one Way, and to the Lands and Rents of the Kingdom the other Way [sic]. (Penn 2002, 317)[50]

Penn's justifications for religious freedom apparently worked as King Charles II granted him a colony wherein Quakers and others were free to pursue their merchant desires. And the merchant desires of the Quakers – known for their industry and commerce – took them far and wide throughout the colonies where they contributed to the growing religious pluralism that eventually prompted greater liberty. More than a century later, Penn's Quaker heirs took it upon themselves to emphasize religious liberty as "the only solid foundation that can be laid for the prosperity and happiness of this or any country" (Religious Society of Friends 1789) in a petition

---

[48] A reference to the Anglican *Book of Common Prayer*.
[49] Originally published in 1679 as "An Address to Protestants of All Perswasions [sic] More Especially the Magistracy and Clergy, for the Promotion of Virtue and Charity."
[50] Originally published in 1686 as "A Perswasive [sic] to Moderation to Church-Dissenters, in Prudence and Conscience."

to President George Washington. This petition was no small matter given that the Quakers were pacifists at a time shortly after the nation had been on war footing. Washington's response was to assure them their rights would be protected.[51]

The relationship between trade and religious freedom also appeared in Virginia, where itinerant Presbyterian preacher Samuel Davies ran into conflict with Anglican officials trying to prevent the poaching of congregants by circuit riders during the Great Awakening. In trying to obtain licenses to use public meetinghouses for purposes of worship, Davies confronted significant resistance in the 1750s.

> A long struggle ensued over the issues of licenses, during which it became clear that the Council [of Colonial Virginia] was determined to hold the dissenters within bounds. President [Thomas] Lee informed the [British] Board of Trade immediately after the refusal of the license that he thought that the liberty Davies sought to extend his preaching activities was "not within the words or intent of the Toleration [Act], and gives great uneasiness to the Clergy and the People. While the bishop of London supported the Council's endeavors [to restrict religious liberty], the Lords of Trade, never very sensitive to the needs of uneasy colonial ruling groups, gave cold comfort. They advised that "a free Exercise of Religion is so valuable a branch of true liberty, and so essential to the enriching and improving of a Trading Nation, it should ever be held sacred in His Majesty's Colonies" (Isaac 1973, 27).

Thomas Lee only partially relented to this general directive from the Board of Trade and although allowing some liberties for itinerant preachers, colonial officials continued to cite circuit riders on "nuisance charges" (Isaac 1973, 27–8).

In New England, the major port city of Boston was exempted as early as the 1650s from laws that required the payment of mandatory religious tithes to the Congregational church (McLoughlin 1971, 118). For aficionados of general political economy, consider this akin to tax and regulatory exemptions granted to spur entrepreneurial growth in "special enterprise zones." Baptist minister Isaac Backus, in appealing to the Massachusetts government in 1778 for an end to religious taxes elsewhere in the region, pointed out the relationship between Boston's wealth and religious freedom (and implicitly noted the level of pluralism in that city).

> By an express law of this government, the *multitude* of people in Boston, have been *left* entirely free, these eighty-five years, to choose what worship they

---

[51] This response is attached to the same document as provided in n. 50.

would attend upon, and not to be compelled to pay a farthing to support any
that they did not chuse [sic]: And there are proofs [sic] enough to show, that
this liberty has greatly contributed to the welfare and not the injury of the
town. (Backus 1778, 11)

The surprising lesson from Boston was that this freedom did not bankrupt
the churches as many had thought (McLoughlin 1968, 1402). Nonetheless, the end of mandatory religious taxation in Massachusetts didn't occur
until 1832, the latest date among the original thirteen colonies. This is
not surprising given the depth that Congressionalists were entrenched in
the various levels of government. But the growing pluralism of the colony
combined with the wealth this pluralism brought, eventually pushed state
officials to deregulate their religious market (cf. McLoughlin 1971, 692).

One of America's first political economists – Tench Coxe[52] – summed
up the relationship between religious liberty and commerce at the dawn of
the new nation.

> Such is the present situation of things in Pennsylvania, which is more or less
> the same in several other of the American stats, viz. New York, Main [sic],
> Virginia, the Carolinas, Georgia, Vermont and Kentucky: but though not so in
> the rest, the principal difference is, that they are so fully peopled, that there are
> no new lands of any value unsold and farming lands, which are improved, are of
> course dearer than with us. In those states, however, agriculture, commerce,
> manufactures, the fisheries, and navigation, afford comfortable sustenance
> and ample rewards of profit to the industrious and well disposed, amidst the
> blessings of civil and religious liberty. (Coxe 1798, 74)

Internal Migration: The Dissenter's Exit Option

Although the policy of the British crown (and Cromwell) allowed for religious dissenters to move from Europe to America in an effort to build a
profitable colony, another form of migration was crucial in augmenting
religious pluralism (and eventually liberty) in the colonies – that is, the
ability to move *internally*. Politically, the cost of monitoring and enforcing religious liberty laws was frightfully high, especially in frontier areas
away from the sight of the established clergy. The persecutions of religious
minorities that did occur usually took place when those dissenters made too
much of a ruckus in a larger town or city, as was the case of Mary Dyer in
Boston. Although some denominations tried to maintain strict control over

---

[52] First but probably not "best known." Perhaps a citation here some two centuries later will
spur a renaissance in the study of Tench Coxe's thought.

the beliefs and practices of the local population, de facto religious pluralism and freedom gradually resulted from the mere fact that people could easily up and leave if they did not like the laws under which they were living (Finke 1990, 612; Bainton 1941, 116). Although attempts were made to enforce strict religious uniformity in Virginia and New England, "[u]nder the harsh conditions of a frontier settlement and in the absence of bishops and ecclesiastical courts, such undeviating procedures [of establishment] were little needed and impossible to maintain in the colony.... As a result, unhampered by any strong centralized episcopacy, those holding various Protestant attitudes were able to adjust local worship to suit their preferences" (Curry 1986, 30).

Perhaps the most famous of all religious dissenters to take the "exit option" in U.S. history was Roger Williams.[53] Concerned that the Puritans of Massachusetts were not puritanical enough, Williams came into conflict with the reigning religious authorities of the colony, particularly John Cotton. Williams's radical nonconformity, wherein he argued that no government could dictate the beliefs of an individual, rubbed against the interests of the ruling Puritan hierarchy who had created a de facto established church in Massachusetts (Stokes and Pfeffer 1964, 13–16). Fearing that their religious haven in New England would be disturbed by Archbishop William Laud, who was cracking down severely on dissent in Old England, the Puritan leaders of Massachusetts thought it in their best political interests to banish Williams in 1635 (Stead 1934, 242). This shows yet another example of how a political calculation – the desire to preserve the colony's charter – dictated policy toward religious groups (all by way of Proposition 3 wherein considerations of political survival impact decisions on religious freedom).

Roger Williams's experience with religious intolerance and his increasingly radical separationist ideals led him to proclaim religious freedom in his settlement of Providence, which in turn attracted a wide array of dissenters including Anabaptists, Quakers, and even a smattering of Catholics, Jews, and French Huguenots. Williams's decision to favor an open religious policy has widely been cited as one of the principal foundations of religious liberty in the United States, influencing the likes of James Madison and Isaac Backus (Noonan 1998, 56). This influence would seem to bolster support for ideational explanations for the rise of religious liberty. As mentioned

---

[53] Williams generally overshadows another important person in the history of Rhode Island – John Clark, who set up the first Baptist church in the settlement of Newport and documented the extent of persecution in Massachusetts in detail (Clark 1652).

in Chapter 2, ideas do influence policy. But often those ideas develop in response to specific interests. Therefore, it must still be observed that political and social considerations played an important role in pushing Williams toward his viewpoint. Of great concern to Williams was social order. In an era where spiritual schism was becoming more socially prevalent, coerced uniformity of opinion would only result in devastating conflict. Bozeman reminds us of a

> little-noticed argument used by Williams in his defense of toleration. For he was one of many persons in the seventeenth century who were [*sic*] sickened at the spectacle of bloody intramural conflicts within "Christendom." The brutal Thirty Years' War had only recently ended, and in England itself, the conflict between Catholic and Protestant policy had produced a host of martyrs. Many had begun to recognize that the age-old premise of religious uniformity had become a *danger to the peace and welfare* of Western society. It is important to recognize that Williams often urged religious toleration as a remedy for the conflicts by which Christendom was slowly being torn to pieces from within. 'Inforced [*sic*] uniformity,' he insisted, 'is the greatest occasion of civill Warre [*sic*].' (Bozeman 1972, 61–2; emphasis added)

The notion that religious pluralism would give rise to war and social unrest was not uncommon in colonial days. This notion has deep historical roots and is often cited as a reason why governments must regulate the religious economy and/or maintain a single state church (cf. Hawkins 1928, 111–22). But given that the irreversibility of the Protestant Reformation meant that religious diversity was going to be a fact of Western life, two political solutions presented themselves. First, the state could try to stave off potential conflict by eliminating nonconformists. The French Wars of Religion, the English Civil War, and persecution of religious minorities throughout the British colonies offer cases in point of how this was a frequently preferred option. Ironically, the more the state, fearing social unrest, tried to stamp out the growth of pluralism, the more society became restive. Understanding this, Roger Williams understood the greater benefits to be gotten from the second policy option – live and let live. If violence and coercion were ineffective in defeating religious dissension and only led to further conflict, then removing the state from regulating spiritual life seemed the better path to social harmony.

Although not widely celebrated at the time as a bold new initiative, Rhode Island's great experiment with religious liberty nonetheless was watched with interested eyes, both in the United Colonies (of Massachusetts, Plymouth, and Connecticut) and England (Harkness 1936, 219). The

Puritan neighbors of Rhode Island were concerned about religious tolerance expanding to their territory, not to mention the fact that they also
wanted to absorb several "renegade Rhode Island towns" (Bozeman 1972,
46–7). The fact that the upstart colony was beset by internal squabbles and
strife left the impression that a territory founded on (relatively) unbridled
religious freedom was doomed to failure in the eyes of their New England
neighbors (Bozeman 1972, 53–4). Williams's experiment was largely saved
by the fact that Oliver Cromwell, a Puritan and empathetic toward religious
rights, emerged victorious in the English Civil War (James 1975, 57). The
climate of religious tolerance that endured in England during Cromwell's
Protectorate provided Rhode Island with the breathing space needed for
the colony to stabilize itself. As Rhode Island grew from a haven for rugged
individualists and religious "malcontents" to a productive colony, it became
apparent that freedom of religion need not necessarily devolve into social
anarchy. In reality, however, Rhode Island moved toward a more controlled
religious environment by the late 1600s in an effort to quell some social
unrest, enacting voting restrictions on Jews and Catholics and cracking
down on Quakers and radical Baptists who refused to bear arms in defense
of the colony (Noonan 1998, 54). As Proposition 1 predicts, there is a tendency for the majority to exercise control over the minority.

The experience of Rhode Island, combined with the creation of Pennsylvania and Maryland as refuges for adventurous religious dissenters, had an
interesting reverse-image effect on religious liberty in the United States.
As Noonan notes, these "colonies demonstrated that the Church of England could tolerate other forms of Christian worship and so prepared the
ground for the English Act of Toleration" (1998, 55).[54] The Toleration Act,
in turn, placed restrictions on the actions of colonists who sought to impose
religious uniformity in their territory and offered up examples for colonial
officials. During the 1740s, "[w]ishing to avoid all impediment to immigration on the frontier, which protected the east from Indian attack, [Virginia]
Governor [William] Gooch construed the Act of Toleration as broadly as
possible, conforming to the attitude of the Crown" (E. Smith 1972, 30).
Lobbying efforts by religious minorities to shake loose from the yoke of a

---

[54] Noonan also included Massachusetts Bay as one of the colonies demonstrating that
Anglicanism could tolerate religious dissent and survive. Given that many Massachusetts
Puritans still considered themselves to be within or representing the "true" Church of
England, it might be a bit of a stretch to include Massachusetts in the mix. Technically
speaking, though, Noonan was referring to the official Church of England back in the
Motherland.

general assessment by Congregationalists (in Massachusetts) and Anglicans (in Virginia) referred back to the Toleration Act (McLoughlin 1971, 108–10). In one of the great ironies of history, although the American colonists fought a hard war of independence against the King of England in the 1770s, it was the British crown nearly a century earlier that helped plant the seeds of liberty.

Religious Pluralism and the End of Mandatory Tithing

The need to attract immigrants and the easy exit from religious persecution meant that religious pluralism increased over time (see Propositions 5a and 5b). This religious pluralism not only included folks such as the Quakers (settling happily in William Penn's colony and then spreading outward), Methodists, and Baptists but also included a substantial number of the religiously indifferent. As Finke and Stark (1992, 31–9) argue, the people most likely to migrate to a new frontier are not necessarily those most likely to attend church. Rather, they tend to be single men and are often "scoundrels and knaves" and high-plains drifters in search of economic opportunity (cf. Sweet 1935, 52–4).[55] Not surprisingly, these folks would tend to chafe under a government that supported an established religion with a policy of mandatory religious taxation. And considering that the "grasping hand" of taxation has often prompted political change throughout history, it is not surprising to see the battle for religious freedom fought on financial grounds. Thus, the growth of pluralism – including both the spiritual and indifferent – inevitably gave rise to a greater demand to end establishment, or at least the financial support it was predicated on, as predicted by Proposition 4c, which claims that when no one religion dominates (i.e., religious diversity increases), regulatory policy will tend not to discriminate among them.

It should come as no surprise that church taxes would be the initial focal point of a movement toward religious liberty. Dissenters who had to pay the mandatory tax to support an established church and then had to contribute to the maintenance of their own parish would undoubtedly be motivated to end payments to a church they either did not use or thought was heretical. The same would be true for the nonreligious. Why pay for something that you don't plan on using? Thus, as religious diversity increased, so too did

---

[55] An easily performed empirical test can provide evidence for this assertion. Next time you are in church, look around and count how many single males ages twenty to thirty years old that you see in the pews, particularly during football season.

the number of individuals agitating for an end to mandatory tithing (Miller 1935, 59–61).

Ironically, the cornerstone to this resistance movement was planted by the Massachusetts's Congregationalists. In a *political* effort to lure a settlement of Baptists in Swansea away from their association with Rhode Island in the 1660s, the Massachusetts legislature exempted the settlers there from the most onerous burdens of Congregational establishment, including a mandatory religious assessment (McLoughlin 1971, 130–6). Congregationalists and Baptists intermingled in Swansea with little incident until the early 1700s when an increasingly "radical" Baptist pastor named Samuel Luther refused to perform or acknowledge infant baptisms (McLoughlin 1971, 136–8).[56] Local Swansea Congregationalists took the opportunity of this controversy to not only lobby for Luther's dismissal but also to propose a general assessment to replace voluntary tithing and then distribute the tax revenue to both Congregationalist and Baptist churches in equal proportion. This petition was successfully resisted in court and religious tithing remained voluntary in the township. Several other attempts by Congregationalists to impose a religious tax also failed, including an attempt to redraw Swansea's boundaries to include several small settlements that would make the city majority Congregationalist (McLoughlin 1971, 140–1). The Congregationalists did score a minor success in getting a religious tax imposed on the neighboring town of Barrington, but it is believed that Baptists were allowed to ignore it with little penalty (McLoughlin 1971, 146). Note that this small but historic shift in policy resulted not from a change in ideology (as mandatory tithing to the Puritan establishment continued in the rest of the Bay colony) but was motivated by a political desire to expand Massachusetts's territory and economic reach. Once the Swansea precedent was established, other dissident communities could refer to it as a means of seeking an exemption.

Other localized battles for exemption to the religious tax, coming from Baptists, Quakers, and Anglicans, occurred throughout New England in the late 1600s and early 1700s, and many of these groups lobbied the British Crown on the basis of the Act of Toleration (Miller 1935, 63). Although the governors of the New England colonies considered it important to support an established Congregationalist church, they also understood that

---

[56] Samuel Luther subscribed to a doctrine known as *antipedobaptism*, a word that does not appear in most word-processing dictionaries. The idea behind this belief is that infants and children are too young to be baptized; baptism must occur when an adult can fully comprehend the grace of God.

they needed to retain their powerful status vis-à-vis the English monarchy (McLoughlin 1971, 263). Experiencing trepidation over having their
colonial charter revoked and losing their influential positions, the ruling
elite in the colonies began to yield to calls for an end to religious taxation.
Not only was the pressure of the Baptists and Quakers important but also
Anglicans played an important role by posing a difficult dilemma for Congregationalists in the new religiously pluralistic environment. "This change
[in tax policy] resulted not from theoretical arguments, but from existing
realities: the fact that New England oppression of dissenters embarrassed
Congregationalists before their brethren in England, who were themselves
oppressed by the established Church of England, and the danger of intervention by the English government to stop Congregationalists, themselves
dissenters, from taxing Anglicans" (Curry 1986, 89–90).

Connecticut was one of the first to succumb to such pressure and implemented its own Toleration Act in 1708 (Miller 1935, 63). Massachusetts
followed suit in 1728 with a law that exempted members of many dissenting
denominations from paying a mandatory tax to support Congregationalist
establishment. It is no coincidence that the First Great Awakening began
just years after this law passed. Freed from a mandatory tax, it became
less expensive for an individual to participate in a nonestablished church.
Previously that person would have had to pay the mandatory tax *and* voluntarily contribute to their own church. The church plantings of the First
Great Awakening were made possible because a change in the regulatory
regime opened up a new avenue of religious demand. Nonetheless, harassment of non-Congregational religions continued for some time, particularly the independent "New Light" churches of the Great Awakening that
were poaching adherents from the established Congregationalists (Finke
and Stark 1992, 60–3; Armstrong 1960, 300).

Virginia experienced a similar controversy over religious taxation, albeit
several decades later. In part the delay can be attributed to the fact that
Anglicans did not protect their establishment with the fervor of their
Puritan brethren to the north (Buckley 1977, 14); religion did not play as
central a role in Virginia's founding as in Massachusetts. This is important.
The religious leaders in Massachusetts originated from the most fervent
dissenting sects in England and could be expected to pursue their religious
interests with zeal. The best clergy in the Church of England, by contrast,
had little incentive to cross the Atlantic. Their career incentives were better
served in England where they could receive more prestigious assignments
and maintain a better chance of ascending in the church hierarchy. As such,
the Anglican clergy in the American colonies were not well unified in their

own defense (Buckley 1977, 10–16). The delayed calls for greater freedom of conscience can also be attributed to the relative lack of religious pluralism that persisted until the mid-1700s. Only after the circuit riders of the Great Awakening tore a path through the southern colonies did Virginia see significant numbers of non-Anglicans (Curry 1986, 134; Buckley 1977, 9). The pace of religious change in Virginia was quite rapid with dissenting denominations becoming a majority within the span of three short decades (1740s to the 1770s).

Despite a lower level of persecution in Virginia, the issue of tithing became salient. Taxation and property rights, after all, have been a mainstay of political upheaval throughout history. With religious dissenters growing rapidly, the cries for an end to mandatory tithing became loud. The Baptists, Mennonites, Presbyterians, and New Lights were joined by a small group of secular rationalists (including Thomas Jefferson and James Madison) who also had little use for a tax that supported a service they did not use.[57] In 1776, amid an environment where the battle cry of "no taxation without representation" was gaining traction, Virginia's Assembly took up the cause of whether to continue the practice of state-enforced tithing (Buckley 1977). With the eloquent Patrick Henry taking up the side of the Anglican establishment and James Madison arguing to terminate religious taxes, the legislature debated the issue for most of 1776. However, with horns locked on what to do with the establishment and a war to fight and finance, a compromise solution emerged that permitted the continuation of the Anglican establishment but suspended mandatory taxation and government-paid clerical salaries (Buckley 1977, 34).

Throughout the course of the war, the issue of establishment sat on the backburner. Some legislators argued for a general assessment that would financially support all recognized denominations, but suspicion of Anglican motives and opposition from the rationalists kept this solution from being accepted. The results of this were predictable. "As the years of revolution lengthened, the break with England, the absence of a bishop, and the suspension of the clerical salaries had a pronounced effect on the church. The supply of English recruits was cut off and the ordination of native vocations impossible. The ranks of the clergy were thinned by resignations and deaths" (Buckley 1977, 44). Without religious leadership to advocate their position, the prospects of reinstating the Anglican establishment waned.

---

[57] In a strategy that is perplexing to me and that counters Proposition 1, Methodists chose to support the Anglican establishment until after the end of the Revolutionary War (Buckley 1977, 29).

The ability of other denominations to financially support their clergy during a time of war added to the argument that government support was unnecessary for religious vitality. The Presbyterians and Baptists – the two largest dissenting denominations – refused to lobby for a general assessment that would extend state support to them (Curry 1986, 137; Buckley 1977, 79).

With non-Anglicans in a majority in Virginia and the ranks of Anglican clergy depleted, the stage was set for a dramatic movement toward religious freedom. Some lawmakers continued stumping for a generic "Christian establishment," which meant that James Madison and Thomas Jefferson's attempts to push a radical religious freedom bill through the Virginian Assembly would fail several times before finally passing in 1786 (Curry 1986, 139; Buckley 1977, passim). Although much has been written regarding the rationalist dispositions of Madison and Jefferson when framing the bill, economic motives for toleration lurked strongly in the background. In his debates with Patrick Henry, Madison

> [e]numerated the states in America where complete freedom of belief prevailed.... If Virginia defied this growing pattern of religious liberty by instituting a policy of establishment, it would be closing the door to immigration and encouraging dissenters to forsake the state for other, freer climes. (Buckley 1977, 99)

It is interesting to note that Madison also chaired the Committee on Commerce in the Virginia Assembly at this time.

Pluralism, Social Conflict, and the Revolutionary War

At the signing of the Declaration of Independence, Benjamin Franklin famously declared that "We must all hang together or assuredly we shall all hang separately." Combined with a high level of denominational pluralism that was facilitated by internal migration, the necessity to form a united front against the British motherland required that all denominations get along if only through mutual disregard. The lesson of the English Civil War was that nations that are fighting among themselves internally cannot aspire to greater prosperity. Historian Roland Bainton astutely observed of both Europe and America that "when the church was definitely atomized, the alternative to religious liberty was mutual extermination" (1936, 430). Another distinguished scholar of American religious history, Perry Miller, drew the connection between pluralism and liberty. "Where a multiplicity of creeds checkmate each other, they find themselves to their surprise maintaining religious liberty" (Miller 1935, 60).

Like Franklin's memorable political cartoon in 1754 wherein a snake was depicted divided into eight parts and the inscription read "join or die," the colonists began to realize that religious differences among comrades were of little consequence during wartime. Facing a common enemy

> the desire for military security accelerated the toleration of dissident groups. In Virginia where the Anglican Church was established, Huguenots, Germans, and Presbyterians were settled on the frontier "to awe the straggling parties of northern Indians, and be a good barrier for all that country."[58] The Baptists in Virginia first obtained toleration in the army, when the need for a united front against England in 1775 led to a concession to dissenting ministers to exhort and celebrate worship for 'scrupulous consciences' among the recruits. (Bainton 1941, 108)

As Bainton points out in the preceding quote, security tended to trump denominational disagreement in the face of a common enemy; the lessons of pioneer migrants facing hostile natives were easily transferred to the situation in the Revolutionary War.

An example of a political trade-off between national security and religious liberty is perhaps nowhere clearer than in the case of Catholics during the Revolutionary War. In a work that echoes the main themes of this book even in its title, Charles Hanson's *Necessary Virtue: The Pragmatic Origins of Religious Liberty in New England* tells a detailed story of how Catholics went from messengers of the Antichrist to helpful allies virtually overnight. Colonial Puritans had consistently maintained a special loathing for the so-called papists throughout most of the colonial era. Even though Catholics were sparse in New England proper, the presence of French settlers in the Canadian provinces was always a looming concern. Tensions were made worse when the English Parliament signed the Quebec Act of 1774 granting the Catholic-dominated province of Quebec extended territorial control of land as far south as the Ohio River Valley. Moreover, this new law officially granted "toleration to Catholics, including the right of the clergy to collect tithes" (Hanson 1998, 11). Outrage erupted among New Englanders, including the likes of John Adams. But less than a year later, the Battle of Lexington changed everything.

---

[58] Citation refers to Henry R. McIlwaine, *The Struggle of Protestant Dissenters for Religious Toleration in Virginia* (1894).

Hanson details how the course of the Revolutionary War led to a number of paradoxes and ironies with regard to religious policy. Initially, the American rebels sought to seize Quebec militarily as it was a British strategic stronghold.[59] That effort failed. And as the war dragged on, it became apparent that the American revolutionaries would need an outside alliance if they had a chance of winning independence. Throughout the next few years, the Continental Congress began negotiations to form an alliance with France, which was eventually concluded in 1778. To wit, members of the Continental Congress had a strategic change in attitude toward Catholics, even to the point of attending a Catholic Mass (Hanson 1998, 97)! Toleration was granted to Catholics living in the rebellious colonies, and the religious provisions of the Quebec Act were reluctantly accepted. An expansion of religious liberty resulted from a direct political calculation and was only justified ideationally ex post facto.

Although beneficial to Catholics per se, this agreement had more strategic implications for dissenters in the colonies at large and New England in particular.

> The existential fact of Protestant-Catholic cooperation against the British strengthened the hand of those who sought to restrict the public role of religious authorities as part of the overall Revolutionary settlement. Even where this did not directly concern the rights of Catholics (of whom there were extremely few in New England throughout the eighteenth century), the boost that the alliances gave to the idea of religious toleration in general proved a useful tool in dismantling the claim to primacy of the Congregationalist Standing Order. (Hanson 1998, 21)

The degree of liberty granted to Catholics should not be overstated. Following the war, Catholics still bore the brunt of legal discrimination – even after the disestablishment of Congregationalism in 1833 – but the tone of criticism subsided and the political space had opened for further gains in religious freedom down the road. By the start of the Industrial Revolution and the growing need for skilled labor, an influx of Catholics into Boston from Quebec, Ireland, Italy, and other places in Europe helped tip the balance in favor of expanded liberty. Catholic immigrants were not welcomed with open arms (something to which my forbearers can attest), but economic necessity and the expansion of their numbers led to their eventual acceptance in society.

---

[59] Quebec was originally settled by the French but became British property in 1763 through the Treaty of Paris.

Following the war, efforts to piece together the disparate colonies meant recognition that religious pluralism was a fact of life. To establish a single national church in a nation where no one denomination held a majority was a recipe for continued strife. Casting ballots to determine if any denomination (or combination of denominations) should be established would only produce instability. As the religious composition of the country shifted – as it did from the early 1600s to the Constitutional Convention – political struggles over religion would consume an inordinate amount of time. The most expeditious solution was to prohibit a national church from being established in the new nation's founding charter – the U.S. Constitution. The Constitution still allowed for religion to be regulated at the state level, and Massachusetts used this point to sustain a Congregational establishment into the 1830s. However, with continued immigration and internal migration, the growing spiritual diversity that ensued, and the gains from trade that could be captured by allowing members of all faiths to engage in commerce freely, Massachusetts eventually succumbed to the pressure of dissenters to allow for greater religious liberty. The eventual disestablishment of Congregationalism ironically was brought about due to growing pluralism within its own ranks.[60] A split between Unitarians and Trinitarians – an admittedly theological debate – provided Baptists, Methodists, and other dissenters with a new ally and enough votes to bring the Congregational establishment to an end (McLoughlin 1971, 1128). Although the Puritans of the early 1600s had hoped to construct a religious utopia based on their brand of Christianity, what eventually evolved was a haven for people of all faiths.

Summary

Religious liberty was born of religious pluralism. In Europe, different rulers begrudgingly tolerated religious factionalization after the Protestant Reformation in order to ameliorate social conflict and focus on consolidating power. However, these rulers were still more favorable to maintaining control over a single church, and policies of toleration were rescinded where the situation allowed (e.g., France in 1685). It is difficult, then, to view the concrete progress of religious liberty as a unilateral trend in intellectual thought. In colonial British America, the pluralism that invariably resulted from the English crown's concern with settlement (and exporting

---

[60] See Stark (2003, 2001) for an argument regarding how schism is endemic in monotheistic religions.

troublemakers) also set the scene for the emergence of religious liberty. Although some religious denominations (e.g., the Puritans in New England and Anglicans in the southern colonies) attempted to re-create established church monopolies on American soil, the growing presence of Quakers, Methodists, Baptists, and others made this objective difficult to maintain. The vast amount of open land meant easy exit for dissenters, and the king's priority to encourage population growth in the region as a bulwark against France and Spain meant that pluralism would become the norm. As the colonies grew, the imperative to promote trade and later to forge a unified front against the British made a policy of religious freedom for all the most attractive option to political leaders. The passage of the First Amendment was not the end of the story. In line with the theory developed in Chapter 2, religious groups worked tenaciously to protect their religious "market share," and this often meant co-opting willing politicians to write legislation making it more difficult for "foreign" faiths to proliferate. Catholics (and later Mormons) faced continued discrimination throughout the nineteenth and early twentieth centuries and even to this day different groups – now including many secular interests – are in a constant struggle to restrict church growth. The story of religious freedom continues to be written in the United States, but the telling of that story must wait for another day.[61] It is now time to venture southward for another glimpse into the origins of religious liberty in a region that proved to be more hostile to such freedom.

---

[61] Readers intrigued by the story to this point are encouraged to keep checking back for more of my inspiring articles and books.

CHAPTER 4

Mexico and Latin America

Religion is the law of conscience. Any law imposed on it annuls it, because when we enforce duty, we remove merit from faith, which is the basis of religion. The precepts and sacred dogmas of religion are useful, luminous proofs of transcendence; we should all profess them, but this obligation is moral, not political.

– Simón Bolívar, *Address to the Constituent Congress* (1826)[1]

ON JANUARY 28, 1992, the Mexican national legislature approved changes to the country's revolutionary 1917 Constitution and effectively reversed eight decades of officially sanctioned hostility toward religious organizations, including principally (and surprisingly) the Roman Catholic Church. Church leaders greeted this new legal framework with a sense of optimism and accomplishment, having obtained the legal recognition and freedom it had sought for many years. Jerónimo Prigione, the papal nuncio who spearheaded the Church's struggle to obtain legal recognition, stated, "We [the Catholic hierarchy] are sincerely appreciative and thankful for the effort of the House of Deputies, and the concern of [President Carlos Salinas], a wise statesman . . . for opening new horizons in the relations between the Church and State [*sic*], channeling the forces of the two societies toward the service of social and religious peace" (Prigione 1992, 24). Archbishop Adolfo

---

[1] Cited in Bolívar (2003, 62).

Suárez Rivera, then president of the Conferencia del Episcopado Mexicano (CEM), declared that this legislation "has marked a new stage in our history. It has been the fruit of a long process... it is undeniable that it has represented a big step that has opened roads to *the freedom of the Church* so that it can better realize its task of evangelization" (Suárez Rivera 1992, 33; emphasis added). Since the passage of this legislation, officials from both the government and the Catholic Church acknowledge that relations between the two have never been better.[2] This legislation also opened opportunities for non-Catholic denominations. Religious liberty finally had taken root in Mexican soil.

For the casual observer of Latin American religion and politics, it may seem odd that Catholic Church officials were celebrating a change in a law that guaranteed their freedom to worship.[3] Latin America is, after all, a predominantly Catholic region and has been since the sixteenth century. One could imagine that Protestants and other religious minorities would have had a rougher go of it, and this is true. Protestants have faced severe limitations on their freedom in many parts of Latin America and slowly have been gaining equal rights over the past century, Simón Bolívar's promise of freedom notwithstanding. The Catholic Church also has been subject to stringent requirements on its behavior from nearly the date when Columbus set foot in the western hemisphere. Many of these legal restrictions on the Church were tempered by a grant of exalted status (and the delivery of financial support), either by the Spanish (and Portuguese) crown or secular politicians following independence in the early 1800s. Such a privileged position was cherished by most bishops and clergy and served to retard the growth of religious pluralism for at least four centuries. But the Catholic Church always had struggled to gain more independence from state control, seeking its own preferred regulatory regime that enhanced its institutional autonomy – freedom of religion for Catholicism – while protecting its social position by limiting the freedom of non-Catholics. This struggle raged most notably in the first several decades after Latin America severed relations with Iberia, but echoes of that battle linger to this day.

---

[2] Various interviews conducted by the author during fieldwork in Mexico City and Puebla in June 1995. Informal conversations with nonpartisan observers reinforced this notion that relations between the Catholic Church and the government were at an apogee.

[3] The freedoms that were reinstated included such things as citizenship rights for clergy, the ability to own property, and permission to hold religious services in public places. These things had been allowed unofficially for about fifty years, though they were not encoded in law. More on this in the following text.

Mexico represents perhaps the most extreme case of state control over religion in the region. Although following a church-state pattern typical of other Latin American territories during the colonial period, and fending off a variety of attacks by the state during the nineteenth century, the Church fell under a highly anticlerical set of constitutional dictates following the Mexican Revolution (1910–20). In fact, the Catholic Church did not *legally* exist in Mexico between 1917 and 1992. Through patience and persistence, the Catholic clergy finally emerged from under such onerous burdens. In the process of securing their freedom, they also opened the door for other denominations, namely Protestants who had been almost invisibly creeping into Mexican society, to gain a foothold in the country. This chapter examines the course of church-state relations in Latin America from colonial times to the present with a particular eye toward understanding the interesting and challenging case of Mexico. In many ways, the 1992 constitutional changes in Mexico represent what the First Amendment meant to the U.S. Constitution in 1789. Although several Mexican political institutions designed after colonial emancipation took inspiration from the United States (Lambert 1967, 320–1),[4] it took roughly two centuries for Mexico to achieve a level of religious freedom comparable to its northern neighbor. Protestants and other religious minorities elsewhere in Latin America only have gained full religious rights in recent decades. Why did it take longer for most Latin American nations to develop broad-based religious freedom? And, with specific reference to the one-faith tradition that culturally prevails over the region, what explains variations in the way that Latin American governments have regulated Catholicism and the Catholic Church? To answer these questions, I begin with a general overview of the region and then turn my attention to a more detailed examination of the Mexican case.

The Colonial Era and Religious Monopoly

Both the United States and Latin America won independence at the tail end of the Age of Enlightenment,[5] where the notions of religious liberty

---

[4] The primary institutional feature borrowed from the United States in Mexico and elsewhere in Latin America was the tripartite division of political power in the form of presidentialism. Although the French Revolution also inspired a number of early-nineteenth-century Latin American intellectuals and politicos, there was a definite tendency to adopt the political institutions of the United States, as can be gleaned from the writings of Simón Bolívar (2003), one of the political giants of the independence era.

[5] The Enlightenment is usually dated to cover the eighteenth century. Technically speaking, then, Latin America broke free from Iberia after this period, although many of the

(from John Locke to James Madison) were well known. The Great Liberator Simón Bolívar held views favoring the separation of church and state similar to that of the United States as is evidenced by the epigraph at the beginning of this chapter. It is also true that Latin American independence came after, and was partially influenced by, the French Revolution, which contained its fair share of anticlericalism (Williams 1920). In France, the separation of church and state usually came upon the clergy as separation of head and body, literally. Elements of anticlericalism were certainly present among the leaders of independence in Latin America (Mecham 1966, 99; Watters 1933, 83). Nonetheless, the *immediate* result of independence was not separation of church and state, the promulgation of religious liberty that would be hospitable to religious minorities, or any widespread anticlerical backlash. All of this would occur in most countries *several decades after* independence, and freedom for religious minorities would take more than a century to develop. The Catholic Church generally maintained its position as monopolistic provider of religious services in society despite losing some of its financial, legal, and social perquisites in the mid-nineteenth century – policies that some scholars claim were influenced by liberal (or even anticlerical) ideas finally taking hold but that could be attributed equally to the financial needs of the state. The reason why the United States and Latin America differed so drastically in their policies toward religious freedom following independence lies in the different conditions each experienced in the colonial era. These differing conditions, emanating from the colonial era, structured the political incentives of national leaders and provided them with little reason to deregulate the religious market.

Of prime importance in Latin America was the absence of religious pluralism and the economic system put in place by Iberia during the colonial era. Whereas the British crown allowed all manner of religious dissenters to populate its American colonies, the Iberian monarchs[6] made their colonial territory the exclusive dominion of the Catholic Church. The defining institutional feature guaranteeing a monopoly status to Catholicism was known as the *patronato real de las Indias* (royal patronage); no other religions

important thinkers and liberators of the period were schooled in the thought of Enlightenment thinkers. Brazil, a Portuguese colonial holding, did not obtain independence until 1890, far past the historical boundaries of the Enlightenment. Other smaller countries such as Belize (British Honduras) and Guyana didn't lose their colonial status until the twentieth century. The discussion here will primarily refer to the major Latin American countries, most of which (excluding Brazil) achieved independence in the early 1800s.

[6] Forthwith I shall mostly refer to the Spanish crown when discussing the colonial period. The church-state relationship in the Spanish and Portuguese colonies was similar enough for purposes of this study that the reader can apply the discussion here to both colonial territories.

would be allowed to proselytize in the Latin American colonies. In addition to exclusive access to the colonial territories, the Church received extensive land grants, and the colonial governors took care to collect and distribute tithes to the Church, a significant advantage in the religious marketplace even if non-Catholics had been allowed to proselytize. Recall Proposition 1 presented earlier (see Appendix). It was hypothesized that hegemonic religions will desire restrictions on religious minorities. The *patronato* delivered such restrictions, and the Vatican cherished the monopolistic status and perquisites that this agreement conveyed. From the vantage point of religious freedom, the *patronato* created a closed and heavily subsidized religious market that benefited only one faith.[7] The opportunity for denominational pluralism to grow, and subsequent pressure by religious minorities to liberalize the market (as in the colonial United States), was severely (if not absolutely) restricted. Put another way, if there were no religious minorities present to demand freedom, a broad-based policy of religious liberty was a moot point. As we shall see in the following text, however, the *patronato* did encroach on the freedom of the Catholic Church (cf. Holleran 1949, 40), and the details of the patronage arrangement favoring secular authority would become a prime point of contention in the nineteenth century.

The origins of the *patronato* date back to the fifteenth century when a weakened Holy See, facing Ottoman encroachment in Europe and the growing consolidation of European kingdoms, found it expedient to trade protection for various concessions (Shiels 1961, 44–71).[8] Although the Vatican had typically farmed out military protection to feudal lords, the negotiating balance between the Church and secular rulers began tipping in favor of the latter in the 1400s. Technological advancements, economic growth, and new political institutions allowed kings to establish greater control over territory than in previous centuries, most evident in Ferdinand and Isabella's unification of Spain by the end of the century. The Protestant Reformation in the early 1500s only strengthened the negotiating power of Catholic monarchs relative to the pope, who now depended

---

[7] I use the term *benefited* loosely here and mostly to refer to the benefits that the Church hierarchy desired. In reality, as was argued in earlier chapters and by Adam Smith (1776), subsidized religious monopolies do not perform very well, and this is neither to the benefit of its parishioners nor the religious institution.

[8] Mecham (1966, 5) dates the first reference to a "right of patronage" granted to a secular authority to the sixth century under Pope Nicholas II. This is completely believable given the difficulty the Church faced in extending its sole influence in far-flung reaches of Europe without assistance from secular leaders who held military power.

more than ever on the good graces of secular rulers to hold their position in Europe. Access to new lands beginning with Columbus in 1492 gave the Spanish and Portuguese monarchies more leverage in that the Vatican's only access to the colonies was through royal ships.

Despite what seemed like a good deal for the Vatican (in terms of privileged access to the New World and other financial perquisites), the *patronato* as negotiated resulted in substantial restrictions on the institutional autonomy of the Catholic Church. With the *patronato*,

> [m]onarchs now selected every cleric who would cross the seas for religious purposes. They singled out the location of each cathedral and minor chapel.... They regulated the procedure of ecclesiastical courts, the manner and time of worship, and rules for lay and clerical behavior, even to causes of excommunication and the lifting of the same. (Shiels 1961, 6–7)

The king also had veto power over papal bulls and other "minute details – officials, edifices, charges, appointments of the churches, provisions, candles, wax, bread, wine, vessels, hours of services, salaries, feasts and tithes" (Holleran 1949, 25; cf. Dussel 1972). The royal control over shipping and communication between Europe and the colonies guaranteed this power not only in law but also in practice. The expulsion of the Jesuits from Brazil in 1759 and Spanish America in 1767 over that religious order's refusal to pay taxes to increasingly impoverished monarchs and their challenge to royal authority indicates clearly that secular power trumped religious influence in the colonies (Brading 1994, 3–19; Bialek 1963, 14).

Despite the greater power of the secular rulers, Church officials – both in Rome and in the Western Hemisphere – fought hard to regain their ability to control their own institution. José Luis Romero observed that the Church "aspired to override political authority each time it could, and was accustomed to make use not only of the prestige it enjoyed with the people, but also of the influence it possessed at Court and the threats of the Inquisition" (1963, 33). The desire for increased autonomy is inferred easily from the Church's constant struggle to control its own appointments and internal policy during the colonial era.

> [M]embers of the hierarchy and ... representatives of the crown often clashed theoretically and even physically, much to the dismay of those looking for an harmonious [*sic*] existence of the two powers.... Colonial records are full of personal altercations between civil and ecclesiastical authorities over issues which today appear childish but which then were full of symbolic meaning to the participants. (Bialek 1963, 13)

Childish disputes over the boundaries of parish lines and other trivial matters (e.g., purchasing candles) actually signified more than symbolic meaning; these conflicts represented a tug-of-war over institutional
sovereignty. Witness the attempt by King Charles III to carve up and create three new dioceses in the Mexican territory in the early 1800s, ostensibly to serve a growing population more effectively. Mexican bishops, even
though appointed by the king, resisted such territorial interference because
it altered the manner in which tithes were collected and managed and
threatened to reduce the funding they would receive (Brading 1994, 173–
5). Hence, although we initially may think that a state-guaranteed spiritual
monopoly removes issues of religious freedom for the dominant church,
there were still issues of institutional autonomy (i.e., freedom) that mat-
tered significantly (Holleran 1949, 40). Conflict over the extent and nature
of regulatory control over the Church would become the focal point of battles for religious freedom following colonial emancipation in the nineteenth
century.

The other major factor inhibiting the growth of religious tolerance and
freedom (compared to the British American colonies to the north) was
the economic system implemented by the two Iberian kingdoms in the
New World. Raw material extraction – be it precious metals or agricultural produce – became the *raison d'etre* of the Latin American colonies
(Bulmer-Thomas 1994, 22–7). Trade was severely discouraged under this
mercantilist system, and the Spanish and Portuguese monarchs went to
great lengths to ensure the colonies' isolation from any country other than
the motherland.[9] Even trade *within* the colonies was discouraged, isolating
the various population centers in the Spanish colonies from one another.
Agriculturally, Latin America was organized around the *latifundio*, a large
estate–based economy that relied heavily on coerced labor either in the
form of debt peonage of the indigenous population or African slaves.[10]
Reliance upon indigenous labor or imported slaves to work on large landholdings, coupled with policies discouraging the growth of artisan crafts

[9] It is arguable that Britain practiced mercantilist economics with respect to its colonies as
mercantilism was all the rage in the seventeenth and eighteenth century. However, the
British American colonies were more open to intracolonial trade (allowing for the creation
of an artisan industry in the New England territories and elsewhere) and foreign trade
with the French and Dutch.
[10] Technically, the *latifundio* was a grant of labor not of land, as the land remained property
of the monarch (Elliott 2006, 40–3). Interestingly, the *latifundio* system encouraged the
growth of larger and more concentrated urban centers in Spanish America than in British
America. Subsequently, the reliance on more numerous smaller townships in North America helped promote greater geographic mobility and intracolonial trade.

and manufacturing, meant that there was less of a need for immigration into Spanish America than in British America (Elliott 2006, 51; Halperín Donghi 1993, 121; Lambert 1963, 62–3).[11]

Contrast all of this with the British colonies in America that were managed by private holding companies and that could not rely on an indigenous supply of labor. Here, immigration was imperative for the economic survival of the colonies. And, as we observed in Chapter 3, the need for immigration – including skilled labor to man the artisan industries in the northern colonies – meant relegating religious homogeneity to a secondary policy position. The British king was willing to allow all sorts of religious malcontents to migrate to America so long as it meant populating the territory. Even Catholics were allowed in Maryland early on! It didn't hurt, either, that Britain at the time was a seething cauldron of growing religious diversity. The imperative for immigration meant a growing religious pluralism and a resulting pressure for toleration and liberty (see Chapter 3). Granted the predominance of the slave plantation economy of the southern British colonies resembled the *latifundio* of Latin America, but the presence of intraregional trade and migration among the Anglo American colonies (lacking in Latin America) pushed Virginia, the Carolinas, and Georgia to accept less regulatory burdens on religious minorities.[12] Had the Iberian monarchs opened Latin America to greater trade with outsiders or encouraged immigration for the development of a skilled-labor manufacturing base, religious pluralism may have developed and resulted in pressures for religious liberty. But given that Spain and Portugal were quite religiously homogenous – having resisted the Reformation – religious diversity probably would not have developed to the extent that it did in British America. When the Spanish crown did begin to allow greater intraregional trade in the latter half of the eighteenth century, there were no non-Catholics to migrate and push for tolerance and liberty. Nonetheless, the economic system put in place by the crown certainly did not help matters any.

---

[11] Elliott, in what represents a brilliant parallel analysis of British and Spanish colonial policy, notes that Spain did encourage emigration from the Motherland to the colonies, but it was more regulated than in the British colonies (2006, 51).

[12] Elliott notes that "British America was eventually to prove a far more geographically mobile society" (2006, 43). Freedom of migration among the British colonies made possible the circuit riding of George Whitefield and others during the First Great Awakening (early 1700s). This in turn prompted pressure for the deregulation of the Anglican establishments in the Southern colonies. See Chapter 3 for details. Although there certainly were people who moved between Latin American settlements, the degree of geographic mobility was substantially lower than in British America. Both geography and colonial policy played a role in this.

Independence and the Battle over Church Autonomy in the 1800s

Immediately follwing independence the Catholic Church retained its privileged position and Protestants were not lovingly embraced despite the proclamations for the separation of church and state by Simón Bolívar; not much changed during the battle for, and the immediate aftermath of, independence (ca. 1810–mid-1820s). The latter may be due to the fact that there were few Protestants to hug anyway. Significant changes in church-state relations were delayed until the 1830s at the earliest (in Venezuela) and mid-century elsewhere. One of the main reasons for this initial lack of action on matters of church and state is undoubtedly due to the immense political and economic turmoil of the independence era. Unlike the United States, which had firmly rooted colonial institutions that provided a reasonably smooth transition to a new regime,[13] most Latin American countries had to begin crafting political institutions from scratch. The wars of independence in Latin America also caused greater economic chaos than in the British colonies, further complicating the task of fashioning new governments. The ensuing battles over how to craft these institutions and who would control them occupied the minds of the elite. No major overhaul of church-state relations was proposed. Most secular leaders assumed the right of *patronato* would automatically devolve to the new republics, a faulty assumption that the Vatican did not share.

Another reason why the liberators did not immediately set about to tinker with church-state relations revolved around the issue of the Church's social influence. Irrespective of the facts that many bishops within the Latin American Catholic hierarchy were loyal to the Spanish crown (having been appointed by the king) and a significant number fled during the wars of independence, many priests within the lower ranks of the clergy joined the revolutionary cause (Bidegain 1992, 87–93). Two Mexican priests in particular – Padres Miguel Hidalgo y Costilla and José María Morelos y Pavón – rallied an army of tens of thousands to the cause of secession under the banner of the Virgin of Guadalupe (Brading 1994, 239–44). Such a potent display of clerical social power did not go unnoticed.

---

[13] I understand that the period under the Articles of Confederacy in the United States could hardly be defined as "smooth sailing." Nonetheless, each state retained its basic governing structure allowing time for the Constitutional Convention to craft a more workable blueprint. And in comparison to the political chaos following Latin American independence, the U.S. transition was undeniably smooth.

Simón Bolívar was an exception among the great leaders of Latin-American independence, for he advocated separation of Church and State [sic]. Nominally a Catholic himself,[14] the "Liberator," ... had drunk deeply of the teachings of the French philosophers and religion at best rested but lightly upon him, until the last few years of his life. Notwithstanding his liberal religious views and his unflagging efforts to have them incorporated into the organic laws of Venezuela and New Granada, Bolívar recognized the political importance of clerical support of the Revolution. No one realized better than he the strength of the hold exercised by the Church over the masses of both high and low degree. He therefore was careful not to antagonize the clergy and put aside personal opinion for the sake of the general good. For example, seeing that separation of Church and State [sic] was unacceptable, he hastened to propose that a diplomatic mission be sent to Rome to conclude a concordat with the papacy. (Mecham 1966, 45)

Moreover, Bolívar fought valiantly to forge the present-day territories of Colombia, Ecuador, and Panama into a single political entity known as Gran Colombia, an effort he later acknowledged was akin to "plowing the sea" (Halperín Donghi 1993, 93). Gaining support of the Church for his goal was crucial as it was the single cultural institution that glued these territories together (Watters 1933, 72). His battle with one-time ally Francisco de Paula Santander only strengthened his resolve to win over the clergy with seemingly nonliberal policies favoring the Church. Santander was trying to curry favor with the clergy while simultaneously control it (Mecham 1966, 90–1, 116–17). Historian Douglass Sullivan-González noted a similar tendency in the liberation of Guatemala in the 1820s, including the fear among the elite that clergymen could possibly lead a popular revolt against their rule (1998, 66–8). All of this clearly illustrated Proposition 4a that hypothesizes a single, dominant religious institution will have enhanced bargaining power when political rivalries are fierce (see Appendix).

As far as defending the Church's status as monopoly provider of religious goods and declaring Catholicism as the state religion, most secular leaders bowed to this demand in the immediate decades following independence. In part, promoting one religion was a means of retaining a single cultural identity that unified people in an era where regional factionalization threatened to tear polities apart, as noted by the failed attempts to establish a Gran Colombia and constant infighting between Mexican provinces. Simon

---

[14] Bolívar received Last Rites and made confession on his deathbed ... just in case (Mecham 1966, 97).

Collier cites Juan Egaña, an early-nineteenth-century Chilean politician, as justifying Catholic institutional hegemony on this and related points:

> 1. The multitude of religion in a single state leads to irreligion; and this is the tendency of our century. 2. Two religions in a state lead to a struggle which must terminate either in the destruction of the state or of one of the two religious parties. 3. *Religious uniformity is the most effective means of consolidating the tranquility of the great mass of the nation.* (Collier 1997, 305; emphasis added)[15]

Bolívar did not necessarily see the point of guaranteeing Catholicism exclusive domain but succumbed to what he saw as the political reality of the day. He wrote, "Knowing that the toleration of no religion except the Catholic would be admitted, I took care that nothing be said upon religion when the Constitution of Colombia was established" (cited in Watters 1935, 306). This exclusion meant that the Church kept its privileges intact.

This pattern of trying to win favor with the Catholic clergy evident early on in the Andean nations held sway elsewhere in the region.

> In the early days of the revolt [against Spain] the political practice in Latin America was to offer to Catholicism respect for its old privileges and exclusions. In the opinion of the great Argentinian constitutionalist [Juan Bautista] Alberdi, this was a tactical concession upon which the success of the Revolution depended. (Mecham 1966, 45–6)

With political secular political rivalries hot, any faction choosing to alienate a segment of the population (clergy) who could rally mass support to one side or another would represent a critical strategic blunder. That the Catholic Church was the only religious institution in the region gave it significant bargaining influence early in the emancipation process despite the ideological desires of some liberators to subvert it.

> The Catholic Church had survived such liberal designs not so much because it was strong, but because it was necessary for a religion to help in controlling social life and to fortify the moral fiber and spirituality of the new nations. Moreover, there had not been other religions that could compete with Catholicism. Had it not been for the ecclesiastical monopoly exercised by the Roman Church during the colonial period, the religious options in Latin

---

[15] Original citation Juan Egaña, *Memoria política sobre si conviene en Chile la libertad de cultos* (Lima 1827), 4. It is interesting to note that Egaña thought religious diversity would lead to the decline of religion in general, a theory common among defenders of religious monopoly and put forth academically by Peter Berger in *The Sacred Canopy* (1969). Berger (1997, 1999) has since backed away from this view.

America would have been very different. But the weight of the Hispanic heritage was much greater than the weight of rationalist ideas among the urban elite [when it came to determining church-state relations]. (Deiros 1992, 405–6)

Of added importance, leaders of the independence movements throughout the region sought official recognition from the Vatican in the hopes that the Holy See would pressure other European countries to recognize the newborn republics, a recognition that would help in their ongoing struggles against the Spanish military and also open economic opportunities for trade (Mecham 1966, 61–87).[16] Not surprisingly, even lacking top leadership the Catholic Church could count on its institutional interests to be respected during the initial power struggles in an independent Latin America in accordance with Propositions 4 and 4a (see Appendix), wherein the bargaining power of a dominant confession increases in an environment of intense political competition. All of this illustrates that despite an ideological predisposition for greater religious freedom (or anticlericalism), leaders like Bolívar chose religious policy strategically based on calculations of political self-interest and not necessarily an inherent ideological disposition.[17]

Despite a strategy to avoid intentionally provoking the Catholic episcopacy and clergy, tension did arise between Church and state related to the status of the *patronato*. For the Catholic Church, officially recognizing the break with Spain created an opportunity to regain autonomy in ecclesiastical affairs, particularly with regards to the naming of bishops. As in the colonial period, Church leaders in the new era of emancipation strongly desired maximum institutional autonomy while demanding financial support and a continued guaranteed monopoly from the state. The efforts of the Catholic Church to retain exclusive dominion over the region while simultaneously securing institutional autonomy are apparent in the workings of the Venezuelan Bishop of Mérida, Rafael Lasso de la Vega.

Curiously enough, it was through the influence of the Bishop of Mérida that Bolívar's policy of making no provision for a state church was followed in [the first] Congress. . . . [T]he primary concern of the Bishop, as he wrote Pius VII and explained at great length later in his published writings, was to secure

[16] The problem of recognition of the independent republics for the pope was complicated by Napoleon's invasion of Spain and the subsequent ascendancy of a short-lived republican legislature (the Cádiz Cortes).

[17] To restate my position on ideology, I do not deny that ideas can motivate political action. Rather, the purpose of this treatise is to demonstrate the power of interest-based behavior that motivates political decisions on regulating religion.

the recognition by the state that the exercise of the patronage should belong
to the church. By opposing a "religion of state," he hoped to bring about
the abolition of state control over the Catholic church [sic], not to establish
liberty of worship. He expected the state to uphold the exclusiveness of the
Catholic church [sic] without exercising any tuition over it. As a member of
the Congress he opposed religious toleration, the extinction of the convents,
restrictions on the privileges of the clergy, and even the abolition of the
Inquisition. (Watters 1933, 83–4)

It is clear from this passage, then, that the issue of religious freedom
throughout most of the 1800s was merely of freedom for the Church to
determine its own appointments and policy. Nonetheless, and as noted
in the preceding text, the Catholic hierarchy still sought to retain all the
material benefits and social advantages of the *patronato* – a policy that was
essentially "give us lots of resources to do what we want"[18] (cf. Castillo
Cárdenas 1968, 1/7).

Determining who had the right to nominate bishops became the most
pressing issue regarding church and state in the postcolonial era. All Latin
American bishops during the wars of independence had been appointed
by the crown and often were born in Iberia, something that put them at
odds with the revolutionary creoles.[19] Many prelates held royalist sympathies, not surprisingly, and even those that did not were often suspected of
favoring the monarchy (Salinas 1992, 298; cf. Dussel 1972, 121). For these
prelates, the prudent response was to flee at the first convenient opportunity, although with Napoleon's troops occupying much of the Iberian
Peninsula, this was not an enticing option either. Add to this the escalat-
ing age of many of the prelates and a lower life expectancy than enjoyed
today. The result was that many bishoprics were vacant in the early decades
of the 1800s (Dussel 1981, 89; Poblete 1965, 18–19). Given that bishops
had influence over the choice of priests, this meant the whole personnel
infrastructure of the Church was severely weakened. It was, in essence, an
institutional hierarchy without leadership.

Once it became apparent that the independent republics of Latin
America were here to stay, the Vatican attempted to regain its sovereignty
over the Latin American Church by declaring what it considered the
most odious portions of the *patronato* null and void (Deiros 1992, 420–5;

---

[18] This is a general policy position shared by basically every political interest group, including
public universities.

[19] Napoleon's imprisonment of Pope Pius VII, his occupation of Spain, and the claim to
governance of the liberal-dominated Cortes when King Ferdinand was in exile made it
impossible for any new bishops to be appointed during these turbulent years.

Aguilar-Monsalve 1988, 236). After all, the *patronato* had been negotiated with the Spanish (and Portuguese) monarch and no more king meant no more deal. Principally, the pope sought to reassert control over the appointments of prelates, the setting of diocesan (and parish) boundaries, and other matters of internal church policy. Of course, the Holy See still demanded that the new republics protect the Church from spiritual competitors (namely the pesky Protestants who cut into Catholic market share in Europe following the escapades of Martin Luther, John Calvin, and others), continued financial support from the state (i.e., the collecting of tithes and other sources of funding), and the preservation of the *fueros eclesiásticos* (special courts that tried clergy for criminal infractions and unbecoming behavior). Secular politicians wanted to keep the Church under their political control. Given the social influence a bishop could potentially wield, rulers wanted to pick close allies they trusted and could influence (cf. Proposition 2 in the Appendix wherein politicians attempt to gain ideological support of the populace). Not surprisingly, politicians also favored continued funding of the Catholic Church as controlling the purse strings of an institution generally meant controlling it politically.

For the most part, an implicit bargain was struck between the republics and the Vatican that kept both parties reasonably satisfied; the Church would be allowed to name bishops and the various presidents would retain an implicit veto over the appointment. So long as the pope chose noncontroversial prelates to fill vacancies, the Vatican could claim its institutional autonomy while politicians still ensured their rule would be unchallenged by activist clergy. *A priori* citizenship requirements were often mandated on the appointment of a prelate, limiting the selection to priests born in the specific country in question. In some cases, the president would recommend a number of candidates that were acceptable to the secular government (Mecham 1966, passim). Such conditions on the selection of bishops sometimes persisted well into the twentieth century (as was the case in Argentina and Colombia), but as time wore on the secular government tended to play less of a role in the process. Moreover, the situation was not as dire as one would imagine given that the Church still monopolized the supply of available clergy capable of becoming bishops; the practice of crass simony common in the Medieval Era had long past.

Despite this controversy over the *patronato*, the Church retained the majority of its privileges during the early years following independence, including its vast landholdings, special judicial status, and monopoly over marriages, funerals, and the registry. Catholicism was widely declared the official religion of the new nations, and little effort was made to ease restrictions on Protestants.[20] It was only in the 1850s that movement against this privileged position was witnessed. In part, the delay was due to incessant civil wars in many places; church-state policy simply never came up on the agenda when many national leaders lasted only months in office before being overthrown. Such intense political rivalries and the resulting instability – known as the era of the caudillos (strongmen) – favored the bargaining power of the Church and no leader sought to alienate it.[21] This is in line with Proposition 4, which hypothesizes that secular power rivalries increase the bargaining power of religious groups. But during the middle part of the century, the Church faced a serious challenge when (primarily) Liberals expropriated Church lands and other financial assets and began, albeit slowly, to deregulate the religious market by making it legal for Protestants to practice their religion freely, though often with prohibitions on proselytizing (Deiros 1992, 435–47; Mecham 1966, passim). Although this could be attributed to the ideological differences between Liberals and Conservatives (who favored the continuation of Church perquisites), the latter rarely reversed these actions when they took power.[22]

The most important factor in the expropriation of Church wealth related to the fiscal health of the state. Because the wars of independence left many national economies in shambles, national governments had to borrow abroad. Unfortunately, the inability to jump-start their economies led many governments to seek quick solutions to liquidity crises. The easiest way of raising revenue was simply to expropriate (often fallow) land from

[20] One of the most interesting examples of this was the continued ban on the sale of Bibles to the general public. Given that Protestants prompt parishioners to read the Bible directly (as opposed to hearing it interpreted only through clerical mediation), the proliferation of Bibles to the laity was considered to be the first step toward a "Latin American Reformation."

[21] An early attempt to limit the judicial powers of the Church in Mexico resulted in a revolt that replaced the executive in short order. See Gill (1999c, 767–8).

[22] A growing political divide between Liberals and Conservatives dominated the latter half of the nineteenth century in Latin America. Liberals – supposedly influenced by European Enlightenment thought – favored urban interests and (ironically) preferred a more federalist form of government, while Conservatives tended to be centralists that represented rural interests. In reality, however, both Liberals and Conservatives shared similar economic interests in promoting free trade (Halperín Donghi 1993, 119). The primary focus of economic conflict between these two factions revolved around how heavily the countryside would be taxed to support urban growth. This generally left religious policy as the key differentiating feature between the two parties, with Conservatives being more "Church-friendly." Beyond this, the Liberal-Conservative divide really reflected conflicts over the access to personal power.

the Catholic Church, the largest landholder in the region.[23] This land was sold to private interests, raising immediate cash.[24] And this is not an inconsequential motive in the early and middle part of the nineteenth century. Throughout Latin America, the first two or three decades following independence were marked by civil unrest, if not outright civil war. With no continuity of leadership or extensive experience with self-governing (like in the British American colonies), various caudillos attempted to take power by force. Upon taking power, these caudillos often found that the government was bankrupt and had little money with which to pay the troops who had helped them win power, a situation that often led various military leaders to shift alliances and thus begin the process of civil unrest anew. By mid-century political leaders quickly learned that raising cash fast to pay the military and other public officials was of critical importance. Mary Holleran, in her study of Guatemalan church-state relations in the 1800s, nicely summarizes the situation for most of the region.

> [P]olitical leaders of the time were not indifferent to the possessions of the religious which might help to replenish a sorely depleted treasury and maintain the army which was helping keep them in power. (1949, 100)[25]

In addition to selling off many of the assets, the government converted several church edifices into governmental buildings including schools, prisons, and mental asylums (Holleran 1949, 59).

Raising funds to pay off public servants wasn't the only financial reason motivating the expropriations at this time. During the early part of the century, many governments took to borrowing money from both private citizens and foreign governments to finance the government. It became difficult to repay these loans with economic growth slow in coming to a region wracked by political instability. Nationalizing church wealth was an easy means of raising the necessary funds to pay back these loans without alienating important political clients.

---

[23] Although the crown had given the Church large land grants during the colonial period, a substantial portion of Church property came from bequeaths and gifts from private citizens. Some of this property included real estate in cities (Holleran 1949, 52).

[24] This is not unlike the strategy surrounding privatization of parastatals during the debt crisis of the 1980s, except that in the 1800s, the state essentially stole the assets that they then privatized. Henry VIII in England and Gustav I in Sweden pursued similar policies under related conditions.

[25] See also Williams (1920). Given the relative poverty of Central America, expropriations tended to come earlier than in Mexico or the Andean states.

> In Colombia ... the radicals were thinking especially in terms of retiring the public debt. In fact on the same day as disamortization, September 9, 1861, General Mosquera [Colombia's caudillo ruler] issued another decree on the public debt which was closely related to the other measure [confiscation of Church property]; the fact that both were issued on the same date was doubtless not simply a coincidence. The proceeds from the sale of the confiscated property were earmarked expressly for the reduction of the internal debt. (Knowlton 1969, 392)

In addition to raising revenue to pay off debt in the short run, selling Church assets to individuals who would make productive use of those assets meant the government created a source of tax revenue in the long run.

Other ecclesiastical revenue streams were also expropriated; for example, the secularization of marriage and funeral services provided a constant (albeit small) source of revenue for local governments because those public officials could charge fees to perform such services, just as clergy had done. The national registry – an important list of births, deaths, marriages, and property ownership – was also taken away from the Catholic Church, giving the state an important bookkeeping apparatus for the purposes of taxation. Opposition from Conservatives to these attacks on the dominant religious institution was probably based more on this material interest than on a burning passion to please the Vatican because they generally objected to any policy that would increase taxation on land. That Conservatives were not quick to yield these privileges back to the Church once they gained power indicates how interests could trump ideology; Conservative rulers benefited just as much from the expropriated Church wealth and functions as the Liberals did. In all these instances, the opportunity cost of continued support for the Catholic Church was a major financial crisis and the possibility of invasion by foreign creditors for failure to pay back debt.[26]

The Liberals' expropriation of Church property and functions during the mid-nineteenth century was accompanied by a significant amount of anticlerical rhetoric. Liberal reformers generally said they were enacting such policies to save Catholicism from a corrupt clergy (Bastian 1992, 319; Powell 1977, 301). References to Enlightenment thinking and the French *philosophes* were also used to justify the "separation of church and state" (Deiros 1992, passim; Mecham 1966, passim). Bishops tended to find allies among Conservative politicians, who were of a more "regal" (i.e., not liberal) mind-set. All of this would naturally lead to the conclusion that ideology

---

[26] France did invade and occupy Mexico during the 1860s for failure to make good on outstanding loans.

played a significant causal role in attacks against the Church. But several things must be remembered. First, even though Liberal politicians talked about separation of church and state, they mostly desired continued control over the ecclesiastical hierarchy by way of the *patronato* (cf. Williams 1920, 122). Although one could argue that they sought to preserve this power as a means of reforming the Church from within, it was more likely that they sought to place their closest allies in positions of social power.[27] Second, the major expropriations of Church wealth tended to come during times of fiscal crisis for the state. Third, the Liberal-Conservative divide became more volatile following land expropriations (Knowlton 1969). When Liberals amortized clerical property, they generally sold it to their political allies and most Conservatives did not gain.[28] The entry of more agricultural land onto the market meant that the economic rents of current *hacendados*, who were generally Conservatives, would be chipped away. Financial self-interest (not necessarily ideology) dictated that Conservatives would seek to prevent this action and, thus, had a strong incentive to ally with the Church in its struggle. Seeing Conservatives join forces with the clergy then provoked Liberals to intensify their attacks on the Church because it was a means of weakening their political rivals (see Proposition 4b regarding a religious group's limited bargaining power when institutionally connected to a secular party). Finally, in regions where the Church lacked significant assets, the attacks on the Church tended to be less severe – most notably in the Southern Cone countries of Argentina, Chile, and Uruguay. Although the Argentine government of Martín Rodríguez (under the guidance of then-minister and later-president Bernardino Rivadavia) did seize Church property, it was neither nearly as extensive nor as violent as it was in Mexico or Colombia (Mecham 1966, 226–7).

The conflict that ensued from the expropriation of Church lands and prerogatives eventually subsided by the end of the century. For the most part, the Church did not suffer immensely from its loss of its estates because much of the land was unproductive in their hands anyway. The loss of buildings was a bit more difficult to swallow, but the ongoing scarcity of

[27] A test of this hypothesis would entail collecting the proposed nominations of secular politicians for various ecclesiastical posts and then tracking the personal linkages between the appointees and appointers, a task beyond the broader scope of this study. It would undoubtedly make for an interesting graduate thesis in history, sociology, or political science.

[28] Conservatives did not benefit from the direct sale of land. They did, however, benefit from the revenue streams that such expropriations generated when they later were to take political power.

clergy and other Church personnel (Poblete 1965) needed to manage this property eased the pain of this defeat. The loss of revenue from marriage and funeral ceremonies was equally painful, but, as history has shown, the Catholic Church did find a way to survive these tribulations. The reason for this was due in part to a series of concordats that were negotiated between the Holy See and various national governments between roughly 1850 and 1900 (Deiros 1992, 458–9).[29] These agreements generally gave the Church the primary authority to appoint bishops albeit under the advisement of the national government, allowed for some degree of state support for the Church, and continued to make it difficult for non-Catholics to spread in the region. Although not ideal from the vantage point of the clergy, these concordats became an acceptable *modus vivendi*, a term frequently used by both parties to denote the new "live and let live" relations between church and state. All of this had the effect of reducing tensions between church and state (Auza 1966, 8/9). Even in nations that did not formally negotiate a concordat (e.g., Mexico), tensions between church and state abated by century's end. A number of nations (e.g., Brazil in 1889 and Chile in 1925), ostensibly declared a separation of church and state, although the Catholic Church retained significant advantages in relation to non-Catholics.[30] In terms of the regulation of religion, by the end of the nineteenth century the Church had generally succeeded in gaining its own decision-making autonomy – an issue of "religious freedom" from the vantage point of one institution. Catholic hierarchs also maintained a moderate level of state support (compared to the colonial past) in most countries. Religious liberty had yet to affect non-Catholics in a serious way. The struggle for religious minorities to obtain equal rights in Latin America became the story of the twentieth century.

Before moving on to the issue of liberty for religious minorities, it is worth mentioning that the Catholic Church continued to seek greater political and social influence during the 1900s. In the early decades of the century, one of the Catholic Church's primary objectives was to rebuild its institutional position relative to the state. One strategy was to strengthen its pastoral outreach among the elite with programs such as Catholic Action that sought to imbue middle- and upper-class children (likely to be the

---

[29] The Vatican continued to renegotiate some of these concordats throughout the 1900s.

[30] E.g., until 2000 the Chilean Catholic Church had a higher legal standing than Protestant churches. The former was legally considered a public institution while the latter were viewed as the equivalent of private clubs (Moreno 1996, 224). This special designation provided Catholic clergy with preferential access to public hospitals, prisons, and the military.

politicians of the future) with strong Catholic values. In an attempt to counter the growing influence of socialist labor unions and political groups, bishops pursued a similar strategy among the working class (Gill 1998, 96–8). With the issues of the *patronato* and property now resolved for all intents and purposes, the Church did see some interesting successes in some countries, illustrating some of the theoretical propositions discussed in Chapter 3, namely that dominant religions often have significant political bargaining power (Propositions 4 and 4a).

In Argentina and Brazil, where the Church had largely been relegated to the sidelines during the first several decades of the twentieth century, Catholic bishops were able to use their social influence during a period of political turmoil to leverage a series of favorable policies. These new privileges included allowing clergy to teach Catholicism in public schools, recognition of religious marriages, increased funding from the state, and laws that made it difficult for Protestants groups to proselytize in society (Lubertino Beltrán 1987, 37–40; Williams 1976, 454–6; Pierson 1974, 177; Canclini 1972, 57–9). The growing influence of the Church followed on the heels of military interventions that displaced elected regimes – Brazil (1930) and Argentina (1943) – and put into power populist leaders – Getúlio Vargas and Juan Perón, respectively. In the case of Brazil, the central Church leader, Cardinal Dom Leme organized a series of mass demonstrations to illustrate the mobilizing power of the Church and then formed an electoral league to keep pressure on national legislatures (Williams 1976, 448–50). What is interesting about this situation is how strategic calculations played a role in the decision of Vargas and his supporters in the legislature to yield to the Church's demands and give them a more favorable position in the new 1934 constitution. Cardinal Leme previously had lobbied the national legislature in the 1920s for similar privileges, but his efforts ended in failure because of fierce opposition from the governor of the populous and powerful state of Rio Grande do Sul – Getúlio Vargas – a publicly avowed atheist who had the audacity to name his two children Luther and Calvin! However, after losing the presidential election of 1930 and then being swept into power by a military coup shortly thereafter, Vargas was in a tenuous political position and saw that appeasing the Church could bolster his popular support in a time of great political uncertainty (Serbin 1995; Williams 1976, 456; Bello 1966, 283–95). Cardinal Leme and the bishops helped their case further by acting as mediators between opposing parties during the coup. Illustrating how the government benefited at the time (in line with Proposition 2), Williams states that Vargas's "regime maintained broad-based support or at least minimized overt hostility by borrowing freely from Catholic rhetoric, by highlighting its close ties to the church and Catholic traditions, and by seemingly acquiring sacred sanctions of its activities ... and cost the government very little" (1976, 457).

A similar situation occurred a little more than a decade later in Argentina. Again, on the heels of a military coup, the new government found itself in a rather shaky situation with regards to public perception of its legitimacy. Given the tenuous nature of the initial military administration and the conflictive rise of Juan Perón (Crassweller 1987, 99–114), it was natural to reach out to a major cultural institution for moral support during the regime's period of consolidation. Though not a devout Catholic, Perón realized that a continued embrace of the Church yielded substantial political benefits. In a speech on June 28, 1944, Perón was quick to make the connection between "the Gospel and the sword" (Lubertino Beltrán 1987, 35). Church support for Perón was reinforced during the national campaign of 1945 when "all the bishops and archbishops prohibited Catholics from voting for a candidate who supported the separation of Church and State [sic], laicism in education and legalized divorce, all policies in the platform of the Democratic Union [Perón's rivals in the election]" (Lubertino Beltrán 1987, 36).[31] In a country where roughly 95 percent of the population was Catholic (though substantially less were devout), episcopal endorsement provided a significant moral advantage in political competition.

The Church's bargaining power increased dramatically with this support and Perón granted them all manner of financial subsidies, access to public schools and hospitals, and – not insignificantly – protection from Protestant competition. The latter restriction on the religious freedom of non-Catholics included such extreme measures as a ban on Protestant radio broadcasting, the creation of a government agency to monitor religious minorities, prohibitions on ministering to the small indigenous population and restrictions on property ownership (D'Amico 1977; Canclini 1972). Ironically, as Perón became more entrenched in power he felt less of a need to bow to Church demands, and in the last two years of his regime conflict arose between the unions and youth groups that he was trying to control and the ones that the Catholic Church was sponsoring, leading to the regime taking oppressive action against the Church and forcing them into the camp of the opposition (Marsal 1955).

---

[31] Although the armed forces came to power in a coup in 1943, and Perón was a member of the army, elections were held in 1945 with Perón receiving the implicit endorsement of the military establishment. The extent to which this and subsequent elections during the Perón era were free and fair is up for substantial debate; many see Perón as a heroic populist while others consider him an oppressive tyrant (cf. Crassweller 1987).

In both the Brazilian and Argentine cases, one of the major demands of the Catholic Church was to restrict non-Catholic religions (predominantly Protestant)[32] from working freely in the country. As noted earlier, the major battles over "religious freedom" in the nineteenth century involved the Catholic Church attempting to gain its own institutional autonomy. Although this may not strike the average person as a matter of "religious liberty," it did involve the freedom of Catholic clergy to run their organization as best they saw fit without state intervention. Recall that the definition of *religious liberty* laid out earlier defined the concept as one of government regulation. Any law or policy limiting the ability of a religious organization to pursue its goals is considered an infringement on religious liberty, and the desire of secular governors to exercise the *patronato* over the Church certainly is such an infringement.[33] Of course, as we saw, the Latin American Church continued demanding state financial support and restrictions upon other faiths, both of which qualify as limitations on religious liberty. Without much of a Protestant presence in the nineteenth century, freedom for non-Catholics was not of major concern for policy makers. But by the next century, the issue of religious freedom for minorities began to take center stage, an issue we shall now consider in greater depth before examining the interesting case of Mexico.

The Emergence of Religious Freedom for Minorities

As put forth in Proposition 1 (see Appendix), hegemonic religions will prefer to keep new religions from entering a market. This certainly was high on the agenda of the Catholic Church from colonial times onward, particularly because they had lost ground to Protestants in Europe. The rise of liberal politicians proclaiming separation of church and state and religious liberty created some apprehension among the clergy as to how successful they might be in protecting their state-guaranteed monopoly. The preceding discussion, however, revealed that the rhetoric of separation of church and state and religious liberty seldom matched with reality as politicians sought to exercise extensive control over the main religious institution – the Catholic Church. Episcopal appointments and property issues dominated the religiopolitical arena for most of the nineteenth century. The lack

---

[32] Interestingly, Cardinal Leme in Brazil actually helped pass a bill allowing for Jewish refugees to settle in Brazil during the Second World War II (Williams 1976, 454).

[33] This may get us into the area of semantics, but I do acknowledge that the Vatican originally agreed to the terms of the *patronato* of its own free will, in essence making this a voluntary restriction on the Church's own liberty in order to get certain benefits in return.

of other faiths, thanks to exclusionary colonial policies, meant that religious liberty for non-Catholics would be of secondary importance (Collier 1997, 305).[34] Nonetheless, "secondary importance" did not mean "no importance." The issue did arise following emancipation, and the limited actions taken early on did have a long-term impact in the cultivation of religious diversity and eventual liberty.

As with the United States, economic trade and immigration became the primary motivation that provided some freedom of maneuver for religious minorities. Following separation from Spain and Portugal, local entrepreneurs drooled over the prospects of expanded markets for their goods.[35] The United States and northern Europe offered the most attractive markets, and both regions were primarily Protestant in orientation. Attracting merchants from these countries meant not locking them up or otherwise persecuting them for practicing a different religion, a lesson learned earlier in colonial British America. Simply put, persecuting merchants is bad trade policy. Most countries were tolerant of Protestants worshiping on their shores so long as they didn't proselytize and worshiped discretely in inauspicious buildings (Winn 1970, 297). But, "even though a non-Catholic foreigner was legally entitled to enjoy the benefits of the protection of his rights, in civil life he suffered fierce ostracism and onerous social pressures because of Catholic mentalities moulded [sic] by three centuries of the colonial Inquisition" (Bastian 1992, 320).

The connection between religious liberty and trade was reinforced by outsiders. Having just gone through emancipation from a colonial power, and understanding the importance of linking economic growth to freedom of conscience, policy makers in the young United States attempted to write guarantees of religious liberty into mercantile treaties with different countries. Various U.S. political leaders in the 1820s and 1830s, including secretaries of state and presidents, considered religious freedom for North American traders and professors who resided in Latin America to be an essential component of any treaty (Bastian 1992, 320; Winn 1970, 1972).

---

[34] Technically speaking, colonial Latin America was not entirely a "Protestant-free zone." The Dutch were able to set up some outposts in northern Brazil and allowed religious freedom, as they did in New Amsterdam. A few other minor exceptions existed, primarily in the Caribbean (Bastian 1992, 314–16).

[35] Commercial trade between Spanish America and the British American colonies and northern Europe existed as far back as the sixteenth century due to Spain's inability to effectively police the waters of the Caribbean (Elliott 2006, 226). However, legal and normalized trade with these Protestant regions was greatly expanded following emancipation as the risks of commerce were reduced with Spain's absence. Pirates still sailed the waters, though.

This was general policy in the United States that applied not only to Latin America but also to Europe. And many of these treaties were based on precedents established by treaties negotiated between Britain, Germany, and various Latin American nations, including Mexico, Colombia, and Brazil (Winn 1970, 297). Although effort was applied to craft strong guarantees of religious freedom, the Catholic Church still held sway in many places resulting in limited versions of the initial proposals. Foreign Protestants were allowed to worship freely, but they were not permitted to spread their version of the Gospel. One of the more creative ways to ensure this was to prohibit Protestant services from being said in Spanish (Collier 1997, 305). *No habla español, no hay conversión.* This was an interesting balancing act for Latin American politicians – to serve their economic interests while placating the social influence of the dominant religion, a situation that shows Propositions 3 and 4a working in conjunction to produce a highly conditional policy of religious freedom.

Chile, the country that perhaps had the most effective law allowing for freedom of religion, happened to be the least accessible country to foreign trade. In 1828, Chile made it illegal to persecute people based on their faith. "It was a standard policy of Chilean governments to maximize overseas trade, and foreigners occupied the dominant position in the import-export houses that sprang up in Valparaiso and elsewhere; it therefore was necessary to handle foreigner's religious sentiments with some care. Guarantees of freedom of worship for foreign nationals were written into commercial treaties concluded with the United States (1833), France (1852), and Britain (1855)" (Collier 1997, 310). Throughout the 1800s, freedoms for Protestants were gradually expanding, including allowing them to maintain their own cemetery and build their own private schools (Sepúlveda 1987, 248). A similar pattern connecting economic trade and religious freedom for foreigners occurred in Argentina (Gill 1998, 152).

Whereas attracting immigrants provided a partial impetus for relaxing regulations on religious dissenters in colonial British America, immigration was not as strong of an impulse in Latin America. It did exist nonetheless. For instance, in Venezuela "[b]y act of Congress (February 18, 1834) freedom of all religious sects was decreed. This action was intended primarily to encourage foreign non-Catholic immigration" (Mecham 1966, 100). Not surprisingly, the nations that were most open to religious freedom – notably Argentina, Brazil, Chile, and Uruguay – were also the least populated, the most in need of immigrants and most desirous of free trade. Chile in particular, given its relatively inaccessible location on the Pacific side of the continent, sought both free trade and immigration and willingly

accommodated Protestants beginning as early as 1818 against the desires of
the Catholic hierarchy (Gill 1998, 130–1). In later decades, Liberal politicians would sometimes seek ways to encourage Protestant migration as a
means of punishing the Church for their alliance with Conservative interests (Considine 1958, 236–7); however Protestantism – particularly the
evangelizing variety – did not become a major social presence until the
mid-twentieth century.

For the most part, Protestantism in Latin America remained an ethnic
immigrant religion until roughly the 1930s.[36] Migrants from Britain, the
United States, Germany, and elsewhere practiced their faith without seeking to spread it to the native population. Missionary work was quite limited
with members of an evangelical conference in Edinburgh in 1910 rejecting
the region as a mission field (Pierson 1974, 87; Considine 1958, 239–40).
Nonetheless, some dissenters set about their own path to demonstrate that
Latin America was ripe for evangelization at their own conference several years later in Cincinnati. Beginning in the late 1910s, Protestant missionaries began to trickle in to the region, little noticed at first given the
general lack of Catholic clergy to sound the alarm bells (Hurtado [1941]
1992; Poblete 1965). Success came to these missionaries a few decades later
as their proselytizing movement became indigenized – spreading not by
foreigners per se but by encouraging local resident to become evangelical
ministers (Considine 1958, 239–43). The closing of the Asian mission fields
in the 1930s due to war led many foreign missionaries to turn their attention to Latin America and embrace the indigenizing strategy pioneered
by earlier missionaries in Brazil and Chile (Gill 1998, 131). The countries
with the greatest degree of religious freedom tended to witness the greatest
growth in non-Catholic religions – most notably Brazil, Chile, Nicaragua,
and El Salvador (Gill 1999a).[37] The expansion of Protestantism – particularly an evangelical and Pentecostal style – shifted the issue of religious
liberty away from one merely dealing with the rights and privileges of the
Catholic Church to one that encompassed all denominations. Pressures by

---

[36] We could include into this mix the smattering of Jews and Muslims that had migrated
to the region, but their numbers were so small as to not make a significant impact on
subsequent developments in religious freedom.

[37] As we shall see in the following text, this did not include Mexico, which had made religious
organizations illegal in its 1917 Constitution. The inability of religions to own property made it near impossible for new denominations to set up shop. In several Central
American countries where the United States had significant influence – namely El Salvador, Nicaragua, and Panama – the governments were willing to yield to demands from
Washington, DC, to open their religious markets to Protestants. Seeking the benefits
that agreement with U.S. policy conveyed on these governments, politicians predictably
opened their markets in line with Proposition 3.

religious minorities for greater freedoms increased as religious denominational diversity grew.

In response to the growing number of Protestants, the Catholic Church sought numerous legal remedies – from attempts to deny visas to foreign missionaries to requests to deny Protestant radio broadcasters licenses to operate. Efforts to restrict property ownership for Protestant churches were also made. And Catholic clergy also enlisted local governments to criminalize posting audio speakers outside of buildings or engaging in religious parades on Sundays, two favored Pentecostal tactics for attracting worshipers to their rather exuberant services (Gill 1999b). Municipal governments where a priest had a great deal of political influence were the most likely to succeed in these tactics. However, national politicians – particularly those secure in their political tenure – were less willing to restrict Protestant activities. This fits with Propositions 5 and 5a, which hypothesize that secular rulers will become more lax in enforcing restrictions on religious minorities considering that such restrictions often entail high enforcement costs. After all, Protestant missionaries (and their indigenous counterparts) often provided much needed economic and social services to poor communities – such as irrigation and literacy projects – at no expense to the government. Tossing out individuals who provided these public goods simply would not be a rational policy, particularly if the Catholic Church could not guarantee any significant political support in return.

In a few cases, the Catholic Church did succeed in catching the ear of politicians; most notably the cases of Argentina and Brazil during the eras of Perón and Vargas, respectively (see preceding text). Perón, in return for support from the Catholic hierarchy, made life substantially more difficult for Protestants by prohibiting their access to radio, forbidding evangelization among the indigenous population, and restricting their ability to construct or rent buildings (Canclini 1972). When the Catholic Church pulled its support from Perón and supported the military coup that toppled him, upper-level clergy became closely identified with anti-Peronist forces within the armed forces, a strategic mistake that they would eventually regret. In the subsequent periods of military rule (1966–73 and 1976–83), the generals returned the favor of support by essentially banning a number of "marginal" Protestant groups (e.g., Jehovah's Witnesses) and making it difficult for other evangelical denominations – largely classified as "sects" – from conducting operations (Marostica 1998, 46; Moreno 1996, 207; Foreign Broadcast Information Services 1979, 1978).

In Brazil, the Catholic Church was able to convince President Vargas from issuing visas for Protestant missionaries in the 1940s in exchange for political support. This action had little effect, however, as Protestants already had a significant foothold, and Vargas wasn't all that committed to the Catholic Church once he secured his power base and expelling the already growing mass of indigenous Protestants would prove logistically infeasible (Proposition 5a). His primary motivation for restricting Protestant entry was to gain bargaining leverage with the United States over Brazil's late entry into World War II (Pierson 1974, 177). The period known as *La Violencia* in Colombia (c. 1948–58) provided the Catholic Church with significant bargaining leverage to counter Protestant advances. For the Catholic bishops' part in helping to bring about a political truce between the Liberal and Conservative parties, the military government that took power in 1953 negotiated a concordat with the Vatican that effectively made Protestantism illegal in 75 percent of the nation's territory (Goff 1968, 3/27–36).[38] In the case of Argentina and Colombia, where the Catholic Church was able to obtain favors from governments seeking legitimacy, Protestant growth was significantly stunted relative to neighboring countries.

Despite efforts of the Catholic Church to hold back the rising tide of Protestantism, religious diversity increased steadily in the region, especially in countries that maintained relatively liberal laws (Gill 1999a).[39] During the authoritarian regimes that dominated the region from the 1960s to the 1980s, Protestants remained relatively quiet, preferring to keep to themselves and focus on matters of spirituality. This strategy of focusing solely on spiritual issues gave them a reputation for being apologetic toward authoritarianism (cf. Ireland 1993).[40] In a few instances where the Catholic

[38] Although it may not seem the Church did a good job in negotiating a truce in 1953 given that "the violence" continued until 1958, the situation was that the main political parties agreed to cease hostilities while some breakaway organizations from each side continued hostilities. The Catholic Church and other political leaders became disillusioned with the Rojas Pinilla dictatorship lasting from 1953–7 and supported the National Pact between the Liberals and Conservatives, which divided up power between the two previously competing parties (Halperín Donghi 1993, 284).

[39] There is a common notion among academics that Protestantism "exploded" on to the Latin American scene beginning in the 1980s. This may be due to David Martin – an acclaimed sociologist of religion – who entitled his book on the subject *Tongues of Fire: The Explosion of Protestantism in Latin America*. In reality, however, Protestantism has been expanding at a relatively steady pace, which through the miracles of compound interest can appear as if it "exploded" from nowhere in roughly five or six decades (cf. Stark 1996, 3–28). Scholars largely overlooked the trend given their ideological bias favoring liberation theology, which had its heyday in the 1970s but fizzled by the late 1980s (Gill 2002b). To his credit, David Martin does note the important contributions of two scholars who noticed the Protestant trend as early as the 1960s and published significant, albeit overlooked, works on the topic (Lalive d'Epinay 1969; Willems 1967).

[40] Protestants associated with the World Council of Churches tended to be critical of the Latin American military regimes, though these mainline churches were not the ones witnessing

Church came out publicly against the military, some Protestant groups were rewarded. This occurred most notably in Chile when Augusto Pinochet's dictatorial regime awarded a group of evangelical ministers with a brand new church building, financial aid, and privileged access to government officials (Fleet and Smith 1997, 177; Smith 1982, 313). Where the Catholic Church became associated with the resistance to authoritarianism, Protestants could largely be guaranteed of being left alone.[41] This is predicted by Proposition 4b wherein a religious group that is institutionally associated with a secular party will not receive much support from that party's secular rival. But in a general climate where freedom did not prevail, these religious minorities generally tempered their requests for greater freedom.

When democracy returned to the region beginning in the 1980s, a new opportunity to lobby for religious freedom presented itself. By the late 1980s, Protestants in most countries were significant enough in number to have an impact on newly competitive elections. Evangelical Protestants who were once perceived of as apolitical began to organize and lobby for greater religious liberty, in line with the predictions of Proposition 1 (religious minorities prefer greater liberty) and Proposition 4 (political competition is beneficial to religious minorities). Although still small in number, Protestants could have a dramatic impact on electoral contests that were tight. The classic case of this occurred in Peru where dark horse candidate Alberto Fujimori won the presidency thanks in large part to the support of an evangelical voting bloc that supported him in the first round of elections in 1990 (Klaiber 1999, 264–6). His campaign staff included a number of prominent evangelicals, and during the course of his ten-year administration, various legal restrictions on Protestants were loosened giving them equal legal status to the Catholic Church.

In Argentina, the Catholic Church emerged from the dictatorial era with a tarnished reputation for having cooperated with an exceedingly brutal military rule (Mignone 1988). However, thanks to restrictive registration laws enacted during the various military regimes, Protestants remained a relatively small portion of the population. During the 1990s, though, a number of evangelical groups have started to organize and pressure the

expansive growth in the region. It was the Pentecostals, Mormons, and Evangelicals that were making the most progress and staying out of the political fray.

[41] As my previous book (Gill 1998) argues, the growth of Protestantism was a key causal factor in prompting the Catholic Church to take up a "preferential option for the poor" and, as a means of winning back credibility among the poor, to oppose military dictatorships. Where Protestant competition among the poor was most intense, the Catholic Church was more responsive to the needs of the poor in an effort to "re-Catholicize" them.

government for greater freedoms.[42] Marostica estimates that "more than one million people joined [evangelical] churches" in the first several years following the last military regime (1998, 45). A greater environment of religious freedom initiated by civilian President Raúl Alfonsín certainly helped to spur this growth in non-Catholic denominations.[43] Fearing a decline in its social influence, the Catholic Church fought back and encouraged politicians to enact tough restrictions on non-Catholic religions including onerous registration requirements that would make it nearly impossible for new and smaller evangelical groups to gain official status (as predicted by Proposition 1) (Marostica 1998, 48). Catholic prelates have attempted to use scandals involving some fringe cults to broadly paint all evangelical Protestant groups as dangerous to society (Frigerio 1993). Through intensified lobbying efforts, the evangelical churches were able to block many of these initiatives. Their physical numbers being still small, the victories have been slow in coming in the political arena as politicians still consider the Catholic Church to be the overwhelming religious actor in society. Nonetheless, since the early 1990s, Argentina has officially separated church and state (although the Catholic Church still receives public funds)[44] and rules requiring the president and vice president be Catholics were eliminated from the constitution (Bonino 1999, 196–203; Moreno 1996, 207–8). Although the political power of evangelical groups has been slow in developing – partially because they are small in number but also because the turbulent political environment in Argentina has provided little time for politicians to take up minor religious reforms – it can be expected that Protestants will continue to make gains toward a status equal to that of Catholicism in the years to come.

Although Colombia technically has not experienced a dictatorship since the 1950s when General Gustavo Rojas Pinilla led a military coup, the "National Front" arrangement to share power between the Liberal and Conservative parties acted as a significant brake on political competition. By the 1970s, this arrangement began to break down and real political rivalries reemerged. During this time evangelical Protestants continued to expand and by the late 1980s several had decided to enter the political

---

[42] Author interviews with members of the Consejo Nacional Evangélico – Eduardo Recio, Juan Passeulo, Emilio Monti, and Noberto Burton – Buenos Aires, November 19, 1996.
[43] Author interview with Angel Centeno, Subminister of Religion, Buenos Aires, November 18, 1996.
[44] Technically speaking, the military government of Juan Onganía reached an agreement to officially terminate the *patronato* in 1968, the last Latin American country to do so. The 1994 constitutional reforms made this agreement with the Vatican official.

arena. With only a short time to organize a political party, the evangelical Christian Union Party – a collection of various evangelical Protestant groups seeking a say in politics – scored a surprising victory in the 1990 election when one of their candidates won the sixth highest number of votes and, through electoral rules, gained an additional seat in the National Constitutional Assembly (Brusco 1999, 250). The representatives of the Christian Union played a significant role in pushing for and achieving a formal separation of church and state in the new 1991 constitution that resulted from the Assembly. With this monumental change in the constitution, the Colombian attorney general declared that the concordat signed with the Vatican in 1953 (see preceding text) was illegal (Brusco 1999, 251). Protestants finally earned the recognition to proselytize freely throughout the country. In one of Latin America's most staunchly Catholic nations, politicians could not help but take notice of the growing clout of a highly unified Protestant bloc. "When a rumor spread during the Colombian presidential elections in 1994 that the Liberal Party candidate, Ernesto Samper Pizano, had secretly promised to name a Protestant as his education minister, the archbishop of Bucaramanga, using language reminiscent of the 1950s, called on Catholic Liberals to cast blank ballots in the election." However, when Samper refused to back down from such threats and stood up for the rights of religious minorities "a dozen Colombian intellectuals, including the Nobel laureate Gabriel García Márquez, released a manifesto for religious freedom" (Brusco 1999, 251). Samper, himself a Catholic by birth, clearly realized the important role that the evangelical voting bloc could play in a tight electoral contest. The success of various evangelical candidates in the legislative elections a year earlier indicated that even though Catholic bishops may have been wary of Protestants, the general population viewed them with some degree of favor; the electoral advantage among a Protestant voting bloc that was intensely interested in issues of religious freedom would outweigh any loss of votes from Catholics who at worst appeared largely indifferent to the issue. Political calculation in an increasingly competitive electoral environment once again prompted changes favorable to freedom of conscience.

To the south in Chile, similar political pressure netted advances in religious freedom. Although Chile has had one of the longest and most liberal regimes regulating religious freedom, there were some arenas where Protestants were excluded due to a technical difference in their legal status relative to the Catholic Church. Unlike the Chilean Catholic Church, which was considered a public entity in the eyes of the law, Protestant churches were categorized equivalent to private clubs (similar to a soccer team). This legal designation meant that Protestant pastors were excluded from ministering to prison inmates, members of the military, and within state-run hospitals. Although such exclusions may seem trivial to outsiders, it was significant enough to Protestants to prompt a growing movement during the 1990s to change the law.[45] In 1999, a major demonstration before the national legislature in Valparaiso caught the attention of lawmakers who nearly unanimously voted to change the law and give religious minorities a legal status equal to that of the Catholic Church.[46] In other countries such as Brazil and El Salvador, the willingness of Protestants to enter politics and run for office has led to significant gains in deregulating the religious market in a way favorable to Protestants (Chesnut 2003, 98–9; Freston 1993).

To summarize, the establishment of religious freedom for non-Catholics has been a long two-century struggle in Latin America. Economic concerns regarding trade and, to a lesser extent, immigration did prompt a limited legal acceptance of Protestants in several countries. However, a general lack of proselytizing zealotry until the 1930s meant Protestant immigrants would remain cloistered in ethnic enclaves. The debate about how religion should be regulated at this time largely revolved around the status, perquisites, and public funding of the Catholic Church. Generally, the Catholic Church survived a variety of assaults on its property and privileges with a privileged status in society. Despite a supposed liberal mind-set that tended to permeate the region during the nineteenth century, numerous restrictions made it difficult for Protestants to preach their brand of Christianity. Politicians were less concerned with promoting a broad-based religious liberty for a diverse set of believers than they were with politically controlling a major social actor, the Catholic Church.

Nonetheless, governments allowed enough freedom in several nations that evangelical Protestants could begin expanding unnoticed in the first half of the twentieth century. With political leaders unwilling to take actions against Protestants who were not much of a social problem – and who could arguably be viewed as a social asset in that they promoted literacy

[45] It is interesting to note that although the dictatorship of Augusto Pinochet offered favors to certain Protestant groups during the 1970s and 1980s (Gill 1998, 143–4), his regime never saw fit to change this law. It was only under a competitive political regime that this significant change was accomplished. The competitive nature of democratic governance is one of the prime engines that promotes civil rights for minorities.

[46] This information comes from a series of interviews that I conducted in Santiago in June 2000 that included Protestant and Catholic activists such as Francisco Anabalón, David Muñoz Condell, Timothy Greenfield, Lee Iverson, and Renato Poblete. See Durán (2000) for a discussion of the new law. For the Catholic reaction to this law, consult Cortínez Castro (1999, 2000).

and community projects – the evangelical movement grew exponentially in the countries with the most tolerant laws toward religious minorities, namely Brazil, Chile, El Salvador, Guatemala, and Nicaragua. In some cases – namely Argentina and Colombia – Catholic bishops were able to convince governments to make life more difficult for evangelizing Protestants by cooperating with secular rulers in times of trouble.[47] Even then, the spectre of Communism and other threatening insurgencies meant these governments, secure in power, would not devote a great deal of attention to weeding out a Protestant population that largely kept to themselves; religious diversity continued to expand. Again, this illustrates Propositions 5, 5a, and 5b wherein over time government will become less concerned with enforcing restrictions on religious minorities, and the result will be the growth of religious pluralism. The real opening for religious liberty came when Latin America began to liberalize in the 1980s.[48] With democratic government returning to the region and elections becoming more closely contested, Protestants discovered that if they could mobilize and vote in a bloc they could gain the attention of politicians seeking election. Their growing influence both as voters and, increasingly, as elected politicians meant that Protestants could influence the policy process and promote a greater degree of religious liberty. As it stands today, the region is largely approaching the level of religious freedom that is enjoyed in the United States, although problems still exist in some localities.[49] The trajectory is in the right direction nonetheless.

We now turn our attention to a more detailed examination of one of the most extreme and unusual cases in Latin America – Mexico. The Mexican case illustrates many of the general themes discussed in the preceding text, particularly as they apply to the struggle to redefine church-state relations in the nineteenth century. However, whereas the Catholic Church was able to regain its privileged social position in most other countries of the region by the early 1900s, the Mexican Church found itself outlawed by the revolutionary 1917 constitution. Protestants suffered alongside Catholics as

---

[47] As noted in the preceding text, Brazil under the Vargas regime during the 1940s could be added to this mix, although Vargas never went as far as the National Front governments in Colombia or the military regimes in Argentina in restricting Protestant actions.

[48] This was not only true of the military dictatorships that "returned to the barracks" but also was true of countries such as Colombia and Mexico (see following text) that began to experience more competitive regimes.

[49] The problems that still remain are less legal in nature than they are in nonenforcement of existing laws. In parts of Argentina, Chile, and Colombia, Protestants are still harassed, and the willingness of public officials to respond is largely determined by the strength of the Catholic clergy.

all religions were denied a legal status and forbidden from owning property. The story of how this happened and how the Catholic Church eventually reclaimed its institutional freedom, and in the process allowed for Protestants to enjoy the same liberty, illustrates a number of the theoretical propositions discussed in Chapter 2.

God in Mexico: The Long Struggle for Religious Freedom[50]

Church-state relations in colonial Mexico resembled the situation elsewhere in Spanish America. The *patronato real* defined the terms between church and state that tended to favor secular control over the episcopacy and Church policy, but the Church did receive a favored monopolistic status in the religious marketplace. Moreover, the Mexican Catholic Church – as elsewhere in the region – had the advantage of running the Inquisition and maintaining its own court system (*fueros eclesiásticos*) where clergy were tried for violations of canon *and* civil law. The Church fared well financially. The colonial state put its coercive force behind collecting the 10 percent religious tithe (*diezmo*), and the Church, through royal grants and inheritance, became the largest landowners in the Mexican territory, which extended up to present-day northern California. Despite this symbiotic relationship wherein the Church legitimized colonial rule and monitored the population through the Inquisition in exchange for the aforementioned perquisites, church-state conflict still existed.

During the mid- to late 1700s, the Bourbon King Charles III increased monarchical control over Church operations in the colonies in an effort to extend his monitoring powers over the colonies. Just as British King George leaned on his American colonies to finance the crown's various military adventures in Europe, the need to increase revenue in Spain prompted Charles to squeeze his colonies. But unlike the British colonies, the presence of a monopoly church already under the thumb of the Spanish crown gave the king another monitoring and enforcement mechanism to ensure colonial compliance. King Charles's increased reach over ecclesiastical affairs prompted a conflict with the Jesuits that led to their expulsion from Mexico and elsewhere (Brading 1994, 3–20). Because of this policy, the bishops who were appointed during the latter half of the eighteenth century became closely associated with the increasingly unpopular Bourbon monarchy.

---

[50] Material from this section is adopted from Gill (1999c). A tip of the hat to Waylon Jennings for inspiring the subtitle.

Interestingly, Mexican independence had a more conservative (monarchical) flavor than the more libertine revolutionaries in Gran Colombia. Fearing the results of the Napoleonic invasion in Spain, the rise of the liberal Cortes of Cádiz, and a populist uprising led by two priests – Padres Miguel Hidalgo and José María Morelos – several bishops encouraged Colonel Agustín de Iturbide to break with the motherland and establish a conservative, independent "empire" in 1821. This quasi-monarchical administration was short-lived, and Iturbide was exiled in 1823.[51]

The first major shift in church-state relations came during the years following Iturbide's abdication. Throughout the war of independence (1810–21) and its immediate aftermath, a majority of the bishops ended up fleeing the country. Those that remained were aged and ended up dying by the late 1820s leaving the Church bereft of leadership (Murray 1965, 109). Filling these vacant benefices became the primary point of contention between church and state. The Holy See argued that the *patronato real* was a right granted exclusively to the Spanish Crown and did not transfer to Mexico's new independent rulers. Rejecting this argument, the first several presidents claimed the *patronato* as a right of national sovereignty. Although these leaders were comfortable with preserving the church's privileged status in society (including state assistance in collecting tithes), they demanded the power to regulate internal church matters, principally the appointment of bishops. The issue was temporarily resolved when President Anastasio Bustamante allowed Pope Gregory XVI to appoint six bishops in 1831 without state interference, setting a weak precedent regarding the Vatican's right to control episcopal appointments (Puente 1992, 221). From the Vatican's standpoint, these appointments were made to the territory (not state) of Mexico, as the Vatican withheld official recognition of Mexican independence until 1836. The intransigence displayed by the Vatican on this issue won the church a temporary victory as Bustamante subsequently relinquished the right to fill bishoprics.

The Church's newfound freedom did not last long, however. In an era of political turbulence, an unregulated and independent church meant that bishops potentially could play the role of power brokers and destabilize governments. As Proposition 4 notes, the presence of secular political rivals

---

[51] The episcopacy had originally searched for a Bourbon prince to rule Mexico, an effort that indicated they wanted to continue the monarchy. Although Iturbide was helpful in bringing about independence, several bishops were not pleased when he declared himself emperor in 1822 (Murray 1965, 96). That Iturbide was reviled was not only revealed by his exiling but also when he tried to return to Mexico – his birth country – in 1824 he was quickly captured and executed. Oops.

increases the power of religious groups. The political faction that could co-opt and/or control this powerful social institution would have a significant advantage at the outset of nation building. With the Mexican Church hierarchy decimated by absences and having a recent history of collaboration with the Bourbon monarchy and Iturbide, the optimal strategy for the more revolutionary liberal forces in the emancipation movement was to exercise control over the Church (cf. Proposition 4b). This concern was particularly on the minds of liberal intellectuals who considered the Church an obstacle to their own political ascendancy. Lorenzo de Zavala, an early-nineteenth-century liberal scholar, claimed "the ecclesiastical hierarchy, with its rents, its *fueros*, and its power, is of such a nature that it is not possible to preserve it in a popular government without destroying at the same time the public peace and the principle of equality" (cited in Mecham 1966, 348). Given this view, the Liberal government that came to power in 1833 undertook the task of bringing the sources of episcopal power under tight control of the state.

The government first tried to reassert its influence over internal Church affairs by demanding the right to approve all ecclesial appointments and communications. However, having renegotiated the terms of the *patronato* so as to get Vatican recognition of the new Mexican state (Casillas 1974, 252–3), political officials lost their ability to manipulate the *internal* workings of the Church, and the Vatican was not of the mind to return this power to the secular state. Controlling ecclesiastical authority thus meant regulating the Church's *external* bases of social power. The government under the control of Valentín Gómez Farías accomplished this by nationalizing the property of various religious orders, closing the Catholic Pontifical University, ending the state collection of the *diezmo* (tithe),[52] and abolishing the *fueros* (special courts). The political machinations surrounding this first round of expropriations – there were still more to come – are instructive as they demonstrate how both religious and secular officials manipulated laws to their advantage. As Murray observes, "when church authorities tried to meet the threat of future attacks by selling or transferring their properties, a congressional act forbade them to do so" (1965, 126). This was as much of a battle over material sources of power as a clash of competing world-views, if not more so; a new government in a new state is typically short on revenue and any chance to fill the coffers is difficult to resist. This is all the more apparent when we consider that Gómez Farías, as a Mexican senator

---

[52] Although state refusal to collect religious tithes would seem to add to church autonomy, the Church's ability to collect revenues from parishioners was vastly inferior to that of the state. "Privatizing" the *diezmo* wreaked havoc on church revenues.

in 1826, issued a statement highly favorable to the Catholic Church declaring the clergy to be honorable, pious and learned, and "very useful to the nation" (Murray 1965, 113). Although Mr. Gómez Farías may have gone through an ideological conversion in the subsequent seven years leading to his first go-around as president, it is more likely that he just wanted the revenue and power when he headed the country.

Interestingly, the Conservative opposition to these anticlerical reforms did not provoke much of a backlash initially, indicating that religious policy was less determined by ideological fault lines than other considerations (namely revenue and power). The liberal experiment to limit Church power, however, came to an end when President Gómez Farías threatened to abolish similar privileges for the military.[53] Army officers and the clergy reacted quickly. Under the battle cry of "*religión y fueros*," a social revolt against the central government broke out (not uncommon for those chaotic times). Just as when Padres Hidalgo and Morelos rallied opposition to colonial Spain decades earlier using the Virgin of Guadalupe as a symbol to inflame the populace's passions, religion proved once again to be a potent countermobilizing force against state action. Showing again that political calculations underlay how religion was regulated the liberal-influenced military hero Antonio López de Santa Anna, who was initially a supporter of Gómez Farías, came out of "retirement" to participate in the rebellion.[54] Being relatively weak, the new government could not repel this challenge and repealed most of the anticlerical legislation. Nonetheless, state officials retained a modified version of the *patronato*, wherein the government would present a list of acceptable episcopal candidates to the pope. As elsewhere, this procedure was not particularly damaging to the Church considering that the limited list of qualified candidates tended to be clergy who had shown their loyalty to the Church and hence were acceptable to the Vatican.[55]

---

[53] Rational choice theory claims that individuals will attempt to maximize utility, but it doesn't rule out that people can make stupid mistakes of judgment. Some may claim this to be evidence of severely bounded rationality. Others might just write it off as temporary stupidity.

[54] Gómez Farías was actually the vice president under military hero Antonio López de Santa Anna who upon ascending to the presidency decided that governing was too boring and "retired" to his hacienda. This was a common pattern for Santa Anna, who apparently enjoyed his military role and playing the role of "king maker," although never staying around long enough in the presidency to relish in the joys of bureaucratic administration.

[55] This is not to say that unqualified candidates could not be advanced. However, this was a much less rare occurrence than during medieval times when benefices were determined more by nobility than fidelity (to the Church).

Battling back the liberal threat did not mean that the Church necessarily was in a stronger position. Though thankful for the moral support of the episcopacy, the leaders of the Conservative reaction still demanded control over society's dominant spiritual institution. Both Liberal and Conservative party leaders "had no intention of adopting a laissez-faire attitude [toward religion] but rather intended to continue the principle of state control inherited from colonial times. Patronage may have been weakening, but not state corporatism; state protection for religion may have been eroding, but not state control over religious affairs" (Schmitt 1984, 360). Although short-lived, the 1833 laws established a new precedent in church-state relations: the primary method of exerting control over the Church shifted from internal domination over ecclesiastical governance, to reducing and constraining its external influence over society.

By the 1850s, the Catholic hierarchy gained the ability to resist further encroachment into its internal affairs, mostly owing to the chaotic political situation.[56] Its financial weight made it a major contender for social authority and gave it a substantial degree of bargaining leverage with political leaders. Although Conservatives were comfortable with this situation, ascendant Liberal forces insisted on the absolute subordination of the Catholic hierarchy. Suspicious that the bishops harbored monarchist sympathies (thanks to the Iturbide interlude) and being an enemy of the Church's prime ally – the Conservatives – Liberals rightly assumed they would not be able to curry ideological support from the prelature (cf. Proposition 4b wherein clergy institutionally committed to one political faction cannot expect support from that faction's rivals). Therefore, it was doubly important – in terms of securing political survival – for Liberals to contain the Church's social power. Given an unstable polity and a stable Church, the only way for them to exert such control would be through a direct attack on the clergy's social bases of power (Meyer 1973, 27). This was accomplished during *La Reforma* (1855–76). During *La Reforma*, Liberals expropriated vast amounts of Church property, regulated sacramental fees, eliminated the *fueros* once and for all, and secularized key sources of clerical social influence (e.g., education) and income (e.g., cemeteries, marriage, the registry, and bequeaths). They even went so far as to convert monasteries into public buildings and

---

[56] To understand the degree of political chaos in Mexico at this time, consider that there were nearly fifty separate national administrations between 1821 and 1860. Santa Anna ruled directly nine times during this period. The situation was probably best summarized by the key figure in *La Reforma*, Benito Juárez, who said, "Under these conditions it is impossible to govern: no-one obeys me and I am not able to oblige anyone to obey" (cited in Brading 1988, 27).

sack churches and sell off sacred objects (Brading 1988, 30). In addition to destroying the Church's economic and political power, the Constitution of 1857 exposed the Church to greater political manipulation through an ambiguous clause in Article 123. This clause allowed for "the intervention of the federal power in religious acts and for external discipline" (Gutiérrez Casillas 1974, 271). Moreover, the government opened Mexico to Protestantism with the intention that this would further check the social power of the Church. As shown in the following text, the episcopacy's inordinate fear of Protestantism became one of the key weapons in the government's arsenal. Unfortunately for the Liberal reformers, and lucky for the Catholic clergy, Protestants didn't have much interest in evangelizing Mexico in the mid-nineteenth century.

The legislation passed during *La Reforma* remained law until 1917, despite the waning fortunes of its Liberal authors. Even the supposedly proclerical Emperor Maximilian (1864–7),[57] although open to negotiations with the papacy, rejected calls to overturn the 1857 Constitution and subsequent *Leyes Reformas*, which dictated the main attacks on the Church (Gutiérrez Casillas 1974, 310–18). Church-state relations eventually improved under President Porfirio Díaz (1876–1911), an "elected dictator" who ostensibly started out a Liberal but governed more by practical considerations for maintaining power. Díaz astutely realized that his own political survival could be bolstered by an appeal to religious nationalism. In his own words,

> there are no uprisings of the people except when they are wounded in their ineradicable traditions and in their legitimate liberty of conscience. Persecution of the Church, whether or not the clergy enter into the matter, means war, and such a war that the Government [*sic*] can only win against its own people, through the humiliating, despotic, costly and dangerous support of the United States. Without its religion, Mexico is irretrievably lost. (cited in Meyer 1973, 44; cf. Murray 1965, 301)

To win Catholic support for his regime, Díaz chose not to enforce the anticlerical articles in the Constitution of 1857. Nonetheless, he shrewdly chose not to revoke them either. This strategy allowed him to co-opt the clergy with promises of nonenforcement, while threatening them with a "sword of Damocles." If at any time the clergy attempted to challenge the civil government's authority, the *modus vivendi* offered by the dictator

---

[57] Emperor Maximilian was an Austrian prince who became ruler of Mexico when the French defeated the Mexican army and imposed him on the nation, largely in part to ensure repayment of debt owed to France.

could be withdrawn and the anticlerical laws enforced. Needless to say, Church leaders remained supportive of President Díaz. Bishops wisely used this respite in church-state hostilities to strengthen their institution by expanding the number of dioceses, seminaries, and social programs (Meyer 1989, 103). It was hoped a stronger institutional base and connection with the populace would give the hierarchy the power to overturn the country's anticlerical laws in the long run. This strategic move would repeat itself a half century later under President Lazaro Cárdenas.

Before the Church could make any legal gains, however, another event took place that significantly impacted the nature of the religious market-place – the Mexican Revolution (1910–20). Concerned mostly with con-solidating his rule, the first revolutionary president – Francisco Madero – made no overt moves against the Church. Nonetheless, in a move to tip the balance of the revolution away from its liberal course, the episcopacy backed a brief counterrevolution in 1913 and confirmed the opinion of most rev-olutionary leaders that Church hierarchs were unremitting enemies of the Revolution. As argued in Proposition 4b (see Appendix), religious organi-zations that commit themselves to one particular political group will likely face punishment when that political faction loses favor.[58] As punishment, the revolutionary 1917 Constitution not only incorporated the provisions of the 1857 Constitution and the *Leyes Reformas* but also further denied basic civil liberties to the clergy, specifically the freedom to vote and criticize the government. The new constitution also prohibited foreign clergy, out-door religious celebrations, property ownership by religious organizations (including schools), and recognition of degrees earned in seminaries. The capstone was the refusal to recognize the legality of any religious organiza-tions, effectively denying the Church and its personnel due process before the law.[59] For those keeping tally, this would represent a step backward in terms of religious freedom. The irony of all this was that the 1917 Con-stitution contained extensive prohibitions against religious organizations that were not legally recognized to exist, while simultaneously proclaiming

[58] Ironically, Emiliano Zapata, the most ideologically radical revolutionary, understood the need to court the Catholic clergy; he may have been suspicious of the hierarchs, but he knew the power of parish priests. Given the grassroots nature of his rebellion, Zapata sensed the deeply held religious values of the popular classes could be harnessed to his advantage. As such, he sought clerical support for his cause and marched on Mexico City carrying the banner of the Virgin of Guadalupe. Upper-class liberal intellectuals, cloistered in their secular surroundings, never fully comprehended the mobilizing capacity of religion despite numerous historical examples to the contrary. Apparently, some things never change.

[59] The full text of the 1917 constitutional articles pertaining to religious organizations can be found in González Fernández (1992).

freedom of worship! The practical result was that the state exercised more regulatory power over religion than at any time since Independence, including over Protestants (who one might think the Liberals would support as a means of countering Catholic power).

The intensity of the anticlerical attack left the Church impotent. Fortunately for the bishops, political problems in consolidating the revolution gave the episcopacy some breathing room for a few years. Politicians facing an uncertain political environment were more concerned with staying in power than in policing and enforcing the new religious laws. This changed once the political situation stabilized. In 1926, President Plutarco Elías Calles – who had effectively neutralized all his rivals to power[60] – began implementing the anticlerical provisions in the 1917 Constitution. All of this supports several of the propositions advanced earlier. When competition for power was intense and political survival was in doubt, as it was between 1910 and the late 1920s, secular rulers avoided alienating the major religious institution and implementation of anticlerical legislation was delayed (Propositions 3, 4, and 4a). However, once political competition subsided, the dominant religious institution – that is, the Catholic Church – lost bargaining power (Proposition 5). Worse yet for the episcopacy, being associated with the counterrevolutionary forces that lost the political battle, the revolutionary victors found it in their interests to implement the provisions in the 1917 Constitution so as to weaken a present and potentially future rival (Proposition 4b).

The Church swiftly responded to Calles's call to arms. The Archbishop of Mexico City forbade the Catholic Mass from being said in the country. This "religious strike" lasted three years. Shortly after the archbishop's pronouncement, a rebellion erupted pitting the central government against a peasant-based guerrilla movement fighting for the glory of *Rey Christo*.[61] The Cristero Rebellion, which contained elements of an agrarian land revolt as much as a defense of Catholicism, arose independent of the Catholic hierarchy and had little, if any episcopal direction (Meyer 1973). Nonetheless, the rebellion was quashed when the episcopacy negotiated a truce in 1929 based on assurances that anticlerical legislation would be applied with benevolence. Despite this agreement, the state assassinated all suspected participants in the uprising. All told, the Cristero Rebellion once again

---

[60] The Mexican Revolution (1910–20) was a remarkably tumultuous period wherein alliances between various revolutionary leaders shifted rapidly. Zapata was betrayed and assassinated shortly after he forced several land reform measures into the 1917 Constitution. Five of seven of the main leaders of the revolutionary force met violent deaths.

[61] Emiliano Zapata was proven correct posthumously.

demonstrated the mobilizing power of religion and reminded politicians that the total subjugation of religion to the state was not possible.

The remaining embers of church-state conflict smoldered to an end during the presidency of Lázaro Cárdenas (1934–40). Realizing that more was to be gained by seeking a truce with the Church, "Cárdenas, the most anticlerical of all the [revolutionary] presidents, renewed the policy [of Porfirio Díaz], using the mediation of the rural priests to govern effectively" (Meyer 1973, 46). Political interest once again trumped ideological conscience. The episcopacy responded in kind by publicly endorsing Cárdenas's decision to nationalize the oil industry in 1938. The new *modus vivendi* persisted until 1992 and served Church interests well. Considering that the religious laws of 1917 would remain in effect for the foreseeable future, the short-term political strategy of the episcopacy was acquiescence with the intent of securing nonenforcement of the laws. From 1940 to the early 1980s, the Mexican hierarchy earned a reputation as the "silent Church," never criticizing government policy and rarely speaking out on the country's major socioeconomic ills. This silence, however, masked a more activist, long-term strategy. The central goal of political silence was to carve out the social space needed to rebuild the Church's institutional strength and press demand for legal change when the political environment was more favorable. Paradoxically, the future political strength of the Church rested in its short-term withdrawal from power. They only had to wait until the political situation became more competitive. The main political party in Mexico – the Partido Revolucionario Institucional (PRI) – overwhelmingly dominated all levels of the government until the 1980s.

As can be seen by this brief history, the struggle between Church and state in Mexico has been one wherein secular leaders have attempted to control the social power of the Church so as to neutralize the most organized threat to their rule. Catholic bishops, for their part, have asserted their social and economic power to maximize institutional autonomy whenever possible, while still trying to preserve the privileged status it had during colonial times. During the early nineteenth century, both Church and state were disorganized and weak, and bargaining power roughly equal. As a result of this political stalemate, bishops regained control of the Church's internal affairs. State officials responded by attempting to control the Church's external social and economic influence. As time wore on, the state – in the guise of various governments – consolidated power more rapidly than the Church. Given that the state's power was based largely on coercion, the socioeconomic influence of the Church was expropriated, often motivated by the need of the state to get out of debt (cf. Proposition 3 – economic interests of politicians often motivate religious policy). However, as the two periods of *"modus vivendi"* show, the social influence of the Church could not be destroyed easily, and peaceful coexistence became the more rational strategy for secular rulers. In the process, religious freedom suffered, not only for Catholics who found their ability to minister to their flock to be constrained by onerous regulations but also for Protestants who sought to break into the religious marketplace. Protestants existed, nonetheless, and expanded slowly under the political radar. By the 1980s, though, an infusion of greater political competition in society shifted the bargaining power to religious groups and created an opening for a new era of religious liberty. Although the new laws were primarily directed at the Catholic Church, Protestants received reasonably equal treatment at the national level.

That new era of religious freedom was ushered in with constitutional changes in 1992 and a series of liberalizing laws known as the Ley Reglamentaria.[62] The roots of Ley Reglamentaria can be traced back to the social space accorded to the Church following the establishment of Mexico's second *modus vivendi* between church and state (1938–92).[63] To understand why this would be so, it is necessary to understand this *modus vivendi* as a bargain, a positive-sum game wherein each side gains something. By relaxing the restrictions on the enforcement of the anticlerical laws contained in the 1917 Constitution, the government obtained the "silence" of the Catholic Church and neutralized "one of the very few institutions, and maybe the only one, capable of confronting the state in an organized way" (Blancarte 1993, 794). This undoubtedly helped Cárdenas and subsequent presidents consolidate and institutionalize their hegemony over the polity. Frayed by a seemingly unrelenting conflict with the state, the episcopacy agreed to

---

[62] Ley Reglamentaria literally translates as *regulatory law*. Officially, the law is known as La Ley de Asociaciones Religiosas y Culto Público, but media outlets referred to it simply as Ley Reglamentaria. In an earlier publication upon which this chapter is based (Gill 1999c), an anonymous reviewer asked why this law was referred to in such a generic way; after all, any regulatory law could earn the title of Ley Reglamentaria. This is a very profound question to which I have no answer, nor could anybody I interviewed in Mexico in June 1995 provide a solid answer. This is not surprising, considering that the main ministry in charge of administering this law had to send an office assistant out to a bookstore to purchase a copy of the law when I requested one!

[63] As a reminder, the first was during the Porfiriato (1876–1910). The bishops' support for the counterrevolution spoiled that *modus vivendi*. As tension still existed between the episcopacy and Cárdenas during the first few years of his administration, some choose to date the beginning of the *modus vivendi* as 1940. Mecham (1966) dates the beginning of the *modus vivendi* in 1929, following the end of the Cristero Rebellion. I prefer 1938 based upon the episcopacy's support for the nationalization of the oil industry, the first time in nearly three decades that church and state agreed on a major policy initiative.

political silence (at least for the time being) in exchange for an opportunity to rebuild their institution. As the original terms of the *modus vivendi* represented an implicit bargain between church and state, it is important to remember that bargains rarely remain static over time. Although not necessarily collapsing, the terms of the original agreement are often modified based on shifts in the relative bargaining power of each actor involved. A shift in bargaining power between church and state, resulting from the decay of the PRI's political dominance, resulted in a deregulation of the religious marketplace.

The initial shift in relative bargaining power emanated from strategic moves made by the Catholic hierarchy. Removed from politics, Church leaders immediately set out to strengthen their institution. From 1950 to 1992, thirty-nine new dioceses were created, the majority established prior to 1970. This gave the central Church greater administrative control over its clergy and rank and file. The episcopacy also engaged in an ambitious series of pastoral programs that enhanced its social influence. Although the hierarchy's pastoral efforts to build social capital originated during the late 1800s, the stability of church-state relations after 1938 allowed these programs to proceed at an expanded pace (Gutiérrez Casillas 1974, 453–6). These projects were spearheaded by two organizations – the Secretariado Social Mexicano (SSM), created in 1920, and Acción Católica Mexicana (ACM), formed eight years later. The ACM was a strictly lay organization and concentrated on indoctrinating members of the middle and upper classes with Catholic values in the hopes of creating political elite friendlier to Church interests. The SSM, under priestly supervision, undertook various social programs such as educational programs, agrarian unions, and financial cooperatives (Concha Malo 1986, 63–4; cf. Eckstein 1986, passim). The PRI tolerated, even encouraged, these activities because they helped alleviate the plight of the poor, thereby reducing social tension.

As time wore on, Church officials grew bolder with the social space they were allotted. Priests began appearing in public with clerical garb, a practice forbidden by Article 130 of the 1917 Constitution. Catholic schools were reopened. Foreign clergy were brought into the country to bolster the Church's pastoral outreach. And, most importantly, bishops began criticizing government policy, albeit cautiously. The first salvo came in 1951 with a pastoral letter denouncing "liberalism in general and the unique form capitalism had assumed in Mexico" to be followed shortly with episcopal criticism of a government textbook program (Blancarte 1993, 798). Other critical episcopal communications followed, including a 1968 pastoral letter that blamed political corruption and the nonparticipatory nature of the political system for the lack of civic maturity that bishops considered endemic among the majority of Mexicans (Conferencia del Episcopado Mexicano 1985a, 53–99). The increasing outspokenness of the clergy throughout this period can be explained with reference to Proposition 5a. This proposition hypothesizes that as political tenure becomes secure, politicians will be less likely to enforce restrictions on religions if those restrictions entail significant monitoring and enforcement costs. Strictly enforcing the regulations of the 1917 Constitution would have been extremely costly, both in terms of monitoring and punishing clerical behavior, but also such prosecutions would not have sat well with devout Catholics. So long as the PRI remained politically dominant, and society remained reasonably docile, government leaders could afford to ignore the sporadic protests of the Church. Should the Church ever become too great of a challenge, they could always drop the Sword of Damocles. As Barranco Villafán and Pastor Escobar astutely noted, "the State [sic] tolerated the organizational and structural recomposition of the Church, leaving the [anticlerical] constitutional articles, a 'legal fiction,' unaltered as a preventative measure" (1989, 18). The strict regulations on religious activity became liberalized de facto, which not only benefited the Catholic Church but also allowed non-Catholics some increased maneuverability within the country. Nonetheless, the state still held an immensely disproportionate share of the bargaining power over religious organizations, making it difficult for the Catholic episcopacy (and Protestant groups) to achieve the goal of greater legal freedom.

Power began to shift marginally in 1968. Just four months after the bishops released their pastoral celebrating the first anniversary of Paul VI's social encyclical Populorum Progressio, student protests broke out in the capital city. The brutal repression of these protests on the heels of the 1968 Olympic Games shook civil society. This was the first major crack in the PRI's unchallenged social control and from this point on the bargaining power of the government began to wane in relation to that of the episcopacy.[64] As social tension mounted during the early 1970s, President Luis Echeverría tried to buoy the legitimacy of the PRI, in part by seeking a better working relationship with the Catholic hierarchy. In addition to meeting frequently with bishops (most likely to forestall any damaging critiques of his administration), the government eliminated reference to contraceptives in its population control policy and contributed funds for a new Basilica of Guadalupe (Grayson 1992, 52–4), one of the holiest sites in the country.

---

[64] Although Protestants were also desirous of religious liberty, they were essentially too small in number to be of any political influence at this time.

Considering that religious groups were not allowed to own property, this was a significant concession – constructing a state-owned building that would serve as a free house of worship for Catholics. Additionally, Echeverría was the first Mexican president to visit the Vatican while in office. These developments are critical as they demonstrate how bargaining relations were shifting. But changes in the constitution were never seriously considered at this time, and the government kept anticlerical legislation in reserve.

The bishops' response to the overtures was conditional on their strategic belief that the time for legal reforms was approaching. Rather than giving the PRI the ideological support it wanted, the CEM responded with a two-pronged strategy. First, they continued lobbying for political democratization, which, in terms of Church interests, meant greater religious liberty. The prelates relied chiefly on public statements and gained greater media access during the 1970s. Public pressure was necessary as PRI officials turned deaf ears to requests for wholesale legal change.[65] Typical of such pressure was a 1973 pastoral that asserted the bishops' right to discuss political issues openly and made a rather unambiguous reference to Article 130 of the Constitution by stating, "priests, as human beings, are subject to political obligations and rights" (Conferencia del Episcopado Mexicano 1985a, 54). As the 1970s progressed, bishops became increasingly concerned with electoral fraud and made it known. This was a perfectly rational strategy given that electoral competition would only help their cause.

Second, the leadership of CEM embarked on a policy of consolidating the political position of the Church. The government easily could exploit internal Church divisions, thus there was a concerted effort to develop a united front. This meant bringing the small but vocal left wing of the Church under control. This segment of the Church, including bishops Sergio Méndez Arceo (Cuernevaca) and Samuel Ruíz Garcia (San Cristóbal de las Casas in the restive region of Chiapas), was proving a nuisance to the PRI.[66] As Michael Tangeman observed, "with progressive lay Catholics increasingly alienated from their hierarchy, the bishops cut all ties to the SSM in 1973, substituting it with [another program], which by virtue of having a bishop as president was more easily controlled" (1995, 54).

---

[65] Archbishop Rosendo Huesca Pacheco, interview with author, Puebla, Mexico, June 17, 1995.

[66] Although liberation theology was a hot topic among academics in the 1970s, Mexico never developed a large leftist Catholic movement as compared to places like Brazil, Chile, and Nicaragua (see Gill 1998). This lack of a significant Catholic left was most likely due to the restrictive regulations on religious organizations.

Two definitive turning points leading to the eventual liberalization of the religious marketplace occurred in 1979 and 1983. The first was Pope John Paul II's visit to Mexico. With relatively little advanced publicity and press, the pontiff attracted millions to his various public appearances. Government officials were stunned, if not terrified. As demonstrated in the past by Padre Hidalgo, the *religión y fueros* uprising and the Cristero Rebellion, religion could mobilize people like no other force in Mexico. Energized by this massive show of social influence, the Mexican episcopacy went on the offensive in the 1980s. Still, the PRI ruling party faced little rivalry to its power and was seemingly strong enough to resist episcopal demands for religious regulatory reform. Things would not change until the political arena became more competitive and the Church could demonstrate that it could sway close elections.

The second event of critical importance to the implementation of the Ley Reglemantaria was Mexico's economic crash in 1982, brought about by a precipitous fall in world oil prices, an equally steep rise in interest rates on foreign loans, and a decision to devalue the peso. This crisis dealt a major blow to the PRI's ruling hegemony. The official party's legitimacy plummeted as fast as per capita income. The PRI's typical method of ensuring loyalty – patronage – became less effective as the government was forced to trim its spending. By the mid-1980s, all this led to something unseen in Mexican politics – serious political competition. And as the PRI's control over the electorate decreased, electoral fraud increased.

The political crisis provided the opportunity for the bishops to assert their social influence and win back their legal rights. The strategy chosen was "good cop/bad cop." Although challenging the legitimacy of the regime publicly ("bad cop"), a select group of bishops engaged in private discussions with PRI officials to modify the laws regulating religion ("good cop"). The former tactic was employed more frequently immediately following the pope's visit and throughout Miguel de la Madrid's administration (1982–8), which on the surface remained closed to negotiations with the Church.[67] References in ecclesiastical documents to "human rights," "social justice,"

---

[67] The key phrase here is on the surface. It would be safe to assume that President Miguel de la Madrid had as much contact with Church officials as previous presidents. Both Presidents José López Portillo and Luis Echeverría kept communications open with bishops, and the former met with at least forty bishops during his election campaign in 1976. However, little is said about high-level contact between Church and state at this time (with one exception noted in the following text). In various interviews conducted in Mexico (June 1995), both Church officials and scholars did not consider such contacts to be worthy of extensive discussions.

"religious liberty," and the country's political situation increased noticeably after 1989 (cf. Conferencia del Episcopado Mexicano 1994).

Perhaps more than any other issue, electoral fraud became a key battleground between the episcopacy and PRI in the mid-1980s. Political competition was in the Church's interest. To the degree that the PRI's rivals gained in strength, the Church gained political leverage. Not surprisingly, bishops from all the country's pastoral regions championed the cause of free and fair elections. On April 25, 1985, the CEM issued a short pastoral regarding election that contains the following advice:

> We trust that the public authority [i.e., the PRI] will, as it has been promised, guaranteed and assured: give freedom and support, equally, to all political parties; make available to the parties the means of communications required for free and truly democratic elections; respect the vote [count] of each party. We also remind [the public authority] that the vote should be free and secret. (Conferencia del Episcopado Mexicano 1994, 220)

Given its monopolization of elected offices, the PRI stood to lose the most in competitive elections; thus the bishops' statement represented a bold attack on the power base of the ruling party and reminded them that the Church had bargaining power in this new political environment.

The PRI, more concerned with preserving its power than securing democratic ideals, ignored the warning. An internal rift within the PRI between more authoritarian hardliners who wanted to use corruption to stifle competition and new "technocrats" who saw a limited political opening as beneficial also distracted the PRI from religious matters. In 1986, election fraud in the northern state of Chihuahua provided the Catholic Church with some leverage against the state. One week after the election, Chihuahuan Archbishop Adalberto Almeida called for "the suspension of Mass and the closing of churches [as] 'a cry of protest and a call to change'" (Ortiz Pinchetti 1986, 15). Only weeks before this incident, a PRI official visited the archbishop to ask his support of the PRI's candidate. Speaking to the press Almeida reported, "of course, I rejected his petition. Then he told me that he wanted to be my friend and offered to visit me frequently. He has not returned; but shortly after that interview he sent me a box of chocolates" (Ortiz Pinchetti 1986, 14). It is clear that the PRI was trying to sweeten its relations with the Church. Almeida's call for a "religious strike" harkened back to the Cristero Rebellion era, which was the last time the Church was able to force a major shift in the government's religious policy (from outright hostility to *modus vivendi*). The entire episcopacy supported his decision. Worried about the effect that such an action could have on the country's political stability, the government was able to stop the strike only by securing the support of the pope (through papal nuncio Jerónimo Prigione) one day before it was to occur (Hinojosa 1986; Pérez Mendoza 1986). Linking this crisis to the episcopacy's desire to improve its legal position, Archbishop Sergio Obeso (president of CEM) loudly declared:

> The bishops will not return to the sacristies, despite that many of the Catholic faithful do not support this view, because they have been influenced by the liberal mentality. The Mexican bishops want extraofficial relations between the Church and the State [*sic*] to become full relations. Constitutional Article 130 should be modified, to recognize the legal personality of the Church.... In no way is it the intention of the ecclesiastical hierarchy to incite new conflicts with the State [*sic*]. The country has sufficient problems that we do not seek to add to them. But we insisted on declaring our rights. (Hinojosa 1986b, 10)

There can be little doubt that the Chihuahuan conflict was used by the CEM to bolster its bargaining power. However, as punishment for defying the ruling party, the PRI passed an electoral law stating that "priests who 'induce the electorate to vote or who act against a candidate or who foment abstention and disorder as a means of pressure' will be subject to a fine of approximately $4,400."[68]

Although the Catholic hierarchy's "bad cop" tactic was visible publicly, the "good cop" strategy took place privately. The diplomatic ability of the Church to press its demands behind the scenes was augmented by the presence of the papal nuncio Jerónimo Prigione, appointed in 1978. Prigione's primary mission was to unify the hierarchy around a single political goal, namely returning legal recognition to the Church (Camp 1997, 230). The Twenty-third Plenary Assembly of Mexican Bishops in Guadalajara (1985) focused specifically on developing a consensus as to what future church-state relations would look like (Conferencia del Episcopado Mexicano 1985b). Ironically, however, it was the divisions within the hierarchy that enabled the "good cop/bad cop" strategy to work. Attacks on the government by "renegade" bishops such as Méndez Arceo and Samuel Ruíz, served to enhance Prigione's bargaining position. The government wanted the progressive Catholic sector silenced. Prigione had the incentive and capacity to do this. As part of the Vatican's policy of bringing the international Church under greater hierarchical control, Prigione's secondary mission was to reign in the Catholic left. The nuncio's political savvy turned potential conflict

---

[68] "Mexico Moves to Silence Church Critics," *Christian Science Monitor* (January 2, 1987), 15. The fine is cited in U.S. dollars.

into mutual grain for the Church and PRI. During his tenure, Prigione influenced more than 30 percent of Mexico's episcopal appointments and clamped down on a number of progressive strongholds, including the Seminario Regional del Sureste, a training center for progressive priests (Camp 1997, 218; Tangeman 1995, 63, 74). He also lobbied for Bishop Samuel Ruíz's removal (Morales y Vera 1995, 12, 17). Catholic progressives paid the highest price for improved church-state relations.[69]

The final break in this process came during the 1988 presidential election. During the campaign, the PRI's candidate Carlos Salinas de Gortari realized his party was in trouble and that the episcopacy would have to be part of any solution. The threatened clerical strike in Chihuahua in 1986 made this abundantly clear. Salinas courted CEM officials with promises of improved relations and constitutional amendments. This election exposed the weakness in the PRI's legitimacy by generating its narrowest margin of victory since the party's inception. There is also reason to believe that Salinas won only through electoral fraud. Either way, it was apparent that something needed to be done to bolster political support for the PRI, especially given that Salinas planned a major overhaul of the economy that would undermine the PRI's traditional corporatist control over society. With massive privatization on the horizon, traditional patronage networks used for securing party loyalty could no longer be counted on. Furthermore, increased coercion would have jeopardized Mexico's goal of becoming a member of the Organization of Economic Cooperation and Development (OECD). It was clear that the PRI needed to win the ideological support of Mexico's most esteemed nongovernmental institution, the Catholic Church. This time, however, Salinas would have to offer more than a box of chocolates.

That Salinas was seeking to trade religious reforms for political legitimacy became apparent immediately after his tightly contested election.[70] First, the president invited important members of the Church hierarchy to his inauguration, where he made bold promises to amend constitutional restrictions on religious organizations and their personnel. In 1990, Salinas

[69] This wasn't a major travesty, though, because the progressive Catholic movement was fizzling out by then anyway (Gill 2002b).

[70] At best, Salinas won by a very slim margin over his left-wing rival Cuauhtémoc Cárdenas, son of the former president who established a truce with the Catholic Church after the Mexican Revolution. There is some suspicion that Salinas actually lost the election and only managed to prevail through fraud, including a power outage that complicated the vote count on election eve. I take no position on this controversy, and it is immaterial for purposes of this book.

greeted Pope John Paul II as he arrived in Mexico for his second visit, an unprecedented act for a contemporary Mexican politician. His next major action on church-state affairs was to visit the Vatican in order to restore ties with the Holy See. In return for this action, Salinas won papal support for his administration as reflected in the following statement by Pope John Paul II:

> I [John Paul II] wish to assure you, Mr. President, that in the Holy See and the Catholic Church you will always find an attentive partner, determined to collaborate – in virtue of her religious and moral mission – with the authorities and the diverse institutions of your country in favour [sic] of the supreme values and the spiritual and material prosperity of the nation.... *Loyal collaboration between the Church and State – through mutual respect and freedom* – produces great good for the whole of Mexican society. (John Paul II 1991, 22; emphasis added)

Loyal collaboration did occur. The Mexican government used its Solidarity program to contribute funds to a variety of church projects, including the construction of cathedrals (Tangeman 1995, 78–9).[71] The Catholic hierarchy returned the favor by participating in a "debt for equity" swap program designed to alleviate Mexico's burdensome foreign debt. Several bishops publicly endorsed the North American Free Trade Agreement (NAFTA). And, the papal nuncio increased pressure on the Catholic left, in part, by vetoing the entry of "radical" foreign priests into the country (Tangeman 1995, 74–81). Obviously, not all bishops or clergy supported these actions, but their voices were being increasingly marginalized by Prigione and the key leaders of CEM. Throughout this time, CEM kept pressuring for legal reforms.

The Church's reward for "loyal collaboration" came in January 1992 with the passage of amendments that eliminated the anticlerical articles of the 1917 Constitution. Ley Reglamentaria implemented these changes on July 15, 1992. For its part, the new laws began by recognizing the corporate identity of churches and other religious organizations.[72] This represented a legal necessity to implementing any other regulations because religious groups did not technically exist prior to 1992. The next major piece of the new legislation provided all registered religions with equal protection before the law, thereby protecting churches and their ministry from

---

[71] Confirmed in an author interview with Archbishop Rosendo Huesca Pacheco, Puebla, Mexico, June 17, 1995.

[72] A full discussion of the Ley Reglamentaria can be found in Gill (1999c, 782–92). The actual text of the law can be found at Secretaria de Gobernación (1992).

capricious attacks by the government and allowing religious minorities to seek legal redress if they are harassed by civilians. Clergy of all denominations now have full citizenship rights and may participate in local and national elections. However, religious personnel are still forbidden from associating with political ends in mind (e.g., promoting a specific candidate). Although still a regulation on religious free speech, this regulation is not any different than what exists in the United States and is usually justified by the religious organization's tax-exempt status. So long as it applies equally to other NGOs with tax-exempt status, such a restriction is not a major burden. One of the other important components of the new law now allows religious groups to own property. Interestingly, all Catholic Church buildings built prior to 1992 were legally the property of the state, usually designated as historical "museums."[73] Nonetheless, the Church used these buildings for religious services free of charge, a significant advantage that further bolsters how the Church benefited from the *modus vivendi* crafted under President Lazaro Cárdenas in the 1930s.[74] And the law has opened up the broadcast airwaves to all denominations, allowing the Word of God to be spread through modern means of communication. In short, the Ley Reglamentaria has led to a dramatic increase in the degree of religious liberty in Mexico, putting it on par with most other Latin American countries that have seen a liberalization of the religious market recently, thanks to a new era of democratic political competition.

Although it is quite obvious that the Catholic Church benefited from the constitutional reforms of 1992, perhaps one of the biggest benefactors from a strict application of the Ley Reglamentaria would be the evangelical Protestant churches that have gained a foothold in Mexico (Isáis 1998). Over the past several decades, they have quietly entered the country and established a presence often by preaching in homes and storefronts.[75] For the most part, the federal government left them alone as they weren't a social nuisance and actually provided needed social services in many cases. By legalizing religious organizations and declaring freedom to worship as

[73] Interviews with Archbishop Rosendo Huesca Pacheco, Puebla, Mexico, June 17, 1995 and evangelical minister Alberto Montalvo Hernandez, Mexico City, Mexico, June 23, 1995.

[74] I am not aware of how the use of church buildings was managed between the Calles and Cárdenas administrations in the late 1920s and early 1930s. The Cristero Rebellion certainly disrupted religious services in many regions of the country (Meyer 1973), but it is not clear whether this was a pattern consistent throughout the country. An interesting histiography of how church property was managed during this historical era needs to be written.

[75] Interview with Rev. Thomas Wynn Drost of the United Pentecostal Church in Mexico City, Mexico, June 23, 1995.

one chooses, the Ley Reglamentaria effectively grants evangelicals equal protection before the law, something that they have always lacked. As evangelical Protestants frequently have been the target of violent persecution and harassment (Isáis 1998; Scott 1992b; *Latin American Weekly Report* 1990), the Ley Reglamentaria now gives them legal protection from such attacks. Perhaps more importantly, the Ley Reglamentaria has provided evangelical organizations with the "psychological boost" needed to continue their expansion throughout the country. Protestant ministers now see themselves as a legitimate part of Mexican society and have organized in ways to effectively assert their right to missionize. For example, realizing that new religious legislation was on the horizon, evangelical minister Alberto Montalvo Hernandez, minister for the Church of God, organized the Foro Nacional de Iglesias Cristianas Evangélicas (FONICE) in 1991 to represent the interests of Protestants.[76] FONICE, although not speaking for all Protestant churches, is at the forefront of defending the legal interests of non-Catholic Christians in Mexico. The record for evangelicals is mixed, however. Harassment, particularly at the local level, still occurs (e.g., Tobar 2005; Lloyd 2001).[77] Such conflict is, unfortunately, to be expected as newer religions displace traditional faiths. Nonetheless, the legal framework is now in place to provide the freedom for all denominations to missionize in ways they see fit. The past several presidents have been open to meeting with evangelical Protestants and listen to their concerns. As reported to me in a personal interview, the Pentecostal Reverend Thomas Drost described attending a breakfast meeting between President Salinas and a group of evangelical ministers wherein the president reportedly said, "you have equal opportunity and now all you have left to do is grow."[78] Religious liberty can open many doors to spiritual opportunity.

Summary

The coming of religious freedom to Latin America took a much longer route than it did in the United States. The region started its modern independent history with a highly regulated religious monopoly inherited from colonial times. The significant absence of religious minorities meant that the primary issue of religious freedom would be the extent of state control

---

[76] Author interview with Alberto Montalvo Hernandez, Mexico City, Mexico, June 23, 1995.
[77] See also "Temple Construction Blocked," *National Catholic Reporter* (April 26, 1996), 7, and "Chiapas Evangelicals Have Little Faith in New Government: Persecution, Arrests, and Killings Persist," *Christianity Today* (February 6, 1995), 46–7 for additional examples.
[78] Author interview in Mexico City, Mexico, June 23, 1995.

over the Catholic Church. The social power of the Church dictated caution among the early liberators and the Church retained its privileged status even among a growing worldview of liberal (and sometimes anticlerical) thought. Political necessity demanded that new rulers not isolate the one institution that could help them win popular support. Conflict did arise over how much control secular rulers would exercise over the Church in exchange for a privileged position. Attempts to influence episcopal appointments through the continuance of the *patronato* brought church and state into conflict shortly after emancipation. The debt crises faced by nearly all governments in the region then pushed government officials to expropriate vast property holdings of the Church and, in the process, helped to reconfigure the religious regulatory landscape. Although losing much of their propertied assets and various revenue-producing functions (e.g., marriage services), the Church was able to reclaim its institutional autonomy by either renegotiating or removing altogether the terms of episcopal appointments in the *patronato*.

Religious liberty for all denominations took a longer time to develop. Initially, the desire to do commercial business with Protestant nations led to a relaxation of restrictive laws on non-Catholics. Protestants slowly built a presence in several countries and by the mid-twentieth century were beginning to show rapid growth in places such as Brazil, Chile, and portions of Central America. As the size of the religious minority populations grew and Latin America experienced a democratic renaissance in the 1980s, Protestants began entering the political arena as a significant voting bloc to push for greater freedom. With more competitive elections, and with some evangelicals even getting elected to office, these Protestants were successful in further liberalizing the religious marketplace. Political freedom prompted success for religious freedom and both have been reinforcing each other.

Not only does Mexico represent many of these general regional trends but it also crystallized many in an extreme form. The expropriations of Church wealth during La Reforma and again shortly after the Mexican Revolution represented the most violent clash between church and state; no other state tried to control religious institutions to the extent that Mexico did, eventually making religious organizations legal nonentities. But as the Mexican revolutionary regime became (ironically) institutionalized and immune from competing political pressures, both Church and government leaders found a way to live side by side. Removing the legal "Sword of Damocles" hanging over the Church's head became a major goal of the Catholic episcopacy, and with the emergence of a competitive political environment in the 1980s, the bishops finally possessed the bargaining leverage to reform the constitutional restrictions on religious groups. Protestants benefited from this turn of events and by the start of the twenty-first century, Mexico along with many other nations in Latin America[79] have witnessed a new and promising era of religious freedom.

Whereas the Mexican revolutionaries of 1917 tried legislating the Catholic Church out of existence, yet were never truly successful in that goal, another group of revolutionaries halfway around the globe proved more successful in subjugating religion. The ultimately tragic Soviet experiment in social engineering largely achieved its goal of eradicating institutional religion from Russian society. Yet, following the fall of the Berlin Wall in 1989 and the collapse of the Soviet Union two years later, it became apparent that the spiritual soul of Russians and East Europeans had not been extinguished fully. A renewed interest in religious life has necessitated the wholesale rewriting of laws regulating religious organizations. Chapter 5 briefly surveys some of the developments pertaining to religious liberty in that region, with an eye to Russia and the infrequently discussed Baltic States of Estonia, Latvia, and Lithuania. It may still be a bit too early to determine what the course of religious freedom will take in those countries as debates are ongoing. But these cases provide an interesting test for the theoretical propositions developed earlier in this study.

---

[79] Cuba remains the biggest holdout in terms of religious freedom. With "elected despots" making a return in Venezuela and a few other Andean countries in recent years, the prospects for political freedom appear to be dimming. However, there is no sign as yet that these nations will backtrack on religious freedom specifically. Only time will tell; as argued in the first two chapters, religious freedom is not a unidirectional historical path. It can move forward as well as falling back.

CHAPTER 5

Russia and the Baltics
(with Cheryl Žilinskas)

Having turned our faces east and west, our wish and prayer now is that the state leadership will at last turn its face to God.

> – Romanian Archbishop Lucian Muresan responding to the election of President Emil Constantinescu[1]

Nineteen hundred and seventeen was a busy year for governments turning their faces from God, at least for the institutional representations of His Word here on earth. Not only did the constitutional council in Mexico effectively outlaw the Roman Catholic Church and other religious denominations but also a group of even more radical state builders seized power in a country halfway around the world. The political and ideological goals of the Russian Bolsheviks revealed an ominous future for religion.[2] By ruthlessly crushing the ROC (even more than what Mexican revolutionaries

---

[1] Cited in Luxmoore (2001, 310). Mureşcan is an official with the Romanian Greek Catholic Church.

[2] Contrary to this book's emphasis on the political incentives behind regulating religious organizations, we do acknowledge that ideology can play an important role in shaping policies (as noted at the end of Chapter 2). The Bolsheviks' attitudes toward religion undoubtedly were influenced by the worldview of Karl Marx who considered spiritual faith to be nothing more than an opiate dulling the senses of "the masses." Some scholars have argued that Soviet Marxism is equivalent to a religion, complete with a myth of salvation (Hanson 1997). Our primary concern here is not to debate whether secular ideologies are

could ever fathom doing to the Catholic Church), the resulting revolutionary government of the Soviet Union drove institutional religion into an emaciated state within a matter of a decade. Although the nationalistic Orthodox Church was allowed to survive throughout the Soviet era, its power and influence was greatly reduced and rigorously monitored. Russia was not the only nation to be affected, though. Upon concluding a nonaggression pact with Nazi Germany, Josef Stalin's Soviet Union gobbled up the Baltic States of Estonia, Latvia, and Lithuania at the outset of World War II. The end of that war brought Soviet influence over most of Eastern Europe; the Soviet-dominated states of that region adopted a similar attitude (to varying degrees) toward institutional religion – churches were a rival source of social influence that needed to be controlled tightly. The iron-fisted rule of the Soviet government along with the country's rapid rise to military superpower status did not bode well for the future of religious freedom. Organized religion in the Soviet Union and Eastern Europe appeared doomed.

Let's fast forward to 1988. As the Soviet monolith began to crack at the seams, the Lithuanian Soviet Socialist Republic was at the forefront of the independence movement. The Catholic Church was largely seen as the most stable national entity and the greatest and most consistent proponent of the national interest. The emerging "reform" Communist government was obliged to show its respect for the struggles of the Catholic Church – not recognizing the Church would have been politically detrimental. In a symbolic act, the newly appointed First Secretary of the Communist Party of Lithuania (soon to be independent Lithuania's first president), Algirdas Brazauskas, returned the national cathedral, used as a museum during the fifty-year occupation, to the Church, its rightful owner (Landsbergis 2000, 123). This was a tremendous victory for the Church and for the political opposition.

By January of 1991, the USSR was nearing its final stages of collapse. In Vilnius, Soviet forces besieged the Seimas, Lithuania's parliament building. A wall of protestors guarded the Seimas against a parade of Soviet tanks while members of the self-appointed opposition government inside attempted (and failed) to make contact with Mikhail Gorbachev, General Secretary of the Communist Party of the Soviet Union. Lithuanians peacefully demanded independence and in doing so boldly invoked religious symbols. Many men and women volunteered to enter the sandbagged building

comparable with religions but rather to focus on the interaction between church and state traditionally defined. We encourage others to take up this debate.

to aid in its defense. But first, they attended confession and Catholic Mass and swore a solemn oath. Outside, by the barricades, stood a statue of the Virgin Mary, traditional Lithuanian roadside crosses, and an altar where various priests came to celebrate Mass. In addition to rallying around patriotic songs, people sang hymns as they waited through the tense hours (Landsbergis 2000, 245). The Soviet Union, not religious faith, was about to meet its doom.

For Lithuania and its Baltic neighbors, Latvia and Estonia, 1991 marked a return to sovereign rule. Each had experienced a short period of independence between World War I and World War II and, like many Western European countries, had developed relatively liberal conceptions of religious freedom, conforming to a liberal intellectual ethos that circulated in some quarters following the "war to end all wars." Nonetheless, in the longer run, power politics still trumped lofty ideals. The religious landscape of the Baltic States was marked by its relationship with imperial Russia and other occupying powers prior to the 1940s and, quite obviously, by the Soviet Union during the latter half of the twentieth century. Although the Soviet empire attempted, in varying degrees, to abolish all forms of religious life, spirituality persisted through the darkest of persecutions only to reemerge in the late twentieth century. In the 1990s, politicians in Russia and the three Baltic States found themselves in an interesting position of having to craft laws regulating religious practice from scratch. With religion now "decriminalized," how would religious organizations be regulated? Who would be allowed official access to the new religious marketplace? And how would formerly oppressed denominations be compensated for their losses (namely expropriated property) under the Communist regime? Answering these questions gives us insight into the political machinations surrounding religious freedom. But explaining the present requires an understanding of the past. Given the intermingling of the politics and history of Russia and the Baltics over the centuries, we present the histories of each in an intermingled fashion focusing first on Russia.

The Pre-Soviet Era

Russia

Christianity came to Eastern Europe, Russia, and the Baltics through the gradual expansion of European culture eastward and northward during the latter part of the first millennium. Russia's adoption of Orthodox Christianity occurred in 988 following the baptism of Prince Vladimir I, ruler of the

Eastern Roman Empire. Given the hierarchical nature that Christianity had developed by this time, it is not surprising that Orthodoxy took on the trappings of a state church because hooking into the political authorities at the time helped facilitate the mass evangelization of subservient people. Although patriarchs of the Orthodox Church jostled with the various tsars for power and influence in the early years of its existence, with the secular rulers generally getting the upper hand, the ROC was finally subsumed under the modern Russian state by Peter the Great in the early 1700s.[3] For the next two centuries, the ROC lived the typical life, for better and for worse, of a state church captured by the secular powers that be.

> [T]he Russian Orthodox Church at once enjoyed extensive privileges and suffered from serious restrictions, both consequent on its legal status as the established religion of the empire. It was supported financially by the government and was defended by law against its religious rivals; it alone had the right to proselytize. Until 1905 defection from the Church by an Orthodox Christian was a punishable offense. The secular authorities welcomed the help of the Church in combating the influence of non-Orthodox denominations. The Church ran an effective system of parish primary schools throughout the empire. Restrictions on it, however, were manifold. It was encumbered with an inefficient bureaucracy. Parish priests . . . from whose ranks the bishops were appointed, suffered from lack of contact with their bishops, who were moved around too frequently to become effective leaders in their diocese. Priests were also burdened with financial poverty and a large number of secular administrative duties. . . . The Russian Orthodox Church, then, was at the same time both protected and compromised. (Walters 1999, 32–3)

This situation should appear to the reader by now as an all-too-familiar story of state churches, albeit in perhaps more of an extreme form. The trade-offs that the ROC faced – between sanctioned protection and financial support and institutional autonomy – mirrors the situation of the Anglican Church in England and the Catholic Church in Latin America detailed in earlier chapters quite well. Moreover, the trade-offs detailed in the preceding passage serve well to support empirically the theoretical axioms and propositions developed here, namely that a dominant religious organization can obtain substantial protection from religious minorities (Propositions 1 and 4a). Politicians frequently enjoy the ability to control such a religious

---

[3] A history of the first eight hundred years of the ROC provides fertile ground for examining the theoretical perspective outlined in the earlier part of this book. However, our present scope is focused on the more contemporary period dating from the mid-twentieth century. We fully hope that some enterprising graduate student, another academic, or independent history buff will take up this challenge.

institution as it provides another means of exercising control over the population (Proposition 2). But as political tenure becomes more secure, the willingness of state rulers to provide everything the state church wants tends to dissipate (Propositions 5 and 5a) and religious pluralism begins to spring from the grass roots of society (Proposition 5b).

In hindsight, the results of the ROC's official status were quite predictable. As noted historian Robert Service observed, the ROC atrophied over time and devout believers in God looked down other avenues of faith to fulfill their spiritual longings when and where they could.

> In the seventeenth century a great schism took place in the Russian Orthodox Church when Patriarch Nikon, with Tsar Alexei's complicity, attempted a reform of the liturgy. As a result there was a vast exodus to the borderlands of the Muscovite state by Russians determined to stay loyal to tradition. The refugees became known as the 'Old Believers.' Although they were the largest group of opponents of the official Church, there were plenty of other denominations of Christianity in Russia and the variety increased in the nineteenth century as Baptists, khlysty, Seventh-Day Adventists and Tolstoians grew in number.[4] Even the Russian Orthodox Church was an unsatisfactory servant of the secular state at the parochial level. Its priests were proverbially needy, drunken and ignorant; frequently they followed the aspirations of their rural congregations more than the instructions of the bishops. Beneath the surface, 'Holy Russia' was a long way from being homogenous. (Service 2002, 47)

This observation goes a long way toward demonstrating the plausibility of Axiom 1, which asserts that religious preferences in society are pluralistic.[5]

---

[4] The *khylsty* (often capitalized Khylsty) were a breakaway mystic sect of Orthodox Christianity who engaged in flagellation and other ascetic rituals (Ramet 1998, 3–4). Their theological beliefs recalled some of the Gnostic sects of earlier Christianity. Formed in the early 1700s, the group remained relatively small until largely disappearing after the Communist revolution. Rasputin, the infamous advisor to the ill-fated Tsar Nicholas II and the Romanov family, counted among the followers of the *khylsty*. The Tolstoians (sometimes Tolstoyans) were followers of the religious thought of Leo Tolstoy (1828–1910) and might be considered a nineteenth-century Orthodox version of liberation theology. Their theology included a preference for pacifism and a belief that the Kingdom of God could be created here on Earth through the perfection of man (cf. Fueloep-Miller 1960). The ROC tried to suppress this radical spiritual competitor throughout the late 1800s (Luukkanen 1994, 39). Despite their progressive (and sometimes anarchistic) attitudes, they were nearly annihilated by the Soviets.

[5] Technically, axioms (or assumptions) are neither true nor false but rather are definitional elements of an argument, with the veracity of the argument resting upon how well the propositions (predictions) generated from the theoretical model match with empirical reality. However, in a more practical sense, a model's assumptions should at least be plausible to some degree.

This point will become important as we eventually move to an examination of the contemporary period. Weakened state churches that have been co-opted by the state can only maintain their hegemonic position in a religiously pluralistic society by gaining the coercive support of the state in restricting religious liberty. The willingness of secular leaders to yield to these demands, and what the dominant religion can provide politicians in return, will determine the level of religious liberty that results. For present purposes, however, it is sufficient to note that the ROC was tightly aligned with the tsarist state for predictable reasons when the Communist revolution swept Russian society in new directions.

It should be noted that an environment favoring religious liberty began to emerge in Russia during the first years of the twentieth century. With Tsar Nicholas II feeling pressure from liberal reformists in the nation, there was a greater willingness to allow foreign missionaries to enter the country. This freedom was enhanced by a law passed by the liberal Duma of 1905 granting non-Orthodox denominations the full legal right to proselytize. A number of missionaries took advantage of this proclamation but their ability to expand in sufficient numbers was limited by the social turmoil of the time and, eventually, World War I. The Provisional government of 1917 began debates regarding the separation of church and state in the summer of that fateful year, but their deliberations became moot after the Bolsheviks seized power in Moscow in October (Walters 1999, 40–1). The eventual fate of Russia would begin anew from that point.

The Baltics

In contrast to Russia, the history of the Baltic nations presents a more varied religious landscape. Catholicism, Orthodox Christianity, Lutheranism, and Calvinism converged in the Baltic lands between the thirteenth and eighteenth centuries. In the thirteenth century, Livonia (approximately modern-day Estonia and Latvia)[6] was gradually taken over by the crusading

[6] In his definitive work, *The Baltic States: The Years of Independence 1917–1940*, Georg von Rauch points out that, "the terminology of Baltic history is not without its pitfalls" (xiii). Livonia generally refers to the region ruled over by the Teutonic Order from 1201–1561 that was comprised of three provinces: Estonia, Livonia, and Courland. Four distinct groups lived in this area – Estonians, Latvians, Livonians, and Courlanders – the latter two eventually assimilating into the former two groups. After the collapse of the Order, Livonia came under Swedish and Polish, then Russian rule. At the end of World War I, Estonia and Latvia emerged as independent states in, approximately, the territory of the former Livonia. Lithuania (though linguistically related to the Latvians) experienced a very different pre–twentieth-century history, uniting with Poland for several centuries and

Sword Brethren (later by the Teutonic Knights) and German merchants, who established the city of Riga as a base for commercial and religious expansion (Raun 2001, 15–16). A social structure of serfdom emerged in Livonia in which the overwhelming majority of vassals were Germans who excluded the local population from the most lucrative sectors of trade, not to mention the hierarchy of the Catholic Church.

The Lithuanians to the south successfully defeated the Teutonic Knights in 1410.[7] Beginning in 1386, Lithuania was united with Catholic Poland through royal marriage and in 1569, the Kingdom of Poland and the Grand Duchy of Lithuania became a commonwealth, Rzeczpospolita, sharing territory, policy, and, officially, Catholic faith.[8] This union endured until 1795 when Russia, Germany, and Austria agreed to partition it to their territorial whims.

Due to Livonia's close proximity to Germany, the Reformation arrived quickly, and people experienced some short-lived advantages. The Reformation here was not liberating in either a political or nationalistic sense as it was to the Germanic lands to the west and north. Far from any spirit of Lutheran egalitarian religious ideals, the Baltic Germans referred to the local people merely as the "Undeutsche" (or non-Germans), not a particularly endearing reference. In the 1520s congregations in Riga were established that preached in the vernacular language, and the church began to recruit non-German clerics (Plakans 1995, 32). The first Estonian-language religious services were conducted in the urban areas in the 1530s. Landed nobility, however, showed little interest in the movement (Raun 2001, 24). The organizational domination of the Lutheran Church, introduced by Baltic Germans, was firmly established during the seventeenth century under Swedish rule, with Baltic Germans trading loyalty to the Swedish crown for continued regional hegemony.

The eighteenth century, however, brought political and social changes that would reverse earlier attempts to accommodate and serve the local peoples. In 1710, Peter I occupied part of Livonia and, eventually, all of the Livonian lands fell under the control of the Russian empire. The organized

---

becoming a sovereign Grand Duchy in its own right. Thus, the Baltic States refer to post-1918 Estonia, Latvia, and Lithuania, whereas the Baltic provinces refer to the territory of the former Livonia.

[7] At the Battle of Žalgiris (also Grünwald, Tannenberg), the mostly Polish and Lithuanian army won a decisive victory against the Germans and the Teutonic Order. Lithuanians are so proud of this historical event that they named their championship basketball team, which was outfitted by the Grateful Dead, after the battle.

[8] In the fifteenth century, the Grand Duchy of Lithuania stretched from the Baltic to the Black Sea, including modern-day Belarus, Ukraine, and the western edge of Russia, and encompassing a vast multicultural and multiconfessional region.

nobility of the regions gained influence over church matters. The churches could not accrue enough wealth to administer themselves, and the Russian government granted nobles the right to take over the task. Estate owners had the right to appoint clergy and would not consider men whose families belonged to the peasant class (Plakans 1995, 65), a situation reminiscent of the Catholic *patronato real* practiced in Southern Europe and Latin America. Again, we see how political and religious exigencies create a situation wherein church and state become closely allied.

The situation in Lithuania was different, however. Reformation ideas initially appealed to the nobility of Poland and Lithuania. The Reformed Calvinist movement made inroads through the Polish nobility, and "by the second half of the sixteenth century, the Lithuanian higher nobility, for all intents and purposes, was Protestant" (Musteikis 1988, 50). But the chancellor of Lithuania, and the leading proponent of the Reformation, Radvila the Black, ultimately wavered between Calvinism, Lutheranism, and Arianism in his later years. When he died in 1565, his and another magnate family returned to Catholicism, breaking the power of Protestantism in Lithuania for good. Musteikis emphasizes the fact that these religious struggles took place almost exclusively in the upper classes. In that regard, choices about the composition of the religious marketplace were made at the elite level irrespective of the preferences of the bulk of potential consumers; and the decisions made were often based more on political alliances than the actual spiritual desires and tastes of the "common folk." After the death of Radvila, "[t]he noblemen were convinced without coercion because, for political reasons, they found it expedient to follow the example of the moguls" (Musteikis 1988, 51). In many respects then, Lithuania has more in common with Catholic Poland than with Latvia and Estonia.

The Baltic provinces in Livonia retained a relatively high level of ethnic homogeneity as the nineteenth century came to a close. However, the Russian Empire – a major player of change on the Eastern horizon – had already begun to affect the confessional makeup of the region. By the mid-1800s, the propagation of Orthodoxy had become a method of Russification, bringing the Baltic region under the increasing influence of mother Russia. Between 1845 and 1848, approximately sixty-five thousand Estonians converted to Orthodoxy, believing that it would free them from certain taxes and military service and provide other means of raising their standard of living at a time when living was hard.

Fueled by rumors that the tsar was offering free land to colonists in the unpopulated parts of the Russian empire, the Estonian peasantry also turned for the first time to the possibility of legal emigration as a solution to its economic problems. In fact, the basis for the conversion movement was not religious, but social and economic. Although the Orthodox prelates in Livland willingly accepted the new converts, no worldly benefits followed. (Raun 2001, 45)

Orthodoxy, then, came to the Baltics through a policy of bait and switch. The trade-off here is an interesting one that fits broadly within the theoretical framework developed in Chapter 2. We can see how Russia was using religious influence to extend its political power over the region (Proposition 2) and offered various material enticements to achieve this end. The people of Livonia weren't necessarily coming theologically to the loving embrace of the Orthodox Church as much as they were trying to accommodate themselves to the economic, political, and military grasp of the Russian state.

Simultaneously, the Baltic Lutheran churches experienced increased problems. Estonians objected to the fact that the German nobles still controlled the appointment of pastors, a majority of whom continued to be German (Raun 2001, 80). Historian David Kirby summarizes well the struggle in the Lutheran church in the nineteenth-century Baltics:

> In the Baltic provinces, the *Landeskirsche* was under threat from those who wished to weaken the privileged status of the Baltic Germans; and although the great majority of Estonians and Latvians remained within the evangelical Lutheran tradition, they could not embrace wholeheartedly the pretensions and precepts of their quondam masters. (1995, 152–3)

Although Lutheranism had become the state confession in many European countries, it was not to happen in the Baltic region – neither while Livonia remained under foreign rule nor when Estonia and Latvia first became independent states in 1918. The growing presence of multiple denominations, including the influence of Russian Orthodoxy, guaranteed that creating a single state church would not be politically wise as it would alienate a significant portion of the population (as per Proposition 4c), particularly if those churches were perceived to be extending the reach of foreign interlocutors.

In this, the Baltic provinces and Lithuania had something in common: "both were subjected to a Russification campaign designed to destroy, not only their growing sense of national identity, but also their confessional allegiance; and both had to assert their social and cultural independence from their Polish or, alternatively, German overlords" (von Rauch 1974, 20). In the late nineteenth century, imperial Russia began efforts to Russify Lithuania; not through obvious enticements to convert to Orthodoxy like in the territories to the north but through attempts to isolate Lithuania from neighboring Poland and to weaken the Catholic Church by forcing it to use the Cyrillic alphabet. An opportunity to pursue this strategy arose following the Emancipation Edict of 1861, a reform measure ostensibly freeing serfs from their conditions of legal and financial slavery (Service 2002, 48). Unfortunately, Alexander II had not kept his promise to provide land for the Lithuanian serfs whom he had freed in 1861. This provided Poles with an argument to incite Lithuanian peasants to join them in their attempt to reestablish the Republic, using religion as a unified rallying cry:

> The Polish Council (*Rzad Narodowy*)... did not appeal to Lithuanian national feelings, but sought the very necessary help of the peasants, promising to provide land for free (the czarist reform of 1861 required that people pay for the land they received) and fervently persuading them that it was necessary to defend the Catholic faith from the Orthodox faith being forced upon them. (Vardys 1997, 223)

Russia responded to this Lithuanian-Polish uprising in 1863 by imposing a ban on the Roman alphabet commonly used in printing the Lithuanian language, a clear signal that Lithuania was Russian (Cyrillic alphabet) territory. The Lithuanian Catholic Church opposed this blatant attempt at Russification and organized the publication of religious materials in Latin script in neighboring Prussia and then smuggled the texts into Lithuania. Not surprisingly, the Catholic Church became an important player in the promotion and preservation of Lithuanian nationalism,[9] a role it would continue throughout the twentieth century, and for which it would be rewarded with favorable legislation after gaining independence briefly following World War I and then after breaking free from Soviet influence in the 1990s.

For the Baltics, the twentieth century witnessed drastic shifts in political power. At the end of World War I, Estonia and Latvia created their first independent states and Lithuania reestablished its sovereignty. Although attention to the question of religious liberty did not gain momentum worldwide until the latter part of the twentieth century, the constitutions of these fledgling republics guaranteed religious freedom and, unlike their Nordic and West European neighbors, did not establish state churches. Predictably, being the hegemonic religion and playing an important political role in resisting outside influence, the Catholic Church was granted special rights

---

[9] This is ironic given that the Polish Council tried to avoid fanning the flames of Lithuanian nationalism by appealing to a common religious heritage.

in the Republic of Lithuania (as per Proposition 4a, which says that hegemonic denominations are often able to get their policy preferences realized).
Catholic clergy saw it as a religious duty to be involved in the political
development of the nation (Vardys 1997). Having religious environments
not dominated by a single confession, Estonia and Latvia shied away from
bestowing such privileges on any particular denomination.

The confessional makeup of interwar Estonia as recorded in the first
census of 1922 reveals a situation of religious duopoly: of a total population
of 1.1 million, 79 percent claimed to be Lutheran, 19 percent Orthodox, and
a mere 0.2 percent Catholic. Despite their small numbers, the 1925 Law on
Religious Associations and Their Alliances, which governed the registration of religious bodies, did not discriminate against Catholics (Salo 2002,
282). Why Catholics would be granted a relatively high level of freedom at
that time can be traced to international politics. As part of their independence, the Baltic States were required by the League of Nations to provide
guarantees to the minorities within their borders, including their former
German and Russian masters (von Rauch 1974, 135–6). The 1920 Estonian
constitution has been praised as remarkable in the extent of its guarantees,
which surpassed the Weimar Constitution on which it was modeled: "It is in
the protection of minorities... that the Esthonian [sic] Constitution is the
best known and most praised. Racial, ethnic, and linguistic minorities are
all given special rights" (Blaustein and Sigler 1988, 389). Nationalist leaders who were on the verge of finally gaining much sought after territorial
independence would surely agree to allow toleration for a small segment
of the population that posed no real threat to other denominations. Cross-
denominational poaching of parishioners presented little problem because
each of the three denominations cited was sufficiently distinct.

By 1918, Latvia had a substantial Orthodox population. Furthermore,
the Counter Reformation in Latgale, the southeastern region of Latvia,
had also been quite successful, raising potential problems of unity for the
fledgling nation. The region of Latgale had come under the rule of the
Lithuanian-Polish commonwealth and developed a strong Catholic iden-
tification. Thus, Latvia witnessed a higher degree of religious pluralism at
the turn of the century than its northern neighbor. The breakdown of confessions reveals less Lutheran dominance than in Estonia: 59 percent of residents were Lutheran, 20 percent Catholic, 9 percent Orthodox, 7 percent
Jewish, 4 percent Old Believers, and 1 percent of the population belonged
to various other small religious groups (Bērziņš 2000, 109).

The question of religious tolerance was central to the potential success
of the newly established independent Latvia; repressing any of the historic confessions potentially meant social turmoil and a lost opportunity

for finally securing sovereignty. As such, the Latvian government signed an agreement with the Holy See guaranteeing the religious freedom of the Catholic population of Latgale. The danger was that Latgallians would fear discrimination in a Lutheran state and decide not to unite with it (Balodis 2000). Thus, Latvia was pulled in three directions – by Orthodoxy from the East, Lutheranism from the West, and Catholicism from the Southeast. Politically speaking, the lack of religious homogeneity and the frailty of the new republic meant that the establishment of a Latvian state church was not a viable option. Fortunately, geographic and ethnic separation of the denominations meant that none truly competed with one another therefore making religious freedom more palatable to leaders of each confession.[10]

Despite a willingness to provide equal freedom for the main historical denominations, Latvian leaders did show concern over some religious newcomers. According to Nikandrs Gills, more than three hundred small denominations were operating in Latvia during the mid-1930s. Gills further noted that the prime concern of Latvian society was the creation of a successful independent state, which gave rise to a situation where the historical churches were allowed substantial freedom. But relatively new religious minorities were viewed with distrust and feared to be agents of foreign influence. For example, the Jehovah's Witnesses, who arrived in Latvia in the early 1920s, acquired legal status in 1933 under the title of the International Bible Students' Association. Yet in 1934, due to protests by state authorities and mainline churches, the organization lost its legal status and was not allowed to renew it in independent Latvia before the ensuing Nazi and Soviet occupations (Gills 2000). The politics of religious freedom, as laid out earlier, are quite transparent. The desire to achieve political sovereignty created the incentive to allow religious freedom for a geographically separate religious oligopoly (lest any group "veto" Latvian unification), but competitive spiritual newcomers faced more restrictive legislation.

All told, the political economy of the Russian and Baltic religious landscapes prior to the Soviet era[11] was similar to that of Europe during the medieval period. Despite the fact that religious preferences among the

[10] Compare this situation with Latin America. The Roman Catholic Church there was never seriously threatened by ethnic Protestant churches that kept to themselves and did not seek to convert Catholics. It was only when evangelical Protestants came to the region with the intent of winning converts that the Catholic Church felt a need to lobby for restrictions on their religion (Gill 1998, 81–95). Such was the case in Latvia where none of the major denominations threatened the flocks of the others.

[11] This era begins with the Bolshevik revolution in Russia in 1917 and the Soviet occupation of the Baltics in 1940 (interrupted for three years by the Nazis).

population may have been diverse, decisions about what faith would institutionally predominate in any region were made by political elites, typically based on strategic calculations related to their political survival and/
or nationalist aspirations. Although the spiritual conversion of Prince
Vladimir's mother to Orthodoxy in Russia may have been truly inspired
by personal faith, it is difficult to argue that the Orthodox Church was not
manipulated and used by future tsars for their own personal benefit. This
is not to say that the ROC was a passive player in all of this. Consistent
with the assumption that hegemonic religions will prefer a tightly regulated
religious market that dampens denominational competition, ROC officials
benefited greatly from their relationship with the monarchy. Schisms did
erupt and some non-Orthodox faiths (e.g., Baptists) found space with which
to survive, revealing that diverse religious preferences did exist below the
state-guaranteed patina of Orthodox hegemony. As for the Baltics, their
geographic location placed them at the crossroads of multiple cultures and
political interests. German and Polish interests mixed and clashed with the
local interests of Lithuanians and the other Baltic regions (i.e., modern-day
Latvia and Estonia) to create a patchwork quilt of religious affiliation, with
some denominations more predominant in certain regions than others. The
resulting confessional makeup of the Baltic region would play a significant
role in determining the laws related to religious freedom at the end of the
twentieth century. But before we get to that point, it is important to understand how the arrival of Communism reshaped the religious scene in ways
that still reverberate to this day.

The Soviet Era

Soviet Russia

The rise to power of the Bolsheviks in Russia in 1917 marked a dramatic turning point for the history of religion in Russia. Almost overnight,
church-state relations were rewritten in dramatic form, first in Russia and
then in the territories that the Soviet Union extended its (direct and indirect) control over. Although the revolutionary Mexican Constitution of
1917 contained elements of religious repression that mirrored what the
Communist Party of the Soviet Union was about to put in force, namely
the legal denial of institutional religion in the country, the Mexican revolutionaries never matched the fury of the Soviets when it came to actually
trying to eradicate religious influence from society. Separation of church
and state came fast and furious in postrevolutionary Russia, even with the

typical chaos following a radical shift in government and a civil war against the counterrevolutionary White Russians drawing the attention of the top Bolshevik leaders. The process of a religious crackdown began in late January 1918, only three months after Vladimir Lenin's followers effectively seized control of the nation. To understand the seriousness with which the Communists pursued their goal of eradicating religion from society, consider that this job was given initially to one of the intellectual kingpins of Russian Communism – Leon Trotsky (Dickinson 2000, 328).[12] Trotsky penned an article in *Pravda* delightfully entitled "Vodka, the Church and the Cinema" (July 12, 1923) wherein he developed an interesting tactic with which to eliminate religion from society. "The cinema competes not only with the tavern but also with the church. And this rivalry may become fatal for the church if we make up for the separation of the church from the socialist state by the fusion of the socialist state and the cinema" (Trotsky 1923).[13] Socialist celluloid icons would replace religious icons in this brave new world.

The first action against religious institutions by the new Communist government was to issue a decree in early 1918 firmly disestablishing the ROC (Luukkanen 1994, 75).[14] This was followed up a few months later with bureaucratic instructions on how to accomplish this disestablishment and laws restricting religious education (G. Young 1997, 56). Although disestablishment could be considered a critical first step on the path toward religious liberty (as it was in colonial Virginia), the Soviets took a different (and more extreme) regulatory path that veered toward severe repression of the ROC and all other religious organizations. The initial policy focused on the closing of churches. In an interesting examination of previously sealed Soviet documents, Anna Dickinson determined that more than twenty-five thousand ROC churches were closed between 1917 and 1936 (2000, 329). David Powell, using perhaps less accurate data due to the closed nature of Soviet governance and society at the time, put the number of closures at nearly fifty thousand (1975, 41). Even at the lower estimate, the number of

---

[12] Although Trotsky held key government and party positions in the early Soviet Union, he was never a purebred Bolshevik and had opposed the Bolshevik's prime leader, Vladimir Lenin, on a number of occasions prior to the revolution. Nonetheless, he did become a close confidant to Lenin. He eventually lost a power struggle against Josef Stalin and was exiled in 1929, eventually ending up in Mexico, the other country that had radically altered its relationship with a dominant religion in 1917. It was in Mexico that Stalin gave Trotsky the axe, literally.

[13] We are grateful to Rimas Žilinskas for making us aware of this document.

[14] See Corley (1996, 17–18) for the exact document, which includes a fascinating compendium of previously secret Soviet communiqués on religion.

church closures was dramatic, if not draconian. Church financial assets were also seized and its publications restricted (G. Young 1997, 148). Neither of the aforementioned actions taken against the ROC include the countless other churches, mosques, and synagogues that felt the brunt of the Soviets' new religious policy.

Confiscating church buildings goes a long way toward diminishing the influence that religious institutions can exert in society. Religious services could only be held at a greatly reduced number of registered sites (Ramet 1998, 230). Without a regular place to congregate congregants will either have to find unofficial locations to meet at great risk of punishment or stop attending religious services altogether. But the Soviets did not just stop with church closures. Their religious policy included the wholesale expropriation and liquidation of other church valuables with the official intent of using those assets to ameliorate the plight of starving and rebellious peasants (Dickinson 2000, 327–8). Even church bells were taken and melted down for the valuable metal they could wield in a beleaguered nation short on raw materials at the time (Luukkanen 1997, 181). It shouldn't come as any great surprise to those familiar with Soviet history that hungry rural folk benefited little from these actions.

And if taking church property proved effective in reducing the influence of the ROC and other denominations, attacking and killing the clergy furthered the cause. Not surprisingly, a number of astute clergy read the writing on the wall early on in the revolutionary era and decided to leave the country post haste (Walters 1999, 41). Many stayed though, not having the means to escape and some went underground to continue preaching (Alexeev 1979, 30), and as Glennys Young notes the rural clergy persevered even with the help of parishioners willing to take on priestly functions (1997, 151–91). Indications early on revealed that the new regime would take a dim view of the ecclesiastical profession, particularly those that found cause in criticizing the government and Communist Party. Following the death of the ROC Patriarch Tikhon in 1925, Soviet leaders arrested his immediate successor along with twenty other ROC hierarchs (Dickinson 2000, 332). The ROC then designated a more reformist bishop – Metropolitan Sergii – to fulfill the role of patriarchal leader. Patriarch Sergii was earlier associated with a schismatic faction of the ROC known as the Renovationist Church (or Living Church), created in the early 1920s by clergy that had been critical of the old tsarist regime and more open to relations with the Bolsheviks (Ramet 1998, 22–3; G. Young 1997, 149–51; cf. Walters 1978). Despite Sergii's predilection toward the new Communist rulers, he refused to excommunicate anti-Soviet members of the ROC who were trying to keep the church going in exile. This recalcitrance landed him in prison for a short time until he agreed to publicly endorse the revolutionary government and its policies toward religious groups (Ramet 1998, 230).

Patriarch Sergii's capitulation to the regime in 1925 bought some temporary goodwill for the church, but Soviet religious policy took a turn for the worse in the 1930s as Josef Stalin sought to consolidate his power. Between 1930 and 1937, 124 ROC hierarchs were jailed or executed. In the city of Ul'yanovsk alone, more than 240 priests were killed between 1937 and 1938 (Dickinson 2000). Priests were routinely among those executed for political reasons throughout the country. Determining that their profession now posed a greater health hazard, many clerics either quit their position or left the country. All of this took its toll on the ROC. "On the eve of the Second World there were 6,376 clergy in the ROC, less than 10 percent of the pre-Revolutionary figure of 66,140. The hierarchy consisted of only four men: two metropolitans and two bishops" (Dickinson 2000, 332), meaning that the ROC was functioning without a designated patriarchal head for a substantial period of time. Clergy from other denominations did not fare any better with certain suspect "sects" (e.g., the Jehovah's Witnesses, Seventh-Day Adventists) being singled out for particularly harsh persecution (Dirksen 2002; Sapiets 1980).

Stalin's crackdown on institutional religion during the 1930s most certainly had its origins in his desire to consolidate power and eliminate rivals (as was true of most of the dictator's actions) (Luukkannen 1997, 159). Nonetheless, it would be improper to deny that Soviet religious policy in general contained an ideological predisposition favoring militant atheism. Both Karl Marx and Friedrich Engels, the intellectual bedrock of the Soviet Union, unabashedly despised religion (cf. Marx 1975). This attitude toward spirituality undeniably trickled down to the leaders of the Russian Revolution, including Lenin and Trotsky. Lenin surely revealed his ideological conviction when he stated "[e]very religious idea, every idea of God, even flirting with the idea of God is unutterable vileness ... vileness of the most dangerous kind. ... Every defense or justification for the idea of God, even the most refined, the best intentioned, is a justification of reaction" (Conquest 1968, 7). With such intense belief, one could only imagine that ideological motivations played a significant role in Lenin's religious policy. Moreover, the Soviet leadership eventually gathered together a committed band of devout nonbelievers into an organization known as The League of Militant Atheists (Froese 2004a). The rabidity with which this group approached its antireligious evangelization indicates that pure ideas did inspire a significant portion of the Soviet bureaucracy.

Nonetheless, political interests and strategy played a significant and substantial role in the formulation of policy. Despite his ideological antipathy toward religion, Leon Trotsky admitted to knowing how religious leaders and institutions could be promoted and manipulated for political ends, a Machiavellian (not pure Marxist) position. In a top secret memo dated May 14, 1922, Trotsky urged the Soviet Politburo to hail the breakaway Renovationist (Living) Church of the ROC as a means of subduing conservative reaction against the Revolution.

> It goes without saying that we now have a complete and total interest in supporting the reformed church group [the Renovationist Church] against the monarchist [conservative ROC group], of course deviating not one iota from our state principle of the separation of the church from the state or, even more, from our philosophical, materialist attitude to religion. Now, however, the great political task consists of ensuring that the reformed clergy do not turn out to be terrorized by the old church hierarchy. . . . One of the tasks of the press in this question at the present time consists precisely in raising the spirit of the loyal clergy and inspiring them with the certainty that within the bounds of their incontrovertible rights the state supports them although, of course, the state is by no means attempting to regulate on purely religious disputes and relations. . . . [I]t is necessary . . . while not hiding our materialist attitude to religion, not to bring it to the forefront however at the present time, that is in the assessment of the current struggle, in order not to push the two sides to a rapprochement, but on the contrary to allow the struggle to turn most bitter and decisive. (Corley 1996, 31–2)

Although an ideological antipathy toward religion certainly informed Trotsky's policy, he was politically shrewd enough to understand that the promotion of some religious leaders would yield significant political gains.

Josef Stalin, too, realized that pursuing religion to the point of extinction, no matter how much he ideologically loathed believers, was not a politically astute move. The repressed often have subterranean means of escaping persecution and can cause great damage as a subversive foe to the regime. Keeping one's foes visible is a wiser strategy and one that was pursued by Stalin.

> The situation of the Russian Orthodox Church toward the end of the 1930s was a tragic paradox: the Catacomb Church, which refused to recognize Metropolitan Sergi as the true head of the Church and went underground, in a sense saved the official Church from complete destruction because the Soviet authorities were afraid to force the entire Russian Church underground through ruthless suppression and so to lose control over it. (Alexeev 1979, 30)

As shown in the following text, the ROC, once subservient to its Soviet masters, also had its advantage as a tool to rally the population in wartime and then to be used as a propaganda puppet in the postwar years.

It wasn't only the state that used the reformist Renovationist Church to its advantage in the early Soviet years. The clergy associated with this breakaway movement wanted to destroy the hierarchical relations within the ROC that they found oppressive.[15] The Bolsheviks helped them accomplish this goal and, ironically, placed members of the Renovationist Church into positions of hierarchical authority abandoned by some conservative ROC leaders (Powell 1975, 28–9). And in a further irony,[16] "the modernist [Renovationist] movement lost its usefulness to the regime within a few years, as the previously recalcitrant Old Church leaders began to adopt an attitude of loyalty toward Soviet rule. Once they professed loyalty, the Bolsheviks withdrew their support from the Living Church, and without official support the Renovationist effort quickly died out" (Powell 1975, 29). Purportedly, the Renovationists could not muster the loyalty of the Orthodox faithful, who refused to recognize their legitimacy. Thus, in order to combat what they saw as an excessively authoritarian church, the Renovationists had to rely on a revolutionary dictatorship to install them in positions of authority only to discover that they lacked authority with their parishioners and would be replaced by the old hierarchs whom they sought to topple initially.

The politically motivated, as opposed to ideologically inspired, manipulation of religious institutions didn't stop with Trotsky's early policies or with Stalin's later purges. The coming of World War II issued in a new, albeit temporary, era in church-state relations that was marked by an easing of persecution and hostilities. The political motivations behind this relaxation of religious repression were quite transparent. With Nazi forces beginning their advance into Soviet territory in 1941, Stalin needed every available resource to rally his population in defense of the homeland. The leaders of the ROC, which had just been brutally repressed in the 1930s, responded to the call and rallied to the cause of war. In addition to saving their own selves from the Nazis, agreeing to support Stalin had a beneficial outcome.

[15] There is some debate as to how sincere the members of the Renovationist Church were in their desire to remake the ROC in a nonhierarchical fashion. That debate is beyond the scope of this study and involves individuals who may not have an impartial scholarly perspective on the matter. For a quick summary of this debate, see Luukkanen (1997, 41).

[16] One of the great natural resources of Russia is a seemingly unlimited supply of irony.

> This support was a major factor in bringing about [a] change in Soviet policy, but it was reinforced by other considerations as well. The Orthodox Church was no longer a threat to the regime, as it had been in the first years after the Revolution. In addition, Stalin was anxious to make a favorable impression on Western public opinion. . . . Most important, Stalin realized that a more liberal policy toward the church would help mobilize popular support within the Soviet Union, both in the German-occupied and Soviet-held territories. (Powell 1975, 32)

Church buildings were reopened, religious feast days were recognized, religious radio broadcasts were allowed and even scarce supplies of lamp oil were provided to the ROC for ceremonial purposes (Powell 1975, 32–3). By the end of World War II, the number of actual churches operating in Russian territory had increased to roughly fourteen thousand (Ramet 1998, 232) from a low of just less than one thousand in 1940 (Dickinson 2000, 329).[17] This *modus vivendi* between Stalin and the ROC was similar to the one negotiated between President Cárdenas and the Catholic Church in Mexico, although prompted by different conditions. In both the case of Mexico and the USSR, an intensified era of religious persecution was followed by liberalization and tolerance at a time when leaders from both countries needed to win support for their foreign policies.[18] But whereas in Mexico this *modus vivendi* would last until the 1992 constitutional reforms favoring religious freedom, allowing the Catholic Church to rebuild its strength, the ROC would have to persist under at least one more onslaught after World War II and prior to its liberation following the Soviet Union's collapse.

In the years immediately following World War II, the ROC and most other religious groups continued to benefit from a thaw in relations with the Soviet state, at least within the pre-1940 boundaries of the country. As detailed in the case of the Baltics in the following text, the USSR's territorial expansion brought with it an iron fist of repression on religious groups and liberal intellectuals alike.[19] Despite this policy in other parts of the Soviet

---

[17] Even after accounting for changed boundaries following the war that would have added some churches to the count, the number of churches that reopened was nothing short of remarkable for a regime that had come close to snuffing out the institutional ROC altogether.

[18] As a refresher of Chapter 4, Cárdenas was pursuing the nationalization of the oil industry from foreign interests at the time he reached out to the Catholic Church in the late 1930s.

[19] Detailing the exact measures taken against religious groups in different Eastern European states is beyond the scope of this study. However, our lack of coverage opens the possibility for some enterprising graduate student or scholar to test the political economic model of church-state relations presented here.

empire, some churches continued to be built within Russian Soviet territories following the war, taxes on monasteries were abolished, and the number of clergy began to increase. A few bishops were even awarded medals for wartime patriotism (Powell 1975, 33)! The only major exception to this détente in church-state relations within the Russian Soviet boundaries related to Jews. Increasing paranoia on the part of Stalin forced a campaign against Jews, which resulted in many being imprisoned, executed, or exiled (Powell 1975, 33–4).

One might rightly wonder why the improved relations that occurred during World War II persisted. In short, the answer can be found in Propositions 3 and 5a. As political tenure of a leader becomes secure (and nobody was thinking of challenging Stalin's authority at this time knowing what had happened to those who had in the past), resources required to enforce restrictions on religious liberty (or to pursue increased repression) could be better used elsewhere. In the Soviet Union, rebuilding a war-torn country, extending administrative control in new lands and attempting to keep pace with the technological might of the United States was more pressing than tamping down a church that really posed no threat to the survival of the regime. The existing ROC hierarchy had proved their patriotic loyalty during the war and learned that with such submission to their Soviet overlords they could actually gain a bit of expanded freedom, just as predicted by Proposition 5a. In fact, "[a]fter 1948 Church representatives were regularly to be found promoting the Soviet concept of peace in international gatherings" (Walters 1999, 43). Despite a relaxation of religious repression, sufficient regulatory restrictions existed on non-ROC churches, largely due the suspicion that Western denominations might be a breeding ground for anti-Communist subversives, that religious pluralism remained stunted, much to the approval of the ROC hierarchs.

Although the churches that were reopened during the war years remained that way through most of the 1950s, there were still powerful incentives in place for people to avoid those houses of worship. Most notably, visibly active members in the ROC were denied membership in the Communist Party. Considering that party membership was really the only pathway to improving one's standard of living – including securing more desirable jobs and housing – it was best for spiritual believers to keep a low profile. Public participation in religious activity remained low. Although it would be difficult to determine for certain how high belief in God remained despite the best efforts of the League of Militant Atheists and other Communist organs to eradicate such "superstition," a census in 1937 – at the height of Stalinist repression – revealed that roughly 56 percent of the population still admitted religious belief (Froese 2004a, 38), a surprisingly high figure given that respondents were responding to members of the Stalinist state apparatus. Following the traumatic events of World War II and the thaw in relations between church and state that persisted for the first decade and a half of the postwar era, it is reasonable to expect that a sense of spirituality persisted among the population.

The religious détente instituted by Stalin during the war continued through the first several years of the reign of Nikita Khrushchev, which began in 1953. However, this came to an abrupt end in 1959. Warning signs of a new wave of repression actually came late in 1958 when the tax-exempt status of Orthodox monasteries – granted in 1945 – was revoked causing many of these institutions to go bankrupt and close. The Soviets again set about the task of closing churches and tightening the registration requirements for new religious groups to the point where it was impossible for small, non-Orthodox groups to survive. The Soviets also overhauled the hierarchical structure of the ROC by assigning the management of parishes to local committees, taking it away from the authority of the priest (Powell 1975, 39–45). Repression didn't stop at the institutional level. Various laws now made it illegal for parents to teach the catechism to their children and prevented baptisms for anyone younger than thirty (Ramet 1998, 233–4; Corley 1996, 184–5). Given that religious belief and practice is a form of human capital that is most effective when instilled at an early age (Iannaccone 1990), delaying an important ritual through legislative decree certainly would diminish the religious intensity among the younger generation of Russians.

The reasons for this renewed repression remain somewhat murky in the scholarly literature. Both Corley (1996) and Ramet (1998) attribute it to Khrushchev's ideological predisposition. "Khrushchev *believed* in the future of Communism and he was determined to push Soviet society toward this goal. One element of this new society would be the absence of religion and he *believed* this process too could be speeded by forcibly rooting out the vestiges of religion in postwar Soviet society" (Corley 1996, 184; emphasis added). Khrushchev undoubtedly subscribed to general tenets of Marxist-Leninism and most likely "worshiped" at the temple of atheism. But given his "true believer" status, the question arises as to why he would have waited nearly six full years to begin his crackdown.

It may have been that growing unrest in Eastern Europe, best exemplified at the time by the 1956 Hungarian uprising, prompted the Politburo to clamp down on any and all sources of possible resistance to Soviet rule. Part of the reformist policies of the Hungarian leader Imre Nagy was to relax restrictions on religious institutions following the death of Stalin in 1953 (Wittenberg 2006, 135–43). As reformist measures in Hungary spiraled out of control, at least in the view of Khrushchev, and toward the withdrawal of Hungary from the Warsaw Pact, Catholic and Reformed clergy in the country began vocalizing the need for expanded religious liberty and gave the impression that they were among the most radical elements of the revolt (Wittenberg 2006, 143–5). Soviet tanks rolled into Hungary in late 1956 putting a premature end to Nagy's experiment. Similar religious upheaval in Poland at the time, including protest marches that used religious imagery and "a mass demonstration of folk piety" surely drew the attention of the Politburo (Ramet 1998, 100). It is plausible to assume that the Soviet leadership took away from these events a realization that religion could play a destabilizing role in socialist society and gave them the motivation to excoriate religious influence anew.[20]

Alternatively, or perhaps concomitantly, the delay in Khrushchev's crackdown simply might be the result of the arduous process of replacing ruling members from the Stalinist era. It is plausible that Khrushchev's immediate need to strengthen his own political position took precedence over his need to pursue a new policy against religious institutions that weren't causing any problems. As Gill and Keshavarzian (1999) demonstrated in the cases of Mexico and Iran, this was a common occurrence in secularizing regimes; the need to consolidate power is more important than pursuing any other particular policy goal. Moreover, eliminating rivals to power, which may include religious leaders, is accomplished best by dealing with them one at a time rather than all at once – a divide and conquer strategy that was used both by Josef Stalin and Nikita Khrushchev in the latter's de-Stalinization campaign. All told, the current available evidence shines little light on what appears on the surface to be a wasted use of state resources (and evidence contrary to Propositions 2 and 5a), particularly considering the docility of the ROC.

The coming of Khrushchev's successor, Leonid Brezhnev, in 1964 shuttled in a new era of *modus vivendi* with the ROC and other religious groups (Walters 1999, 44).[21] Having once again decimated religious institutions under Khrushchev, there was little need to keep devoting scarce resources to this goal (as predicted by Propositions 5 and 5a). Moreover, members of

[20] Exploring this linkage between the role of churches in the Hungarian revolt, Poland, and the new wave of repression against religious groups would make for a fine dissertation.

[21] By this time, most non-ROC religious groups were inert at best given the fact that many of them were viewed as sources of Western imperialism or, worse yet, subversion (cf. Dirksen 2002).

the ROC hierarchy, dating back to the Stalin era, had adjusted to their new reality and came to understand that their survival and personal role in society depended on unquestioned cooperation with the state. Several bishops and clergy cooperated so extensively that they became collaborators with the Soviet secret police – that is, the dreaded KGB (Committee for State Security) (Corley 1996, 358–84; Dunlop 1995, 28–32; Pospielovsky 1995, 51; Polyakov 1994, 148; Meerson 1981, 106–8). The following excerpt from a declassified KGB document reveals the chilling extent of this collaboration:

> *March 1983.*[22] In December of last year a group of monks from the Pskov Cave monastery expressed their dissatisfaction with regulations in the monastery and complained to patriarch Pimen about the superior of the Pskov Cave monastery. By means of agents 'Drozdov' and 'Skala', educational work was conducted among the monks of the Pskov Cave monastery.... The situation at the present time has been normalized. (cited in Corley 1996, 369)

It is doubtful that the complaining priests considered the situation "normal."

ROC leaders also helped to market a positive image for the USSR abroad, claiming that freedom of religion truly existed, and to support the activities of Western peace movements in light of Soviet strategic goals (Walters 1999, 43; Corley 1996, 358–84 passim). As KGB documents reveal, they were rather successful in infiltrating different international peace and religious organizations.

> *October 1968.* To provide counter-intelligence coverage of the work of the Christian Peace Conference and for the conducting of agent-operational measures ... [the KGB] traveled 12 agents of the organs of state security. In the course of measures unfavourable changes of personnel were prevented, and politically favourable final documents were adopted as well as amendments to the Statute.

> *February 1969.* As part of the delegation of the ROC the agents 'Svyatoslav', 'Antonov' and 'Kuznetsov' traveled to Poland to take part in the work of the international religious organization the 'Christian Peace Conference' with counter-intelligence and intelligence tasks. They presented materials on the political situation in this organization in connection with events in the CSSR [Czechoslovakia].

> *August 1969.* The agents 'Svyatoslav', 'Adamant', 'Altar', 'Magistr', 'Roshchin' and 'Zemnogorsky' traveled to England to take part in the work of

[22] Corley (1996) breaks these KGB documents down by month. The text of the documents cited here and others contained in Corley's work make for fascinating reading.

the CC [Central Committee] of the World Council of Churches [WCC]. The
agents were able to counter hostile activity and to promote agent 'Kuznetsov'
to a leading post in the WCC. (all cited in Corley 1996, 362–3)

This close association would come back to haunt slightly the ROC in the
post-Soviet era; collaboration with a previously repressive regime did not
bode well for building trustworthy relations with post-Soviet leaders. But,
ironically, this relationship would help in establishing bonds with former
Communists in the new Russian parliament that would help the ROC return
to an exalted state-church status in 1997.

The depressurization of religious repression created a result predicted by
Proposition 5b – religious activity and pluralism began increasing. Meerson
goes so far as to call the increased religious participation a "revival," noting
that it encompassed "tens of thousands of young people who belong to the
second and third generation of Soviet citizens and who have received atheist education" (1981, 105; cf. Anderson 1983, 27). To the extent that this is
true, it demonstrates how difficult it is to eradicate the spiritual longings that
seem almost innate in human beings. The ROC certainly benefited from
the relaxation in oppression and the subsequent "revival," but many non-
Orthodox groups also benefited. Underlying the easy repression and state
control of the highly visible ROC, "unregistered congregations continued
with unabated vigour and their activity was difficult to monitor, especially
when these congregations had no fixed meeting place" (Rowe 1979, 6).
The photographs accompanying Rowe's article reveal large crowds gathered along riverbanks waiting to be baptized.[23] In order to bring these
nearly invisible organizations under the influence of the Communist Party,
government officials realized that coercion did not produce the desired
results and only forced congregations underground where they were more
difficult to monitor. The Brezhnev regime offered "positive inducements":

In Chernovtsky, Ukraine, newly registered Pentecostal and Baptist churches
were both given unused church buildings for their services. Local authorities
[were] empowered to make church buildings available free of rent but [did] not
usually do so.[24] ... Officials even [went] so far as to offer registration without

[23] That such photographs exist is simply stunning to us. Given the brutality of the repression
that believers faced under both Stalin and Khrushchev, the act of simply taking a photo
that could fall into the state's hands would qualify as an act of immense courage.
[24] Although this may seem like local Soviet officials were disobeying orders higher up the food
chain to ease restrictions on churches, there was actually another rational logic at work –
one that was completely explicable under a command economy. Given that building space
was scarce and hence valuable, local officials required that "'most new churches [had]
to be built at the believers' expense ... and [would] automatically become the property

THE POLITICAL ORIGINS OF RELIGIOUS LIBERTY

demanding that a congregation commit itself to observing the legislation on religious cults, that is the congregation [could] be registered without accepting any restrictions on its activities.... Permission to meet without formal registration [was] another form of registration without conditions. It [was] in effect a declared truce, during which the authorities hope[d] that the congregation [would] get used to meeting freely and ultimately prefer to register than resume an illegal existence. (Rowe 1979, 7–8)

Brezhnev's more liberalized policy toward religion also allowed the importation of Bibles and other religious literature and the resumption of religious youth education (Rowe 1979, 10). Although strong disincentives (and a fear of renewed repression) still kept religious participation low, a new environment of religious pluralism was starting to take root in Russia and the other territories of the USSR.[25] This incipient spiritual diversity would come to haunt the ROC in the post-Sovietera and play a role in ushering in new restrictions in 1997.

The final chapter in the Soviet-era story of the ROC was to be written by Mikhail Gorbachev, who became general secretary of the Communist Party in 1995. Facing a troubled economy and a recalcitrant bureaucracy, Gorbachev fatefully engaged in a series of liberalizing political reforms (*glasnost*) that would ensure his economic restructuring (*perestroika*) of society. His apparent political strategy with respect to *glasnost* was to send credible signals to potential allies buried deep within the bureaucracy that he was serious in his desire for reform (Anderson 2001).[26] Part of the reform included a liberalization of regulations on religious groups. Moreover, Gorbachev wanted ROC leaders to publicly endorse *perestroika* (Bourdeaux 1995a, 115); much the way Mexican president Carlos Salinas traded greater

of the State" (Rowe 1979, 7). Ironically (once again), Soviet planners were using private initiative to add to the stockpile of resources that they controlled! Those local officials were responding positively to the mandate to allow greater religious activity but in a way that supported their own economic well-being, a result fitting well with the general theory of this work.

[25] One should not overestimate the size of this "revival" and growing pluralism. Practicing religion in the USSR was still a dangerous and materially unrewarding activity. The growth of religious believers remained extremely small.

[26] This should be considered in contrast to the "Let a Hundred Flowers Bloom" campaign in Maoist China wherein scholars and bureaucrats were encouraged to criticize the regime for the sake of making improvements. The only problem was that once Chairman Mao determined that the criticism had gone too far, the flowering critics were brutally mowed down. The tight ideological control of totalitarian regimes such as this tends to create a great deal of skepticism toward official policies of reform and creates an aura of "preference falsification" wherein no one is willing to reveal their own true preferences leading to a situation wherein no one knows who is really speaking the truth (Kuran 2004).

religious freedom for support of his economic trade policies. This is a clear indication of religious policy being made in the interests of securing a politician's political and economic goals (through Proposition 3).

The ostensible goal for loosening the reins on the ROC was the upcoming millennial celebration in 1988 of Prince Vladimir's baptism and official arrival of Christianity in Russia. This symbolic milestone and public celebration created an opportunity for Gorbachev to introduce the 1990 law "On Freedom of Conscience and Religious Organizations," which reiterated the long-standing law in the USSR that said people were free to worship as they chose. However, this law actually added some teeth to that previously hollow declaration and allowed clergy to participate in politics, made registration of new religious groups easier, and even gave the green light to denominations wishing to construct their own educational facilities (Berman 1999, 272–5). Religious political parties – such as the Christian Patriotic Union and the People's Orthodox Movement of Russia – were allowed to form (White et al. 1994, 74). A more specific and liberal law was implemented in the Russian Federation the same year as Gorbachev's initiative (Knox 2004, 91). What is important to note, though, is that this new legislation was not motivated by a deep-seated desire by Gorbachev for religious liberty.[27] Rather it was part and parcel of his larger *glasnost* strategy of saving the Soviet empire from economic stagnation and buying support for his other economic reforms. As John Basil asserts:

> Responding to gradually building pressures from international organizations in favor of religious freedom, and looking for collaborators at home to help bolster its flagging energy, the tottering regime introduced the first substantial legal changes since the early 1920s. . . . [T]he Soviet leadership under Mikhail Gorbachev was clearly 'playing the religious card' as part of its survival tactics. (2005, 152)

As Proposition 3 predicts, these religious reforms (and the other components of *glasnost*) were created with the end goal of trying to invigorate the USSR's economy and save Soviet Communism from being relegated to the dustbin of history. But again, dipping into the mine shaft of Russian irony, these reforms – unforeseen to Gorbachev and virtually all Soviet observers – only hastened the demise of a world superpower.

---

[27] One might plausibly question this statement based upon the revelation that Gorbachev had been baptized as a youth (White et al. 1994, 73) and that his mother was a regular churchgoer (Bourdeaux 1990, 24). However, the direct trade-off noted by Bourdeaux (1995, 115) indicates that there were political and economic motives at play.

One final item relevant to the course of post-Soviet affairs needs mentioning. Gorbachev's new religious law did not only apply to Orthodoxy but was designed to apply to all faiths. Even nonmainstream groups such as the Hare Krishna benefited as noted in the passage from a 1990 document prepared by M. V. Kornilov, Commissioner of the Council for Religious Affairs in the Yaroslavl region.

> I consider that the question of the registration of the given religious association [Krishna Consciousness] should be resolved positively, proceeding from the fact that official registration would allow full control over their activity, would exert a positive influence on the members of the group and would hold them to loyal positions in relation to the state and society. (Corley 1996, 356)

First, this passage clearly indicates that in addition to being part and parcel of the liberalizing strategy of *glasnost*, new religious laws also had the advantage of allowing Soviet bureaucrats to exercise some degree of monitoring and control over these groups. But more importantly, although the ROC initially welcomed this new legislation and the operational freedom it allowed, the legalization of groups like the Hare Krishna and other non-Orthodox faiths created a new set of problems for the hierarchy. Weakened by decades of Communist torment and only knowing life as a state-supported church, the leaders of the ROC were unprepared institutionally to deal with the onslaught of missionaries, new religious movements, and other confessional rivals ushered in by this law. Their response to this new competitive religious economy was typical of previously hegemonic state churches – seek the support of the state in curtailing the religious rights of others. Before completing this story, we must first examine how Soviet religious policy affected other regions to where it was spread – namely the Baltic States of Estonia, Latvia, and Lithuania.

The Soviet Baltics

For the Baltic States, having started down a democratic path in 1918, the secret 1939 Molotov-Ribbentrop Pact negotiated between their neighbors to the east and west guaranteed their nascent freedom would be short lived. Crushed beneath the onslaught of Soviet tanks the following year was also the hope that religious liberty would flourish. Continuing a strategy perfected earlier in Russia under Stalin, the Soviet invaders immediately implemented policies designed to destroy (or, at a minimum, seriously weaken) the churches. Although Germany's duplicity in the Molotov-Ribbentrop Pact and military advance eastward interrupted the Soviet occupation a year later, Stalin had time to bear down harshly on all religious institutions during what was known as a "year of terror." A Latvian exile in Stockholm reported, "In the summer of 1941, the Russians had hastily to leave Latvia, and their plans for the destruction of the Christian Church remained unfinished" (cited in Talonen 2004, 198). Upon their return in 1944, the Soviets swiftly consolidated power and recommenced their antireligious activities. Yet Stalin's policy of a religious "thaw" in Russia during the war and in the years immediately thereafter created a rather ambiguous situation for churches in the now Soviet-dominated Baltics.

Riho Altnurme, utilizing Soviet-era documents from the Estonian State Archives, the State Archives of the Russian Federation, and the Estonian Evangelical Lutheran Church (EELC) Consistory archives, noted similar trends in Estonia as in Soviet Russia during 1944–9.

> There was a certain ambiguity in the church-state relationship during this period, after the shift in Stalin's religious policy during the war. Religious tolerance was granted in order to preserve good relations with the allies. Yet this was just a front: religious policy had the same aim as before: to cut the ties between church and society, to destroy the religious traditions which had become national traditions. (Altnurme 2003, 269)

But unlike in Russia where the ROC had been largely tamed as an instrument of the state, the churches in the three Baltic nations were still considered unpredictable at best. Being that the Soviet Union had just installed its dominion over these countries, there was also the possibility that the churches could be a source of nationalist resistance. For that reason, religious institutions came under greater scrutiny and control by the Soviets than what the subjugated ROC experienced in Russia at the time. Put another way, what the Soviets did to religious institutions in Russia in the 1920s and 1930s had to be repeated in the newly conquered Baltics.

In Estonia, an agency known as the Council for the Affairs of Religious Cults was established by the Soviets to "monitor" churches.[28] The department nationalized church property, "registered" churches, and developed case files on clergy, seminarians, and lay believers. Johannes Kivi, Soviet Commissioner of the Council for the Affairs of Religious Cults for Estonia from 1945–54 used a combination of mechanisms, which limited the freedom of churches, including official registration and property nationalization, although the churches were still able to use much of their property until 1949. Individually, pastors were burdened by higher income taxes than

---

[28] This agency was present in the two other Baltic nations as well.

the rest of the population. Confirmation classes continued through 1948, but the minimum age of participants was raised from sixteen to eighteen, which had the paradoxical effect of increasing participation.[29] Not surprisingly, this was met with the initiation of an atheist campaign by the department of ideology in the Estonian Communist Party. After mass deportations of clergy in 1949, confirmation classes were "liquidated." Apparently, increased participation in confirmation classes was frowned on by the Communists. Lutheran pastors reacted by taking their training of young people and the teaching of theology underground (Altnurme 2003, 271–3).

But the response of the Estonian clergy was not unified. Some searched for a theological explanation for the Soviet occupation as punishment that would lead to repentance; others hoped for a war of liberation and supported the partisan resistance. As in Russia, a number of clergy were recruited by the security apparatus to report on colleagues. Among them were true collaborators and "untrustworthy" agents who were eventually punished. Between 1944 and 1949, twenty-three clergy were arrested (Altnurme 2003, 273–4).

The attempt to rein in religion took on an interesting denominational flavor with the belief that encouraging Orthodoxy would help to bring non-Orthodox believers under the same control the Soviets exercised over the ROC. For instance, as soon as the Soviets called for religious groups to register under the new regime, the Moravian Brethren, once quite influential in the Baltic provinces, tried to maintain their status by registering as branches of Lutheran or other congregations. The Ministry of Security attempted, but failed, to lure some uncompromising congregations of the Brethren to join the Orthodox Church in order to increase its influence against the Lutherans. Joining the EELC with the ROC was also proposed as a means of weakening the influence of the former. EELC leader Jaan Kiivit ultimately rejected the idea, as did Soviet authorities who feared that the Orthodox Church in Estonia would eventually be overwhelmed by the Lutherans (Altnurme 2003, 274–5), a result that would have been the opposite of what they were trying to achieve – that is, making Lutherans more Orthodox (and passive). Despite this failed policy of trying to make everyone Orthodox, restrictions on churches and religious organizations in Estonia did take their toll. Restrictions on religious freedom seriously dampened enthusiasm for religious practice and by 1977 attendance in any

[29] An attitude of nationalist defiance might explain this paradox. Conquered populations do not always subjugate easily, and one could imagine defiant young adults attending confirmation classes merely to spite the new law that tried to prevent such behavior.

of these registered denominations represented less than 1 percent of the population (Plaat 2003, 56).

In Latvia, as Soviet troops returned and German forces retreated, many clergy, recalling the deportation and murder of some church leaders in the first Soviet occupation, fled to Germany and Sweden. The exile of Latvian priests was not always voluntary though. With Hitler's military campaign stalling on the eastern front and the Soviets making territorial gains, German security police (for reasons unclear) forcibly deported several of the most important Evangelical Lutheran, Orthodox, and Roman Catholic leaders to Germany. By the beginning of 1944, more than half of clergy within the Latvian Evangelical Lutheran Church alone became refugees. The losses were worse up the church hierarchy, with roughly four-fifths of its district leaders being exiled or assassinated, some killed by advancing Russian soldiers. The majority of the faculty at the College of Theology also fled to the West (Talonen 2004, 208–12). Thus, by the time the Soviets arrived, the Lutheran Church was institutionally decimated and could offer little resistance to what was to come. Not only Lutheran clergy were affected: the combination of the resettlement of Baltic Germans and Estonian-Swedes, border changes with the Soviet Union, and emigration of pastors due to the threat of persecution and deportation caused major losses for the Orthodox Church. Although the Lutheran Church took the greater hit, losing 85 percent of its clergy between 1939 and 1945, the Orthodox Church saw its ecclesiastical ranks cut roughly in half. The coming Soviet deportations of 1944–5 and 1949 further diminished the ranks of the clergy, including those of minority churches (Salo 1978, 193–4).

In heavily Catholic Lithuania, the Soviet regime's initial strategy involved severing the Church's ties with Rome, creating a national, "autocephalous" church that would no longer be under the umbrella of the pope. The plan shifted to ensuring that religious institutions would "act within the limits of liturgical practice" and provide support for the regime's domestic and foreign policy (Streikus 2003, 278). The Soviets pressured the Church hierarchy to denounce the partisan resistance but to no avail. Because of their refusal, Bishop Borisevicius was sentenced to death, Bishop Ramanauskas was sentenced to ten years in a forced labor camp, and Bishop Matulionis and Archbishop Reinys were sentenced to seven years in the Vladimir prison (Streikus 2003, 279). Conditions in Soviet prisons were difficult; Reinys died in prison six years later (Misiūnas and Taagepera 1993, 124). These persecutions left Lithuania with only one prelate, Kazimieras Paltarokas. By 1954, half of Lithuania's clergy had been deported (Anderson 1994, 54). Beyond interrogating and harassing priests and laypeople, the

Soviet regime pursued other antireligious strategies including the closure of churches often turning them into museums,[30] shutting down or severely restricting entrance into seminaries, and charging churches more than six times more than other cultural institutions (e.g., museums, schools) for basic services like electricity.

Efforts to crush the Church in Lithuania succeeded by many measures; eliminating the ecclesiastical staff of a religious institution goes a long way toward reducing its social efficacy. The tenacity of Soviet propaganda and harassment certainly took its toll on many individuals. Soviet agents of the Council of Religious Cult Affairs could claim some rather significant victories. Archival records include written declarations by a priest named Vytautas Starkus who bowed to pressure and traded his priestly duties for apartments and a peaceful life. At first, Father Starkus merely wanted to trade his *ecclesiastical career* for a simple apartment:

> Because of the fact that I have firmly decided to quit my priestly duties in the nearest future and to sacrifice my efforts and talents for scientific, atheistic propaganda, I ask you to be my mediator in the appropriate institutions to provide me and my mother a residence in the city of Vilnius. I plan to start a family in the future. I will announce my resignation from the priesthood in the press. Therefore, because of reasons known to you, I cannot stay in my former place of residence. (Lithuanian Central State Archives 181/6/43)

But apparently this was not enough for state officials and in order to secure himself a better station in life, Vytautas completely renounced his connection to the *spiritual world* in a statement a short time later.

> I constantly observed the reality of the Soviet life, and deepened my knowledge. All of this has changed my attitude toward faith. I consciously understood that religious dogmas do not have any real foundation, and all that is taught by the Church has no basis in reality. Not wanting to go against my conscience, and beliefs and further mislead people.... I request that you, comrade commissioner, cross out my name from the list of registered priests. (Lithuanian Central State Archives 181/6/42)

Concurrent with the drop in clergy, the onslaught of atheist propaganda and various political and economic disincentives to being a practicing Catholic, participation in Catholic rites dropped significantly. Although such a decline may not reveal the true spiritual longings of the population who were after

---

[30] It is an interesting historical coincidence that the Mexican revolutionary government, inspired by its own radical Constitution of 1917, also transformed churches into public museums.

all being provided with myriad disincentives for attending church,[31] there is no doubt that religious groups were losing ground because of the heavy-handed secularism promoted by the Soviets.

Although Soviet policy was proving successful in the ways just mentioned, in other ways it backfired, a result not surprising given the strong Lithuanian nationalism that had informed Lithuanian politics over the past century (Sapiets 1979). A significant portion of the population remained defiant and religion became an integral part of that defiance. Certain Church activities went underground – for example, training priests in a secret seminary, illegally catechizing children, and eventually establishing one of the most widely distributed *samizdat* (underground) journals of the Soviet era, the *Kronika* (*The Chronicle of the Lithuanian Catholic Church*). But not all religious activity took place in secret, and it often mingled with political dissent. During the period from 1965–78, 10.3 percent of all political protests occurred in Lithuania despite the fact that Lithuanians represented only 1.3 percent of the USSR's overall population. And between 1970 and 1977, two-thirds of the demonstrations in Soviet-controlled Lithuania were specifically religious in nature (Misiūnas and Taagepera 1993, 84; cf. Sapiets 1979). Courageous religious leaders were becoming heroes of the resistance, a fact that would be noted and amply rewarded when the battle for independence was won a decade later.

International awareness of human-rights abuses gave the Lithuanian resistance a point of leverage in its struggle, and freedom of conscience played a central role in their struggle. Their efforts were bolstered when the Soviet Union joined in signing the Helsinki Agreements in 1975. After that time, the USSR was under increased pressure to prove that reports of the abuse of human and religious rights were not true. Gradually, religious groups in Lithuania and the Baltics more generally were granted increased freedom to gather for worship. With this they began to make more demands on the regime (Sapiets 1979).

The Helsinki Group in Lithuania was founded by a Jesuit priest and supported by other Catholic clergy, laypeople, and nonreligious intellectuals. The group defended the rights not only of Catholics but also members of

---

[31] Kuran (1995) provides a stark reminder that under repressive conditions, people have a strong incentive to falsify their true feelings in a public setting. His own analysis of the USSR and its collapse is instructive when it comes to examining "official" statistics from the Communist era. The "rebirth" of religious life following the liberation of the Baltics in 1990 and the collapse of the Soviet Union in 1991 indicate that many people kept their true religious desires hidden out of the lack of knowledge that others felt as they did and a palatable fear that others would punish them for expressing such views.

Protestant sects (though there were admittedly few) to worship in freedom. In June of 1977, the group issued a statement regarding the discrimination of a Pentecostal family (Petkus 1999, 31).[32] Ironically, when independent Lithuania drafted its 1995 Law on Religious Communities and Associations (LRCA), Pentecostals were considered a nontraditional and suspicious religious cult, not worthy of full freedoms. Despite the irony, this action was consistent with Propositions 1 and 4a, which state that dominant religions will favor restrictions on religious minorities and will tend to have greater bargaining power during periods of political competition (as was the case in Lithuania during the 1990s). The Helsinki Group also intervened on behalf of the Lutheran church, complaining that worshipers had nowhere to gather (Petkus 1999, 72). Although Evangelical Lutherans did make the list of traditional religions in 1995, the Lithuanian Catholic Church still demanded and received greater privileges in education and legislation than their Protestant brethren. Institutional and political concerns matter quite extensively when formulating policy preferences in the religious arena. Different political contexts quickly can make competitors out of former allies.

The Communist era proved to be difficult for religious organizations within Russia and throughout all the territories of the Soviet empire. Many a faithful cleric often made unseemly compromises to preserve not only the survival of their own church, but often their own lives. Through all of this, though, religion survived. When the chains of Communism were tossed aside, it would become quite clear that the grand atheistic plan of Marxist-Leninism was a failure. But as religious belief frequently requires a social and institutionally organized form, the battle over which confessions would gain supremacy in the post-Soviet era would make for some interesting political battles.

Free at Last? The Post-Soviet Era

The collapse of the Berlin Wall in 1989 and subsequent demise of the Soviet Union two years later took the world, including nearly all academics, by surprise. Since that time, the study of transitions from Communist rule has become a major topic of interest among social scientists. The design of various political and economic institutions and their relative performance has been the primary focus of these scholars, and for good reason. The rapid

---

[32] Viktoras Petkus went on trial and was imprisoned several times for his religious resistance to Soviet rule in 1947, 1957, and again in 1977. See the appendix in Sapiets (1979) for a discussion of his history under persecution.

collapse of a major empire and the need to create new rules and institutions from scratch throughout a wide range of nations – including Eastern Europe and the nations contained in the former Soviet Union – provided scholars the opportunity to test a wide range of theories in an environment approaching a natural experiment. Such an opportunity motivated this chapter even though the principal author is not an expert on the region. Nonetheless, the chance to test the theoretical propositions put forth in Chapter 2 in this new and exciting political environment proved too enticing to pass up. As such, we examine how policy toward religious institutions has been constructed during the 1990s and into the early twenty-first century in Russia and the Baltic States of Estonia, Latvia, and Lithuania. Although a full comparison of all the nations of Eastern Europe and the former Soviet Union would be ideal, time and space considerations determined that we would limit our focus to the aforementioned countries.[33] Our goal is to provide an initial test of the theoretical propositions put forth in Chapter 2, demonstrate their initial plausibility, and encourage other scholars or enterprising graduate students to extend the analysis into other contexts.

Russia

Russia's post-Soviet religious policy is a fairly straightforward story of movement from laissez-faire freedom to a tightly regulated religious economy that fits well with the theoretical propositions developed earlier. Although finally welcoming freedom from Soviet tyranny, the ROC quickly came to realize that it was not institutionally prepared to compete with a rush of non-Orthodox competitors that flooded into the nation. Being the historically dominant denomination and now being put on the defensive meant that ROC hierarchs quickly came to favor creating regulations that limited the ability of religious newcomers (and many preexisting non-Orthodox groups) to gain new followers. With the political scene being turbulent and uncertain, ROC leaders were finally able to find the support of a political faction that rode a wave of nationalism to power and granted the ROC's wishes in exchange for their political cooperation. Ironically,[34] this political faction contained many former Soviet Communists who took a rather dim view of spirituality in the heyday of the USSR. Let us examine how this story unfolded in greater detail.

---

[33] One could add to this list the primary author's unfamiliarity with the region as a reason for limiting the analysis.

[34] As mentioned earlier, there is no shortage of irony in Russia.

The liberalization under Gorbachev's era of *glasnost* formed the basis of religious policy early on in post-Soviet Russia. For the most part, the general policy under Russia's first post-Soviet president, Boris Yeltsin, was a live and let live attitude. Considering that the entire political and economic structure of a nuclear superpower basically evaporated overnight, Yeltsin had more pressing concerns than what to do with churches. The easiest road to travel was simply to continue with the path established by Gorbachev's 1990 legislation "On Freedom of Conscience and Religious Organizations." Arguably, too, he was concerned with presenting a credible face to the United States and Western Europe that showed how things were really changing in Russia and that the new government would honor its international commitments, including those advocating freedom of conscience (Anderson 2003, 128).

The ROC hierarchy was as surprised as anyone else by the fast-moving events of 1989–91. Not surprisingly they welcomed the greater religious freedom established by the 1990 law, but almost immediately they were concerned about their historical (pre-Soviet) status as an official state church. Their vocal anxiety on this matter was propelled by a remarkable explosion of religious pluralism, which had been taking shape gradually over the last several decades of the Soviet regime, and the quick interest foreign missionaries showed in the country. From the vantage point of missionaries, Russia offered potentially ripe pickings – a nation with a spiritual thirst that had been denied holy water for more than seventy years. The extent to which atheism had taken hold was not fully known at the time, but indications of a minor religious revival under Brezhnev (as noted in the preceding text) and Gorbachev offered significant hope.[35] One of the most astute and longtime observers of Soviet religion argued that this religious revival had been brewing since the 1960s, and "[w]hat Gorbachev did was to take the lid off a seething cauldron, facilitating the rebirth of religious institutions nationwide and giving voice to the pent-up spiritual aspirations of the Russian people" (Bourdeaux 2000, 13).

The hope of a religious revival in the post-Soviet era was quickly realized (Froese 2004a, 2004b; Bourdeaux 2000; Filatov 2000; Greeley 1994). Not only did the population show a renewed interest in Orthodoxy (Ellis 1996), the most familiar religion to ethnic Russians, but also the upsurge in religion was seen throughout all confessions including Catholicism, Protestantism,

[35] The authors are aware that there were two general secretaries of the Communist Party between Brezhnev and Gorbachev – Yuri Andropov and Konstantin Chernenko. But to paraphrase Ronald Reagan, these leaders died so fast that they aren't worth talking about.

Buddhism, Islam, and even paganism (Bourdeaux 2000; Filatov 2000). As Elliott and Deyneka point out,

> Quickest to take advantage of new opportunities were parachurch ministries, which are more flexible than church bureaucracies [like the ROC]; ministries headed by Slavic immigrants from the region, whose leaders understood the region's languages and cultures firsthand; and ministries with worldwide programs, which could rapidly redeploy substantial resources and personnel to former Soviet Bloc states.... In 1993, British author Patrick Johnstone published an admittedly conservative estimate of 1,113 foreign missionaries in the former Soviet Union.... In 1995, survey work conducted by the East-West Church and Ministry Report determined that the twenty-five largest sending agencies, by themselves, had 3,190 nonindigenous missionaries in the former Soviet Union.... At the same time, hundreds of other smaller agencies appeared to be sponsoring an average of four missionaries each in the mid-1990s. In late 1996, an East-West Church and Ministry Report survey indicated a one-year increase of 31 percent in the number of Western denominational missionaries in the former Soviet Union. (1999, 199–200)

Elliott and Deyneka go on to mention that domestic Protestant denominations were forced to register under one name – the Evangelical Christian Baptist church – and the arrival of new freedoms led to a proliferation of groups from Pentecostals to Mennonites (1999, 201). As in Latin America (cf. Gill 2002a, 1999b), indigenous groups have tended to fare better than foreigners in the proselytizing and conversion game (Filatov 1999). Although precise estimates are difficult to obtain, the frenetic nature of missionary activity – both foreign and homegrown – is quite evident, particularly to those who have a direct interest in what the religious landscape looks like – namely the ROC.

Despite the success of non-Orthodox recruitment, which has been sound but not resounding (cf. Filatov 1999), the leaders of the ROC have seized on the new presence of various denominations as a serious challenge to their traditional spiritual hegemony. One prominent leader in the ROC – Metropolitan Kirill of Smolensk and Kaliningrad – noted as such in a 1996 speech before the World Council of Churches.

> As soon as freedom for missionary work was allowed, a crusade began against the Russian church, even as it began recovering from a prolonged disease, standing on its feet with weakened muscles. Hordes of missionaries dashed in, believing the former Soviet Union to be a vast missionary territory. They behaved as though no local churches existed.... They began preaching without even making an effort to familiarize themselves with the Russian cultural heritage or to learn the Russian language. In most cases the intention was not

to preach Christ and the Gospel, but to tear our faithful away from their traditional churches and recruit them into their own communities. (Kirill 1999,
73; cf. Kuznetsov 1996)

Just as General Motors felt threatened by an invasion of fuel-efficient cars
from Japan in the 1970s, so too does the ROC sense the pressure from more
agile spiritual competitors in Russia. "Metropolitan Kirill clearly believes
that the Russian Orthodox Church should be free to reevangelize the traditional Orthodox believers on its own 'canonical territory.' A central problem
here, however, is the failure of the Russian Orthodox Church in postcommunist times to rise to the challenge of effective witness to its own nominal
flock. It is arguably this failure, as much as the aggressive 'proselytizing'
activities of non-Orthodox denominations, which gives Orthodox denun-
ciations of 'sheep-stealing' their strident character" (cf. Knox 2004, 93–4;
Walters 1999, 48).

Given that the once dominant ROC existed in stasis for most of the
twentieth century and considering that it exists as a highly bureaucratic
organization, less agile than many of its Christian competitors, it should be
the case – according to Proposition 1 – that the ROC hierarchy would seek
legal limitations on the activities of non-ROC confessions and financial support to compete more effectively. Shortly after the Soviet Union collapsed
and the competitive nature of the religious economy became apparent, the
Orthodox hierarchy pleaded for state assistance.

> Archpriest Viacheslav Polosin, then chairman of the Russian parliament's
> Committee on Freedom of Conscience, noted in August 1993 that Patriarch
> Aleksii had recently given President Yeltsin a direct ultimatum: either the
> president must sign a new law passed by the legislature restricting the activites
> of foreign missionaries in Russia, or "the Russian Orthodox Church would
> go into the opposition," that is it would officially link up with the Red-Brown
> coalition. (Dunlop 1995, 32)

The Red-Brown coalition consisted of former members of the Communist
Party and a number of new quasi-Fascist politicos who favored extreme
Russian nationalism. The leaders of the ROC actively played their political
support card. Thinking that they had substantial credibility among the
population, this strategy seemed quite appealing. The overarching political
goal of the ROC hierarchy became reversing the religious freedoms that
were established under Gorbachev and Yeltsin in the early 1990s.

That the ROC hierarchs would have to threaten President Yeltsin with
defection to another political alliance indicates that Yeltsin was noncom-
mittal or hostile toward their policy requests (Verkhovsky 2002, 334). This

is interesting considering that in a situation as politically fluid as Russia was at the time, Proposition 4a – which states that a hegemonic church gains in bargaining power when political competition is high – leads us to hypothesize that Yeltsin would bow to the demands of Patriarch Aleksii. There were two factors operating in Russia at the time, however, that affected such an outcome. First, it was not at all clear that the ROC represented anything close to being hegemonic. True, Orthodoxy had a millennial history in Russia, but the spiritual revival occurring within Russia since the 1960s tended to favor non-Orthodox confessions and leveled the playing field. White et al., note this trend:

> Religious affiliations were themselves undergoing a substantial change in the late communist period. . . . There was a considerable decline . . . in support for the Orthodox Church: partly in response to the reports that were emerging of its close relationship with the Soviet government and the KGB, but partly also because of a more general movement toward other religious beliefs including Catholicism or (much more commonly) toward a nondenominational identification with 'Christianity in general.' (1994, 6–7)

The rapid expansion of non-Orthodox groups certainly gave the impression that the ROC was just one among many denominations vying for social influence. Orthodoxy may have been the largest of these denominations, and the one with the longest history in the country, but it certainly was not commanding hegemonic loyalty of the population. Add to this the fact that the ROC had a hard time speaking with one voice. A substantial reformist movement that was challenging the authority of the reigning Orthodox hierarchs came to the fore in the early 1990s (Knox 2004, 101–5). This group revealed, through its public criticism of the existing ROC hierarchs, that the patriarch and his immediate entourage did not command loyalty even of the population of Orthodox adherents. In an environment wherein multiple religious denominations (or factions) exist, it is best to award a wide degree of freedom to all if you are going to provide liberty to any (Proposition 4c).

The underlying reason why Orthodox reformers were critical of the Church's hierarchy points to the second reason why Yeltsin was at best ambivalent toward the policy demands of the patriarch. As noted in the preceding text, clergy within the ROC, reaching all the way to the top, were active agents of the Soviet secret police (KGB). An examination of KGB files in 1991 revealed

> [t]hat four of the six current permanent members of the Moscow Patriarchate Holy Synod are, or at least until very recently were, KGB agents: Patriarch

Aleksii II (agent code name "Drozdov"); Metropolitan Iuvenalii of Krutitsy
("Adamant"); Metropolitan Kirill of Smolensk ("Mikhailov"); and Metropolitan Filaret of Minsk ("Ostrovskii").... It should be stressed that an "agent" of
the former KGB was considerably more than an informer, he or she was an
active operative of the Committee for State Security, in effect a nonuniformed
officer of that organization. Successful agents were wont to receive official
awards. In February 1988, for example, "agent Drozdov" (Partriarch Aleksii)
was given a letter of commendation for his activities by the KGB chairman.
(Dunlop 1995, 30; cf. Corley 1996, passim)

Being so closely attached to the security apparatus of the regime Yeltsin
had just helped to topple could only create a hesitation on his part. By way
of Proposition 4b, a church that was credibly linked to a deposed political
faction can hardly expect to be showered with great favors.

The actions of the ROC hierarchy during the 1991 coup attempt that
sought to depose Gorbachev, but that eventually proved to be Yeltsin's
shining moment and the end of the Soviet Union, did not inspire confidence
with Yeltsin. The statement issued by the ROC patriarch on the first day
of the coup was extremely ambiguous and called for citizens to listen to
the voice of Gorbachev (who was under house arrest by armed members
of the military).[36] A subsequent statement did claim that the ROC could
not "give its blessing to illegality, violence and acts of bloodshed" but did
not clearly take a side in the standoff (Polyakov 1994, 145–6). Although
the Orthodox leadership might be forgiven for being gun shy in taking
sides, lest they pick the wrong team and suffer renewed repression, the
patriarchate's statements should be contrasted with the statement on the
part of the Russian Evangelical Lutheran Church.

> We call on you [the Russian people] to support President B. N. Yel'tsin and
> the Russian Parliament. In the current crisis they are the only power which
> can stop the plotters of the Committee, who are trying to take us back to the
> bloody nightmare of the communist past. May the Lord God preserve us to
> live a worthy life. (cited in Polyakov 1994, 146)

From Yeltsin's viewpoint, it is not hard to understand his ambivalence
toward the ROC hierarchy. Nonetheless, Polyakov does note that the ROC
leadership did oppose military intervention in Lithuania and "distinguished

---

[36] In the Orwellian world of totalitarian governance, it is often difficult to tell what is really
being said. To say that the population should listen to Gorbachev at the moment when
a gun was being held to his head made it difficult to know whether the patriarchate was
really supporting Gorbachev or the leaders of the coup.

itself by hero after the event" through various statements and actions in support of Yeltsin once the dust had settled (1994, 147 passim).

Given the unpopularity of Communist rule in Russia by the late 1980s, and Boris Yeltsin's heroic role in bringing that regime to an end, one might rightfully expect Yeltsin to be the modern Russian equivalent of George Washington and enjoy unheralded popularity. Unfortunately, the political and economic chaos resulting during the transition from command economy to market economy did not result in Yeltsin's secular deification. As Russia's economy descended into chaos, Yeltsin's popularity diminished, and many a Russian longed for the stability of the old Communist system. Amid this turmoil, the opportunity arose for the ROC to strike a new deal with ascendant parliamentarians and other political leaders. With weak parties and a system unable to coalesce into a stable two-party system, throwing support to even minor political factions could have big payoffs for the ROC.[37] The most logical political train for the ROC hierarchs to jump on was the one that carried an exceedingly nationalist, almost xenophobic, cargo. After all, a thousand-year history in Russia made it the perfect institution for ardent nationalists to rally around. Ironically, many of these new ultranationalists turned out to be members of the old Communist guard – the first half of the Red-Brown coalition noted in the preceding text – that were seeking access to power once again. For the ROC hierarchy, which still viewed Orthodoxy as the historical and hegemonic church of all Russians, there was a direct connection between supporting this communist-patriotic coalition and the attempt to restrict the freedom of non-Orthodox faiths.

It is frequently said that the main reason why the bishops of the ROC fight against non-Orthodox organizations is that they are afraid of competition. This is said to be the reason why they subject the Muslims or the Baptists, who are not engaged in active proselytism, to incomparably less condemnation than the 'rapidly multiplying' Jehovah's Witnesses. There is a good deal of truth in this view, but it is not the whole reason. We simply need to recall, for example, the fact that in 1993, when the major competitive threat to the ROC was posed by the 'indigenous' White Brotherhood (*Beloye bratstvo*) and

---

[37] In multiparty parliamentary systems, small factions holding only a few seats can wield substantial power. Throwing their support to larger blocs within the legislature can create majority coalitions. Likewise, withdrawing from such a coalition can drive a parliament into gridlock. Small parties or factions can thus leverage significant favors on numerous issues, many of which may be peripheral to the larger parties. In the case of religious liberty (or restrictions thereupon), the ROC could (and did) leverage the general concern for large economic and political reforms to obtain legal limitations on minority sects.

Mother of God Centre (*Bogorodichny tsentr*), the main demand from the ROC
was still to introduce restriction on foreigners. (Verkhovsky 2002, 335)

Politically speaking, it is much easier to restrict the activities of foreigners
than one's own countrymen, but "foreign" influence could broadly be construed to mean "alien" theologies held by indigenous citizens. Any direct
competitor to the ROC became a "foreign influence" and felt the brunt of
the 1997 law that successfully restricted the rights on all but a small set of
historic confessions (Elliott and Corrado 1999).[38]

Sensing Yeltsin's initial intransigence in supporting restrictions on religious liberty, the ROC hierarchy moved their lobbying activity to the local
level.[39] There the clergy could use its former political connections to win
various favors. This strategy proved beneficial to old Communist politicians
in that it permitted "the de facto revival of the careers of former officials
of the Soviet-era Council for Religious Affairs, many of whom were reap-
pearing as expert advisers to local administrations" (Anderson 2003, 129).
Anderson further notes that these local administrators, resurrected in their
careers, engaged in "tightening of procedures for the legal recognition of
religious communities, intrusive monitoring of religious life, discrimination
against 'foreign' groups, limits on the use of public space and free speech"
and general harassment contrary to the laws of the Russian republic (1999,
129). The most visible and perhaps famous *quid pro quo* occurred in 1995
when the Orthodox clergy actively supported the election of the Moscow
mayor in exchange for funding to construct a new cathedral (*Financial Times*
1995). Other politicians in the mid-1990s tried to buy the political support
of the Orthodox clergy in a similar manner (cf. Orttung 1996).

A local political strategy, although proving successful in some areas, could
only bring about a patchwork of regulations restricting religious minorities.
Non-Orthodox denominations could still carve out geographically specific
spaces within the national territory to proselytize and grow. A national
solution to this problem remained on the legislative agenda of the ROC
hierarchy. The first attempt at changing Gorbachev's laissez-faire 1990 law,
which still remained in effect, came in 1993 when the ROC gained the

[38] See particularly Elliott and Corrado's appendix providing a list of various persecutions
against non-ROC confessions. This list includes several indigenous religious movements,
such as the Old Believers. Given the religious pluralism that was beginning to appear in
pre-Soviet times (see preceding discussion), it is difficult to effectively distinguish between
indigenous and foreign sects, such as Pentecostals and Methodists.

[39] This strategy is remarkably similar to how the Roman Catholic Church has attempted
to limit the influence of proselytizing Protestants in Latin America despite national laws
protecting the rights of religious minorities (Gill 1999b).

support of Sergei Stankevich, a noted nationalist, to propose a series of restrictive amendments to the law (Marsh and Froese 2004, 139; Anderson 2003, 138). Key among the proposals was a provision preventing "foreign-based organizations" to operate in the country "without an invitation from an officially recognized indigenous religious organization" (Anderson 2003, 128; see also Basil 2005; Berman 1996). Given that many religious groups that had been operating in the country for several decades – including Catholics, Pentecostals, and Baptists – could be considered foreign, the changes proved to be threatening to a wide array of non-Orthodox denominations. Interestingly, and quite predictably, the proposed changes received support from Muslim leaders (Anderson 2003, 128). The ROC hierarchy was most concerned about direct competitors to their (potential) parishioner base. Muslims had the same fears with the onrush of Christian missionaries that came quickly after the Soviet Union collapsed. But Muslims and Orthodox are not direct competitors being geographically separated for the most part. (There have been some indications, however, that Muslims have been making some inroads in parts of Orthodox Russia lately.) They shared a common enemy – foreign Christian evangelists from abroad. Although numerous non-Orthodox (and non-Muslim) groups vocalized their opposition to the proposed changes, the parliament passed them with a large majority. Yeltsin, however, refused to sign it perhaps realizing that he had received little support early on from the Orthodox Patriarchate. Ongoing negotiations about the bill proved to be for naught, though, as Yeltsin dissolved parliament later in the year,[40] and no further action was taken on the religious legislation (Anderson 2003, 128–9).

By 1995, the ROC again had built up enough support in the national parliament to block legislation reaffirming the tenets of the 1990 legislation granting religious freedom (Anderson 2003, 130). And with a presidential election the following year, and an economy experiencing the growing pangs of a market transition, Yeltsin was feeling enough heat from rivals that he succumbed to pressure from the Orthodox hierarchy and accepted their support (Paretskaya 1996). Throughout late 1995 and into 1996, a variety of drafts similar to the proposed legislation in 1993 were put forth. Substantively, little changed between the 1993 proposed legislation and what was being debated in the State Duma, Russia's lower house of parliament. The ROC Patriarchate held its ground and the recently elected Boris Yeltsin remained firm, at least initially. However, bowing to a majority within the Duma favoring the new legislation and strong ROC pressure, Yeltsin caved

---

[40] The parliament was still known as the Supreme Soviet at the time.

in and accepted the 1997 law entitled On Freedom of Conscience and Religious Associations.

The provisions of the 1997 law, applying to the Commonwealth of Independent States (CIS) and detailed in Anderson (2003), Gunn (1999), and Elliot and Corrado (1999),[41] reaffirm the rights of individual conscience, but create two categories of religious groups – privileged denominations that have historic or "traditional" roots (known as religious *organizations*) and other religious affiliations not falling into the former category (termed religious *groups*). Four faiths are contained in the religious organization category, including the ROC, Islam, Buddhism, and Judaism. The Vatican, although generally favoring open religious freedom for all in Russia, also tried unsuccessfully to get Roman Catholicism declared as a historic faith.[42] It is revealing that none of the four recognized historic confessions compete with one another, the way that evangelical Protestants do. Buddhism is geographically concentrated in the eastern section of the CIS, and conversions are not common throughout its theological boundaries. Judaism, whose adherents are primarily mixed among the Orthodox in Russian territory, no longer is a proselytizing religion. Islam, like Buddhism, tends to be geographically concentrated (in the southern portions of the CIS). Although there have been some efforts (and limited success) by Muslims to convert ethnic Russians, these numbers are small compared to the inroads that Protestants and Catholics are making. Thus, from the vantage point of the ROC, these three non-Orthodox religions are relatively "safe" (not withstanding any particular theological dislike that the clergy may have toward them). Catholicism is a direct competitor to the ROC, primarily among the "nominal" (or "cultural") Orthodox.

This is not to say that the Orthodox Church or the Russian government remain unconcerned with Islam, Judaism, or Buddhism. Islamic extremism in places such as Chechnya remains a serious concern for the Kremlin, and one that is probably shared by the Orthodox hierarchs. And despite being part of a recognized religious "organization," Muslims have faced increased public attacks and bureaucratic roadblocks in the early part of

[41] For the full English text of the law, see http://en.rlinfo.ru/documents/onfreedom.html (accessed May 24, 2007).
[42] This fits with the observation in Chapter 2 that the Vatican pursues a restrictive strategy on religious minorities in Latin America where it is the hegemonic spiritual institution and favors less restrictions where it is a minority, such as in Russia. However, the Catholic Church's lobbying effort to be included as a historic church, had it been successful, would have allowed them to pursue restrictions on Protestant minorities even though Catholics are a minority faith in Russia.

the twenty-first century (United States Commission on International Religious Freedom [USCIRF] 2005, 1). Likewise, Jews and Buddhists have faced government harassment. In early 2005, "nineteen members of the Russian Duma published a virulently anti-Semitic letter calling for banning all Jewish organizations in Russia" (USCIRF 2005, 1). Although this legislation was never passed and the letter was quickly withdrawn, it does indicate the presence of anti-Semitism within the halls of government. And the Dalai Lama, the exalted leader of Buddhism, has been blocked continually from entering the country (USCIRF 2005, 1). Despite such unofficial harassment and repression, the current 1997 law remains in place giving all of these faith traditions an officially sanctioned status. Many evangelical Protestants face similar persecution but without the benefit of a similar level of legal recognition.

For nonfavored denominations (i.e., religious *groups*), the 1997 law contains a number of key provisions that make life more difficult. Article 9.1 of the law contains the terms under which a group is officially recognized as being a religious organization (and hence subject to the other portions of the law).

> No fewer than ten citizens of the Russian Federation may be founders of a local religious organization, joining together as a religious group which must have confirmation from the organs of the local government that it has existed on the given territory for no less than fifteen years, or confirmation from a centralized religious organization of the same creed that it forms part of its structure. (cited in Gunn 1999, 240)

This section is reminiscent of Article 7 of the Mexican Ley Reglamentaria that places historical conditions on the legal recognition of churches, places them in a Catch-22 dilemma and exposes them to the whims of local officials (see Gill 1999c, 783–4). For a church to be legally recognized it must be present for a given period of time but without any legal recognition (or specific rules delineating what constitutes legal presence) it becomes contentious as to how long the organization has actually existed.[43] Other provisions of the 1997 Russian law prohibit nonofficial religious groups from owning property, obtaining tax exemptions, receiving government subsidies, operating schools, conducting charitable activities, gaining access

---

[43] The Mexican regulation places a property-ownership requirement on a church that makes the situation doubly frustrating as government building permits generally require the owner to specify the use of the building. However, specifying that the building will be used for religious purposes is not a possible option considering that a religious group is not legally recognized until it owns property.

to government institutions (e.g., military, prisons, hospitals), and inviting foreign preachers or owning and using mass media outlets (Gunn 1999, 246–7). It is clear how each of these limitations on religious groups would create significant roadblocks on the path to gaining members.

As clearly predicted by Proposition 1, the dominant church (along with three other nonthreatening "historical" confessions) sought restrictions on religious minorities, limiting their ability to compete for members. What may not be clear, however, is why Yeltsin (and various members of the Duma) would yield to such restrictions in an environment of growing religious pluralism (as noted in the preceding text). There are several related answers to this question. First, the local strategy of the ROC, particularly being connected to government officials during Soviet days who were seeking election to the Duma and/or gaining their bureaucratic jobs back, meant that the patriarchate could wield disproportionate influence among locally elected officials. Second, although the ROC had been battered by Soviet rule, the number of individuals affiliated with Orthodoxy still significantly outnumbers the non-Orthodox population (see Barrett et al. 2001). Granted, many of those claiming to be Orthodox are probably only nominal (as compared to regular practitioners); the larger number still represents a significant political constituency that *might* care about legal protections for the ROC. Finally, the lobbying pressure against the bill by religious minorities proved to be "counterproductive" (Anderson 2003, 130), in large part because a substantial portion of the opposition came from outside of Russia, confirming the arguments of Russian nationalists that the country's sovereignty was under assault. Because local politicians need not concern themselves greatly with foreign individuals who are not their constituents, it can be claimed that the ROC still has a significant hegemonic presence in the political arena despite growing pluralism. This, as such, confirms the prediction of Proposition 4a wherein the dominant church has succeeded in wielding its political and social influence to its advantage in a competitive political environment.

If there is a bright spot for religious minorities in Russia following the 1997 law, it is that "successively lenient official interpretations of this law at the federal level neutralized some of its harsher provisions." In large part, this has been because "[t]hose in the Kremlin (where, under President Vladimir Putin, power has become increasingly concentrated) who are authorized to take decisions impacting on religious freedom are normally immersed in mainstream political issues, which they no doubt consider to be far more pressing" (Fagan 2003, 1). This observation directly supports Propositions 5 and 5a wherein over time laws restricting religious minorities are not enforced. Following through on this, Proposition 5b would predict that although religious groups face many legal difficulties, a lack of enforcement will allow them to continue growing and religious pluralism will slowly increase in Russian society. Hopefully, this will lead to greater political opportunities for these minorities to modify the law to their advantage. How long this may take, we offer little prediction, but the experience of the United States, Latin America, and other countries around the world leaves us optimistic.

The Baltics

When the Soviet empire collapsed, there was a resurgence of traditionally dominant churches in the Baltics and new religious movements arrived from both East and West (Hoppenbrouwers 1999, 163; Ramet 1998, 266–7; Goeckel 1995, 210–11).[44] Legislators and religious leaders alike claimed that the sudden combination of old and radically new religious ideas threatened to become a combustible mixture. Just as in Russia, nationalist politicians and priests (to varying degrees in each country) cited fears of dangerous "sects" and appealed to religious traditions as a means of solidifying their reborn national identities. To a certain extent, when drafting regulations for religious communities, the republics modeled their laws on preexisting, interwar legislation. After all, why reinvent the wheel? Although separated by two generations of citizens, the interregnum between the Soviet occupation and liberation was still much shorter than in Russia and resentment over Soviet occupation kept the memory (and hope) of the interwar years alive. The freedom won by the Baltics in the interwar period represented a highpoint in a Baltic history dominated by foreign intervention. Moreover, it is important to remember that the Baltics were still part of the USSR in 1990 when Gorbachev implemented his remarkably liberal religious reforms (Marshall 2000, 198).

Just as in Russia, the promise for greater religious freedom had finally arrived reversing decades of Soviet persecution. For the most part, all three Baltic States exhibit reasonably high levels of religious freedom both on paper and in practice, a situation reminiscent of Russia from the last years of Gorbachev until the restrictive 1997 laws went into effect (Barnett 2001, 96). Lithuania represents perhaps the biggest exception in that the Catholic

---

[44] For reasons unknown, Hoppenbrouwers calls this increase in religion *paradoxical* (1999, 163), but it should not be surprising that religious activity would increase when highly repressive laws restricting religious activity are liberalized.

Church has been granted a more privileged position relative to other confessions and has lobbied for stricter requirements regarding official church registration.

Despite favorable levels of religious freedom in the Baltics, traditional churches that scraped by under Soviet repression have felt it difficult to compete in this new and open environment. The result of this has been predictable in line with Proposition 1; historical churches have called for governmental support of their denominations (Goeckel 1995, 210) and have tried to limit the proselytizing ability of relatively new and/or foreign religions by making it difficult to register or own property. And even in some cases, previously registered religious communities were no longer recognized, a fact that violated the ideological spirit of religious liberty that supposedly flourished in the interwar years but that really revealed the institutional concerns of the clergy. With freedom returning, each of the historic confessions jockeyed for position to reclaim the allegiance of people who had drifted away from religious life. Any advantage they could secure for their institution would help them down the road. Add to this a new complication in the religious landscape. The increased influence of the ROC, as a result of massive Soviet deportations and population transfers intended to "Russify" the Baltics, further politicized already tense relations between the republics and the Moscow Patriarchate (Goeckel 1995). Although having a rooted presence in the three states to varying degrees, many native Baltic residents viewed the ROC as a foreign bully associated with Soviet interference in their affairs. Although each country proclaimed religious freedom and toleration for its citizens, in many cases, their new laws, explicitly or not, favored "traditional" religions and imposed tighter restrictions on others, especially those led by foreigners.

Even before the Baltic republics became officially independent in 1991, there was a revival of religious interest, mirroring the situation in Russia – no matter how much the Communists tried, and despite success in significantly reducing active church participation, they could not fully extinguish the spiritual flame that burned within many citizens. Missionaries from established foreign churches and new religious movements alike entered the region. When the veil of repression was lifted in 1991, it became apparent that the religious landscape had been altered in several places. According to Estonian historian, Toivo Raun, "[a] striking feature of the phenomenon of religion in postcommunist Estonia was its pluralism" (Raun 2001, 261). Fifty new religious movements had appeared by the early 1990s. Though many were small, it became apparent that religious diversity was something that political and religious leaders could not ignore.

In 1993, Estonia passed ostensibly the least restrictive regulations of religious groups of all of the Baltic States. The Law on Churches and Congregations stated that all religious communities are considered equal and congregations of twelve or more people must register with the government. Founding members do not have to be Estonian citizens but must have residence permits and need to have lived in Estonia for minimum of five years, which is much less restrictive than the Russian requirement of fifteen years (Barnett 2001). Of course, the question of difficulty in obtaining visas and residence permits must be factored into understanding this law, but there is no mention of "traditional" or more acceptable religious groups in the Estonian law.

The 2000 report by Paul Marshall, senior fellow at Freedom House's Center for Religious Freedom praised the former Soviet republic: "Estonia broke the shackles of Communism with remarkable rapidity and currently demonstrates a model of religious liberty. Church leaders have not exhibited the paranoia about the activities of foreign evangelists that has been evident in other newly independent countries" (Marshall 2000, 131). Although the report alludes to a rift between the government and the Orthodox Church, it does not mention the ten-year period in which one branch of the Estonian Orthodox Church (subordinated to the Moscow Patriarchate) was de facto unrecognized.

The controversy began in 1993, with the registration of the Estonian Apostolic Orthodox Church (EAOC), which had been subordinated to the Patriarchate of Constantinople since it broke with the ROC in 1920. The question surrounded the EAOC's right to be legal successor to the Orthodox Church in post-Soviet Estonia and to have expropriated church properties returned. The leadership of the EAOC had been maintained in exile under Metropolitan Alexander, who fled in 1944 as the Soviet army approached. Both the EAOC and the Estonian Orthodox Church subordinated to the Moscow Patriarchate claimed to have operated in continuity throughout the period, and each claimed to be entitled to church properties.

After the reestablishment of Estonian independence, the formerly exiled church was granted official recognition by the Estonian government in August 1993. Soon after, the ROC also attempted to register under the name Estonian Orthodox Church Moscow Patriarchate (EOCMP). The government did not allow the registration, claiming that the name was too similar and that there was no need for two Orthodox churches in Estonia. The more important political and economic problem underlying this decision was related to property rights. Returning expropriated church property to its rightful owners became a contentious issue throughout Eastern

Europe. Governments naturally coveted the real estate and were reluctant to return it to any claimant.

The 1993 decision clearly represented a desire on the part of the Estonian government to disassociate itself from Moscow. With an ethnic Russian population of approximately 25 percent, the new government most likely felt pressure from ethnic Estonians to prove the nation's independence from its one-time oppressor. The Estonian ROC was not formally recognized until 2002. The Freedom House study was also published too early to take into account the politics that would lead to the adoption of a revised statute on religious organizations in 2002. In 2001, the Estonian Riigikogu passed legislation that would amend the 1993 law and included provisions to prohibit the registration of religious organizations whose leadership was located outside Estonia. The only exception to the new article was the Roman Catholic Church, which could remain registered through a prior special agreement with the Estonian government. Of course, the heretofore unrecognized EOCMP would fall into this category along with various Protestant groups and other religious movements.

Although the parliament passed the previously mentioned measure, it was vetoed by two successive presidents, Lennart Meri and Arnold Ruutel. The exclusion of foreign-based religious organizations from registration was removed clearing a path for the registration of the Moscow-based ROC. Interestingly, responsibility for registering churches and religious groups shifted from the Interior Ministry's Department of Religious Affairs to local courts, a process that may prove cumbersome for some denominations but in no way represents a significant barrier to religious freedom. This process required the reregistration of all religious organizations by July 1, 2004. In 2002, there were 593 registered religious organizations in total. Religious groups are not required to register, but they cannot then enter into contracts as a community or get tax-exempt status (Corley 2002).

The EOCMP (Russian Orthodox) was finally granted registration in April 2002, after ten years of legal wrangling. Among those who lobbied for the recognition of the Moscow-led Church were Estonian businessmen who had been led to believe by Russian authorities that such a move would end the practice of charging twice the rate on customs tariffs. This did not happen, however, but Estonian businessmen were officially recognized by the Church for their efforts. The link between trade and religious freedom once again proved to be salient as it has been throughout time and throughout space. Though the controversy of registration has ended, Ringo Ringvee noted that, given the long history of conflict, it "would be too early to say that the 'religious controversy' has been overcome" (Ringvee 2003).

All told, Estonia remains, however, the only one of the three Baltic countries that recognizes no traditional religions and has no special agreements with any religious group. The reason for this was both the country's multiconfessional history and a lack of significant influence of any particular church on the national identity. Even though Lutherans tend to predominate nominally, the social influence of the EELC is rather limited. One estimate places the number of affiliated Lutherans (55,000) just under the number of affiliated Orthodox (60,000), indicating a relative parity between the two largest faiths (Hoppenbrouwers 1999, 164). In a population of roughly 1.5 million, each denomination has active adherents of less than 4 percent of the population. With no previous commitments to any particular confession and no truly hegemonic religion, government actors are beholden to no one – the ideal environment for a laissez-faire form of religious liberty (see Proposition 4c).

Similar to Estonia, the Lutheran tradition in Latvia was greatly weakened by its connection to German occupation and the flight of many clergymen at the onset of World War II. At the time of the Soviet occupation, Latvia was roughly divided into thirds: Lutherans, Russian Orthodox, and Roman Catholics. Soviet attempts to Russify Latvia through population transfers created a situation wherein roughly a third of the citizenry was of recent Russian descent. Of all the Baltic States, ethnic tensions in Latvia have remained highest since independence. However, given that these ethnicities map closely onto religious lines, none of the three major confessions are in direct competition with one another. Favoring any one particular faith over the others would only serve to fan the flames of ethnic rivalry thereby making an unregulated religious market a safe political bet for politicians.

According to Solveiga Krumiņa-Konkova, "religious life in contemporary Latvia could be characterized by the coexistence of five equally strong Christian confessions that claim to represent the priority of the Christian tradition in the life of Latvian society and are regarded by public opinion as the traditional confessions of Latvia" (2000, 289). The 1995 Law on Religious Organizations passed by the Latvian Saeima recognizes the plurality of these traditional religious denominations – Lutheran, Roman Catholic, Orthodox, Old Believers, Baptists, and Jews (Marshall 2000, 198). Religious groups are not required to register, although registration is required to own property, receive tax benefits, and freely organize public gatherings. The law also stipulates that no splinter group (a second group within the same confession) may register. Other restrictions include requirements that foreign religious workers have a certificate of theological education or ordination and that they be invited by a domestic religious organization in order to hold meetings and proselytize (Barnett 1999, 97–8).

The more specific restrictions of Latvia's religious code and the preferential treatment for certain confessions are reminiscent of the interwar decision to not declare any official state religion. In post-Soviet Latvia, in order to keep the peace among an ethnically and spiritually diverse population, it seems logical to grant special status particularly to these three main religious groups. However, "Latvia . . . distinguishes between traditional religions . . . and nontraditional religions, and grants certain privileges to the former such as the right to teach in public schools. Generally religious organizations are exempt from property tax, from tax on donations, and from tax on receipt of humanitarian aid. However, for nontraditional religions the current practice appears to be that to qualify for tax exemptions they must reapply for tax-exempt status each year" (Barnett 2001, 98). These restrictions on other religious groups apply mostly to proselytizing denominations and "cults." Although Latvia's list of requirements led Freedom House to give it a ranking of "3," the lowest possible ranking within the "free" category (Marshall 2000), it should be emphasized that Latvia still offers significant protections for religious liberty. Their laws are none the more restrictive than many in Western Europe, a point emphasized by Barnett (2001) in his comparison of the Baltics with other European states.

In general, it is difficult to find examples of serious violations of religious rights in Latvia. Even the Jehovah's Witnesses, one of the most closely watched "sects" by governments around the world, were permitted to register as a church in 1998 after being denied that right since 1993, even though the group had been registered during Latvia's first period of independence. When the Witnesses reapplied in 1995, the Court of Zemgale determined that their registration in 1933 as the "International Society of Bible Researchers" warranted their being considered as an "old" religion. This was overturned by the Supreme Court on June 28, 1995. But in 1998, three congregations of Witnesses were permitted to register, although they must reregister annually for ten years before being granted full recognition by the state. By 2000, eleven of their congregations were registered (Krumiņa-Konkova 2000, 292).

The Ministry of Justice also considered revoking the registration of the United Evangelical Congregation of God, claiming that the group is intolerant of other religions (especially Catholics) and forbids children from participating in extracurricular activities, isolating its members from society. The Law on Religious Organizations still requires that religion may be taught in public schools only by representatives of the Evangelical Lutheran,

Roman Catholic, Orthodox, Old Believer, Baptist, and Jewish religious communities (Krumiņa-Konkova 2000, 290).[45] Clearly the major traditional denominations fear an invasion of evangelizing organizations that they would have to compete with, but their political clout is sufficiently weak that their desires are only acted on in the most superficial manner. Latvia, then, fits within the pattern wherein a religious pluralistic society endorses broad religious freedoms, yet concern by the more traditional (and less competitive) churches has led to some restrictions on proselytizing denominations considered outside of mainstream Christianity (e.g., Jehovah's Witnesses, Christian Scientists). To put this in perspective, it should be acknowledged that conflict with such groups frequently arises in countries such as the United States and Canada (Gill 2003).

Religion has played a stronger political role in Lithuania than in the other two Baltic States. The highly visible and active presence of the Catholic Church, which claims the allegiance of more than 80 percent of the population (Barrett et al. 2001, 260), would qualify it as the dominant religious institution in the country. Not surprisingly, as per Proposition 4 and 4a, we would expect politicians to be more attentive to the needs of an active religious population and reward the dominant confession with a more privileged legal position. As compared to Estonia and Latvia, work on legislation governing religious activity began quite early in Lithuania, taking a cue from the Gorbachev reforms implemented in 1990. Initially, the proposal developed reflected the general openness of Gorbachev's law and looked toward the United States for inspiration. In the words of Donatas Glodenis, former senior specialist in the Lithuanian Ministry of Justice's Registration Department:

> The draft of 1990 was a joint effort between the former regime's atheist philosophers and representatives of different religious communities to establish freedom of both belief and unbelief and the free exercise thereof. It is possible that at the time anything seemed better to the social representatives as well as to all religious communities than the previous Soviet restrictions. Consequently, the 1990 draft was as liberal as possible. (2005, 1)

This version of the law, however, was never passed by Lithuania's legislative body. Catholic Reverend Vaclovas Aliulis, a work group leader who participated in drafting the 1990 law (and the subsequent 1992 and 1993 versions)

---

[45] Krumiņa-Konkova (2000) documents a few other cases including restrictions placed on Christian Scientists justified as being a sect with practices that endangered the lives of others (2000, 291).

noted that the first draft was based on the North American model, without differentiation among religious groups. Later, however, a more "European approach" that privileged historic denominations and sought more cooperative relations between church and state was used both as a model and as a defense against criticism (Glodenis 2005). Some influential Catholics believed that refusing to grant the same rights to unknown religious movements as bestowed on established traditional ones was justifiable, especially because other European countries have a long history of this practice.

The LRCA was not passed until 1995. By then, the initial draft proposal dating back to 1990 had been modified so many times as to render it unrecognizable. The LRCA defined nine "traditional" religions and set forth restrictions upon the registration of other religious groups. The nine traditional denominations include Latin Rite Catholics, Greek Rite Catholics, Evangelical Lutherans, Evangelical Reformed Church members, Orthodox Christians (Moscow Patriarchate), Old Believers, Jews, Sunni Muslims, and Karaites (a small Jewish sect). Each of these religious groups has been present in Lithuania for at least three hundred years and has, according to the reasoning behind the law, made a lasting contribution to the country's culture. This designation entitles them to certain benefits including special tax breaks and access to schools and other public institutions. As with Estonia and Latvia where a set of historic religions receives a favored designation, it is important to note that none of these historic churches directly compete with each other for members in any serious way.

Although nine historical churches in Lithuania receive special privileges, the Roman Catholic Church stands out as being the one confession that is more equal among equals. The Seimas, Lithuania's parliament, officially recognized this special status by signing a concordat with the Catholic Church in May of 2000 that grants the Church certain privileges, noting the "special role of the Catholic Church, especially in strengthening the moral values of the Lithuanian nation, as well as its historical and current contribution to the social, cultural and educational spheres" (Ministry of Justice of the Republic of Lithuania 2005). The concordat, among other things, guarantees the Church's right to own real estate and other property and to provide pastoral care in hospitals, prisons, orphanages, and other institutions. It also states that the government will support the Church's publishing activities in the same way that it would any other NGO. The state also declares that Sundays and six specific Church feast days will be public holidays. This ability of the Catholic Church to gain such status derives from the recognition that the overwhelming majority of Lithuanians identify themselves as Catholic. The Church's privileged status also reflects the active role the Catholic Church played in resisting foreign occupation over the past two centuries.

Moreover, Catholicism is well represented through official channels in the post-Soviet political arena. Although this presence certainly is a function of the Church's long historical resistance to foreign occupation, it was institutionally accelerated in the Sąjūdis movement that formed in 1988 to press for Lithuanian independence. "Sąjūdis in Lithuania had the closest relations with the national church [Catholicism] of any in the Baltics. Sąjūdis allocated representation to the Catholic Church at its congresses and sought to recruit priests as candidates. Although the church refused to permit priests to enter electoral competition, it actively supported Sąjūdis" (Goeckel 1995, 211–12). One of the key leaders of the Sąjūdis movement, Vytautas Landsbergis, was the speaker of the Seimas when Lithuania declared independence, effectively representing the head of government at the time of independence. Landsbergis understood the importance of religion in social and political life and was the one to champion the initial religious reforms in 1990, at a time when he was declaring independence from the Soviet Union for Lithuania (Bourdeaux 1995b, 10–11). The Catholic Church's encouragement of lay Catholic involvement in Sąjūdis prompted many of those individuals to establish confessional political parties in Lithuania in 1991.

Although the Catholic Church and other historical denominations have been granted certain advantages in the legislation arena, burdens on religious minorities (known as "nontraditional religions" in the country) have not been particularly onerous; the nation still maintains a relatively open religious market earning it "2" in Freedom House's rankings, just between Estonia (most free) and Latvia. It is important to understand that Freedom House considers all these countries to have substantial religious freedom and the difference between the numerical rankings are certainly matters of minor degree, particularly compared with Russia's new religious regime (rated as a "4" – partly free).[46] In 2001, Barnett assessed the situation as follows:

> There are no differences between traditional and nontraditional religions in relation to property rights and religious activity, though traditional religions can receive state aid for the renovation of religious buildings. The tax regime is favourable to all religious communities and associations in Lithuania. Income received for the construction, restoration and repair of religious buildings is free of income tax provided it is used for such purposes. Religious

---

[46] See Marshall (2000) for a discussion of Freedom House's rankings.

literature and other necessities imported from outside Lithuania by religious associations or communities are free from customs duty (2001, 97).

However, a June 2006 law changed the situation regarding property ownership. The administrative and charitable real estate assets held by *nontraditional* churches became taxable property, whereas similar buildings and assets owned by *traditional* denominations remained tax exempt. Such a law poses a significant restriction on new religious movements and has placed a roadblock in front of many foreign missionary movements.

To a large extent, the biggest regulatory barriers for nontraditional churches involve the process of being recognized as a traditional church and gaining the added state support that such status entails. Such recognition entails being present in the country for twenty-five years after initial registration. Although the initial registration process is slightly more complex for nontraditional churches, religious communities need only fifteen adult members to qualify and a religious association (which is the entity that would be recognized for traditional status) needs to include only two communities (e.g., parishes) (Barnett 2001, 97). Certain religious organizations continue to attempt to prove that they fall within the boundaries of the definition of a "tradition religion." In 2005, the Lithuanian parliament heard arguments from the head of its Human Rights Commission in favor of the official recognition of the Lithuanian Union of Evangelical Christians, a group that includes Pentecostals, Evangelical Lutherans, Reformed Evangelicals, Baptists, Anglicans, and Methodists (*Delfi News Service* 2005). As of this writing, their case remains unresolved. In fact, United Methodists in Lithuania have recently gone on a two-pronged evangelistic campaign: first, to share the gospel and, second, a public relations campaign to remind people that the Justice Department declared that the United Methodists are not a cult. More than a decade of suspicion about small and foreign-based religious groups has left a lingering mark. Given the twenty-five-year presence required to become a traditional religion, and considering that no religious organizations were allowed to register during the Soviet period, only groups that had been registered during the interwar period from 1918–40 could qualify for such historical status. Determining the historical continuity of a church opens the door to ambiguous interpretations.

Conclusion

The pattern of church-state regulatory relations in Russia and the Baltics has followed a path similar to those of many Western European nations that have maintained established state churches over the course of their history. Political considerations made by elites largely determined the religious composition of the population, at least officially. In Russia, cultivating the Orthodox Church proved useful both to the tsar and the Orthodox hierarchy. With a history of foreign incursion and domination, the religious marketplace that resulted was more varied in the Baltics, particularly in Estonia and Latvia. Although the Communist leaders of the Soviet Union attempted to quash all religious affiliation and belief, their efforts inevitably failed. Religious participation did drop precipitously during the Soviet era due to harsh repression and strong disincentives for openly affiliating with a religious organization. However, the revival of religious life following the collapse of the USSR reveals that religious belief is resilient even amid the worst of conditions. The post-Soviet history of Russia and the Baltics, at least up to this point, fits well within the theoretical framework developed earlier. Historically hegemonic churches have found it difficult to compete in the religious economy after years of oppression and attenuation. As such, they have sought, and achieved to varying degrees, legislation that limits the rights of religious minorities. This situation has been more pronounced in Russia where the Orthodox Church has been able to use local political connections to build national support for restricting non-Orthodox faiths, particularly those in direct competition for their (nominal) membership. In the Baltics, however, a history of religious pluralism has resulted in legislation more favorable to the rights of religious minorities. As noted in the preceding text, the growth of religious liberty is a contentious process that takes time. The lack of Russia's willingness to enforce many of its most extreme regulations over religious minorities and the relative freedom extended to nontraditional religions in the Baltics provides an opportunity for new religious groups to grow. As they do, it is likely their social and political influence will increase, which will lead to greater demands for religious liberty. Only time will tell, and time offers no guarantees, only surprises.

CHAPTER 6

We Gather Together: The Consequences
of Religious Liberty

> We gather together, to ask the Lord's blessing;
> He hastens and chastens His will to make known.
> The wicked oppressing, now cease from distressing.
> Sing praise to His name; He forgets not his own.
>
> – Traditional hymn

EASTRIDGE CHRISTIAN ASSEMBLY sits just outside the city limits of Issaquah, a growing suburban town in western Washington State. Like many of his fellow clergymen, Pastor Steve Jamison wants to grow his ministry to meet the demands of a rapidly expanding community of suburban families. This requires a larger church building. Unfortunately for the pastor, the county government has limited his ability to expand. Currently, the Eastridge Christian Assembly church building uses a septic system that limits the number of people who can use the facility at any given time and hence restricts the size of the church's physical structure.[1] In order to get county permission to enlarge his building, Pastor Jamison needs a special permit to

---

[1] For urban folks who do not know what a septic system is, think of it as an outhouse wherein you don't have to go out of the house. Waste material is collected in a large tank outside of the main building, where it eventually breaks down. However, to ensure that the tank does not overflow or the pump system isn't overloaded, strict limits on building size need to be imposed.

connect his facility to a sewer system. Unfortunately, county administrators have denied the church's request to hook up to a sewer line, despite the fact that a sewer pipe runs directly through an easement on the church's own property. What complicates the situation further is that the sewer running through the church's property is connected to a public school bus barn on the adjacent lot. Given that both buildings rest on unincorporated (rural) land, one might expect county permitting regulations to apply equally. They don't. And it is the church that is subject to more onerous conditions.

This regulatory dispute may seem trivial, but it is not an isolated incident. Just a dozen or so miles north of Eastridge Christian Assembly sits another church restricted by the same septic regulations. Additionally, that church is bound by a "conditional use permit" that prevents it from having a sign visible from the road, putting in recreational facilities such as a gymnasium or ball field, or even maintaining a large kitchen.[2] All of this goes to the heart of religious liberty. Most religious groups seek to expand their membership. Spreading the Word of God requires gathering people together. And deepening one's faith also goes hand in hand with publicly worshiping with others. This, in turn, often necessitates more spacious buildings where folks can congregate for a variety of activities. Restrictions on building size may interfere with the clergy's ability to publicly worship and reach a wider audience of believers. Crowded pews (and parking lots) may deter new members from joining simply due to space considerations.[3] And efforts to add other services, such as day-care facilities or elementary schools, could easily hinder the church's ability to cultivate youth members, who represent the future base and leadership of the church, or attract families. Moreover, the ability to build a church in a location of one's own choosing, free from discriminatory zoning laws specifically targeting churches, can have a significant impact on whether a congregation (and the larger denomination it may be affiliated with) flourishes or fails.

Now consider the story of the Cottonwood Christian Center.[4] For years, this group of devout evangelical Christians saved money to buy a parcel of land in Cypress, California that would allow them to build a three hundred thousand square foot building that contained a large sanctuary, day-care center, gymnasium, and other facilities. Their application for a land-use

---

[2] The congregation in question happens to be the author's own church.

[3] Alternatively, crowded pews – like crowded restaurants – have the effect of signaling that the denomination is popular. If a church building is bursting at the seams with people waiting anxiously for the Sunday sermon, it must be pretty good.

[4] Details of this case can be found at the Beckett Fund's Web site http://www.becketfund.org/index.php/case/46.html (accessed June 14, 2006).

permit was denied by the city council, who then granted the rights to the
real estate to the CostCo Corporation, a "big box" retailer. In his legal
rebuke of the Cypress City Council, U.S. District Judge David O. Carter
wrote:

> Preventing a church from building a worship site fundamentally inhibits its
> ability to practice its religion. Churches are central to the religious exer-
> cise of most religions. If Cottonwood could not build a church, it could not
> exist.[5]

Although the case was eventually settled with an agreement allowing the
Cottonwood Christian Center to purchase a comparable piece of nearby
land, three years of legal proceedings certainly complicated the ability of
this group to carry out its pastoral mission. A smaller, less dedicated group
may have chosen to give up the fight.

The seemingly indirect connection between property-rights regulations
and religious liberty is such a hot topic in the United States today that
it spawned a major piece of federal legislation known as the Religious
Land Use and Institutionalized Persons Act (RLUIPA) of 2000 (Gaubatz
2005; Storzer and Picarello 2001).[6] Cash-strapped governments are often
tempted to grant building permits to residential or commercial development projects that will fill the public coffers with property-tax revenue
instead of allowing tax-exempt religious denominations to build on prime
real estate. Public education officials who worry about religious schools
skimming off students (and per pupil budgetary allotments) also have a
strong incentive to use building and other regulations to stymie the spread
of churches. And "no-growth" environmentalists or neighborhood activists fearing Sunday traffic congestion have been known to oppose church
plantings.[7]

As we have discovered in previous chapters, land-use regulations are not
the only way governments can inhibit the practice and growth of religion. In
both the history of the United States and Mexico, religious tests were used
to determine citizenship and eligibility to serve in public office. Currently,

---

[5] See *Cottonwood Christian Center v. Cypress Redevelopment Agency*, 218 F. Supp. 2d 1203; 2002
U.S. Dist. LEXIS 14379 (August 6, 2002).

[6] See http://www.rluipa.org (accessed May 24, 2007) for an excellent summary of this legislation and a listing of related legal cases.

[7] These insights are based on numerous informal discussions that I have had with religious
ministers and local government officials in King County, Washington. Readers anxious for
me to go into greater detail on the connection between property rights and religious liberty
will have to wait until my next book on the subject. Consider this concluding chapter to
be the trailer of coming attractions.

governments in Latin America and Europe tinker with the definition of what constitutes an officially recognized denomination. Manipulating the required size of membership – be it two hundred members or two thousand – can have a significant impact in determining which religious groups qualify for tax-exempt status and/or legal privileges. Other regulations such as whether religious groups can broadcast on radio or television airwaves, import religious literature, or conduct prayer services on government property all affect the abilities of religions to prosper.

Admittedly, the task of regulating religious organizations is a difficult job for governments. Leonard Trelawney Hobhouse, a famous classical liberal theorist writing in his classic tome *Liberalism* at the beginning of the twentieth century, recognized the intricate balancing act between freedom of conscience and assembly and protection of the public's welfare.

> What...is the primary meaning of religious liberty? Externally, I take it to include the liberties of thought and expression, and to add to these the right to worship in any form which does not inflict injury on others or involve a breach of public order. (Hobhouse [1911] 1942, 29)

A completely unregulated religious economy would invariably include all sorts of faiths from ones that engage in relatively innocuous activities to those practicing human sacrifice, drug use, or rituals that could infringe on existing laws and the public order. Reasonable individuals would surely conclude that restricting groups that pursue violent activities that could bring serious injury to innocent bystanders or unwilling participants is a legitimate use of government regulatory power. But beyond that, the line gets rather murky. Is restricting the right of Jehovah's Witnesses to knock on doors in Russia or Mexico in order to preserve the historical legacy of Orthodoxy or Catholicism a proper form of government regulatory power? Can courts require that Sikhs wear hard helmets in compliance with occupational safety laws while on construction sites even though this would create problems with their religious turbans (cf. Beaman 2003)? Should governments investigate the private activities of "strange" new religious cults with the suspicion that the leaders of those groups may be defrauding or harming the welfare of their members? None of these questions have easy answers and are subject to ongoing scholarly and legal debate. The pursuit of institutional and career interests by both politicians and clergy certainly make that debate all the more contentious and irresolvable. Although the public interest may be served best by some theoretically given degree of religious liberty, both priest and politician have an incentive to deviate from the optimal level of freedom.

As we have seen throughout this book, clergy tend to be most concerned with proselytizing and protecting the institutional interests of their
church.[8] In many cases, they will seek to restrict the freedom of upstart
spiritual movements. This was true in colonial Massachusetts, postcolonial
Latin America, and contemporary Russia. Dominant churches sought (and
often still seek) to use government power to restrict the liberties of religious minorities. Political actors, for their part, are typically interested in
their own political survival, be it getting democratically elected to office
or remaining in authoritarian control of a dictatorship. Beyond this, these
political actors are concerned with increasing their own fiscal resources,
promoting a growing economy, and minimizing social unrest, all of which
determine the survivability of the ruler. When it comes to determining how
religious groups will be regulated in society – and hence the level and nature
of religious liberty – all of these interests come into play. Politics is a game
of trade-offs, and regulating (or deregulating) the religious economy will
depend on how well such regulation enhances the survival and well-being of
politicians. The process is never straightforward, and the path of religious
liberty runs forward and back. The framework presented here, however,
would seem to indicate that religious freedom will prevail over time. And
empirically, just as democratic governance has marched onward, sometimes
against unbelievable odds, history seems to be charting an optimistic course.
This does not mean liberty is inevitable, but as long as there are people
continually willing to fight for freedom, hope always remains bright.

It cannot be doubted that religious freedom matters for the health of
any society. As noted earlier, numerous scholarly studies have shown a
strong connection between religious liberty and the strength and diversity
of religious organizations. This only makes sense. When there are fewer
governmentally imposed barriers to the organization of religion, religious
organizations will be able to pursue their proselytizing goals at a lower
cost. They will be able to build church buildings in which to congregate,
print and distribute literature however they please, and educate children in
a manner in which they deem best. This is not to say that all religions will
flourish under an environment of religious liberty; inefficient or unpopular denominations will find it difficult to attract and retain members when
more superior religious alternatives are allowed to exist. As basic economic
theory would predict, and as Adam Smith observed more than two centuries

---

[8] The obvious caveat, again, is that not all religions are proselytizing (e.g., Judaism), but the
leaders of such religious groups will still have an interest in maintaining the institutional
integrity and strength of their organizations.

ago, more people will be satisfied when numerous organizations compete for their loyalty and attempt to offer the best services possible. In a world where many people are worried that civil society and bowling leagues are becoming weaker (cf. Putnam 2000), and recognizing that religious organizations have long been at the heart of civil society, it would make sense that promoting religious freedom and the spiritual vitality that results from it would be desirable public policy.[9] May our government leaders always keep that in mind, and, in the event they don't, may our citizens be ever vigilant in the protection of their natural rights and liberties.

O Lord, make us free.

---

[9] I do recognize that a great many atrocities have been committed in the name of religion and that religious groups can sometimes cause more harm than good. However, my personal belief is that the balance sheet for religions throughout the ages has been overwhelmingly positive. Major shortcomings of religious individuals or organizations are newsworthy events, often because they are rare. The everyday acts of charity, kindness, and redemption seldom make headlines. Perhaps that is how it should be, so let's just keep it our little secret.

List of Definitions, Axioms, and Propositions

Definitions

Definition 1: Religious goods are fundamental answers to the deep philosophic questions surrounding life that have as their basis some appeal to a supernatural force.

Definition 2: A *religious firm* (i.e., a church or denomination) is an organization that produces and distributes religious goods.

Definition 3: A *religious marketplace* is the social arena wherein religious firms compete for members and resources.

Definition 4: Religious liberty (or freedom) represents the degree to which a government regulates the religious marketplace.

Axioms

Axiom 1: Religious preferences in society are pluralistic.

Axiom 2: Proselytizing religious firms are market-share maximizers; they seek to spread their brand of spiritual message to as many followers as possible.

APPENDIX

232

Axiom 3: Politicians are primarily interested in their personal political survival.

Axiom 4: Politicians will also seek to maximize government revenue, promote economic growth, and minimize civil unrest.

Axiom 5: Politicians seek to minimize the cost of ruling.

Propositions

Proposition 1: Hegemonic religions will prefer high levels of government regulation (i.e., restrictions on religious liberty) over religious minorities. Religious minorities will prefer laws favoring greater religious liberty.

Proposition 1a: In an environment where no single religion commands a majority market share, the preferences of each denomination will tend toward religious liberty.

Proposition 2: Politicians will seek ideological compliance of the population when possible.

Proposition 3: To the extent that political survival, revenue collection, economic growth, and social stability are hindered by restrictions on religious freedom or subsidies to a dominant church, religious regulation will be liberalized or not enforced (de facto liberalization). In other words, deregulation of the religious market results when restrictions on religious liberty have a high opportunity cost as measured in terms of political survival, government revenue, and/or economic growth. Concomitantly, restrictions on religious freedom will increase if it served the aforementioned political and economic interests of policy makers.

Proposition 4: The presence of viable secular rivals to power increases the bargaining power of religious organizations, *ceteris paribus*.

Proposition 4a: If one religious organization commands hegemonic loyalty among the population and is not tied to any secular political actor, the bargaining power of that church increases, *ceteris paribus*. Regulatory policy toward religion is likely to favor the dominant church and discriminate against minority denominations.

Proposition 4b: If a church is institutionally linked (or credibly committed) to one political faction, regulatory policy will favor that denomination if the affiliated faction holds power. Conversely, religious deregulation, punishing the dominant church and rewarding spiritual competitors, is likely when the church's favored faction loses.

Proposition 4c: If several competing denominations exist (none with hegemonic dominance) regulatory policy will tend not to discriminate among them (i.e., increased religious liberty). In other words, the presence of competing religious denominations reduces the bargaining leverage of any one particular group, leading politicians to attempt to curry favor with all denominations.

Proposition 5: As political tenure becomes more secure, the bargaining power of a religious group wanes.

Proposition 5a: Given that restrictions on religious liberty entail monitoring and enforcement costs, politicians will be less likely to enforce them as their political tenure becomes secure.

Proposition 5b: As enforcement of restrictions on religious freedom decreases, religious pluralism increases in society (by way of Axioms 1 and 2).

Bibliography

Aguilar-Monsalve, Luis. 1988. "Breaking the Bonds of Church and State: The New Religious Freedom in Ecuador," *Thought* 65 (250): 236–49.

Ahlstrom, Sydney E. 2004. *A Religious History of the American People*. 2nd ed. New Haven: Yale University Press.

Alexeev, Wassilij. 1979. "The Russian Orthodox Church 1927–1945: Repression and Revival," *Religion in Communist Lands* 7 (1): 29–34.

Altnurme, Riho. 2003. *Soviet Religious Policy toward the Lutheran Church in Estonia (1944–1949)*. Symposium of the Commission of Latvian Historians, vol. 9. Riga: Latvian History Institute Publishers: 269–77.

Anderson, John. 2003. *Religious Liberty in Transitional Societies: The Politics of Religion*. Cambridge: Cambridge University Press.

———. 1994. *Religion, State and Politics in the Soviet Union and the Successor States*. Cambridge: Cambridge University Press.

———. 1983. "Soviet Religious Policy under Brezhnev and After," *Religion in Communist Lands* 11 (1): 25–9.

Anderson, Richard D. 2001. "Why Did the Soviet Empire Collapse So Fast – and Why Was the Collapse a Surprise?" In *Political Science as Puzzle Solving*, Bernard Groffman, ed. Ann Arbor: University of Michigan Press.

Arkin, Marc M. 1995. "'The Intractable Principle': David Hume, James Madison, Religion and the Tenth Federalist," *The American Journal of Legal History* 39 (2): 148–76.

Armstrong, Karen. 2000. *The Battle for God*. New York: Knopf.

Armstrong, Maurice W. 1960. "The Dissenting Deputies and the American Colonies," *Church History* 29 (3): 298–320.

Armstrong, Megan C. 2004. *The Politics of Piety: Franciscan Preachers during the Wars of Religion, 1560–1600*. Rochester, NY: University of Rochester Press.

Auza, Néstor Tomás. 1966. *Católicos y liberales en la generación del ochenta*. SONDEOS, nos. 6–7. Cuernavaca, Mexico: Centro Intercultural de Documentación.

Azzi, Corry and Ronald Ehrenberg. 1975. "Household Allocation of Time and Church Attendance," *Journal of Political Economy* 83 (1): 27–56.

Backus, Isaac. 1778. *Government and Liberty Described and Ecclesiastical Tyranny Exposed*. Boston: Powars and Wills.

———. 1771. *A Letter to a Gentleman in the Massachusetts General Assembly, Concerning Taxes to Support Religious Worship*. Boston: AAS Copy.

———. 1770. *A Seasonable Plea for Liberty of Conscience, against some late Oppressive Proceedings; Particularly in the Town of Berwick, in the County of York*. Boston: Philip Freeman.

Bainton, Roland H. 1941. "The Struggle for Religious Liberty," *Church History* 10 (2): 95–124.

———. 1936. "Changing Ideas and Ideals in the Sixteenth Century," *The Journal of Modern History* VIII (4): 417–43.

Baird, Henry M. 1895. *The Huguenots and the Revocation of the Edict of Nantes*. 2 vols. New York: Charles Scribner's Sons.

Balodis, Ringolds. 2000. "Valstybės ir Bažnyčios santykiai Latvijoje." Conference proceedings, Religija ir teisė pilietinėje visuomenėje, Vilnius, Lithuania, May 7–8, 2000. http://www.tm.lt/religija/turinys.htm (accessed August 5, 2006).

Barnett, Simon. 2001. "Religious Freedom and the European Convention on Human Rights: The Case of the Baltic States," *Religion, State and Society* 29 (2): 91–100.

Barrett, David B., George T. Kurian, and Todd M. Johnson. 2001. *World Christian Encyclopedia*. 2 vols. Oxford: Oxford University Press.

Barronco Villafán, Bernardo and Raquel Pastor Escobar. 1989. *Jerarquía Católica y modernización en México*. México, DF: Palabra Ediciones.

Barro, Robert J. and Rachel M. McCleary. 2004. "Which Countries Have State Religions?" NBER Working Paper 10438.

Bastian, Jean-Pierre. 1992. "Protestantism in Latin America." In *The Church in Latin America, 1492–1992*, Enrique Dussel, ed. Maryknoll, NY: Orbis Books.

Bates, Robert H., Avner Greif, Margaret Levi, Jean-Laurent Rosenthal, and Barry R. Weingast. 1998. *Analytic Narratives*. Princeton: Princeton University Press.

Beaman, Lori G. 2003. "The Myth of Pluralism, Diversity and Vigor: The Constitutional Privilege of Protestantism in the United States and Canada," *Journal for the Scientific Study of Religion* 42 (3): 311–25.

Becker, Gary S. 1994. *Human Capital: A Theoretical and Empirical Analysis, with Special Reference to Education*. Chicago: University of Chicago Press.

Bello, José María. 1966. *A History of Modern Brazil, 1889–1964*. James L. Taylor, trans. Stanford: Stanford University Press.

Berger, Peter. 1997. "Epistemological Modesty: An Interview with Peter Berger," *The Christian Century* 114 (October 29): 972–75, 978.

———. 1969. *The Sacred Canopy*. New York: Doubleday.

Berger, Peter L., ed. 1999. *The Desecularization of the World: Resurgent Religion and World Politics*. Grand Rapids, MI: William B. Eerdmans.

Bergin, Joseph. 2004. *Crown, Church and Episcopate under Louis XIV*. New Haven: Yale University Press.

―――. 1991. *The Rise of Richelieu*. New Haven: Yale University Press.

Berman, Harold J. 1999. "Freedom of Religion in Russia: An Amicus Brief for the Defendant." In *Proselytism and Orthodoxy in Russia: The New War for the Souls*, John Witte Jr. and Michael Bourdeaux, eds. Maryknoll, NY: Orbis Books.

―――. 1996. "Religious Rights in Russia at a Time of Tumultuous Transition: A Historical Theory." In *Religious Human Rights in Global Perspective: Legal Perspectives*, Johan D. van der Vyver and John Witte Jr., eds. The Hague: Martinus Nijhoff Publishers.

Bērziņš, Valdis, ed. 2000. *20. Gadsimta Latvijas vēsture I: Latvija no gadsimta sākums līdz neatkarības pasludināšanai 1900–1918*. Riga: Latvijas vēstures institūta apgāds.

Bialek, Robert W. 1963. *Catholic Politics: A History Based on Ecuador*. New York: Vantage Press.

Bidegain, Ana María. 1992. "The Church in the Emancipation Process." In *The Church in Latin America, 1492–1992*, Enrique Dussel, ed. Maryknoll, NY: Orbis Books.

Blackman, Peter. 2003. "Communications Act – Just!" Churches' Media Council (United Kingdom), http://www.churchesmediacouncil.org.uk/cmec/commsact/comms_Act_full.htm (accessed August 25, 2005).

Blancarte, Roberto J. 1993. "Recent Changes in Church-State Relations in Mexico," *Journal of Church and State* 35 (4): 791–805.

Blaustein, Albert P. and Jay Sigler. 1988. *Constitutions That Made History*. New York: Paragon House Publishers.

Bolívar, Simón. 2003. *El Libertador: Writings of Simón Bolívar*. Frederick H. Fornoff, trans. Oxford: Oxford University Press.

Bonino, José Míguez. 1999. "Argentina: Church, State, and Religious Freedom in Argentina." In *Religious Freedom and Evangelization in Latin America*, Paul E. Sigmund, ed. Maryknoll, NY: Orbis Books.

Bossy, John. 1991. "English Catholics after 1688." In *From Persecution to Toleration: The Glorious Revolution and Religion in England*, Ole Peter Grell, Jonathan I. Israel, and Nicholas Tyacke, eds. Oxford: Clarendon Press, 369–88.

Bourdeaux, Michael. 2000. "Religion Revives in All Its Variety: Russia's Regions Today," *Religion, State and Society* 28 (1): 9–21.

―――. 1995a. "Glasnost and the Gospel: The Emergence of Religious Pluralism." In *The Politics of Religion in Russia and the New States of Eurasia*, Michael Bordeaux, ed. London: M. E. Sharpe.

―――. 1995b. "Introduction." In *The Politics of Religion in Russia and the New States of Eurasia*, Michael Bordeaux, ed. London: M. E. Sharpe.

―――. 1990. *Gorbachev, Glasnost and the Gospel*. London: Hodder and Stoughton.

Bozeman, Theodore Dwight. 1972. "Religious Liberty and the Problem of Order in Early Rhode Island," *The New England Quarterly* 45 (1): 44–64.

Bradford, William. [1650] 1909. *Bradford's History of the Plymouth Settlement, 1608–1650*. Rendered into modern English by Valerian Paget. London: Alston Rivers.

Brading, D. A. 1994. *Church and State in Bourbon Mexico: The Diocese of Michoacán 1749–1810*. Cambridge: Cambridge University Press.

———. 1988. "Liberal Patriotism and the Mexican *Reforma*," *Journal of Latin America Studies* 20 (1): 27–48.

Brusco, Elizabeth E. 1999. "Colombia: Past Persecution, Present Tension." In *Religious Freedom and Evangelization in Latin America*, Paul E. Sigmund, ed. Maryknoll, NY: Orbis Books.

Buckley, Thomas E. 1977. *Church and State in Revolutionary Virginia, 1776–1787*. Charlottesville: University Press of Virginia.

Bulmer-Thomas, Victor. 1994. *The Economic History of Latin America since Independence*. Cambridge: Cambridge University Press.

Camp, Roderic Ai. 1997. *Crossing Swords: Politics and Religion in Mexico*. Oxford: Oxford University Press.

Canclini, Santiago. 1972. *Los Evangélicos en el tiempo de Perón: Memorias de un pastor bautista sobre la libertad religiosa en la Argentina*. Buenos Aires: Editorial Mundo Hispano.

Casanova, José. 1994. *Public Religions in the Modern World*. Chicago: University of Chicago Press.

Castillo Cárdenas, Gonzalo. 1968. *The Colombian Concordat in the Light of Recent Trends in Catholic Thought Concerning Church-State Relations and Religious Liberty*. SONDEOS, no. 22. Cuernavaca, Mexico: Centro Intercultural de Documentación.

Chadwick, Owen. 1975. *The Secularization of the European Mind in the 19th Century*. Cambridge: Cambridge University Press.

Chaves, Mark and David E. Cann. 1992. "Regulation, Pluralism and Religious Market Structure: Explaining Religion's Vitality," *Rationality and Society* 4 (3): 272–90.

Chesnut, R. Andrew. 2003. *Competitive Spirits: Latin America's New Religious Economy*. Oxford: Oxford University Press.

Chong, Dennis. 1991. *Collective Action and the Civil Rights Movement*. Chicago: University of Chicago Press.

Chwe, Michael Suk-Young. 2001. *Rational Ritual: Culture, Coordination and Common Knowledge*. Princeton: Princeton University Press.

Clark, John. 1652. *Ill Newes from New England*. London: Henry Hill.

Coffey, John. 2000. *Persecution and Toleration in Protestant England 1558–1689*. Harlow, UK: Pearson Education.

Collier, Simon. 1997. "Religious Freedom, Clericalism, and Anticlericalism in Chile, 1820–1920." In *Freedom and Religion in the Nineteenth Century*, Richard Helmstadter, ed. Stanford: Stanford University Press.

Collins, Jeffrey R. 1999. "The Restoration Bishops and the Royal Supremacy," *Church History* 68 (3): 549–80.

Concha Malo, Miguel. 1986. *La participación de los cristianos en el proceso popular de liberación en México*. México, DF: Siglo Veintiuno.

Conferencia del Episcopado Mexicano. 1994. *Documentos colectivos del episcopado mexicano: Volumen II, 1976–1986*. México, DF: Ediciones CEM.

———. 1985a. "Carta pastoral del episcopado mexicano sobre el desarrollo e integración de nuestra patria en el primer aniversario de la 'Populorum Progressio.'"

In *Documentos Colectivos del Episcopado Mexicano: A Diez Años del Concilio Vaticano II*. México, DF: Ediciones CEM.

——. 1985b. *Sociedad Civil y Sociedad Religiosa: Compromiso recíproco al servicio del Hombre y bien del País*. México, DF: Ediciones CEM.

Conquest, Robert, ed. 1968. *Religion in the U.S.S.R.* New York: Praeger.

Consejo Episcopal Latinoamericano (CELAM). 1984. *Las Sectas en América Latina*. Buenos Aires: Editorial Clarentiana.

Consodine, John J. 1958. *New Horizons in Latin America*. New York: Dodd, Mead and Company.

Corley, Felix. 2002. "Estonia: Registration Transferred from Interior Ministry to Courts." *Keston News Service* (July 4). http://www.starlightsite.co.uk/keston/kns/2002/020704ES.htm (accessed August 5, 2006).

——. 1996. *Religion in the Soviet Union: An Archival Reader*. London: MacMillan.

Cortínez Castro, René. 2000. "Críticas a la nueva ley de iglesias," *Mensaje* (May): 46–8.

——. 1999. "¿La razón de la sinrazón?" *Mensaje* (July): 48–50.

Coxe, Tench. 1794. *A View of the United States of America, in a Series of Papers*. Philadelphia: William Hall and Wrigley and Berriman.

Crassweller, Robert D. 1987. *Perón and the Enigmas of Argentina*. New York: W. W. Norton.

Curry, Thomas J. 1986. *The First Freedoms: Church and State in America to the Passage of the First Amendment*. Oxford: Oxford University Press.

D'Amico, David F. 1977. "Religious Liberty in Argentina during the First Perón Regime, 1943–1955," *Church History* 46 (4): 490–503.

Deiros, Pablo A. 1992. *Historia del Cristianismo en América Latina*. Buenos Aires: Fraternidad Teológica Latinoamericana.

——. 1991. "Protestant Fundamentalism in Latin America." In *Fundamentalisms Observed*, Martin E. Marty and R. Scott Appleby, eds. Chicago: University of Chicago Press, 142–96.

Delfi Internet News Service. 2005. "Siūloma suteikti valstybės pripažinimą Evangelinio tikėjimo krikščionių sąjungai. http://www.delfi.lt/news/daily/lithuania/article.php?id=6255040 (accessed March 15, 2005).

Della Cava, Ralph. 1993. "Financing the Faith: The Case of Roman Catholicism," *Journal of Church and State* 35 (1): 37–59.

Dickinson, Anna. 2000. "Quantifying Religious Oppression: Russian Orthodox Church Closures and Repression of Priests 1917–41," *Religion, State and Society* 28 (4): 327–35.

Dillon, Francis. 1975. *The Pilgrims*. Rev. ed. Garden City, NY: Doubleday.

Dirksen, Hans Hermann. 2002. "Jehovah's Witnesses under Communist Regimes," *Religion, State and Society* 30 (3): 229–38.

Dolan, Jay P. 1992. *The American Catholic Experience: A History from Colonial Times to the Present*. Notre Dame: University of Notre Dame Press.

Drake, Paul W. and Matthew D. McCubbins. 1998. "The Origins of Liberty." In *The Origins of Liberty: Political and Economic Liberalization in the Modern World*, Paul W. Drake and Matthew D. McCubbins, eds. Princeton: Princeton University Press, 3–12.

Dunlop, John B. 1995. "The Russian Orthodox Church as an 'Empire-Saving' Institution." In *The Politics of Religion in Russia and the New States of Eurasia*, Michael Bordeaux, ed. London: M. E. Sharpe.

Durán, Victor Hugo. 2000. "Promulgan reglamento de nueva ley de culto." *La Tercera* (May 27). Internet edition (accessed June 5, 2000).

Durham Jr., W. Cole. 1997. "Perspectives on Religious Liberty: A Comparative Framework." In *Religious Human Rights in Global Perspective: Legal Perspectives*, Johan D. van der Vyver and John Witte Jr., eds. The Hague: Martinus Nijhoff Publishers, 1–44.

Dussel, Enrique. 1981. *A History of the Church in Latin America: Colonialism to Liberation (1492–1979)*. Alan Neely, trans. Grand Rapids, MI: William B. Eerdmans.

————. 1972. "The Appointment of Bishops in the First Century of 'Patronage' in Latin America (1504–1620)," *Concilum* 77: 113–21.

Eckstein, Harry. 1975. "Case Study and Theory in Political Science." In *Handbook of Political Science*, vol. 7. Fred Greenstein and Nelson Polsby, eds. Reading, MA: Addison-Wesley, 79–137.

Eckstein, Susan. 1988. *The Poverty of Revolution: The State and the Urban Poor in Mexico*. Princeton: Princeton University Press.

Ekelund, Robert B., Rebert F. Hébert, Robert D. Tollison, Gary M. Anderson, and Audrey B. Davidson. 1996. *Sacred Trust: The Medieval Church as an Economic Firm*. Oxford: Oxford University Press.

Elliott, J. H. 2006. *Empires of the Atlantic World: Britain and Spain in America 1492–1830*. New Haven: Yale University Press.

Elliott, Mark and Sharyl Corrado. 1999. "The 1997 Russian Law on Religion: The Impact on Protestants," *Religion, State and Society* 27 (1): 109–34.

Elliott, Mark and Anita Deyneka. 1999. "Protestant Missionaries in the Former Soviet Union." In *Proselytism and Orthodoxy in Russia: The New War for the Souls*, John Witte Jr. and Michael Bourdeaux, eds. Maryknoll, NY: Orbis Books.

Elster, Jon. 1983. *Sour Grapes*. Cambridge: Cambridge University Press.

Fagan, Geraldine. 2003. "Russia: Religious Freedom Survey, July 2003." *Forum 18 News Service* (July 29). Oslo, Norway: Forum 18. http://www.forum18.org (accessed July 30, 2003).

Filatov, Sergei. 2000. "Protestantism in Postsoviet Russia: An Unacknowledged Triumph," *Religion, State and Society* 28 (1): 93–103.

————. 1999. "Sects and New Religious Movements in Post-Soviet Russia." In *Proselytism and Orthodoxy in Russia: The New War for the Souls*, John Witte Jr. and Michael Bourdeaux, eds. Maryknoll, NY: Orbis Books.

Financial Times. 1995. "Moscow Puts Its Faith in a Capital Projectt," *Financial Times* (August 24): 2.

Finke, Roger. 1990. "Religious Deregulation: Origins and Consequences," *Journal of Church and State* 32 (3): 609–26.

Finke, Roger and Laurence R. Iannaccone. 1993. "Supply-side Explanations for Religious Change," *Annals* 527: 27–39.

Finke, Roger and Rodney Stark. 2005. *The Churching of America: Winners and Losers in Our Religious Economy*. New Brunswick: Rutgers University Press.

Fleet, Michael and Brian H. Smith. 1997. *The Catholic Church and Democracy in Chile and Peru*. Notre Dame: University of Notre Dame Press.

Földesi, Tamás. 1996. "The Main Problems of Religious Freedom in Eastern Europe." In *Religious Human Rights in Global Perspective: Legal Perspectives*, Johan D. Van der Vyver and John Witte Jr., eds. The Hague: Martinus Nijhoff Publishers.

Foreign Broadcast Information Service (FBIS). 1979. "La Tribuna Discusses Banning of Jehovah's Witnesses" (January 9): H1.

———. 1978. "Jehovah's Witnesses Banned" (February 16): B3.

Fox, Jonathan and Shmuel Sandler. 2005. "Separation of Religion and State in the Twenty-First Century: Comparing the Middle East and Western Democracies," *Comparative Politics* 37 (3): 317–35.

Freston, Paul. 1993. "Brother Votes for Brother: The New Politics of Protestantism in Brazil." In *Rethinking Protestantism in Latin America*, Virginia Garrard-Burnett and David Stoll, eds. Philadephia: Temple University Press.

Frigerio, Alejandro. 1993. "La invasion de las sectas: el debate sobre nuevos movimientos religiosos en los medios de comunicacion en Argentina," *Sociedad y Religion* 10/11: 24–51.

Froese, Paul. 2004a. "Forced Secularization in Soviet Russia: Why an Atheistic Monopoly Failed," *Journal for the Scientific Study of Religion* 43 (1): 35–50.

———. 2004b. "After Atheism: Religious Monopolies in the Post-Communist World," *Sociology of Religion* 65 (1): 57–75.

———. 2003. "The Great Secularization Experiment: Assessing the Communist Attempt to Eliminate Religion." PhD diss., University of Washington.

Froese, Paul and Steven Pfaff. 2005. "Explaining a Religious Anomaly: A Historical Analysis of Secularization in East Germany," *Journal for the Scientific Study of Religion* 44 (4): 397–422.

———. 2001. "Replete and Desolate Markets: Poland, East Germany and the New Religious Paradigm," *Social Forces* 80 (2): 481–508.

Fueloep-Miller, Rene. 1960. "Tolstoy the Apostolic Crusader," *Russian Review* 19 (2): 99–121.

Gaubatz, Derek L. 2005. "RLUIPA at Four: Evaluating the Success and Constitutionality of RLUIPA's Prisoner Provisions," *Harvard Journal of Law and Public Policy* 28 (2): 504–607.

Geddes, Barbara. 1994. *Politician's Dilemma: Building State Capacity in Latin America*. Berkeley: University of California Press.

Gill, Anthony. 2003. "Lost in the Supermarket: Comments on Beaman, Religious Pluralism and What It Means to Be Free," *Journal for the Scientific Study of Religion* 42 (3): 327–32.

———. 2002a. "Religiöse Dynamik und Demokratie in Lateinamerika," *Politische Vierteljahresschrift* 33 (3): 478–94.

———. 2002b. "Studying Liberation Theology: What Next?" *Journal for the Scientific Study of Religion* 41 (1): 87–89.

———. 2001. "Religion and Comparative Politics." In *Annual Review of Political Science*, vol. 4, Nelson W. Polsby, ed. Palo Alto, CA: Annual Reviews.

———. 1999a. "Government Regulation, Social Anomie and Protestant Growth in Latin America: A Cross-National Analysis," *Rationality and Society* 11 (3): 287–316.

————. 1999b. "The Struggle to Be Soul Provider: Catholic Responses to Protestant Growth in Latin America." In *Latin American Religion in Motion*, Christian Smith and Joshua Prokopy, eds. New York: Routledge, 17–42.

————. 1999c. "The Politics of Regulating Religion in Mexico: The 1992 Constitutional Reforms in Historical Context," *Journal of Church and State* 41 (4): 761–94.

————. 1999d. "The Economics of Evangelization." In *Religious Freedom and Evangelization in Latin America*, Paul E. Sigmund, ed. Maryknoll, NY: Orbis Books.

Gill, Anthony and Arang Keshavarzian. 1999. "State-Building and Religious Resources: An Institutional Theory of Church-State Relations in Iran and Mexico," *Politics and Society* 27 (3): 430–64.

Gill, Anthony and Charles M. North. 2005. "Crowded Pews or Crowded Out? The Effect of State Social Welfare Spending on Religious Attendance in the United States," unpublished manuscript, University of Washington.

Gills, Nikandrs. "Jehovah's Witnesses in the Social and Cultural Context of Contemporary Latvia." Conference paper CESNUR (Center for Studies on New Religions) 14th international conference, Riga, Latvia, August 29–31, 2000. http://www.cesnur.org/conferences/riga2000/gills.htm (accessed August 5, 2006).

Girnius, Saulius. 1997. "Katalikų Bažnyčios vaidmuo nepriklausomos Lietuvos visuomenėje." In *Krikščionybė Lietuvoje*, Vytautas Vardys, ed. Chicago: Lietuvos krikščionybės jubiliejus komitetas, 270–99.

Glodenis, Donatas. 2005. "Legislation on Religion and the Challenge of Pluralism in Lithuania." http://www.religija.lt/en/showarticle.php?articleID=17 (accessed August 5, 2006).

Goeckel, Robert F. 1995. "The Baltic Churches and the Democratization Process." In *The Politics of Religion in Russia and the New States of Eurasia*, Michael Bordeaux, ed. London: M. E. Sharpe.

Goff, James E. 1968. *The Persecution of Protestant Christians in Colombia, 1948–1958*. SONDEOS, no. 23. Curenavaca, Mexico: CIDOC.

González Fernández, José Antonio. 1992. *Derecho Eclesiástico Mexicano*. México, DF: Editorial Porrúa.

Gould, Andrew. 1999. *Origins of Liberal Dominance: State, Church, and Party in Nineteenth Century Europe*. Ann Arbor: University of Michigan Press.

Grayson, George W. 1992. *The Church in Contemporary Mexico*. Washington, DC: Center for Strategic and International Studies.

Greeley, Andrew. 1994. "A Religious Revival in Russia?" *Journal for the Scientific Study of Religion* 33 (3): 253–73.

Greene, Evarts B. 1941. *Religion and the State: The Making and Testing of an American Tradition*. New York: New York University Press.

Greene, M. Louise. 1970. *The Development of Religious Liberty in Connecticut*. New York: Da Capo Press.

Grell, Ole Peter, Jonathan I. Israel, and Nicholas Tyacke, eds. 1991. *From Persecution to Toleration: The Glorious Revolution and Religion in England*. Oxford: Clarendon Press.

Grim, Brian J. 2004a. "The Cities of God versus the Countries of Earth: The Regulation of Religious Freedom." Paper delivered at the annual meeting of the

Association for the Study of Religion, Economics, and Culture, Kansas City, MO.

_____. 2004b. "The Cities of God versus the Countries of Earth: The Restrictions of Religious Freedom (RRF) Index," unpublished manuscript, Pennsylvania State University.

Grim, Brian J. and Roger Finke. 2006. "International Religion Indexes: Government Regulation, Government Favoritism, and Social Regulation of Religion," *Interdisciplnary Journal of Research on Religion* 2 (Article 1). http://www.religjournal .com (accessed January 17, 2007).

Grose, Clyde L. 1937. "The Religion of Restoration England," *Church History* 6 (3): 223–32.

Gunn, T. Jeremy. 1999. "The Law of the Russian Federation on the Freedom of Conscience and Religious Associations from a Human Rights Perspective." In *Proselytism and Orthodoxy in Russia: The New War for the Souls*, John Witte Jr. and Michael Bourdeaux, eds. Maryknoll, NY: Orbis Books.

Gura, Philip F. 1984. *A Glimpse of Sion's Glory: Puritan Radicalism in New England, 1620–1660*. Middletown, CT: Wesleyan University Press.

Gutiérrez Casillas, José. 1974. *Historia de la Iglesia en México*. México, DF: Editorial Porrúa.

Gwin, Carl R. and Charles M. North. 2004. "Religious Freedom and State Religion in an International Panel," unpublished manuscript, Baylor University.

Halperín Donghi, Tulio. 1993. *The Contemporary History of Latin America*. John Charles Chasteen, trans. Durham, NC: Duke University Press.

Hanson, Charles P. 1998. *Necessary Virtue: The Pragmatic Origins of Religious Liberty in New England*. Charlottesville: University Press of Virginia.

Hanson, Stephen E. 1997. *Time and Revolution: Marxism and the Design of Soviet Institutions*. Chapel Hill: University of North Carolina Press.

Harkness, R. E. E. "Principles Established in Rhode Island," *Church History* 5 (3): 216–26.

Harmin, Carol Lee. 2005. "A New Framework for Promoting Religious Freedom in China," *The Brandywine Review of Faith and International Affairs* 3 (1): 3–10.

Harris, Joseph Claude. 1993. "Pennies for Heaven: Catholic Underachievers," *Commonweal* (April 9): 8–9.

Hawkins, L. M. 1928. *Allegiance in Church and State: The Problem of the Nonjurors in the English Revolution*. London: George Routledge and Sons.

Hecther, Michael. 2000. *Containing Nationalism*. Oxford: Oxford University Press.

Helmstadter, Richard, ed. 1997. *Freedom and Religion in the Nineteenth Century*. Stanford: Stanford University Press.

Hinojosa, Oscar. 1986a. "Prigione, enlace de Bartlett para reprender a obispos críticos," *Proceso* (August 18): 6–11.

_____. 1986b. "La mission evangélica ordena dejar la sacristía, afirma Sergio Obeso," *Proceso* (September 8): 10.

Hirschman, Albert O. 1970. *Exit, Voice and Loyalty: Responses to Decline in Firms, Organizations and States*. Cambridge, MA: Harvard University Press.

Hobhouse, Leonard Trelawny. [1911] 1942. *Liberalism*. London: Oxford University Press.

Holleran, Mary P. 1949. *Church and State in Guatemala*. New York: Columbia University Press.

Holt, Mack P. 1995. *The French Wars of Religion, 1562–1629*. Cambridge: Cambridge University Press.

Hoppenbrouwers, Frans. 1999. "Romancing Freedom: Church and Society in the Baltic States since the End of Communism," *Religion, State and Society* 27 (2): 161–73.

Hungerman, Daniel M. 2005. "Are Church and State Substitutes? Evidence from the 1996 Welfare Reform," *Journal of Public Economics* 89 (11–12): 2245–67.

———. 2004. "Comparing Government Expansion and Contraction: Are All Crowd Out Stories the Same?" unpublished manuscript, Duke University.

Hunter, Ian. 1998. "Religious Toleration and the Pluralisation of Personhood: Christian Thomasius' Program for the Deconfessionalisation of Society," *Southern Review* 31 (1): 38–53.

Hurtado, Alberto. [1941] 1992. *¿Es Chile un país católico?* Santiago: Editorial Los Andes.

Hutson, James H. 1998. *Religion and the Founding of the American Republic*. Washington, DC: Library of Congress.

Iannaccone, Laurence R. 1995. "Voodoo Economics? Reviewing the Rational Choice Approach to Religion," *Journal for the Scientific Study of Religion* 34: 76–88.

———. 1991. "The Consequences of Religious Market Structure: Adam Smith and the Economics of Religion," *Rationality and Society* 3 (2): 156–77.

———. 1990. "Religious Practice: A Human Capital Approach," *Journal for the Scientific Study of Religion* 29 (3): 297–314.

Instituto de Investigaciones Jurídicas. 1996. *La Libertad Religiosa: Memoria del IX Congreso Inernacional de Derecho Canónico*. México, DF: Universidad Nacional Autónoma de México.

Ireland, Rowan. 1993. "The *Crentes* of Campo Alegre and the Religious Construction of Brazilian Politics." In *Rethinking Protestantism in Latin America*, Virginia Garrard-Burnett and David Stoll, eds. Philadelphia: Temple University Press.

Isaac, Rhys. 1973. "Religion and Authority: Problems of the Anglican Establishment in Virginia in the Era of the Great Awakening and the Parsons' Cause," *The William and Mary Quarterly* 30 (1): 3–36.

Isaacson, Scott E. 2003. "A Practical Comparison of the Laws of Religion of Colombia and Chile," *The International Journal of Not-for-Profit Law* 6 (1). http://www.icnl.org/JOURNAL/vol6iss1/rel_isaacsonprint.htm (accessed August 28, 2005).

Isáis, Juan M. 1998. "Mexico: Out of the Salt Shaker," *Christianity Today* (November 16): 72–3.

Jaffa, Harry V. 1990. *The American Founding as the Best Regime: The Bonding of Civil and Religious Liberty*. Claremont, CA: The Claremont Institute.

James, Sydney V. 1975. *Colonial Rhode Island: A History*. New York: Charles Scribner's Sons.

Jenkins, Philip. 2002. *The Next Christendom: The Coming of Global Christianity*. Oxford: Oxford University Press.

John Paul II. 1991. "Continue the path of dialogue," *L'Osservatore Romano*, English ed. (July 22): 22.

Johnson, Paul. 1976. *A History of Christianity*. New York: Macmillan Publishing.

Jordan, W. K. 1932. *The Development of Religious Toleration in England: From the Beginning of the English Reformation to the Death of Queen Elizabeth*. Cambridge, MA: Harvard University Press.

_____. 1936a. *The Development of Religious Toleration in England: From the Accession of James I to the Convention of the Long Parliament (1603–1640)*. Cambridge, MA: Harvard University Press.

_____. 1936b. *The Development of Religious Toleration in England: From the Convention of the Long Parliament to the Restoration (1640–1660)*. Cambridge, MA: Harvard University Press.

_____. 1936c. *The Development of Religious Toleration in England: Attainment of the Theory and Accommodations in Thought and Institutions (1640–1660)*. Cambridge, MA: Harvard University Press.

Juergensmeyer, Mark. 2000. *Terror in the Mind of God: The Global Rise of Religious Violence*. Berkeley: University of California Press.

Kalyvas, Stathis N. 1996. *The Rise of Christian Democracy in Europe*. Ithaca, NY: Cornell University Press.

Ketola, Mikko, "Some Aspects of the Nationality Question in the Lutheran Church of Estonia, 1918–1939," *Religion, State and Society* 27 (2), 1999: 239–43.

King, Gary, Robert Keohane, and Sidney Verba. 1994. *Designing Social Inquiry*. Princeton: Princeton University Press.

Kirby, David. 1995. *The Baltic World 1772–1993: Europe's Northern Periphery in an Age of Change*. London: Longman.

Kirill, Metropolitan. 1999. "Gospel and Culture." In *Proselytism and Orthodoxy in Russia: The New War for the Souls*, John Witte Jr. and Michael Bourdeaux, eds. Maryknoll, NY: Orbis Books.

Klaiber, Jeffery. 1999. "Peru: Evangelization and Religious Freedom." In *Religious Freedom and Evangelization in Latin America*, Paul E. Sigmund, ed. Maryknoll, NY: Orbis Books.

Knowlton, Robert J. 1969. "Expropriation of Church Property in Nineteenth Century Mexico and Colombia: A Comparison," *The Americas* 25 (4): 387–401.

Knox, Zoe. 2004. "Postsoviet Challenges to the Moscow Patriarchate, 1991–2001," *Religion, State and Society* 32 (2): 87–113.

Krumina-Konkova, Solveiga. 2000. "New Religious Minorities in the Baltic States," *Nova Religio* 4 (2) (April): 289–98.

Kuran, Timur. 2004. *Islam and Mammon: The Economic Predicaments of Islamism*. Princeton: Princeton University Press.

_____. 1995. *Private Truths, Public Lies: The Social Consequences of Preference Falsification*. Cambridge: Cambridge University Press.

Kuru, Ahmet. 2006. "Dynamics of Secularism: State-Religion Relations in the United States, France, and Turkey," PhD diss., University of Washington.

Kutznetsov, Anatoly. 1996. "Ecumenism, Evangelism, and Religious Freedom in Russia and the Former Soviet Republics," *Religion in Eastern Europe* 16 (2): 8–14.

Kwilecki, Susan and Loretta S. Wilson. 1998. "Was Mother Teresa Maximizing Her Utility? An Idiographic Application of Rational Choice Theory," *Journal for the Scientific Study of Religion* 37 (2): 205–22.

Lalive d'Epinay, Christian. 1969. *Haven of the Masses: A Study of the Pentecostal Movement in Chile*. London: Lutterworth Press.

Lambert, Jacques. 1967. *Latin America: Social Structures and Political Institutions*. Helen Katel, trans. Berkeley: University of California Press.

Landsbergis, Vytautus. 2000. *Lithuania: Independent Again*. Anthony Packer, trans. Seattle: University of Washington Press.

Latin American Weekly Report. 1990. "Worrying rise of religious strife: In Mexico clashes claiming lives" (October 4): 6–7.

Lave, Charles and James March. 1975. *An Introduction to Models in the Social Sciences*. New York: Harper and Row.

Leege, David C. 2004. "Roman Catholics in American Catholic Politics: A Contesting and Contested Group," unpublished manuscript.

Levi, Margaret. 1988. *Of Rule and Revenue*. Berkeley: University of California Press.

Levy, Leonard W. 1999. *Origins of the Bill of Rights*. New Haven: Yale University Press.

Lewis, Mike. 2001. "County Councilman Takes on School, Church Moratorium," *Seattle Post-Intelligencer*. http://seattlepi.nwsource.com/local/moratorium26.shtml (accessed August 25, 2005).

Lichbach, Mark Irving. 1995. *The Rebel's Dilemma*. Ann Arbor: University of Michigan Press.

Lindley, Keith. 1998. *The English Civil War and Revolution: A Sourcebook*. London: Routledge.

Lithuanian Central State Archives (*Lietuvos Centrininis Valstybės Archyvas–LCVA*) [untitled response to request for information on Catholic rituals] F. R-181 Ap. 1 B. 145 L.11–12.

Lithuanian Statistical Department (Lietuvos Statistikos Departamentas). http://www.std.lt/lt/news/view/?id=292 (accessed July 30, 2006).

Lloyd, Marion. 2001. "Mexican Hamlet Presses Evangelicals," *The Boston Globe* (September 20): A10.

Locke, John. [1689] 1955. *A Letter Concerning Toleration*. Indianapolis: Bobbs-Merril.

Lodwick, Robert E. 1969. *The Significance of the Church-State Relationship to an Evangelical Program in Brazil*. SONDEOS, no. 40. Cuernavaca, Mexico: CIDOC.

Lohrenz, Otto. 1970. "The Virginia Clergy and the American Revolution, 1774–1799," PhD diss., University of Kansas.

Lubertino Beltrán, María J. 1987. *Perón y la Iglesia (1943–1955)*. 2 vols. Buenos Aires: Centro Editor de América Latina.

Luukkanen, Arto. 1997. *The Religious Policy of the Stalinist State: A Case Study*. Helsinki: Suomen Historiallinen Seura.

———. 1994. *The Party of Unbelief: The Religious Policy of the Bolshevik Party 1917–1929*. Helsinki: Suomen Historiallinen Seura.

Luxmoore, Jonathan. 2001. "Eastern Europe 1997–2000: A Review of Church Life," *Religion, State and Society* 29 (4): 305–30.

Lyon, Thomas. 1937. *The Theory of Religious Liberty in England, 1603–39*. London: Cambridge University Press.

Manning, Brian, ed. 1973. *Politics, Religion and the English Civil War*. London: Edward Arnold.

Marcinkevičius, Andrius and Saulius Kaubrys. 2003. *Lietuvos stačiatikių bažnyčia 1918–1939 m.* Vilnius: Vaga.

Marostica, Matthew. 1998. "Religion and Global Affairs: Religious Activism and Democracy in Latin America," *SAIS Review* 18 (2): 44–51.

Marsal, Pablo. 1955. *Perón y la Iglesia.* Buenos Aires: Ediciones Rex.

Marsh, Christopher and Paul Froese. 2004. "The State of Freedom in Russia: A Regional Analysis of Religion, Media and Markets," *Religion, State and Society* 32 (2): 137–49.

Marshall, Paul, ed. 2000. *Religious Freedom in the World: A Global Report on Freedom and Persecution.* Nashville, TN: Broadman and Holman.

Martin, David. 1990. *Tongues of Fire: The Explosion of Protestantism in Latin America.* Cambridge: Basil Blackwell.

Marx, Karl. 1975. *On Religion.* Moscow: Progress Publishers.

Mayhew, David. 1974. *Congress: The Electoral Connection.* New Haven: Yale University Press.

McCallum, Jane Y. 1929. *Women Pioneers.* Richmond, VA: Johnson Publishing Company.

McConnell, Michael W. 1990. "The Origins and Historical Understanding of Free Exercise of Religion," *Harvard Law Review* 103 (7): 1409–517.

McGrath, Alister. 2001. *In the Beginning: The Story of the King James Bible and How It Changed a Nation, a Language and a Culture.* New York: Anchor Books.

McLoughlin, William G. 1971. *New England Dissent 1630–1833: The Baptists and the Separation of Church and State.* 2 vols. Cambridge, MA: Harvard University Press.

_____. 1968. "Isaac Backus and the Separation of Church and State in America," *The American Historical Review* 73 (5): 1392–413.

Mead, Sidney E. 1956. "From Coercion to Persuasion: Another Look at the Rise of Religious Liberty and the Emergence of Denominationalism," *Church History* 25 (4): 317–37.

Mecham, J. Lloyd. 1966. *Church and State in Latin America: A History of Politico-Ecclesiastical Relations.* Chapel Hill: University of North Carolina Press.

Meerson, Michael Aksenov. 1981. "The Russian Orthodox Church 1965–1980," *Religion in Communist Lands* 9 (3–4): 101–9.

Meyer, Jean. 1989. *Historia de los cristianos en América Latina: Siglos XIX y XX.* México, DF: Editorial Vuelta.

_____. 1973. *La Crisiada: El conflicto entre la Iglesia y el estado, 1926–1929.* México, DF: Siglo Veintiuno.

Mignone, Emilio F. 1988. *Witness to the Truth: The Complicity of Church and Dictatorship in Argentina, 1976–1983.* Phillip Berryman, trans. Maryknoll, NY: Orbis Books.

Miller, Perry. 1956. *Errand into the Wilderness.* Cambridge, MA: Harvard University Press.

_____. 1935. "The Contribution of the Protestant Churches to Religious Liberty in Colonial America," *Church History* 4 (1): 57–66.

Miller, William Lee. 2003. *The First Liberty: America's Foundation in Religious Freedom.* 2nd ed. Washington, DC: Georgetown University Press.

Ministry of Justice of the Republic of Lithuania. 2005. "Šventojo Sosto ir Lietuvos Respublikos sutarties dėl santykių tarp Katalikų bažnyčios ir valstybės
teisinių aspektų," signed May 5, 2005. http://www.tm.lt/min/default.asp?load=
ti_sut_teis_aspektai.htm (accessed March 5, 2005).
Misiūnas, Romuald J. and Rein Taagepera. 1993. *The Baltic States: Years of Dependence
1940–1990*. Berkeley: University of California Press.
Modie, Neil. 2001. "Compromise Plan on Rural Church Ban," *Seattle Post-
Intelligencer* (April 6). http://seattlepi.nwsource.com/local/17543_rural06.shtml
(accessed August 24, 2005).
Monsma, Stephen V. and J. Christopher Soper. 1997. *The Challenge of Pluralism:
Church and State in Five Democracies*. Lanham, MD: Rowman and Littlefield.
Montgomery, T. S. 1979. "Latin American Evangelicals: Oaxtepec and Beyond." In
Churches and Politics in Latin America, Daniel H. Levine, ed. Beverly Hills, CA:
Sage Publications.
Moore, Barrington. 1996. *Social Origins of Dictatorship and Democracy*. Boston:
Beacon Press.
Morales, Sonia y Rodrigo Vera. 1995. "Samuel Ruíz ha resistido desde 1960,
hosigamientos, acusaciones, condenas, agresiones, injurias," *Proceso* (February
27): 12–17.
Moreno, Pedro, ed. 1996. *Handbook on Religious Liberty around the World*. Char-
lottesville, VA: Rutherford Institute.
Mullett, Charles F. 1938. "Some Essays on Toleration in Late Eighteenth Century
England," *Church History* 7 (1): 24–44.
Murray, Paul V. 1965. *The Catholic Church in Mexico: Historical Essays for the General
Reader*, vol. 1. México, DF: Editoríal E. P. M.
Musteikis, Antanas. 1988. *The Reformation in Lithuania: Religious Fluctuations in the
Sixteenth Century*. New York: Columbia University Press.
Noonan Jr., John T. 1998. *The Lustre of Our Country: The American Experience of
Religious Freedom*. Berkeley: University of California Press.
Norris, Pippa and Ronald Inglehart. 2004. *Sacred and Secular: Religion and Politics
Worldwide*. Cambridge: Cambridge University Press.
North, Douglass C. 2005. *Understanding the Process of Economic Change*. Princeton:
Princeton University Press.
———. 1981. Structure and Change in Economic History. New York: W. W.
Norton.
Olson, Mancur. 1993. "Dictatorship, Development and Democracy," *American
Political Science Review* 87 (3): 567–76.
———. 1965. *The Logic of Collective Action*. Cambridge, MA: Harvard University
Press.
Ortiz Pinchetti, Francisco. 1986. "Campaña orquestada, las críticas a la suspension
de misas: El Arzobispo Almeida," *Proceso* (July 21): 14–15.
Orttung, Robert. 1996. "Zyuganov Promises to Back Church," *Open Media Research
Institute Daily Digest* (April 12).
Pajas, Petr. 2003. "The Impact of New Czech Laws on Churches," *The International
Journal of Not-for-Profit Law* 6 (1). http://www.icnl.org/JOURNAL/vol6iss1/rel_
pajasprint.htm (accessed August 24, 2005).
Paretskya, Anna. 1996. "More Support for Yeltsin," *Open Media Research Institute
Daily Digest* (May 16).

Park, Charles E. 1954. "Puritans and Quakers," *The New England Quarterly* 27 (1): 53–74.

Pauck, Wilhelm. 1946. "The Christian Faith and Religious Tolerance," *Church History* 15 (3): 220–34.

Penn, William. 2002. *The Political Writings of William Penn*. Intro. and annotations by Andrew R. Murphy. Indianapolis: Liberty Fund.

Pérez Mendoza, Jaime. 1986. "Por petición de Bartlett El Vaticano ordenó que hubiera misas en Chihuahua," *Proceso* (August 4): 6–13.

Pestana, Carla Gardina. 1991. *Quakers and Baptists in Colonial Massachusetts*. Cambridge: Cambridge University Press.

Petkus, Viktorus, Živilė Račkauskaitė, and Mindaugas Uoka, eds. 1999. *Lietuvos Helsinkio grupė: dokumentai, atsiminimai, laiškai*. Vilnius: Lietuvos gyventojų genocido ir rezistencijos tyrimo centras.

Pierson, Paul Everett. 1974. *A Younger Church in Search of Maturity: Presbyterianism in Brazil from 1910 to 1959*. San Antonio, TX: Trinity University Press.

Plaat, Jaanus. 2003. "Religious Change in Estonia and the Baltic States during the Soviet Period in Comparative Perspective," *Journal of Baltic Studies* 34 (1) (Spring): 52–73.

Plakans, Andrejs. 1995. *The Latvians: A Short History*. Stanford, CA: Hoover Institution Press.

Poblete, Renato. 1970. "The Church in Latin America: A Historical Survey." In *The Church and Social Change in Latin America*, Henry A. Landsberger, ed. Notre Dame: University of Notre Dame Press.

———. 1965. *Crisis Sacerdotal*. Santiago: Editorial del Pacífico.

Polyakov, Yevgeny. 1994. "The Activities of the Moscow Patriarchate during 1991," *Religion, State and Society* 22 (2): 145–63.

Pope, Robert G. 1969. *The Half-Way Covenant: Church Membership in Puritan New England*. Princeton: Princeton University Press.

Pospielovsky, Dimitry V. 1995. "The Russian Orthodox Church in the Postcommunist CIS." In *The Politics of Religion in Russia and the New States of Eurasia*, Michael Bourdeaux, ed. Armonk, NY: M. E. Sharpe.

Powell, David E. 1975. *Antireligious Propaganda in the Soviet Union: A Study of Mass Persuasion*. Cambridge, MA: MIT Press.

Powell, T. G. 1977. "Priests and Peasants in Central Mexico: Social Conflict during 'La Reforma,'" *The Hispanic American Historical Review* 57 (2): 296–313.

Poynter, J. W. 1930. *The Reformation, Catholicism and Freedom: A Study of Roman Catholic and Other Martyrs, and of the Struggles for Liberty of Conscience*. New York: The Macmillan Co.

Prigione, Jerónimo. 1992. "Mensaje Inicial." In *La Iglesia Católica en el Nuevo Marco Jurídico de México*. México DF: Ediciones de la CEM.

Puente, María Alicia. 1992. "The Church in Mexico." In *The Church in Latin America, 1492–1992*, Enrique Dussel, ed. Maryknoll, NY: Orbis Books.

Pufendorf, Samuel. [1687] 2002. *Of the Nature and Qualification of Religion in Reference to Civil Society*, Simone Zurbuchen, ed. Indianapolis: Liberty Fund.

Pullerits, Albert, ed. 1935. *Estonia: Population, Cultural and Economic Life*. Tallinn, Estonia: State Central Bureau of Statistics.

Putnam, Robert. 2000. *Bowling Alone: The Collapse and Revival of American Community*. New York: Simon and Shuster.

Ramet, Sabrina P. 1998. *Nihil Obstat: Religion, Politics, and Social Change in East-Central Europe and Russia*. Durham, NC: Duke University Press.

Raun, Toivo. 2001. *Estonia and the Estonians*. Stanford: Hoover Institution Press.

Religious Society of Friends. 1789. "To the President of the United States. The address of the religious society called Quakers, from their yearling meeting for Pennsylvania, New Jersey, Delaware, and the western parts of Virginia and Maryland." Philadelphia: Daniel Humphreys Pinter.

Ringvee, Ringo. 2003. "Orthodox Churches in Estonia," *Estonian Culture*. http://www.einst.ee/culture/I_MMIII/ringvee.html (accessed August 5, 2006).

Romero, José Luis. 1963. *A History of Argentine Political Thought*. Stanford: Stanford University Press.

Rowe, Michael. 1979. "Soviet Policy toward Evangelicals," *Religion in Communist Lands* 7 (1): 4–12.

Salinas, Maximiliano. 1992. "The Church in the Southern Cone: Chile, Argentina, Paraguay and Uruguay." In *The Church in Latin America 1492–1992*, Enrique Dussel, ed. Maryknoll, NY: Orbis Books.

Salo, Vello. 2002. "The Catholic Church in Estonia 1918–2001," *The Catholic Historical Review* 88 (2): 281–92.

———. 1978. "The Struggle between State and Church." In *A Case Study of a Soviet Republic: The Estonian SSR*, Tönu Parming and Elmar Järvesoo, eds. Boulder, CO: Westview Press, 192–3.

Sandler, S. Gerald. 1960. "Lockean Ideas in Thomas Jefferson's Bill for Establishing Religious Freedom," *Journal of the History of Ideas* 21 (1): 110–16.

Sapiets, Marite. 1980. "V. A. Shelkov and the True and Free Seventh-Day Adventists of the USSR," *Religion in Communist Lands* 8 (3): 201–10.

———. 1979. "Religion and Nationalism in Lithuania," *Religion in Communist Lands* 7 (2): 76–85.

Schmitt, Karl M. 1984. "Church and State in Mexico: A Corporatist Relationship," *The Americas* 40 (3): 349–76.

Schweikart, Larry and Michael Allen. 2004. *A Patriot's History of the United States*. New York: Sentinel.

Scott, David Clark. 1992a. "Mexico's Churches Dispute Details of New Law on State and Religion," *Christian Science Monitor* (July 24): 6.

———. 1992b. "Christian Sects Clash in Latin America," *Christian Science Monitor* (April 1): 14.

Scoville, Warren C. 1952. "The Huguenots and the Diffusion of Technology," *The Journal of Political Economy* 60 (4): 294–311.

Secretaria de Gobernación (México). 1992. "Ley de Asociaciones Religiosas y Culto Público," *Diario Oficial de la Federación* (July 15): 1.

Segers, Mary C. and Ted G. Jelen, eds. 1998. *A Wall of Separation? Debating the Public Role of Religion*. Lanham, MD: Rowman and Littlefield.

Sepúlveda, Juan. 1987. "El nacimiento y desarrollo de las Iglesias evangélicas." In *Historia del pueblo de Dios en Chile*, Maximiliano Salinas, ed. Santiago: Ediciones Rehue.

Serbin, Kenneth P. 1995. "Brazil: State Subsidization and the Church since 1930." In *Organized Religion in the Political Transformation of Latin America*, Satya R. Pattnayak, ed. Lanham, MD: University Press of America.

Service, Robert. 2002. *Russia: Experiment with a People*. Cambridge, MA: Harvard University Press.

Sharansky, Natan. 2004. *The Case for Democracy: The Power of Freedom to Overcome Tyranny and Terror*. New York: Public Affairs.

Shiels, W. Eugene. 1961. *King and Church: The Rise and Fall of the Patronato Real*. Chicago: Loyola University Press.

Sigmund, Paul E. 1999. *Religious Freedom and Evangelization in Latin America: The Challenge of Religious Pluralism*. Maryknoll, NY: Orbis Books.

Smith, Adam. [1776] 1976. *An Inquiry into the Nature and Causes of the Wealth of Nations*, vol. II. Indianapolis: Liberty Fund.

Smith, Brian H. 1982. *The Church and Politics in Chile: Challenges to Modern Catholicism*. Princeton: Princeton University Press.

Smith, Elwyn A. 1972. *Religious Liberty in the United States: The Development of Church-State Thought since the Revolutionary Era*. Philadelphia: Fortress Press.

Smith, George L. 1973. *Religion and Trade in New Netherland: Dutch Origins and American Development*. Ithaca, NY: Cornell University Press.

Stark, Rodney. 2005. *The Victory of Reason: How Christianity Led to Freedom, Capitalism, and Western Success*. New York: Random House.

_____. 2003. *For the Glory of God: How Monotheism Led to Reformations, Science, Witch-Hunts, and the End of Slavery*. Princeton: Princeton University Press.

_____. 2001. *One True God: Historical Consequences of Monotheism*. Princeton: Princeton University Press.

_____. 2000. "Religious Effects: In Praise of 'Idealistic Humbug,'" *Review of Religious Research* 41 (3): 289–310.

_____. 1996. *The Rise of Christianity: A Sociologist Reconsiders History*. Princeton: Princeton University Press.

_____. 1992. "Do Catholic Societies Really Exist?" *Rationality and Society* 4 (3): 261–71.

Stark, Rodney and William Sims Bainbridge. 1987. *A Theory of Religion*. New York: Peter Lang Publishing.

Stark, Rodney and Roger Finke. 2000. *Acts of Faith: Explaining the Human Side of Religion*. Berkeley: University of California Press.

Stark, Rodney and Laurence R. Iannaccone. 1994. "A Supply-Side Reinterpretation of the 'Secularization' of Europe," *Journal for the Scientific Study of Religion* 33 (3): 230–52.

Stead, George Albert. 1934. "Roger Williams and the Massachusetts-Bay," *The New England Quarterly* 7 (2): 235–57.

Stepan, Alfred. 1988. *Rethinking Military Politics: Brazil and the Southern Cone*. Princeton: Princeton University Press.

Stokes, Anson Phelps. 1950. *Church and State in the United States*. 3 vols. New York: Harper and Row.

Stokes, Anson Phelps and Leo Pfeffer. 1964. *Church and State in the United States*. Rev. ed. New York: Harper and Row.

Storzer, Roman P. and Anthony R. Picarello Jr. 2001. "The Religious Land Use and Institutionalized Persons Act of 2000: A Constitutional Response to Unconstitutional Zoning Practices," *George Mason Law Review* 9 (4): 929–1001.

Streikus, Arūnas. 2003. "The Lithuanian Catholic Church and the Soviet Regime in 1944–1953." Symposium of the Commission of Latvian Historians, vol. 9. Riga: Latvijas vēstures institūta apgāds: 278–86.

Suárez Rivera, Adolfo A. 1992. "Mensaje de Apertura." In *La Iglesia Católica en el Nuevo Marco Jurídico de México*. México DF: Ediciones de la CEM.

Subačius, Giedrius. 2005. "Development of the Cyrillic Orthography for Lithuanian in 1864–1904," *Lituanus* 51 (2): 29–55.

Sullivan-González, Douglass. 1998. *Piety, Power and Politics: Religion and Nation Formation in Guatemala 1821–1871*. Pittsburgh: University of Pittsburgh Press.

Swatos, William H. and Daniel V. A. Olson, eds. 2000. *The Secularization Debate*. Lanham, MD: Rowman and Littlefield.

Sweeney, Ernest S. 1970. *Foreign Missionaries in Argentina 1938–1962*. SONDEOS, no. 68. Cuernavaca, Mexico: CIDOC.

Sweet, W. W. 1935. "The American Colonial Environment and Religious Liberty," *Church History* 4 (1): 43–56.

Talonen, Juoko. 2004. "The Latvian Evangelical-Lutheran Church during the German Occupation in 1941–1945." Symposium of the Commission of Latvian Historians, vol. 11. Riga: Latvijas vēstures institūta apgāds: 197–220.

Tangeman, Michael. 1995. *Mexico at the Crossroads: Politics, the Church and the Poor*. Maryknoll, NY: Orbis Books.

Taylor, Michael. 1982. *Community, Anarchy and Liberty*. Cambridge: Cambridge University Press.

Temple, William. 1690. *Observations upon the Provinces of the Netherlands*. London: Jacob Tonson and Awnsham Churchill.

Tibi, Bassam. 1998. *The Challenge of Fundamentalism: Political Islam and the New World Disorder*. Berkeley: University of California Press.

Tierney, Brian. 1996. "Religious Rights: An Historical Perspective." In *Religious Human Rights in Global Perspective: Religious Perspectives*, Johan D. Van der Vyver and John Witte Jr., eds. The Hague: Martinus Nijhoff Publishers.

Tobar, Hector. 2005. "One Faith Fits All – Or Else," *Los Angeles Times* (December 15): A1.

Trotsky, Leon. 1923. "Vodka, the Church and the Cinema," *Pravda* (July 12). Internet translation by Sally Ryan. http://www.marxists.org/archive/trotsky/works/women/23_07_12.htm (accessed August 10, 2006).

Tyacke, Nicholas. 1991. "The Rise of Puritanism and the Legalizing of Dissent, 1571–1719." In *From Persecution to Toleration: The Glorious Revolution and Religion in England*, Ole Peter Grell, Jonathan I. Israel, and Nicholas Tyacke, eds. Oxford: Clarendon Press, 17–50.

United States Commission on International Religious Freedom (USCIRF). 2005. "Russia: Eyes Wide Open" (February 23). http://www.uscirf.gov/mediaroom/press/2005/february/02232005_russia.html (accessed November 22, 2006).

United States State Department. 2004. *International Religious Freedom Report*. http://www.state.gov/g/drl/rls/irf/2004 (accessed June 10, 2006).

van der Vyver, Johan D. and John Witte Jr., eds. 1996. *Religious Human Rights in Global Perspective: Legal Perspectives*. The Hague: Martinus Nijhoff Publishers.

Verkhovsky, Aleksandr. 2002. "The Role of the Russian Orthodox Church in Nationalist, Xenophobic and Antiwestern Tendencies in Russia Today: Not Nationalism, but Fundamentalism," *Religion, State and Society* 30 (4): 333–45.

Von Rauch, Georg. 1974. *The Baltic States: The Years of Independence 1917–1940*. Gerald Onn, trans. London: C. Hurst.

Walters, Philip. 1999. "The Russian Orthodox Church and Foreign Christianity: The Legacy of the Past." In *Proselytism and Orthodoxy in Russia: The New War for the Souls*, John Witte Jr. and Michael Bourdeaux, eds. Maryknoll, NY: Orbis Books.

———. 1978. "The Living Church 1922–1946," *Religion in Communist Lands* 6 (4): 235–44.

Wanniski, Jude. 1978. "Taxes, Revenue and the 'Laffer Curve.'" *The Public Interest* Winter (50): 3–16.

Warner, R. Stephen. 1993. "Work in Progress toward a New Paradigm for the Sociological Study of Religion in the United States," *American Journal of Sociology* 98 (5): 1044–93.

Watters, Mary. 1935. "Bolívar and the Church," *The Catholic Historical Review* 21 (3): 299–313.

———. 1933. *A History of the Church in Venezuela, 1810–1930*. Chapel Hill: University of North Carolina Press.

Welsh, Frank. 2002. *The Four Nations: A History of the United Kingdom*. New Haven: Yale University Press.

White, Stephen, Ian McAllister, and Ol'ga Kryshtanovskaya. 1994. "Religion and Politics in Postcommunist Russia," *Religion, State and Society* 22 (1): 73–88.

Willems, Emilio. 1967. *Followers of the New Faith: Cultural Change and the Rise of Protestantism in Brazil and Chile*. Nashville: Vanderbilt University Press.

Williams, Margaret Todaro. 1976. "Church and State in Vargas's Brazil: The Politics of Cooperation," *Journal of Church and State* 18 (3): 443–62.

Williams, Mary Wilhelmine. 1920. "The Ecclesiastical Policy of Francisco Morazán and the Other Central American Liberals," *Hispanic American Historical Review* 3 (2): 119–43.

Wilson, Bryan. 1966. *Religion in Secular Society*. London: C. A. Watts and Co.

Wilson, J. Peter. 2003. "Why Christian Broadcasting Is Difficult in the Country," *Crossrythms* (February 27, 2003). http://www.churchesmediacouncil.org.uk/cmec/commsact/comms_Act_full.htm (accessed August 25, 2005).

Winn, Wilkins B. 1972. "The Efforts of the United States to Secure Religious Liberty in a Commerical Treaty with Mexico, 1825–1831," *The Americas* 28 (3): 311–32.

———. 1970. "The Issue of Religious Liberty in the United States Commercial Treaty with Colombia, 1824," *The Americas* 26 (3): 291–301.

Wittenberg, Jason. 2006. *Crucibles of Political Loyalty: Church Institutions and Electoral Continuity in Hungary*. Cambridge: Cambridge University Press.

Young, Glennys. 1997. *Power and the Sacred in Revolutionary Russia: Religious Activists in the Village*. University Park: Pennsylvania State University Press.

Young, Lawrence A., ed. 1997. *Rational Choice Theory and Religion: Summary and Assessment*. New York: Routledge.

Zweirlein, Frederick J. 1910. *Religion in New Netherland*. Rochester, NY: John P. Smith Printing Company.

Index

Act of Settlement, 90
Act of Toleration, 1–2, 82n29, 89–90
  in British America, 105, 106
Act of Uniformity, 88
Alberdi, Juan Bautista, 124
Aleksii, Patriarch, 204–6
Alexander II, Tsar (Russia), 177
Alexei, Tsar, 172
Alfonsín, Raúl, 142
American colonies. *See* British
  American colonies
Anabaptists. *See also* Baptists
  in Massachusetts, 98
  in New Amsterdam, 94
  in Rhode Island, 102
Anderson, John, 7
Anglican Church. *See* Church of
  England
Anglicans
  exempted from taxation, 106–7
  in New England, 65, 104n54
  persecuted under Cromwell, 87
  in Virginia, 2

anticlericalism
  under communism, 3
  in France, 117
  in Latin America, 125
  in Mexico, 116, 148–9, 152–4
Argentina
  appointment of bishops in, 127
  expropriation of property in, 131
  immigration and religious liberty,
    137
  Perón and Catholic Church, 134
  Protestants in, 141–2, 145
  religious liberty in, 38, 39
  restrictions on religious minorities,
    17
  support of Catholic Church, 19

Backus, Isaac, 65, 71–2, 102
Baltic States, 4, 5, 39, 169. *See also*
  Estonia, Latvia, Lithuania
  post-Soviet era, 221–2
  pre-Soviet era, 173–80
  under Soviet Union, 194–200

Baptists
  and Act of Toleration, 89
  in Carolina colonies, 95
  in England, 86
  ideas about religious liberty, 35
  and immigration, 105
  in Latvia, 217
  in Lithuania, 222
  in Massachusetts, 112
  in New England, 2, 69–71
  and religious pluralism, 74
  and religious taxation, 67, 106–9
  in Rhode Island, 104, 106
  in Russia, 172, 207, 209
  in Soviet Union, 191
  in Virginia, 62n4, 96, 110
Becker, Gary, 27
Bible bans, 13, 128n20
Bolívar, Simón, 117, 122–6
Bolsheviks, 168, 173, 182, 185
bowling leagues, 229
Bradford, William, 63
Brazauskas, Algirdas, 169
Brazil
  immigration and religious liberty,
    137
  Protestants in, 139–40, 144–5, 166
  separation of church and state, 132
  support of Catholic Church, 133–4
Brezhnev, Leonid, 189, 191, 202
Britain. See England
British American colonies, 2–3, 60–75,
    113, 121
Buddhism, 203, 210
Bustamante, Anastasio, 147

Calles, Plutarco Elías, 153
Calvert, Cecil, 73, 92–3
Calvin, John, 35
Calvinism. See also Pilgrims, Puritans
  in Baltic States, 173
  in England, 62, 82
  in France, 78
  in Lithuania, 175
Cárdenas, Lazaro, 152, 154–5
Carolina colonies, 73, 95, 121
Catholic Action, 132–3, 156

Catholic Church. See Roman Catholic
    Church
Catholics. See Roman Catholics
Charles I, King (England), 62, 64, 78,
    86, 92
Charles II, King (England), 88, 97, 99
Charles III, King (Spain), 146
Chile
  expropriation of property in, 131
  immigration and religious liberty,
    137
  Protestants in, 14, 141, 145, 166
  separation of church and state, 132
China, 6, 12, 30
Christian Peace Conference, 190
Chronicle of the Lithuanian Catholic
    Church, 4, 199
Church of England
  in British America, 17, 91
  in Carolinas, 95
  disestablishment in Virginia, 39
  in England, 27, 82–3, 88
  and English Civil War, 86
  incentives of clergy, 108
  in Maryland, 74
  in New England, 104n54
  and Puritans, 63–5, 78, 85, 92
  in Virginia, 2, 72–3, 96, 109
circuit riders, 66n13, 73, 74, 100, 108,
    121n12
citizenship requirements, 127
Clark, John, 35, 70–1
Colombia
  appointment of bishops in, 127
  property expropriations in, 130
  Protestants in, 140, 142–3, 145
  religious liberty in, 38
commerce. See trade
Communist Party (USSR), 4, 18, 187,
    191
Conferencia del Episcopado Mexicano
    (CEM), 115, 158, 160–3
Congregationalists. See also Puritans
  and religious taxation, 106–7
  in Rhode Island, 106
Connecticut. See also New England
  religious taxation in, 66–7, 107

Conservatives
  in Latin America, 39, 128, 128n22, 131
  in Mexico, 148–51
Conventicle Act, 88
Corporation Act, 88
Cottonwood Christian Center, 225
Coxe, Tench, 101
credence goods, 51, 54
Cristero Rebellion, 153–4, 159
Cromwell, Oliver, 70, 87–8, 101, 104
Cuba, 12, 167n79
Czechoslovakia, 190
Czech Republic, 14–15

Davies, Samuel, 100
de la Madrid, Miguel, 159
Delaware, 94
Díaz, Porfirio, 151–2
Dignitatis Humanae, 45
Dyer, Mary, 60–2, 71, 101

Eastern Europe, 4, 39, 169
ecclesiastical courts. *See fueros eclesiásticos*
Echeverría, Luis, 157–8
economic trade. *See* trade
Ecuador, 38
ecumenism, 46
Edict of Nantes, 1, 38, 78–81
  revocation of, 5, 12, 80–1
education, religious, 20–1, 133, 156, 171, 181, 192, 193, 211, 218, 220
Egaña, Juan, 124
Elizabeth, Queen (England), 82–3
El Salvador, 138, 144, 145
Engels, Friedrich, 183
England
  religious dissenters in, 82–91
  religious persecution in, 62–4
  religious pluralism in, 82–3
  religious toleration in, 1, 82–91
English Civil War, 36, 78, 86, 109
Enlightenment, 7, 34, 36, 37, 116, 130
Erasmus, 35

Estonia. *See also* Baltic States, Livonia
  constitution (1920), 178
  post-Soviet era, 217
  religious liberty in, 4–5, 178
  religious pluralism in, 214
  Soviet persecution of religion in, 195–7
Estonian Orthodox Church Moscow Patriarch (EOCMP), 215–16
expropriation of religious property
  compensation for, 170
  in Estonia, 195
  in Latin America, 3, 128–32
  in Lithuania, 198
  in Mexico, 148–51, 166
  in Soviet Union, 182

Falun Gong, 6
Finke, Roger, 7, 27, 75
First Amendment (U.S. Constitution), 2, 23, 35, 61, 74–5, 113
First Great Awakening. *See* Great Awakening
France
  and Edict of Nantes, 1, 78–81
  and Muslims, 15
  in North America, 75, 84
  and Protestant Reformation, 77
  separation of church and state, 117
French Protestants. *See* Huguenots
Froese, Paul, 27
fueros eclesiásticos, 3, 127, 146, 148
Fujimori, Alberto, 141

Georgia (America), 73, 121
Germany, 169, 197
  in Lithuania, 174
  religious taxation in, 20
glasnost, 192–3, 202
Glorious Revolution, 89
Gómez Farías, Valentín, 148–9
Gorbachev, Mikhail, 192–3, 201–2, 206, 208, 213, 219
Great Awakening
  building restrictions and, 73
  economic trade and, 100
  and religious liberty, 35, 66n13

Great Awakening (*cont.*)
  and religious pluralism, 74
  religious taxation and, 67, 107
  in Virginia, 108
Great Britain. *See* England
Gregory XVI, 147
Guatemala
  expropriation of property in, 129
  independence of, 123
  Protestants in, 145
  religious liberty in, 38

Half-Way Covenant, 69
Hanson, Charles, 7, 75, 110
Hare Krishna, 194
Helsinki Agreements (1975), 199
Helsinki Group (Lithuania), 199
Henry IV, King (France), 1, 79
Henry VIII, King (England), 77, 82
Henry, Patrick, 39, 108–9
Hidalgo y Costilla, Miguel, 122, 147,
  149, 159
Hobhouse, Leonard Trelawney, 227
Holy See. *See* Vatican
Huguenots
  in Carolina colonies, 95
  and Edict of Nantes, 1, 78–81
  in the Netherlands, 90
  in Rhode Island, 102
  in Virginia, 110
Hume, David, 35
Hungary, 30, 189
Hutchinson, Anne, 71

Iannaccone, Laurence, 27
Ill News from New England, 70–1
immigration
  in Latin America, 121
  and religious liberty, 92–6, 121, 138
Institutional Revolutionary Party. *See*
  Partido Revolucionario
  Institucional
Iran, 189
Ireland, 82n29, 87
Islam. *See* Muslims
Issaquah, 224
Iturbide, Augustín de, 147

James I, King (England), 62–4, 82–5,
  92
James II, King (England), 89–90
Jamestown, 84, 92
Jefferson, Thomas, 2, 21, 39, 108–9
Jehovah's Witnesses, 16, 139, 179, 183,
  207, 218, 227
Jesuits
  in Latin America, 119, 146
  in Lithuania, 199
  in Maryland, 74
Jews
  in Brazil, 135n32
  in Germany, 20
  in Latvia, 178, 217
  in Lithuania, 220
  in New Amsterdam, 94
  in Rhode Island, 102, 104
  in Russia, 210–11
  in Soviet Union, 187
John Paul II, 159, 162–3
Juárez, Benito, 150n56
Judaism. *See* Jews

KGB. *See* Soviet secret police
khlysty, 172
Khrushchev, Nikita, 188–9
Kirill, Metropolitan, 203, 206

Landsbergis, Vytautas, 221
La Reforma, 150–1, 166
latifundio system, 120–1
Latin America, 3, 39
  colonial era, 3, 117–21
  expropriation of religious property,
  128–32
  independence, 3, 117, 122–8
  Protestants in, 12, 135–45
  in twentieth century, 135
Latvia. *See also* Baltic States, Livonia
  post-Soviet era, 217–19
  religious liberty in, 4–5, 178–9
  Soviet persecution of religion in,
  195, 197
Laud, William, 86, 102
League of Militant Atheists, 183,
  187

Leme, Cardinal Dom, 133–4
Lenin, Vladimir, 181, 183
Leyes Reformas, 151, 152
Ley Reglamentaria, 155, 159, 163–5, 211
Liberals
  in Latin America, 128, 128n22, 131
  in Mexico, 148–51
liberation theology, 140n39, 158n66
Lithuania. *See also* Baltic States
  and collapse of USSR, 170
  post-Soviet era, 221–2
  religious liberty in, 4
  Soviet persecution of religion in, 197–9
Living Church. *See* Renovationist Church
Livonia, 173–5. *See also* Estonia, Latvia
Locke, John, 34–6, 39, 90, 91
Lord Baltimore. *See* Calvert, Cecil
Louis XIII, King (France), 79–80
Louis XIV, King (France), 1, 80–1, 88
Luther, Martin, 35, 76, 76n26, 77
Lutherans
  in Baltic States, 173–4, 176
  in Estonia, 5, 178, 196–7, 217
  in Latvia, 178, 197, 217
  in Lithuania, 175, 200, 220, 222
  in New Amsterdam, 94
  in Nordic countries, 17
  in Russia, 206

Madero, Francisco, 152
Madison, James
  and Anglican disestablishment, 39, 73
  and *Federalist*, 4, 8
  on immigration and religious liberty, 96
  influence of Englightenment on, 35
  and religious taxation, 108–9
  Roger Williams's influence on, 102
marriage, religious, 21, 127, 130, 133
Marx, Karl, 32, 168n2, 183
Maryland
  and Act of Toleration, 104
  Anglican establishment in, 74, 93

religious liberty in, 92–3
  trade and religious liberty in, 94
Massachusetts. *See also* New England
  disestablishment in, 74–5, 112
  religious persecution in, 61, 69–72
  religious policy of, 64–72
  religious taxation in, 62n4, 66–8, 101, 106–7
Mather, Cotton, 66–7
Mazarin, Cardinal, 80, 86
media restrictions, 17
Méndez Arceo, Sergio, 158, 161
mercantilism, 120–1
Methodists
  and Act of Toleration, 89
  and immigration, 105
  in Lithuania, 222
  in Massachusetts, 112
  and religious pluralism, 74
Mexican Constitution (1917), 5, 114–15, 152–3, 155, 158, 163
Mexican Revolution, 3, 116, 152–3, 166
Mexico, 145–65
  anticlericalism in, 54, 116, 148–9, 152–4
  constitutional revisions, 114–15
  election fraud in, 159–62
  independence, 146–7
  registration requirements in, 15
  religious liberty in, 3, 38
migration (domestic). *See also* immigration
  and religious liberty, 101–5, 121
missionaries, 56n49
  in Baltic States, 214
  in Latin America, 138–9
  in Lithuania, 222
  in Russia, 12, 138, 173, 202, 204, 209
modernization theory. *See* secularization theory
Montesquieu, 39
Moore, Barrington, 25
More, Thomas, 35
Morelos y Pavón y Pavón, José María, 122

Morelos y Pavón, José María, 147, 149
Mormons, 91n41, 113
Mother Teresa, 30n8, 40, 40n24
Mureşan, Lucian, 168
Muslims
  and Christian missionaries, 209
  in Europe, 6
  in France, 15
  in Germany, 20, 38n17
  in Lithuania, 220
  in Netherlands, 38n17
  in Russia, 203, 207, 209–10

Nagy, Imre, 188
Netherlands
  colonial religious policy, 94–5
  and Huguenots, 81
  in Latin America, 136n34
  Pilgrims flee, 85
  religious pluralism in, 78, 89
  religious taxation in, 20
  religious tolerance in, 2, 62, 90–1
New Amsterdam (New York)
  religious toleration in, 94–5
New England. *See also* Connecticut,
    Massachusetts, Plymouth, Rhode
    Island
  religious persecution in, 69–72
  religious pluralism in, 69
  voting restrictions in, 36
New Jersey, 94
Nicaragua, 38, 138, 145
Nicholas II, Tsar (Russia), 172n4, 173
Nikon, Patriarch, 172
North American Free Trade
    Agreement (NAFTA), 163

Obeso, Sergio, 161
Old Believers, 172, 178, 217, 220
Olson, Mancur, 27
opportunity costs, 53, 55
Orthodox Christianity. *See* Russian
    Orthodox Church
Orthodox Church. *See* Russian
    Orthodox Church
Oxnam, G. Bromley, 9, 16

Partido Revolucionario Institucional
    (PRI), 154, 157–62
patronato real, 117–20, 125–7, 131, 135,
    147–8, 166
Paul VI, 157
peace movements, 190
Penn, William, 35
  on immigration and religious liberty,
    95
  on trade and religious liberty, 98–100
Pennsylvania, 2, 73, 94, 95, 104
Pentecostals. *See also* Protestants
  in Latin America, 45, 138
  in Lithuania, 4, 200
  in Russia, 209
perestroika, 192
Perón, Juan, 17, 19, 39, 134, 139
Peru, 141
Peter the Great, 171, 174
Pfaff, Steve, 27
Pilgrims, 2, 61–3, 65, 84–5
Pius VII, 125
Plymouth
  religious taxation in, 67–8
  religious toleration in, 63
Poland, 174, 177
political rulers
  preferences of, 47–53
Portugal, 84
prayer in public school, 15
Presbyterians
  in England, 2, 82
  and religious taxation, 108–9
  in Virginia, 33, 110
Prigione, Jerónimo, 114, 161–3
property rights, 15–17, 108, 211, 214.
    See also zoning regulations
Protestant Reformation, 35, 76–8, 103,
    112, 118, 175
Protestants. *See also* specific
    denominations
  in Argentina, 133, 134, 139, 141–2
  in Brazil, 140, 166
  in Chile, 132n30, 138, 141, 144, 166
  in Colombia, 140, 142–3
  in Estonia, 216
  in France. *See* Huguenots

in Latin America, 3, 13, 17, 115, 128, 135–45, 166
in Mexico, 116, 151, 153, 155, 157, 164–5
in Peru, 141
in Russia, 202–4, 208–9, 211
in Soviet Union, 191–2
Puritans
emigration to America, 84–6, 92
in England, 82–7
in New Amsterdam, 94
in New England, 17
and Oliver Cromwell, 87
persecution of, 62–4, 83–4
Putin, Vladimir, 212

Quakers. *See also* Dyer, Mary
and Act of Toleration, 89
as business owners, 94
in Carolina colonies, 95
in England, 2
ideas about religious liberty, 35
and immigration, 105
in New Amsterdam, 94
in New England, 2
as pacifists, 100
persecuted in Massachusetts, 69, 71
persecuted in New England, 71–2
persecuted under Cromwell, 87
in Rhode Island, 102, 104
taxed in New England, 67, 106
and trade, 97–100
Quebec Act, 110

Radvila the Black, 175
Rasputin, 172n4
rational choice theory, 22, 27–31, 40–1, 45n32
and ideas, 59
Red-Brown coalition, 204, 207
Reformation. *See* Protestant Reformation
registration requirements, 13–15, 193, 211, 214, 215, 217, 227
religious freedom. *See* religious liberty
Religious Freedom Restoration Act, 6n3, 14n18, 46n36

religious human capital, 58
Religious Land Use and Institutionalized Persons Act (RLUIPA), 6n3, 226
religious liberty. *See also* specific countries, regions
definition of, 9–12, 43–4
as government regulation, 10–12, 135
government subsidies and, 18–21
and modernization, 32–9
restrictions on, 12–18
religious marketplace, 41–3
religious minorities. *See also* specific countries, denominations
and dominant religion, 8
and political power, 55
political preferences of, 45–7
religious monopoly
political preferences of, 8, 44–6
and state regulation, 42–3
religious persecution. *See* specific countries
religious pluralism
in British America, 47, 113
causes of, 47, 55–6, 145
and Edict of Nantes, 79
in England, 82
in Estonia, 214
and immigration, 121
in Latin America, 115, 117
in Latvia, 178–9
in Massachusetts, 68–9
and migration, 101–2
in New Amsterdam, 94
in Pennsylvania, 2
in post-Soviet Russia, 212, 213
and Protestant Reformation, 76–8
and religious liberty, 7, 46–7, 56, 75, 95, 99
in Rhode Island, 2
in Russia, 172–3, 202–5
and social conflict, 79, 103
in Soviet Union, 187, 191–4
religious toleration
definition of, 43n31
Renovationist Church, 182–5

Revolutionary War (United States), 2, 75
religious liberty and, 109–12
Rhode Island
  and Act of Toleration, 104–5
  conflict with New England, 97–8, 106
  religious liberty in, 2, 71, 73, 96, 103–4
  and restrictions on religious liberty, 104
Richelieu, Cardinal, 39, 79–80, 86
Rivadavia, Bernadino, 131
Roman Catholic Church
  in Estonia, 216
  in France, 1
  in Latin America, 167
  in Latvia, 217
  in Lithuania, 4, 170, 177–8, 197–200, 214, 221–2
  in Mexico, 146–65
  and Protestant Reformation, 76–7
  and religious liberty, 45
  in Russia, 205
Roman Catholics
  in Baltic States, 173–4
  in British America, 2–3
  in colonial British America, 110–11
  in England, 82n29, 83
  in Estonia, 178
  in France, 1
  in Latin America, 3
  in Latvia, 178
  in Maryland, 2, 73–4, 92–3
  in Mexico, 3
  in New Amsterdam, 94
  persecuted in England, 62, 88
  in Rhode Island, 102, 104
  in Russia, 202, 209, 210
  and U.S. Revolutionary War, 110–11
  in U.S. Revolutionary War, 75
Ruíz, Samuel, 158, 161, 162
Russia. See also Soviet Union
  1997 law restricting religious liberty, 210–13
  in Baltic States, 176–7
  in Lithuania, 174

  in Livonia, 174–6
  post-Soviet era, 201–13
  pre-Soviet era, 170–3
  religious liberty in, 4, 173
  religious revival in, 202–3
Russian Orthodox Church
  in Baltic States, 173, 214
  clergy persecuted, 182–3
  in Estonia, 178, 196, 215–16
  under Khrushchev, 189
  in Latvia, 178, 197, 217
  in Lithuania, 220
  in Livonia, 175–6
  post-Soviet era, 4, 45, 201–13
  in pre-Soviet era, 173
  under Soviet Rule, 168–9
  and Soviet secret police, 190–1
  under Soviet Union, 180–94
  during World War II, 187

Salinas de Gortari, Carlos, 114, 162–3, 192
Samper, Ernesto, 143
Santa Anna, Antonio López de, 149
Santander, Francisco de Paula, 123
Saudi Arabia, 30
Scotland, 83, 86, 87
Second Vatican Council. See Vatican Council II
secularism, 15, 18, 21, 38n17
secularization theory, 7, 31–7
  critique of, 37–40
separation of church and state, 21
Separatists. See also Pilgrims, 61–3
septic systems, 224–5
Sergii, Patriarch, 182
Seventh-Day Adventists, 172, 183
Smith, Adam, 26–7, 44–7, 49n40, 50n41, 228
Smith v. Oregon, 15
Soviet secret police (KGB), 190–1, 205–6
Soviet Union, 180–94
  persecution of religion in, 4, 17, 54, 168–9
  separation of church and state, 21
Stalin, Josef, 169, 183–8, 194

Stark, Rodney, 25, 27
Sweden, 6, 174, 197

taxation
  religious, 2, 3, 19–20, 65, 66n13, 68, 69, 74, 89, 98, 100, 105–9, 118, 146
  secular, 10n13, 82n29, 86, 96, 130, 175, 195, 211, 218, 220, 221, 226
televangelism, 17
Test Act, 88
Teutonic Knights, 174
Tikhon, Patriarch, 182
tithing. *See* taxation, religious
Toleration Act. *See* Act of Toleration
trade, 120–1, 125
  and religious liberty, 2, 6, 75, 84, 100–1, 136–7, 166, 216
Trotsky, Leon, 181, 183–5
Turkey, 15, 16

United Nations, 4
United States Constitution, 2, 74–5, 112
Universal Declaration of Human Rights, 4
Uruguay, 30, 131, 137
USSR. *See* Soviet Union

values
  and rational choice theory, 59
Vargas, Getúlio, 133–4, 139
Vatican
  and England, 82
  and Latin America, 3, 118–19, 125–7, 132
  and Latvia, 179
  and Lithuania, 4
  and Mexico, 147–8, 158, 161
  and Russia, 210
Vatican Council II, 45
Venezuela, 122, 137, 167n79
Virginia
  Anglican disestablishment in, 108–9
  religious persecution in, 72–3
  religious taxation in, 62n4, 107–9
  trade and religious liberty, 100, 121
Vladimir, Prince (Russia), 170, 180, 193
vodka, 181
voting
  religious restrictions on, 68, 104

wall of separation, 21
Warner, Carolyn, 27
Wealth of Nations, The, 26–7
whack-a-mole, 76
Whitefield, George, 35n12, 66n13, 121n12
William of Orange, King (England), 1, 82n29, 89
Williams, Roger, 35, 70, 71, 72n23, 102–4
Winthrop, George, 66
Winthrop, John, 64, 85
World Council of Churches, 140n40, 191, 203

Yeltsin, Boris, 202, 204, 206–10, 212

Zapata, Emiliano, 152n58
zoning regulations, 8n9, 11, 16–17, 224–6